LAW AND THE MEDIA

FIRST EDITION

By

PROFESSOR DUNCAN BLOY,
B.A., L.L.M., P.G.C.E.
*Schools of Journalism, Media and Cultural Studies and Law
at Cardiff University*

and

SARA HADWIN
M.A. (Oxon)
*Professional Tutor, School of Journalism, Media and Cultural Studies at
Cardiff University (former newspaper editor)*

LONDON
SWEET & MAXWELL
2007

First edition 2007

Published in 2007 by
Sweet & Maxwell Limited of 100 Avenue Road,
http://www.sweetandmaxwell.co.uk
Typeset by Servis Filmsetting Ltd, Manchester
Printed and bound in Great Britain by
TJ International Ltd, Padstow, Cornwall

No natural forests were destroyed to make this product;
only farmed timber was used and re-planted.

British Library Cataloguing in Publication Data

A CIP catalogue record for this book
is available from the British Library

ISBN 978–1–84703–215–7

PREFACE

"Lawyers tell it how it is; journalists how they would like it to be." Since we became colleagues over three years ago that simple aphorism seems to have permeated most of our conversations. In trying to instil best practice into budding journalists, we have regularly had to put both sides of the argument. The journalist can see no obvious reason why something cannot be broadcast or printed yet the lawyer urges caution. A good example is the law on contempt. The Contempt of Court Act 1981 warns journalists not to create a substantial risk of serious prejudice to pending legal proceedings in pre-trial reporting. Yet only eight months ago, the Lord Chief Justice in the *R. v Abu Hamza* is on record as saying that we can trust our juries to ignore apparently detrimental pre-trial publicity and reach objective decisions based purely on the evidence. The Act warns against trial by media. The ruling in *Hamza* suggests that there is no such thing. The Attorney General in a speech to the Reform Club Media Group in May 2007 called for research into the effect upon juries of pre-trial publicity. That, briefly, is the dilemma that we have tried to address in this book. The law has the capacity to change unbelievably quickly. The developing law in favour of greater Art.8 (ECHR) protection with the corresponding restrictions on freedom of expression is perhaps the best recent example. Throughout this book, we have endeavoured to state the current legal principles in many of the everyday situations faced by journalists. We are conscious of the fact that copyright has not been given prominence but space limitations have meant that certain intellectual property issues had to be sacrificed.

The text essentially offers two perspectives. The major legal principles are stated together with a number of pertinent quotations from major cases. An experienced editorial eye is then cast over those principles in an endeavour to explain just what could or should not be attempted without risking a breach of the law. The text is aimed at both trainee journalists and those studying media law at undergraduate level, but we hope that it may prove to be of interest to a wider media audience as a reference text. A healthy democracy requires both an acceptance of the rule of law and a thriving and responsible fourth estate. Lawyers and journalists may not always agree but at least we can keep the dialogue open, ongoing and friendly!

We would both like to thank our Cardiff students for demanding answers to many of the questions addressed in this book. Sara Hadwin would like to thank Santha Rasaiah for inspiring a fascination with media law; a succession of in-house media lawyers for helping to rescue most legally-dubious stories from the spike and her father for teaching her that, whatever the legal advice and however much you pay for it, the final decision and responsibility is the editor's.

Duncan Bloy would like to wish Hannah and Vern a safe and fulfilling 'rite of passage' as they travel the world. Thanks also to Sue Hodgkinson for her much appreciated secretarial support over the past four years.

We also wish to thank Nicola Thurlow at Sweet & Maxwell simply because nothing seems to have been too much trouble for her and as authors that was music to our ears!

We have endeavoured to state the law as at August 20, 2007.

Duncan Bloy
Sara Hadwin

Addendum

Roberts & Another v Gable & Others [2007] EWCA Civ 721

Since our manuscript was typeset, the Court of Appeal has delivered an extremely significant decision on the media defence of 'reportage' within the context of the *Reynolds Public Interest* defence. (See Ch. 2, p.70). The following represents a brief summary of the decision.

When running a *Reynolds* defence, the publisher will normally have to show that reasonable steps were taken to verify the truth and accuracy of what has been published. There is no public interest in receiving misinformation. However, if reportage is relied upon, then there is no need to ensure the accuracy of what has been published. Why should this be the case? Lord Justice Ward said:

> "To qualify as *reportage* the report, judging the thrust of it as a whole, must have the effect of reporting, not the truth of the statements, but the fact that they were made. If upon a proper construction of the *thrust* of the article the defamatory material is attributed to another and *is not being put forward as true*, then a responsible journalist would not need to take steps to verify its accuracy. He is absolved from the responsibility because he is simply reporting in a *neutral fashion* the fact that it has been said *without adopting the truth*." (Italics added.)

He goes on:

> "This protection is lost if the journalist adopts the report and makes it his own or if he fails to report the story in a fair, disinterested and neutral way."

This however does not mean that the *Reynolds* defence is lost, because he can still go on in an attempt to show that he acted in a responsible manner in all the circumstances even though he did not check on accuracy. The test for reportage is objective. The reporter may say that he was attempting to write in a neutral way, but that will not be decisive. The court will look at all the evidence and reach a conclusion on whether it was *reasonable* to conclude that the piece, taken as a whole was neutral and disinterested.

Whether lawyer or journalist we would urge you to refer to the nine-point approach to reportage at para.61 of the report. To us this appears as a significant judgment, pro-media and in keeping with the spirit of the *Reynolds* decision and the concept of responsible journalism. Ward L.J. even acknowledges the pressures placed on editors when deciding, at short notice, whether to run a story. Reportage equally applies whether there are time constraints or no time pressures.

As the judge said:

"Public interest is circumscribed as much by events as by time and every story must be judged on its merits at the moment of publication."

However, we urge a modicum of caution. Do note that the application of the reportage rule will have an impact on the *repetition* rule and as a result, there may be a tendency for judges to seek to interpret reportage in a restrictive way.

For the latest analysis of the principles governing privacy, see *Murray v Express Newspapers Plc & Another* [2007] EWHC 1908 (Ch).

Duncan Bloy
Sara Hadwin
August 20, 2007

ACKNOWLEDGMENTS

Grateful acknowledgment is made to the following authors and publishers for permission to quote from their works:

Culture, Media Sport and Culture Select Committee, 5th Report, *www.culture.gov.uk.*

European Court of Human Rights: *Selisto v Finland* [2004]; *B and P* [2001]

Frankel, Maurice, Director of Campaign for Freedom of Information, *www.cfoi.org.uk.*

Guardian, quotation from Duncan Lamont, *www.guardian.co.uk.*

Holdthefrontpage, Judgment of Sir Igor Judge, *www.holdthefrontpage.co.uk.*

Incorporated Council of Law Reporting: *Bonnard v Perryman* (1891); *Lewis v Daily Telegraph Ltd* [1964]; *Montgomery v HM Advocate* [2003]; *Campbell v MGN* [2004].

Judicial Communications Office, quotation from Sir Nicholas Wall, *www.judiciary.gov.uk*

Judicial Studies Board, Reporting Restrictions in the Magistrates' Courts, *www.jsboard.co.uk.*

Media Lawyer, Mostyn Memorial Lecture at Gray's Inn, (Lord Falconer); and Commons Constitutional Affairs Committee, (Mumby J.), *www.media lawyer.press.net.*

Observer, quotations from Mary Riddell and Simon Jenkins, *observer.guardian.co.uk.*

Press Complaints Commission, PCC Report on Subterfuge and Newsgathering, *www.pcc.org.uk.*

Thomas, Richard, Information Commissioner's Office, 'What Price Privacy', *www.ico.gov.uk.*

CONTENTS

TABLE OF CASES

TABLE OF STATUTES

INTRODUCTION: IT'S THE HUMAN RIGHTS ACT, STUPID

Law is learnt as a litany of bans and restrictions; terrible tales of journalists' undoing, massive legal bills and expensive apologies. It is good,
and indeed vital, that those lessons are learnt. Warning bells need to ring
for journalists, but learning law must not end with a list of stories that
can't be told. Journalists need to turn to statute and to informed legal
judgments in order to realise what is required in terms of investigative
procedure and the wording of their reports so that a story can be safely
put in the public domain. Media law is something journalists can't avoid
but we can learn to work more effectively within it.

Ignorance of the law can certainly be expensive in terms of damages,
costs and even a spell in prison. But adopting an informed attitude to
working within the law will protect a responsible journalist seeking
genuinely to serve the public interest where a legal challenge arises.
This greatly improves their chances of telling the stories that need to be
told and providing the public with the fullest possible story within the
law.

Most stories can be told in a legally safe form by employing legal
insights, ingenuity and rigorous journalistic method. But this requires
judgement. Risk must be acknowledged but it can be minimised with the
benefit of legal advice. Ignore it at your peril but use it to your advantage.

The implications of the law must be borne in mind for all stories, for it
applies to all. Journalists have a tendency to see defamation, for instance,
as applying only to in-depth exposés rather than to seemingly innocuous
club reports or letters to the editor.

They recognise that legal training is required for reporting courts but
fail to see its significance for health, education, council or human interest coverage.

Law is not a series of absolutes. Grey areas increase risk but also create
room for manoeuvre in individual cases. Media law is about much more
than relevant legislation. Case law, especially in the wake of the Human
Rights Act (HRA), has significant impact on journalists. Barely a week
goes by without a hearing which challenges the boundaries of journalistic activity; what can and can't be printed and increasingly what is
expected of journalists claiming any protection from the law for what
they publish.

Law is changing at a sometimes alarming pace, mainly by virtue of
judicial rulings more than legislation. As a result, journalists need to
keep up to date with the ramifications of these decisions for their work.
They also need to know where they can take advantage of methods and
wordings which will keep them on the right side of the law.

Journalists may wish that legislation and case law were less intrusive in our work, but the trend is strongly towards greater scrutiny not less. Journalists who want to push the limits of the law to tell stories that the public really do have a right to know can expect to have to justify their working practices as well as what they say.

This trend is set to continue and even accelerate for some time to come given the enormous impact of the adoption into the Human Rights Act of the principles of the European Convention on Human Rights, which now lie at the heart of all media law. All legislation and related judicial rulings are now required to be convention-compliant. So the Act has ushered in a series of judgments seeking to create a new methodology for resolving media-related cases. Since 2000 and from now on, cases will be judged in terms of pitting the journalist's Art.10 rights against other human rights, particularly the Art.8 rights of individuals to protect their privacy and the Art.6 rights to a fair trial.

These responses to the Human Rights Act have largely determined the contents of this book in that we have focused on those areas of direct impact, primarily defamation, privacy and contempt, but also looked at associated questions of regulation and statutory developments such as the Freedom of Information Act.

We have featured the areas of media law which are changing most in the 21st century and where emerging case law is having the most significant impact on working journalists and their news organisations. Those areas of media law which are relatively "fixed" in comparison have been left to existing textbooks to outline.

Only by keeping abreast of these developments can a journalist expect to operate within the law while not allowing it to create more curbs on reporting than need be.

Journalists respect the law and would generally seek to work within it. They are certainly not above it and are likely to face swift retribution where they behave as if they were. The jailing of News of the World royal editor, Clive Goodman, in 2007, has provided a stark reminder to journalists of the price they may pay for breaking the criminal law. They claim their rights to freedom of expression as individuals and it is, generally, as individuals that they are called to account, as anyone else would be, if they disobey the law.

Many journalists, and editors, will come across a story which they want to tell badly enough—for principled and/or commercial reasons—to take that risk. Some will pay a heavy price.

But far more frequently massive legal bills are racked up because the legal ramifications of a story are not thought through, because defences are not marshalled or because, when it comes to the crunch, the journalistic process as a whole does not stand up to scrutiny. Don't let that happen to you.

Each chapter of this book aims to capture not just the 21st century trends in media law but the continuing debate and tensions between the law and the journalist. Each chapter commences with Duncan Bloy discussing the major legal principles and concludes with Sara Hadwin providing a practical journalistic perspective. While neither of us can claim to be particularly typical of our "breed", we both consciously and sub-consciously interpret media law in ways which reflect our respective callings. We hope this will prove illuminating and go some way to stimulating the dialogue between the law and the media which remains crucial to democratic debate and to what kind of democratic society we will become.

For each chapter of the book, relevant legislation and the thinking behind it are discussed. Key definitions and landmark cases are given. These legal underpinnings are then viewed from a working journalist's perspective in an attempt to illustrate the impact on day-to-day practice, including general advice on how stories can be run without falling foul of the law. The inclusion of recent case law provides the most up-to-date guidance we can for journalists. We acknowledge the time constraints of a textbook but we would strongly urge journalists to carry forward this habit of tracking relevant judgments which are published on a variety of legal websites as they emerge. See Bibliography for details.

This book is part source book for budding media lawyers; part advice guide for practising journalists and hopefully a catalyst for informed debate about the interrelationship between the law and the media in the 21st century.

We believe this is a crucial time for journalists to grapple with the issues raised by the judicial responses to the Human Rights Act. If the right to freedom of expression is to be upheld, journalists need to know where it can be advanced and where it is under threat. They need to think long and hard about their role in a democratic society and know how the law protects or hinders it. Hopefully by tracking 21st century media case law, we can provoke journalists and their news organisations into playing a still more active role in testing the boundaries of our freedom of expression and the public's right to know.

As the authors we can inform. We can challenge. We can urge that any risk taken be a calculated risk and we can help you to make that assessment. But, however much legal advice is sought, the ultimate decision on what to run remains with your editor.

CHAPTER 1
FREEDOM OF EXPRESSION

From a personal perspective, 1948 is a significant date. It was the year of Duncan Bloy's birth. From a professional perspective it is also an important date because in December of that year the United Nations General Assembly "adopted and proclaimed" the Universal Declaration of Human Rights. Member countries at that time were invited to disseminate the Declaration principally through educational institutions. The young of each nation were to be asked to embrace the terms of the Declaration in the hope that future generations would benefit from the foresight of their elders. Sadly there have been many examples over the years of breaches of many of the Articles. However, nations have consistently reaffirmed the commitment to freedom of expression. Article 19 states:

"Everyone has the right to freedom of opinion and expression; this right includes freedom to hold opinions without interference and to seek, receive and impart information and ideas through any media regardless of frontiers."[1]

It was reported that, in 2006, there were 155 "murders, assassinations and unexplained deaths of journalists and media workers."[2] The unsurprising conclusion was that "the killing of journalists threatens everyone's human rights by closing the door to *free expression*."[3]

The first part of each of the chapters in this book endeavours to describe and comment upon the *legal context* within which the press has to operate in this country. We then comment on the practical implications of the law for the working journalist. In discussing freedom of expression and the value of a free press to a modern western democracy, we examine the legislation, case law and judicial comments relevant to these concepts. The United Nations Universal Declaration of Human Rights was closely followed in Europe when, in 1950, the European Convention on Human Rights was signed. The signatories proclaimed that they were:

"Reaffirming their profound belief in those Fundamental Freedoms which are the foundations of justice and peace in the world and are best maintained on the one hand by an effective political democracy

---

[1] United Nations Declaration of Human Rights, 1948.
[2] International Federation of Journalists: Journalism Put to the Sword 2006. (Brussels, 2007).
[3] ibid., p.2.

and on the other by a common understanding and observance of the
Human Rights upon which they depend. "[4]

We are primarily concerned with Art.10 of the Convention:

"1. Everyone has the right to freedom of expression. This right shall
include freedom to hold opinions and to receive and impart information and ideas without interference by public authority and regardless
of frontiers.
    2. The exercise of these freedoms, since it carries with it *duties and
responsibilities*, may be subject to such *formalities, conditions, restrictions
or penalties* as are *prescribed by law* and are *necessary* in a democratic
society, in the interest of *national security, territorial integrity or public
safety*, for the *prevention of disorder or crime*, for the *protection of health or
morals*, for the *protection of the reputation or rights of others*, for *preventing
the disclosure of information received in confidence*, or for maintaining the
authority and *impartiality of the judiciary*."

Even the most cursory examination of this provision tells us that freedom
of expression is subject to limitations. That in itself does not undermine
the value to a democratic society of the first part of Art.10, but is more of
a reminder to governments that, while freedom to express views and
opinions can be curtailed, it should only occur when absolutely necessary. *Necessary* is indeed the defining word. In *Kommersant Moldovy v
Moldova [2007]*,[5] the European Court of Human Rights stated that the test
of "necessity" required the court to:

"determine whether the interference complained of corresponded to
a pressing social need, whether it was proportionate to the legitimate
aim pursued and whether the reasons given by the national authorities to justify it are relevant and sufficient."[6]

This strong statement of principle is hardly something new. The court
cited the *Sunday Times v United Kingdom* case (1979) as its authority and
the words will be familiar to all those who over the years have had more
than a passing interest in the legal working of Art.10. In the *Moldova* case,
the applicant newspaper had been critical of the government's response
to the establishment of the Moldavian Republic of Transdniestra. The
government's response was to prosecute the newspaper for endangering national security and public safety. In effect, the authorities' view was
that the newspaper was acting in a way that was tantamount to promoting treason by demonstrating hostility towards its own government. The
relevant legal background was Article 32 of the Moldovan Constitution,
which deals with freedom of opinion and expression. Each citizen is

---

[4] Preamble: European Convention on Human Rights: Rome, November, 1950.
[5] [2007] ECHR 9
[6] ibid., at para.33.

guaranteed freedom of thought, of opinion, as well as freedom of expression in public through words, images or through other available means. However freedom of expression should not harm "the honour or dignity of others or the right of others to have their own opinion".

Article 32(3) states:

"The law prohibits and punishes the contestation and defamation of the State and the nation, calls to war and aggression, national, racial or religious hatred, and incitement to discrimination, territorial separatism, or public violence, as well as other expression which endangers the constitutional order."

So what is giveth by the one hand can be taketh away by the other.

Moldova also has a Press Act 1994. Article 4 was relevant to this case. Publishers of periodicals are given discretion as to what they publish, but then the article repeats word for word the second part of Art.10 of the European Convention on Human Rights.

The Moldovan courts ordered that the newspaper should close on the grounds there had been a systematic violation of the Press Act although, strangely, the courts were extremely vague as to which of the many outpourings of the newspaper had created the problem for which they were being closed down. The newspaper appealed. The European Court of Human Rights had little difficulty in concluding there had been a violation of Art.10.

The Court reiterated the well-known general principles relating to this area of law:

1 That freedom of expression constitutes one of the essential foundations of a democratic society.
2 Safeguarding the press is of particular importance. However the press must not "overstep the bounds set."
3 It is incumbent on the press to "impart information and ideas of public interest."
4 There is a corresponding right on behalf of the public to receive such information and ideas.
5 The press has a vital role to play as "public watchdog."
6 It is incumbent on the Court of Human Rights to engage in the "most careful scrutiny" when a national authority has acted in such a way as to discourage "the participation of the press in debates over matters of legitimate public concern."
7 The right to freedom of expression includes the right to communicate ideas and opinions that ". . . offend, shock or disturb the State or any section of the community."
8 Journalistic freedom ". . . covers possible recourse to a degree of exaggeration, or even provocation."

The Court is always at pains to confirm that Art.10 does not admit of "unrestricted freedom of expression" even when matters of serious public concern are being highlighted. The press must be aware of the "duties and responsibilities" listed in Art.10(2). These duties and responsibilities said the court in the Moldova case "assume significance when . . . there is a question of endangering national security and the territorial integrity of the State."

A number of authorities are quoted to support the above propositions. The press role as public watchdog is supported by the *Observer and Guardian v United Kingdom (1991)*[7] (the aftermath of the *Spycatcher* litigation in the United Kingdom) and *Busuioc v Moldova (2004)*.[8]

The court's approach when press freedom is under challenge by national authorities is supported by the precedents of *Lingens v Austria* (1986),[9] *Bladet Tromso and Stensaas v Norway* (1999)[10] and *Thorgeir Thorgeirson v Iceland* (1992).[11]

Freedom to express views forcefully and to offend the State is regarded as a "right" within the proper ambit of Art.10. The Court in Moldova cites *De Haes and Gijsels v Belgium* as authority for the proposition.[12] The strongly held views of the authors, the editor and a journalist with HUMO magazine criticising the decision of the judges in the Antwerp Court of Appeal were held to be consistent with Art.10.

> "Although Mr De Haes' and Mr Gijsels' comments were without doubt severely critical, they nevertheless appear proportionate to the stir and indignation caused by the matters alleged in their articles. As to the journalist's polemical and even aggressive tone, which the Court should not be taken to approve, it must be remembered that Article 10 protects not only the substance of the ideas and information expressed but also the form in which they are conveyed."[13]

Of course, Art.10 does not give a guarantee of wholly unrestricted freedom of expression. The duties and responsibilities of the press are likely to be drawn into sharper focus when writing about issues that the state believes could adversely affect national security or territorial integrity. *Han v Turkey (2005)*[14] is cited as the supporting authority for this proposition in the *Moldova* case. It is worth pointing out that, whatever safeguards are comprehended by Art.10, they are subject to the proviso that journalists are ". . .acting in good faith in order to provide accurate and reliable information in accordance with the ethics of journalism."[15]

The court cites *Goodwin v United Kingdom* (1996) for the proposition that the "necessity" for any restriction on the freedom of the press has to

---

[7] [1991] ECHR 49, para.59.
[8] [2004] ECHR 695, para.56.
[9] [1986] ECHR 7, para.59.
[10] [1999] ECHR 29, para.64.
[11] [1992] ECHR 51, para.63.
[12] [1997] ECHR 7, para.46.
[13] ibid., para.48.
[14] (2005) ECHR 588.
[15] *Moldova* case [2007] ECHR 9, at para.32.

be "convincingly established."[16] In *Sunday Times v United Kingdom (No2)* (1991)[17] the court said that the word *"necessary"* implies a *"pressing social need"*. States have a *"certain margin of appreciation"* in coming to a conclusion as to whether such a need exists. Whatever the wording or approach, the European Court of Human Rights must ensure that any *restriction in the exercise* of Art.10 rights is "reconcilable with freedom of expression as *protected* under Article 10."[18]

It will be apparent that the *Moldova* case has been taken as one of the latest cases to be decided at the time of writing. It has no particular significance in terms of general principles other than the fact that it states the major principles that are applicable to these issues at the beginning of 2007. In any future study of this topic readers should ensure that they consult the latest ECHR cases on the exercise of Art.10 rights.

The numerous decisions of the ECHR leave us in no doubt about its views on the importance of a free press to a democratic society. What of the English judiciary? This is what Lord Justice Brooke said in *Greene v Associated Press* [2004][19]:

"In this country we have a free press. Our press is free to get things right and it is free to get things wrong. It is free to write after the manner of Milton, and it is free to write in a manner that would make Milton turn in his grave. Blackstone wrote in 1769 that the liberty of the press is essential in a free state, and this liberty consists in laying no previous restraints on publication. 'Every freeman,' he said, 'has an undoubted right to lay what sentiments he pleases before the public: to forbid this is to destroy the freedom of the press.' "[20]

Lord Hoffmann was typically forthright in *Campbell v MGN Ltd* [2004][21]:

". . . the press is free to publish anything it likes. Subject to the law of defamation, it does not matter how trivial, spiteful or offensive the publication may be."[22]

The Master of the Rolls in *Loutchansky v Times Newspapers Ltd* [2004][23] is of the opinion that there is a public interest:

". . . in a modern democracy in free expression and, more particularly, in the promotion of a free and vigorous press to keep the public informed. The vital importance of this interest has been identified and

16 [1996] ECHR 16 at para.40.
17 [1991] ECHR 50.
18 ibid., para.40.
19 [2004] EWCA 1462.
20 ibid., para.1.
21 [2004] UKHL 22.
22 ibid., para.56.
23 [2001] EWCA 1805.

emphasised time and again in recent cases and needs no restatement here.''[24]

Judicial support in the UK for a free press is strong and consistent. Perhaps all the more surprising then that Sir Christopher Meyer, the chairman of the Press Complaints Commission, should tell his audience in November 2006 that press freedom was "being eaten away." He went on:

"I believe the boundaries of freedom of expression seem to be closing in a bit on newspapers and magazines in a way that may not be healthy. I'm not a conspiracy theorist, I don't believe in government plotting to curb freedom of expression but when you read that after two years, there are proposals to make it more difficult to obtain information under the Freedom of Information Act, you have to worry."[25]

It is apparent that, while the principle of a free press is lauded by judges, one has to ask exactly what does having a free press entail and what responsibilities are cast upon the media. Rights and responsibilities do, after all, tend to go hand in hand. The issue was graphically raised by the 2005 publication in Jyllands-Posten, a Danish newspaper, of cartoons which depicted the Prophet Mohammed. The editor of the newspaper was bound to be aware that graphic depictions of the Prophet would provoke extreme reactions from Muslims, particularly as one of the cartoons showed the Prophet with a bomb in his turban. The implication was obvious . . . Islam and therefore all Muslims are linked to terrorism. The Danish government responded to criticism by commenting that, in a democratic country which embraced freedom of expression, the newspaper was free to publish what it liked subject of course to any laws which specifically prohibited the publication of such material. Protests spread throughout the Islamic world and inevitably this led to damage to property and loss of life.

The cartoons were reprinted in many newspapers throughout Europe and the western world as part of the process of disseminating the news and in some cases simply to demonstrate the right to freedom of expression.

The cartoon issue raised a number of questions about the interrelationship between a free press, freedom of expression and a government's duty to protect religious freedom and promote religious tolerance.

For a government to suppress speech that it finds distasteful or offensive will inevitably lead to accusations of censorship and political interference. One might do well to heed the words of Lord Nicholls of Birkenhead when dealing with the limits of the defence of fair comment in English Law:

---

[24] ibid., para.36. Cited with approval by Lord Scott of Foscote in *Jameel v Wall Street Journal Europe Ltd.* [2006] UKHL 44 at para.134.
[25] Quoted in the Guardian Tuesday, November 14, 2006.

"... the comment must be one which could have been made by an honest person, however prejudiced he might be, and however exaggerated or obstinate his views: see Lord Porter in *Turner v. Metro-Goldwyn-Mayer Pictures Ltd [1950]* ... It must be germane to the subject matter criticised. Dislike of an artist's style would not justify an attack upon his morals or manners. But a critic need not be mealy-mouthed in denouncing what he disagrees with. He is entitled to dip his pen in gall for the purposes of legitimate criticism."[26]

Without at this stage entering into a discourse on the defence of Fair Comment, the purpose of such a defence is to:

"... facilitate freedom of expression by commenting on matters of public interest. This accords with the constitutional guarantee of freedom of expression. And it is in the public interest that everyone should be free to express his own, honestly held views on such matters ..."[27]

Lord Nicholls goes on to state:

"The public interest in freedom to make comments within these limits is of particular importance in the social and political fields. Professor Fleming stated the matter thus in his invaluable book on The Law of Torts, 9th edition, p.648: '... untrammelled discussion of public affairs and of those participating in them is a basic safeguard against irresponsible political power. The unfettered preservation of the right of fair comment is, therefore, one of the foundations supporting our standards of personal liberty.' "[28]

Under Art.10(2) of the European Convention one accepts that, through the due process of law, a state may seek to inhibit or proscribe particular aspects of free speech. In the United Kingdom, Parliament has made it a criminal offence intentionally to stir up religious hatred. This may be achieved by the use of words or behaviour or written material or publishing or distributing the same. However, under the schedule to the Racial and Religious Hatred Act 2006 which inserts a new Pt 3A into the Public Order Act 1986, Parliament, through s.29J, reaffirms its commitment to freedom of expression:

"Protection of Freedom of Expression
Nothing in this Part shall be read or given effect in a way which prohibits or restricts discussion, criticism or expressions of antipathy,

---

[26] *Albert Cheng v Tse Wai Chun Paul* [2000] HKCFA 88.
[27] ibid., per Lord Nicholls.
[28] ibid., per Lord Nicholls. See also the comment of Chief Justice Li in the same case:"The freedom of speech (or the freedom of expression) is a freedom that is essential to Hong Kong's civil society. It is constitutionally guaranteed by the basic Law. The right of fair comment is a most important element of freedom of speech."

dislike, ridicule, insults or abuse or particular religions or the beliefs or practices of their adherents, or of any other belief system or the beliefs or practices of its adherents, or proselytising or urging adherents of a different religion or belief system to cease practising their religion or belief system."[29]

So would the publishers of the cartoons have committed an offence under the Act if published initially in the UK rather than Denmark? In all likelihood the answer would be no because there was no evidence that the publishers intended to stir up religious hatred although that would depend very much on whether the editor foresaw that "religious hatred" would be the consequence of his actions. Secondly the written material so displayed would have to be "threatening" and at the time of writing this word still requires judicial determination. If all else failed then the publishers could still argue that their actions were consistent with s.29J.

The theoretical perspective in favour of freedom of speech rests squarely with John Stuart Mill (1806–1873). Arguably the most famous British philosopher of the 19th century, he embraced logic, philosophy, economics, politics, ethics and religion. His treatise *On Liberty*, published in 1859, was one of his most controversial works. He expressed the view that society should not have to keep defending the "liberty of the press." Press freedom was necessary to protect society "against corrupt or tyrannical government." Referring to the suppression of free expression as a "particular evil" he opines that the human race is being "robbed" of something of value. If the opinion is "right" then the people are "being deprived of the opportunity of exchanging error for truth: if wrong, they lose, what is almost as great a benefit, the clearer perception and livelier impression of truth, produced by its collision with error . . .".[30] He goes on to advocate that "the necessity to the mental well-being of mankind (on which all other well being depends) of freedom of opinion and freedom of expression of opinion . . ." is well recognised. There are four distinct grounds:

1. Truth should never be denied a platform.
2. Through expressing opposing opinions the truth may emerge.
3. The truth should be "vigorously and earnestly contested."
4. Suppression of opinion inhibits the growth of "any real and heartfelt conviction." Both the individual and the nation are the losers.

Professor Eric Barendt's classic work *Freedom of Speech*[31] takes a modern-day perspective on the notion of free speech pitting the "purely" philosophical arguments in favour of freedom of speech against the more "specific" arguments that courts have to take into account when acting constitutionally.

---

[29] Racial and Religious Hatred Act 2006. Sch.1: s.29J.
[30] On Liberty: Ch.2.
[31] Oxford University Press, 2nd edn, March, 2007. (PBK).

The theoretical nature of the discussion is underpinned by reference to four justifications of free speech which warrant the conclusion that free speech deserves special legislative protection. The first drawing upon Mill's analysis resonates around the idea that opinions should never be suppressed otherwise individuals will rarely be able to discover the truth. Even falsehoods should be articulated so that they can be shown up for what they are. As Wendell Holmes J. so famously stated in his dissenting judgment in *Abrams v United States*[32]:

"... the ultimate good desired is better reached by free trade in ideas—that the best test of truth is the power of the thought to get itself accepted in the competition of the market, and that truth is the only ground upon which their wishes safely can be carried out ... we should be eternally vigilant against attempts to check the expression of opinions that we loathe and believe to be fraught with death, unless they so imminently threaten immediate interference with the lawful and pressing purposes of the law that an immediate check is required to save the country."

The pursuit of truth as an overriding justification for supporting a principle of free expression is shown by Barendt if not to be fallacious, then certainly to be a cause that can be logically challenged. He points out that the Weimar Republic in the 1920s generally supported free political expression yet led to the Nazi regime establishing itself in Germany in the early 1930s. The collective myopia of much of the German nation to the holocaust bears testimony to the fact that not so much the free expression of opinions but exposure to graphic pictures and newsreels was the catalyst to the ultimate acceptance of the truth.

The second argument put forward by Barendt is that free speech makes a contribution to individual self-development and fulfilment. That aspect of freedom of expression would seem to complement the recognition inherent in Art.8 of the European Convention on Human Rights that the right to a private life includes a person's physical and psychological integrity. Over zealous reliance by the media upon Art.10 rights to reveal information about private lives has recently come under critical surveillance not just from the European Court of Human Rights but also the English courts including the House of Lords.[33] A primary objective of the Convention is to ensure "the development, without outside interference, of the personality of each individual in his relations with other human beings . . . There is therefore a zone of interaction of a person with others, even in a public context, which may fall within the scope of 'private life.' "[34] The amount of money that the state pours into education would seem to suggest that government accepts the need for

---

[32] [1919] USSC 2.
[33] *Von Hannover v Germany* [2004]; *Campbell v MGN Ltd* [2004]; *McKennitt v Ash* [2005/6]; *HRH The Prince of Wales v Associated Press* [2006].
[34] *Von Hannover v Germany* [2004] ECHR 294 at para.50.

intellectual self-fulfilment through the development of ideas, opinions and the ability to communicate one's views to others.

Eric Plutzer tells us that"most young citizens start their political lives as habitual non-voters but they vary in how long it takes to develop into habitual voters."[35] This sentiment would strike a chord with Barendt's third argument in favour of freedom of speech, that of encouraging people to take an inclusive approach to the democratic processes of their country. As he says:". . . citizen participation in a democracy . . . is probably the most easily understandable, and certainly the most fashionable, free speech theory in Western democracies." In order to make an informed choice at the ballot box, one must not only be capable of intellectually comprehending the various manifestos on offer, but also be aware of the detail contained in the manifestos through extensive publicity and debating of the issues. This is the argument that sustains the major rationale for the First Amendment to the American Constitution—the desire for the populace to embrace self-government through representation and the ballot box.

Finally, and perhaps not unexpectedly, the notion of free speech permits the populace to be vigilant against governmental attempts to "limit radical or subversive views." This section of Barendt's first chapter is headed "Suspicion of Government" and the author rightly poses the question of whether in this all pervasive media age we need to be any more suspicious of government than we do of other organisations which have the power to censor free speech such as the huge media conglomerates. It is ironic that the very organisations upon whom we depend for information may in fact be disseminating information that is itself selective and non-critical. This in turn brings us back to the Millian argument that we need to hear as many opinions as possible to be able to determine where the truth lies.

Unlike the United States, this country has an unwritten constitution and therefore freedom of expression has no greater standing than any other principle in English law. The Human Rights Act 1998 does though include a section entitled "Freedom of Expression" which purports to emphasise to the judiciary the importance of the concept. In assessing whether to grant any relief which might affect the exercise of Art.10, the court has to take a number of factors into account. When the respondent in any action is not present or represented in court, no relief is to be granted unless all reasonable steps have been taken to notify the respondent of the action, unless there are *compelling* reasons for not so doing. A court is directed to have "particular regard" to "the importance of the convention right to freedom of expression" when the respondent wishes to publish "journalistic, literary or artistic material."

In 2004, the House of Lords had the opportunity to consider the meaning of s.12(3) of the Human Rights Act. This sub-section appears to support the rule against prior restraint. (See p. 20) This means that a

---

[35] *Becoming a Habitual Voter: Inertia, Resources and Growth in Young Adulthood.* American Political Science Review (2002), 96: 41–56, Cambridge University Press.

publication will not be subject to injunctive relief prior to publication unless a court is satisfied that the applicant's prospects of success at any subsequent trial "are sufficiently favourable to justify such an order being made in the particular circumstances of the case."[36]

The UK position should be contrasted with the United States where freedom of speech is protected by the First Amendment to the United States Constitution. Ratified on December 15, 1791, it reads:

> "Congress shall make no law respecting an establishment of religion, or prohibiting the free exercise thereof; or abridging the freedom of speech, or of the press; or of the right of the people peaceably to assemble, and to petition the Government for a redress of grievances."

It is worth noting that the Amendment doesn't actually refer to the word "expression." The "freedoms" protected are speech, assembly and the ability to petition government but arguably the use of the word "expression" covers all three rights identified by the First Amendment. Freedom of speech is clearly protected but only against interference by Congress and by the 14th Amendment of the Constitution, not state legislatures. In *New York Times v Sullivan* [1964][37] the Supreme Court was required for the very first time to decide the extent to which "the constitutional protections for speech and press limit a State's (Alabama's) power to award damages in a libel action brought by a public official against critics of his official conduct."The newspaper had carried an advertisement urging its readers to "Heed Their Rising Voices." Its purpose was to elicit funds to assist with the promotion of civil rights campaigns in the southern states of America. The respondent was one of three elected Commissioners of the City of Montgomery in Alabama and held the position of Commissioner of Public Affairs. He sued on the basis that he had been libelled by statements in the advertisement. Although he was not identified by name, he claimed that the criticism of the police force in Montgomery were a direct reflection on him. Here is an example of what was written:

> "In Montgomery, Alabama, after students sang " 'My Country, 'Tis of Thee' " on the State Capitol steps, their leaders were expelled from school, and truckloads of police armed with shotguns and tear-gas ringed the Alabama State College Campus. When the entire student body protested to state authorities by refusing to reregister, their dining hall was padlocked in an attempt to starve them into submission.
>
> "Again and again, the Southern violators have answered Dr King's peaceful protests with intimidation and violence. They have bombed his home, almost killing his wife and child. They have assaulted his person. They have arrested him seven times—for speeding, loitering

---

[36] *Cream Holdings Ltd v Banerjee* [2004] UKHL 44.
[37] [1964] 376 US 254.

and similar offences. And now they have charged him with perjury—
a felony under which they could imprison him for ten years . . ."

The threat of civil action for libel undoubtedly induces the potential for
the "chilling effect" on the media to raise its head. The Court in *Sullivan*
determined that a public official could only succeed in an action for libel
if it could be shown the newspaper in question was actuated by malice.
Lest it be thought that *Sullivan* has no influence on the English courts one
needs to consider the speech by Lord Keith in *Derbyshire County Council
v Times Newspapers Ltd* [1993].[38] The House of Lords agreed that it was of
vital importance in a democratic society to be able to criticise public
bodies without the constant fear of a defamation action hanging over the
media. Not only did he endorse the decision in *Sullivan*, he quoted with
approval from the earlier US decision in *City of Chicago v Tribune Co*
(1923),[39] in which it was held that the city could not bring an action for
libel against the media. Thompson C.J. stated:

"The fundamental right of freedom of speech is involved in this litigation and not merely the right of liberty of the press. If this action can
be maintained against a newspaper it can be maintained against every
private citizen who ventures to criticise the ministers who are tem-
porarily conducting the affairs of his government. "

The judge was of the opinion that the threat of civil action against the
media was "as great if not a greater restriction than a criminal prosecution." He went on to say:

"It follows, therefore, that every citizen has a right to criticise an inef-
ficient or corrupt government without fear of civil as well as criminal
prosecution. This absolute privilege is founded on the principle that it
is advantageous for the public interest that the citizen should not be
in any way fettered in his statements, and where the public service or
due administration of justice is involved he shall have the right to
speak his mind freely.'"[40]

1. Public Interest

The above statement reinforces the view that free speech/expression is
in the public interest. This raises the question of what is legally meant by
the words *public interest* because it is this very concept that the media
consistently relies upon to justify publication of sometimes extremely

[38] [1993] 1 All E.R. 1011.
[39] (1923) 307 Ill 595.
[40] ibid., pp.607–08.

contentious material. When the media applied to intervene in the recent
McKennitt v Ash case,[41] one of the issues identified by counsel was that
the definition of public interest needed to be restated particularly when
balancing personal privacy against the media's right to expose what
might be regarded as essentially private information. That of course is a
narrow issue whereas the original point was that the media consistently
relies upon the concepts of freedom of expression and "public interest"
to defend its right to publish. The context is very often the legal basis
upon which a judge will decide between two competing public interests.

In the privacy field it is likely to be between the public interest in protecting confidentiality, whether personal or commercial, and the public
interest in publishing information, i.e. utilising the right of free expression and free speech. As Lord Justice Stephenson said in *Lion Laboratories
v Evans*,[42] the countervailing interest is of the public being kept informed
of matters that are of "real public concern." There were, he said, four
further considerations:

> "1. There is a wide difference between what is interesting to the public
> and what it is in the pubic interest to make known.
> 2. The media have a private interest of their own in publishing what
> appeals to the public and may increase the circulation or the numbers
> of their viewers or listeners and as a result they are 'particularly vul-
> nerable to the error of confusing the public interest with their own
> interest.'
> 3. The public interest may be best served by an informer giving infor-
> mation not to the press but to the police or other responsible body.
> 4. It is in the public interest to disclose grave misconduct or wrongdo-
> ing or to put it another way there is no confidence 'as to the disclosure
> of iniquity.'"[43]

In this case two ex-employees of Lion Laboratories had released to the
press information based upon confidential company documents that
indicated that Lion, the maker of breath-testing equipment, was aware
there were doubts as to the reliability and accuracy of the instruments.
The court held that injunctions granted to the company to prevent
publication of the information should be lifted. The court confirmed
that it was "well accepted" that there was a public interest defence to
actions of breach of confidence and breach of copyright providing that it
could be shown that it was in the public interest to publish confidential
information.

Much the same reasoning applied in the *McKennitt* case albeit in a
different context. McKennitt was a folk singer of some repute whose
erstwhile friend was intent on publishing a book about her life. For
commercial reasons publishers will expect revelations in such a book

---

[41] [2005] EWHC 3003 and [2006] EWCA 171.
[42] [1984] 2 All E.R. 417.
[43] ibid., at p.423.

and Ash was intent upon not disappointing them. McKennitt sought and injunction and damages for breach of confidence. In this chapter we are not concerned with the current state of the privacy laws (see Chapter 4), but looking at whether such a publication would be construed as being in the public interest. It will be obvious that much of what Ash intended to publish could have been gleaned only because of her close friendship with McKennitt. In other words it was argued by the applicant that there had been a breach of confidentiality. The trial judge, Eady J. took the view that there was "little public interest in the matters addressed in the book" and "certainly no public interest sufficient to outweigh Ms McKennitt's Art.8 right to respect for her private life."

In response, Ms Ash argued that McKennitt was a public figure and "for that reason alone" there was a legitimate public interest in her affairs. The second argument, of which more in the privacy chapter, centres on the "putting the record straight" theory. This theory is based on the premise that 'if a public figure misbehaves' then the public have a right to have the record corrected. The premise is not in doubt and has been supported by the courts for many years. In precedent terms, the most influential case is the decision of the House of Lords in *Campbell v MGN Ltd* [2004].[44] All five Law Lords held that it was in the public interest that the Daily Mirror inform its readership of Ms Campbell's use of drugs. Not only was she a public figure but she had maintained that, unlike other supermodels, she did not use drugs; a fact that the Mirror exposed as a lie when she was photographed by long lens coming out of Narcotics Anonymous in London. However the House went on to conclude, by a 3:2 majority, that the Mirror was breaching Ms Campbell's privacy by using a surreptitiously obtained photograph to illustrate the story.

The Court of Appeal in rejecting Ms Ash's arguments expressed surprise that McKennitt should be considered a public figure. The court followed European jurisprudence from the Court of Human Rights[45] in reaching that conclusion. The "European" view is that while it is accepted that the press has an:

"... important role ... in dealing with matters of public interest ... a distinction was then to be drawn between the watchdog role in the democratic process and the reporting of private information about people who, although of interest to the public, were not public figures."[46]

It follows that there will always be a degree of subjectivity when assessing whether a publication is in the "public interest." However, what seems to be clear is that, if the media is exercising its "watchdog" role, then there is every likelihood that the publication will be deemed to be

---

[44] [2004] UKHL 22.
[45] *Von Hannover v Germany* [2004] EMLR 379
[46] [2006] EWCA 171 at para.58.

in the public interest. Exposing corruption, examining the actions of state-funded bodies, matters of constitutional importance, rooting out crime and of course keeping a watchful eye out for potential abuses of trust or office by politicians is in all probability going to serve the media well if challenged by an aggrieved applicant.

The Press Complaints Commission (PCC) Code of Practice provides a definition of public interest. After stating the various elements of best practice for newspaper and magazine journalists, the Code makes the following assertions:

1   The public interest includes, but is not confined to:
   i. detecting or exposing crime or serious impropriety
   ii. protecting public health and safety
   iii. preventing the public from being misled by an action or statement of an individual or organisation.

The Code goes on to confirm that, in the PCC's view, there is a public interest in freedom of expression itself. (In fact, it would have been difficult to have made any other statement, given the strong endorsement from the English and European courts.) As a matter of good practice, once an editor has invoked the public interest as a justification for publication, then the onus is placed upon the editor to justify that decision. In other words there must be tangible evidence to support the conclusion. One factor that will clearly influence editors is whether or not the information is already in the public domain. However, with the recent developments in the privacy laws this may not be the trump card that one would expect. (See Chapter 4, *X & Y v Person or Persons Unknown* [2006])

The Broadcast Code takes a slightly different approach.[47] Nowhere is there to be found a "generic" definition of public interest. Rather the Code identifies certain situations where the public interest is a necessary concomitant of good broadcasting practice. For example at cl.8.13, which deals with surreptitious filming and recording, broadcasters are told that such filming will only be warranted if "there is prima facie evidence" of a story in the public interest. Another example at cl.8.1 works on the same assumption as 8.13. In this case, a breach of privacy may be warranted if it is in the public interest and "the broadcaster should be able to demonstrate that the public interest outweighs the right to privacy."

As one might expect, discussion of the public interest concept is evident in a number of cases. These will appear throughout this book. However at this introductory stage it is perhaps worthwhile suggesting one looks for the highest judicial reasoning. We have already mentioned *Campbell v MGN Ltd*. It is also fruitful to refer to the House's decision in *Cream Holdings Ltd v Banerjee [2004]*.[48] As Lord Nicholls said, the material the newspaper wished to publish was "incontestably" a matter of serious

---

[47] Ofcom Broadcasting Code: May 2005. Available at *www.ofcom.org.uk*.
[48] [2004] UKHL 44.

public interest and the story was one that no court could properly suppress. The case hinged upon whether the former finance officer of Cream
Holdings was acting in the public interest to remove confidential documentation when dismissed by the company.

The documentation was delivered to the Liverpool Post and Echo
and purported to show that there was illegal and improper activity by
the company including an allegation of a corrupt relationship between a
director of the company and a local council official. The House denied
injunctive relief to the company. The newspaper was undertaking its
"watchdog" role in bringing into the open the allegation of impropriety.

So the concept of the public interest goes to the very heart of media
operations. This and the right to exercise freedom of expression are vital
factors to consider if the media is faced with an application for an injunction to prevent the publication or broadcasting of material that the applicant would rather did not receive a public airing.

2. The Rule Against Prior Restraint

Lord Justice Brooke, in the case of *Greene v Associated Newspapers Ltd*
[2004],[49] was blunt in his defence of free speech. Our press, he said:

> "... is free to get things right and it is free to get things wrong. It is
> free to write after the manner of Milton, and it is free to write in a
> manner that would make Milton turn in his grave."

This sentiment has its historical roots in the writings of the English
jurist Sir William Blackstone (1723–1780) and his famous *Commentaries
on the Laws of England* published in four volumes from 1765–1769. He
wrote:

> "The liberty of the press is indeed essential to the nature of a free
> state: but this consists in laying no previous restraints upon publica-
> tions, and not in freedom from censure from criminal matter when
> published. Every free man has an undoubted right to lay what senti-
> ments he pleases before the public: to forbid this is to destroy the
> freedom of the press: but if he publishes what is improper, mischie-
> vous or illegal, he must take the consequences of his own temerity."[50]

The principle therefore seems to have strong foundations. The US courts
are not averse to quoting the principle in support of the First Amendment
to the Constitution. "Any system of prior restraints of expression comes
to this court bearing a heavy presumption against its constitutional

---

[49] [2004] EWCA Civ 1462.
[50] Commentaries on the Laws of England Vol. 4, p.151.

validity."[51] The Government "thus carries a heavy burden of showing justification for the imposition of such restraint."[52] In *New York Times v US*
(1971),[53] the government had sought injunctions to prevent the New York
Times and the Washington Post from publishing government documents
relating to the conduct of the Vietnamese war. The Supreme Court was
having none of it. As Brennan J. so forcefully put it:

> "The error that has pervaded these cases from the outset was the
> granting of any injunctive relief whatsoever, interim or otherwise. The
> entire thrust of the Government's claim throughout these cases has
> been that publication of the material sought to be enjoined 'could,' or
> 'might,' or 'may' prejudice the national interest in various ways. But the
> First Amendment tolerates absolutely no prior restraints of the press
> predicated upon surmise or conjecture that untoward consequences
> may result."[54]

Of course the UK does not have the benefit of a written constitution, but
the rule against prior restraint was given judicial acknowledgement in
respect of libel in *Bonnard v Perryman* (1891).[55] Lord Coleridge C.J. stated:

> "... it is obvious that the subject matter of an action for defamation is
> so special as to require exceptional caution in exercising the jurisdic
> tion to interfere by injunction before the trial of an action to prevent
> an anticipated wrong. The right of free speech is one which it is for the
> public interest that individuals should possess, and, indeed that they
> should exercise without impediment, so long as no wrongful act is
> done; and, unless an alleged libel is untrue, there is no wrong com
> mitted; but on the contrary, often a very wholesome act is performed
> in the publication and repetition of an alleged libel. Until it is clear that
> an alleged libel is untrue, it is not clear that any right has been
> infringed; and the importance of leaving free speech unfettered is a
> strong reason in cases of libel for dealing most cautiously and warily
> with the granting of injunctions ...".

The rule is still as potent now as it was in 1891. Lightman J. in *Service
Corporation International Plc v Channel Four Television* [1999][56] said:

> "The reason that defamation is not and cannot be invoked is because
> no interlocutory injunction could be granted on this ground in view of
> the defendant's plain and obvious intention to plead to any such claim
> the defence of justification."[57]

[51] *Bantam Books Inc v Sullivan* (1963) 372 US 58 at p.70.
[52] *Organisation for a Better Austin v Keefe* (1971) 402 US 415 at p.419.
[53] [1971] 403 US 713.
[54] ibid., p.714.
[55] (1891) 2 Ch.269.
[56] [1999] EMLR 83.
[57] ibid., p.89.

To that may be added that an intention to plead fair comment and qualified privilege will invariably lead to the same conclusion.[58] The prevailing view is that it is up to the media to publish at their own risk. As Lord Denning said in *Fraser v Evans*,[59] if the media is guilty of libel or breaches of confidence or copyright, then that can be determined by a post-publication action and damages awarded against the media organisation.

The rule against prior restraint would therefore seem to sit easily with the idea of a free press and freedom of expression. In legal terms it would appear to be compatible with Art.10 of the European Convention of Human Rights. The European Court in its judgment in the notorious Spycatcher case (*The Observer and the Guardian v United Kingdom* [1991][60]) stated:

"... the dangers inherent in prior restraints are such that they call for the most careful scrutiny on the part of the Court. This is especially so as far as the press is concerned, for news is a perishable commodity and to delay its publication, even for a short period, may well deprive it of all its value and interest."[61]

However the court did add, by reference to Art.10(2), that the imposition of prior restraints was not prohibited under Art.10. A number of the judges expressed the opinion that any such restraint should only be imposed in "wartime and national emergency."

The approach that had been adopted in respect of the granting of interim injunctions was that the applicant had to establish a prima facie case. In practice, this meant he had to prove that on the evidence before the court *at that time* and on the balance of probabilities he would succeed at any subsequent trial. The so-called "balance of convenience" test was then conceived by the House of Lords in the non-media case of *American Cyanamid v Ethicon Ltd* [1975].[62] In essence judges were to be satisfied that the applicant's claim for an injunction was not "frivolous or vexatious." If that "threshold" was passed then the court had to consider where the "balance of convenience" lay. As Lord Nicholls said in the *Cream Holdings* case, where matters were evenly balanced then a court was likely to take "such measures as are calculated to preserve the status quo."[63] In other words, to grant the interim injunction. Enter the Human Rights Act and s.12(3), a section designed to "allay (the) fears" that, if the conventional Cyanamid test was applied, then prior restraint could almost become a formality. As Lord Nicholls so eloquently put it:

[58] See for example *Fraser v Evans* (1969) 1 Q.B. 349.
[59] ibid., at p.363.
[60] [1991] 14 EHRR 153.
[61] ibid., at para.60.
[62] [1975] AC 396.
[63] *Cream Holdings Ltd v Banerjee* [2004] UKHL 44, at para.14.

"Its principal purpose was to buttress the protection afforded to freedom of speech at the interlocutory stage. It sought to do so by setting a higher threshold for the grant of interlocutory injunctions against the media . . ."[64]

So what is the current position and what will an applicant have to establish to obtain an interim restraint order against the media? Lord Nicholls again:

"Section 12(3) makes the likelihood of success at the trial an essential element in the court's consideration of whether to make an interim order . . . There can be no single, rigid standard governing all applications for interim restraint orders . . . the court is not to make an interim restraint order unless satisfied the applicant's prospects of success at the trial are sufficiently favourable to justify such an order being made in the particular circumstances of the case."[65]

In assessing the meaning of the words "sufficiently favourable" the general approach should be that courts will be exceedingly slow to make interim restraint orders where the applicant has not satisfied the court he will probably (more likely than not) succeed at the trial.[66]

In broad terms the court must consider the following:

- The strength of the applicant's case at that time.
- Whether the media intends to plead justification, fair comment or privilege.
- The importance of Art.10.
- Any countervailing Convention rights in particular Art.8.

In adopting this approach it also means that, as Lord Steyn said in *Re S (FC) (A child)* [2004],[67] no one article in the Convention has precedence over the another and this is becoming increasingly the case when Arts.8 and 10 come into conflict.

As a result of this, the issue of prior restraint has taken on a new dimension in recent years because of the increasing influence of the European Convention on Human Rights upon English law. Many of the applications for interim injunctions resulted in judges having to decide between the respective public interest in maintaining confidentiality and supporting free expression. The "modern" dimension has encompassed the twin rights of freedom of expression under Art.10 and the right to respect for private life under Art.8. If there is a story to tell why should a person be prevented from informing the public of the details through the active support of the media? This aspect will be further developed in the chapter

---

[64] ibid., para.15.
[65] ibid., para.22.
[66] ibid., para.22.
[67] [2004] UKHL 47, at para.17.

dealing with privacy and confidentiality but deserves passing mention here because of the recent nature of the case law.

Eady J. in *CC v AB* [2006][68] has recently revisited the principles in a most unusual context. The claimant had conducted an adulterous affair with the defendant's wife. The defendant wished to gain revenge by telling his side of the story to the media. The claimant sought and was granted an interim injunction and the judge expressed himself satisfied that the injunction was likely to be made permanent if and when the case went to full trial. (See Chapter 4 for more detail on the privacy aspects of this case.) The following points relating to prior restraint were raised in the judgment:

- If the claimant was basing his case on libel then 'there would be no prospect of an injunction' if the defendant raised the defence of justification. (*Bonnard v Perryman* being cited as the authority.)
- The *Observer and Guardian v United Kingdom* (1991) is cited as authority for the proposition that "the dangers inherent in prior restraint are such that they call for the most careful scrutiny." Also *Wingrove v United Kingdom* (1996) highlighted the fact that "special scrutiny by the court" is required in such cases.[69]
- "... what is sought is an interlocutory injunction and I need to take into account the requirements of s.12(3) of the Human Rights Act and its interpretation by the House of Lords in *Cream Holdings Ltd v Banerjee* [2005] 1 AC 253."[70]

The temporary injunction was granted but one should be careful not to treat this case as laying down any new points of principle. It was decided very much on its own particular facts. Newspapers editors would be extremely keen in most circumstances to reveal the cuckolded husband's unique insight into the relationship. However in this case they held off because of the potential that press intrusion into what was already a difficult family situation might exacerbate the claimant's wife's fragile mental health and result in a suicide attempt.

There are numerous other cases that could be mentioned at this stage concerning the approach to prior restraint. Suffice to say that those cases will be referred to at other points in this book. The working principle is that courts will be most reluctant to impose temporary injunction restraining the press from putting material into the public domain unless it is clear from the evidence that an injunction is likely to be granted at a full trial. Given that many of these applications are 11th hour attempts by celebrities to restrict the "fabled" excesses of the Sunday tabloid market, the required evidence is most unlikely to be available and therefore the claimant is faced with the prospect of having to read about his or her legal failure the following morning over breakfast.

---

[68] [2006] EWHC 3083.
[69] ibid., para.16.
[70] ibid., per Eady J. at para.34.

3. Forum Shopping

The vast majority of legal actions affecting the media will commence in the High Court in London. The assumption is that the correct forum to resolve a dispute is that in which the "wrong" occurred. Therefore, if we are discussing the "tort" of defamation, it would appear to be relatively straightforward to determine which jurisdiction should be seized of the case. If the alleged defamatory comments are contained in a national newspaper or broadcast on the BBC or another national broadcaster then once again there will be no problem.

However, with the advent of online journalism and the rapid expansion of the internet there is more likely to be a degree of uncertainty as to where any legal action may be commenced. This problem was addressed for the first time in 2004 by the Court of Appeal in the case of *Lennox Lewis v Don King*.[71] This case is a fertile source of information about the legal criteria upon which jurisdictional issues will be determined. The background is that King, a boxing promoter with an international reputation, alleged he had been defamed. Two articles had appeared on boxing websites hosted in California. They had been placed there by Judd Bernstein, a New York lawyer, among whose clients were Lennox Lewis and his production company Lion Promotions. In the articles Bernstein referred to the "clearly anti-Semitic tone" of his (King's) comments. King argued that the articles portrayed him as a ". . . persistent, bigoted, and unashamed or unrepentant anti-Semite."

King wished to bring an action in the High Court in London basing his claim on the fact that he had a reputation within this jurisdiction. Yet the facts are that a New York lawyer posted articles on Californian websites criticising a United States citizen. We are entitled to ask what this has to do with London.

The answer of course is that Don King is well known in this country. His reputation could, as a result of the postings, be damaged in this country. Logically therefore a person with an "international" reputation could literally sue in any jurisdiction in the world if he could prove that his reputation has been damaged.

The Court of Appeal examined the relevant law in order to determine the appropriate *forum conveniens*. The following is a digest of the court's assessment of the law.

1 Two points are to be established at the outset based upon the reasoning of the House of Lords in the case of *Spiliada Maritime Corp v Consulex Ltd*.[72] The first is that the matter of which jurisdiction is "pre-eminently a matter for the trial judge . . . An appeal should be rare and the appellate court should be slow to interfere."[73]

---

[71] [2004] EWCA 1329.
[72] [1987] A.C. 460.
[73] ibid., at p.465 F-G.

The second proposition is that the burden of proof rests upon the claimant to persuade the court that England". . . is the appropriate forum for the trial of the action (and) that he has to show that this is clearly so."

2 Other authorities, particularly *The Albaforth*,[74] establish three 'strands' which in essence are discretionary matters. The first 'strand' is that there is an initial assumption that the appropriate forum for trial will be the courts of the place where the tort is committed. Lord Steyn approved this statement in the *Berezovsky v Michaels & Others* case,[75] stating that the approach was "unobjectionable in principle." The second strand follows from the first and it is that "the more tenuous the claimant's connection with this jurisdiction (and the more substantial any publication abroad) the weaker this consideration becomes." The third strand deals with so called "trans-national" libels. This includes libels originating from the internet. The court refused a request to adopt special rules for the internet. It must be remembered that no media organisation is forced to utilise cyberspace. Those that do, choose to do so and for a variety of reasons. The old English authority of *Duke of Brunswick v Harmer*[76] established the principle that in respect of defamatory material each publication constituted a separate tort. Therefore actions could lie in numerous jurisdictions assuming the claimant has a reputation and there has been a publication of the alleged defamatory material within the jurisdiction.

The Australian High Court in *Gutnik v Dow Jones*[77] saw no reason to depart from the long-established approach to libel in saying: "If a publisher publishes in a multiplicity of jurisdictions it should be understood, and must accept, that it runs the risk of liability in those jurisdictions in which the publication is not lawful and inflicts damage." (The position of Internet Service Providers in the context of transmitting defamatory material will be considered in the Defamation chapter (Ch.2).)

So the Court of Appeal is rejecting a "single publication rule." Publishers using the internet will have to consider the likely outcome of choosing that medium and take the consequences if they are sued in a number of jurisdictions. In practice though a claimant will have to have tremendous stamina and deep pockets to pursue actions in a number of jurisdictions.

The fourth strand relates to what the courts call the "juridical advantage," in other words, seeking to choose a jurisdiction in which to commence an action that is likely to be favourable to the claimant. The Court of Appeal considered the first three strands not to be rules of law but

---

[74] [1984] 2 Ll L.R. 91.
[75] [2000] 1 W.L.R. 1004.
[76] (1849) 14 Q.B. 185.
[77] [2002] H.C.A. 56.

factors to be considered by the trial judge in exercising discretion. This last "strand" however should be considered as a matter of law. The juridical advantage may relate to the potential for higher damages awards or perhaps a more generous limitation period or a more complete process of discovery. The solution as Lord Goff's speech in *Spilida* emphasised was that the venue should reflect the interests ". . .of all the parties and for the ends of justice" to be achieved. The other factors discussed will help the judge make the final decision. "The underlying principle requires that regard must be had to the interest of all the parties and the ends of justice."[78]

Therefore the media needs to exercise caution when communicating via the internet. The rules for terra firma apply equally to the internet.

A slightly more recent example is the case of *Dow Jones & Co Inc v Jameel*.[79] The libel action against the company related to an article posted on web servers in New Jersey. The company claimed that there was no publication in England, arguing that the publication took place in the United States. The court recognised that Dow Jones had removed the article from its website and from the archive and therefore no repetition was likely to occur. There had been what the court called "insignificant publication" in this jurisdiction (five people, of whom three were known to the claimant) but recognised that this jurisdiction could nevertheless be the *forum conveniens*. However adopting a pragmatic approach it ruled that it would be an abuse of process to proceed as damage to reputation was unlikely in the circumstances. The proceedings were stayed.

The warning to the media is obvious. Be aware of the potential legal consequences of what is published and be prepared for legal action to be commenced in this country even though neither the media organisation nor the claimant is based in this jurisdiction.

4. Conditional Fee Arrangements

Conditional fee arrangements are discussed within the ambit of freedom of expression because they have had a profound impact on the overall cost of defending actions brought against the news media which may have a "chilling" effect on its reporting.

To mount an action against a media organisation requires a fair amount of resource. For example, legal aid is not available for defamation suits. Over the past decade, conditional fee arrangements have become widespread. The scheme was introduced by the Courts and Legal Services Act 1990 and modified by the Access to Justice Act 1999. The idea is to provide greater access to justice as in cases such as defamation where legal aid is not available to claimants.

[78] ibid., pp.482D–484B.
[79] [2005] EWCA 75.

In broad terms, such agreements permit lawyers to engage in "no win, no fee" arrangements. The benefit to the client is that if he or she loses the case no fee would be charged although the claimant would be liable for disbursements and the winning side's costs. If the claimant is successful then fees are payable but in practice the losing side will be liable for the costs of the case. In addition, the lawyer will also be able to claim a *"success"* fee which is calculated on a percentage basis of the normal professional fees.

This may sound like a good deal for the litigant and indeed, it is. It can also be rewarding for the lawyers involved because although they have to shoulder the risk of losing, if they were to win the case, the *"success"* fee can be has high as 100 per cent. However, it will be obvious that this is not such good news for the defendant media organisation faced, as it will be, with a massive hike on the conventional fees that would be paid if the claimant were not acting under a CFA. Media organisations have argued forcefully that the mere existence of the success fee regime is contrary to the principles of Art.10 of the European Convention on Human Rights. It is argued the higher costs that an organisation will have to pay if successfully sued will act as a deterrent to publication, i.e. freedom of speech will be restricted.

The CFA regime does not impose any means testing on the claimant. So the scheme is available to prince or pauper as confirmed by the House of Lords in *Campbell v MGN Ltd (Costs)* [2005].[80] It will be recalled that the super model Naomi Campbell sued the Daily Mirror for breach of confidence. She succeeded and was awarded £3,500 in damages and her legal costs but of course the case was appealed first to the Court of Appeal and then to the House of Lords. She prevailed by a 3:2 majority in the House of Lords. If one considers the figures it is immediately understandable why the defendants took umbrage at the costs bill. Ms Campbell's solicitors claimed the following in costs:

1. £377,070 for the trial;
2. £114,755 for the appeal to the Court of Appeal;
3. £594,470 for the appeal to the House of Lords.

Total Costs: £1,086,295.

An important point to recognise when considering the media's argument is that only costs that have been "proportionately and reasonably incurred and which are proportionate and reasonable in amount will be recoverable against the paying party."[81]

Until the Access to Justice Act 1999, such "success" fees were to be paid by the successful litigant and the fee could not be recovered from the loser, but that was changed as a result of s.27 of the 1999 Act inserting a new s.58A into the Courts and Legal Services Act 1990.

---

[80] [2005] UKHL 61.
[81] ibid., *per* Lord Hoffmann at para.4.

Lord Hoffmann had no doubts regarding the intent underpinning this new approach. He thought there was "no doubt that a deliberate policy of the 1999 Act was to impose the cost of all CFA litigation, successful or unsuccessful, upon the unsuccessful defendants as a class."[82] The fact that Ms Campbell might have been able to afford to pay any costs when deciding to take this case to the House of Lords was largely irrelevant said Lord Hoffmann. The fact that on occasions an individual might be in a strong financial position should not set a precedent for restricting the scheme on a means tested basis. As Lord Hoffmann put it:

". . . concentration on the individual case does not exclude recognising the desirability, in appropriate cases, of having a general rule in order to enable the scheme to work in a practical and effective way."[83]

Having established the principle, Lord Hoffmann went on to consider the "problems which defamation litigation under CFAs is currently causing and which have given rise to concern that freedom of expression may be seriously inhibited." He went on to highlight the 'blackmailing' effect of CFA litigation. CFAs may be used by 'impecunious claimants' who do not take out after the event insurance presumably because they cannot afford the premiums. The second problem relates to the "conduct of the case by the claimant's solicitors in a way which not only runs up substantial costs but requires the defendants to do so as well." A good example of this latter point is the first case in the *Henry v BBC* litigation.[84] The BBC applied for a cost capping order which was refused by Gray J. on the basis that the application was made too late in the process. The judge identified the "predicament" the BBC found itself in:

"If the case goes to trial, the BBC's own costs will be £515k. If the BBC wins at trial . . . the BBC will not be entitled to recover more than 20% of its costs (under the ATE insurance). The combined assets of the claimant and her husband come to about £235,000 most of which consists in the equity in the matrimonial home. The claimant's share is therefore only £117,000. Conversely if the claimant wins at trial the BBC will be faced with a bill of the claimant's costs which, inclusive of uplift, will total in the region of £1.6 million. On the other hand the BBC will also have to pay its own costs."

It will be recalled that the BBC eventually won the case at the second attempt after pleading justification.

There are recent examples of the potential misuse of the CFA regime alluded to by Lord Hoffmann. In late January 2007, Clarke J. terminated a libel action brought by Patricia Tierney against the Sun newspaper after it alleged that she had sex with the footballer Wayne Rooney while

[82] ibid., para.16.
[83] ibid., para.26.
[84] *Henry v BBC* [2005] EWHC 2503.

working as a prostitute in a Liverpool massage parlour. She admitted
working as a "receptionist" but denied being a sex worker. At the outset
of the trial, the newspaper was able to introduce a statement she had
made to Liverpool police five years earlier in which she admitted she was
a sex worker. The Sun had been facing costs in the region of £500,000 and
the claimant sought damages of £250,000. The judge regarded her
conduct as an attempt to pervert the court of justice. He said that her
claim had been "conceived in falsehood and continued in deceit." Costs
were awarded against her but as she lived on benefits and had no assets
it was unlikely that any costs would be recovered.

In March 2007, a claimant withdrew her action against Associated
Newspapers after claiming that she had been libelled by the Evening
Standard. An undercover investigation had claimed that the nursing
home that she owned mistreated its patients. In 2005, the case had been
subject to a cost capping order when the claimant's lawyers working on
a CFA had accumulated costs that were estimated to be in the region of
£500,000. This was another case where there was no ATE insurance in
place. As it was, the newspaper would have to absorb its own costs estimated to be around £100,000.[85]

Access to justice is a laudable principle but there are clearly serious
concerns over some aspects of the CFA arrangements, which, as the Sun
commented, was tantamount to "access to injustice."

At the heart of the costs regime will be the issue of proportionality in
relation to the amount of damages at issue. In *Cox and Carter v MGN Ltd*
[2006],[86] this issue was considered by the court as the aftermath of the
privacy claim against MGN by Sara Cox and her husband in which a settlement of £50,000 was agreed without the need for a trial of the issues.
The case is instructive as it focuses attention on how quickly costs may
escalate. The claimants were represented under a CFA agreement. There
was a dispute over the hourly fees charged by the claimant's lawyer.
Should it be £300–315 per hour or £400–450? Also under contention was
the "correct" percentage for the success fee. The Costs judge thought 40
per cent, the claimant's solicitor 95 per cent uplift and the newspaper five
per cent. There was not much basis for compromise when one looks at the
different aspirations of those involved. The court dismissed each of the
appeals but the judgment is instructive as it reviews the main factors to
be considered, including the potential "chilling effect" upon the media, in
determining the appropriate costs level. Reference should be made to the
"proportionality test" in the case of *Lownds v Home Office [2002]*.[87]

The Court referred to a two-stage approach; the "global" and the "item
by item." In broad terms the "global" approach will indicate whether the
total sum claimed is or appears to be disproportionate to the sum
claimed. If so then one moves on to the second stage and takes an "item
by item" approach to assess whether the individual costs are reasonable.

---

[85] *Matadeen v Associated Newspapers* (Unreported).
[86] [2006] EWHC 1235.
[87] [2002] EWCA Civ 365.

This section has outlined the risks currently inherent for media organisations facing opponents who are proceeding under the CFA regime. While there appears to be no tangible evidence to prove that the "chilling effect" is having a noticeably negative impact on freedom of expression, it must be a consideration when editorial judgement is being exercised.

5. Freedom of Expression in Practice

Freedom of speech, like many of our civil liberties, is at worst derided and, at best, predominantly taken for granted.

A UK journalist adopting the moral high ground by claiming to be upholding a fundamental human right is likely to provoke hollow laughter in most circles. The trivialisation of the news agenda, particularly but not exclusively in print, has strengthened the sense that little of significance is at stake. The concept of media ethics is dismissed as an oxymoron and the "me" generation assumption is that self-interest is the only genuine driver of the actions of journalists.

Yet the commitment is genuine. A journalist has to believe that, as a general rule, disclosure is the best policy. People want and need to know what is happening in their world, if they are to understand it and be able to play their part in it, not just in an overtly political context but in a day-to-day, sometimes mundane, way of using information to improve their lot, to seize opportunities, to make sense of the world and to make the most of their lives.

Upholding the public right to know inevitably involves exercising freedom of expression. For many journalists this is manifested in the daily battle to overcome the welter of obstacles put in the way of placing information in the public domain. The vast majority of journalists working up and down the country 24/7 will never bring down a government or even topple a corrupt local official but that does not make their contribution insignificant. Journalists toiling away in the backwaters may not even themselves consider their work fundamental to the successful workings of democracy but that must not obscure the fact that it is.

6. Human Rights Act in Practice

Asked if they have had "a good day at the office, dear", journalists are certainly not likely to say what a cracking time they spent exercising their Art.10 rights. Few will realise yet what an impact the Human Rights Act is having, and will increasingly have, on their ways of working and their role in society. Its operation challenges the journalistic mindset and news values and marks a significant shift in the whole field of media law.

Traditionally, journalists, like any other citizens, could pretty much act as they liked except in those areas specifically subject to legal sanction. This partly explains why media law is synonymous with restraint. Media law has historically told us what we can't do; or at least what we can expect to be punished for doing.

The Human Rights Act challenges that pattern. Journalists should arguably welcome it with open arms as, in the absence of a written constitution, it comes as close as we can get to a fundamental declaration of the right to freedom of expression. It falls a long way short of the US First Amendment but it is more than we have had in the past. It includes a variety of phrases to gladden any journalist's heart by recognising a free press as an essential player in a healthy democracy. This provides a strong legal card and means the public interest in freedom of expression per se and in any particular case has to be recognised by the courts.

But we certainly don't get it all our own way. All the freedoms 'guaranteed' by the Act's adoption of the European Convention on Human Rights are subject to limitations and these aren't even in the 'small print.' All the Articles—particularly those establishing the right to privacy and the right to a fair trial—have specific implications for journalists which will be discussed throughout this book. However, taken as a whole, the message of the Convention means that media law now relies explicitly on a balancing act. Exercising any fundamental right such as freedom of expression can involve impinging on the rights of others and where it does, it is for the courts to decide where the balance lies.

This is in many ways startlingly obvious. A key challenge for any healthy democracy is to operate a complex system of checks and balances on power. The Articles of the Convention provide the check and, where rights compete or where grounds for restricting those rights are advanced, the courts will decide the balance to be struck. The work of journalists so often butts up against the rights of others, our right to exercise freedom of expression is bound to be challenged frequently in court where judges will decide our fate. As a Tom Stoppard character says in his play Night and Day: "I'm with you on the free press; it's the newspapers I can't stand."[88] Similarly, although journalists may recognise the absolute value of an independent judiciary, we remain nervous of our fate being in the hands of individual judges.

Any statute is open to interpretation and that task has always been a matter for the courts. However, any statute which is founded on the concept of a balancing act, of what the courts call proportionality, is going to be even more dependent on judicial views and, for journalists, effectively a small group of Supreme Court media specialists. Names

---

[88] Stoppard, Tom, *Night and Day* quoted by himself in *My love affair with newspapers*, British Journalism Review, Vol.16, No.4, 2005, p.19–29, (interestingly as not being indicative of his general attitude to newspapers. Nevertheless it remains a pithy encapsulation of the kind of ambivalence towards the news media in the upper echelons of British society).

such as Lord Hoffmann, Lord Nicholls, Baroness Hale, Mr Justice Eady and Master of the Rolls, Sir Anthony Clarke, are set to loom large in journalists' lives as they will in this book. The legal future of the news media is in their hands.

7. The Lessons of Case Law

The range of the latest key judgments relating to Freedom of Expression explored earlier in this chapter highlight the trends in the application of the Convention and thereby our UK Human Rights Act. Article 10 rights do not give journalists anything like free rein to publish anything they deem to be in the public interest. Countervailing rights will put a check on that. But the Act, provides the framework for decision-making in the courts from now on. Any 20th century (or earlier) judgment can be re-assessed or even dismissed as not Convention-compliant so the 21st century becomes a whole new world for media law. These are early days in legal terms, but each case that goes all the way to the Lords establishes a powerful legal precedent which can have a significant impact on how we exercise our freedom of expression—what sorts of stories we run, who and what we cover and what we can report within the law.

Journalists can reasonably celebrate the outcome of *Kommersant Moldovy v Moldova* (2007), where a newspaper successfully fought back against State efforts to close it down. This was a classic case of the news media standing up to effective censorship by a Government, one of the more blatant challenges to Art.10 rights as exercised by journalists.

But there are concerns too. Moldova, like many governments, tried to rely on the exemption clause, Art.10(2), specifically that it could restrain freedom of expression in the interest of *national security, territorial integrity or public safety*. These are the standard opt outs which governments, particularly the more repressive ones, rely on more or less disingenuously to justify suppression of the media. There is a deep-set suspicion among journalists that playing the "national security" card is all too often the last resort of a government desperate to keep embarrassing secrets hidden.

The national security or territorial integrity exception is also why journalists are right to challenge catchphrases such as the War on Terror. One doesn't have to apply the full Orwellian conspiracy to see that it could be tempting for those in power to fall back on such justifications to save themselves under the cloak of national security: "If you run that you'll undermine national security and, oh dear, we can't tell you why, that would undermine national security too." There are situations where that is genuinely the case but striking the balance is tough. Language should be used with precision. To use the terminology of war when the country is not at war is inimical to civil and media liberties.

The European Court of Human Rights made some supportive moves in finding against Moldova, partly by dwelling on the proviso in the exception clause that it must be necessary—that there must be a pressing social need for the restraint and that it must be proportionate. Its main complaint was that the State had not done enough to explain how the material run by the newspaper jeopardised national security. Unfortunately this suggests that, had the State been slightly less high-handed and come up with a more detailed justification, its action could have been upheld.

The tone of the judgment is less than complimentary of the newspaper and there is much stress on duties and responsibilities, good faith, ethics, accuracy and reliability. Cavalier journalists are warned not to expect a sympathetic hearing.

8. Public interest in Practice

Few concepts are more to the fore in current media law judgments than the notion of public interest. Yet there is no one all-embracing definition of it and often its meaning is almost assumed as in the Ofcom broadcasting code.

Information is power and information empowers the public, particularly as voters but also in their daily lives. There is a public interest in the free flow of information. There is recognition of a public interest in freedom of expression itself, but given that there is a public interest in upholding all the other human rights too, this does little to advance the journalist's cause because in practice most disputes involve a clash of rights.

The limitations outlined in *Lion Laboratories v Evans* suggest a scepticism on the part of the courts regarding media claims to be running a story in the public interest. Obviously, for a journalist, there would be no point running any story if it wasn't of some public interest, but that is nowhere near enough for the courts. When the news media seeks to defend a story, its case tends to be considered more in terms of its interest in telling it rather than in the public's interest in knowing it.

Certainly there is a temptation to be disingenuous and confuse self-interest with public interest, but news organisations deserve a more sophisticated appreciation of their position than that.

Selling newspapers, or attracting "eyeballs" to any platform, is not just a matter of self-interest. It is only by attracting an audience that the news media can inform the public. There is no public interest in covering stories in such a way that they are ignored.

The pursuit of audience may have led some to abandon genuine issues in favour of celebrity gossip and other trivia, but it is not an ignoble aim in itself. One of the greatest challenges for any journalist committed to serving the public's right to know is that of "making the significant interesting."[89]

Information about weighty issues has to be communicated success-fully and that may involve telling stories in a human interest style, perhaps using celebrity examples, which will draw the public to the story and engage their attention. Without a consideration of how to make issues accessible, a high-minded journalist may not be serving the general public any better than one devoted entirely to "tittle-tattle."

One of the most encouraging contributions is from Lord Nicholls in *Reynolds v Times Newspapers Ltd* [1999] where he says:

> "The court should be slow to conclude that a publication was not in the public interest and, therefore, the public had no right to know . . . . Any lingering doubts should be resolved in favour of publication."[90]

More generally, and particularly in privacy rather than defamation actions, the higher courts are reining back on various fronts and creat-ing effective hierarchies of public interest depending on the topic of any story, who it involves and the scope and level of detail it reveals.

In *Campbell v MGN*, in the context of freedom of expression, Baroness Hale advances a hierarchy of different types of speech. She says:

> "There are undoubtedly different types of speech, just as there are dif-ferent types of information, some of which are more deserving of pro-tection in a democratic society than others. Top of the list is political speech. The free exchange of information and ideas on matters rele-vant to the organisation of the economic, social and political life of the country is crucial to any democracy. Without this, it can scarcely be called a democracy at all. This includes revealing information about public figures, especially those in elective office, which would other-wise be private but is relevant to their participation in public life.

> "Intellectual and educational speech and expression are also important in a democracy, not least because they enable the development of indi-viduals' potential to play a full part in society and in our democratic life. Artistic speech and expression is important for similar reasons, in fos-tering both individual originality and creativity and the free-thinking and dynamic society we so much value. No doubt there are other kinds of speech and expression for which similar claims can be made."[91]

But she goes on to say:

> "But it is difficult to make such claims on behalf of the publication with which we are concerned here. The political and social life of the

---

[89] Kovach, Bill and Rosenstiel, Tom, The Elements of Journalism, p.13.
[90] [1999] UKHL 45.
[91] *Campbell v MGN* [2004] UKHL 22, at para.148.

community, and the intellectual, artistic or personal development of individuals, are not obviously assisted by pouring over the intimate details of a fashion model's private life."[92]

She did however acknowledge that using a model's story as an example of the battle to overcome drug addiction could have a "beneficial educational effect."

The Press Complaints Commission Code of Practice[93] provides the most frequently quoted examples of what is in the public interest, although it pointedly uses the phrase "includes but is not confined to" to keep the door open to argue for a wider definition. The three areas are broadly: wrongdoing, health and safety, and preventing the public from being misled.

The PCC factors all help to establish the area of public interest, but the extent of the public interest depends on the circumstances in each case. A whole matrix is building up. A small misdemeanour by a Government Minister might help Art.10 rights to "win", but even a serious impropriety by a B-list celebrity might not, and the chances are diminishing with every landmark judgment. If the impropriety involves criminal activity, such as drug-taking, a celebrity might be enough, but if it is only sexual shenanigans, again it probably won't. Even putting the record straight is not the trump card it used to be; it depends how actively the public is being misled and how much it matters whether they have accurate knowledge or not.

The wrongdoing element of the PPC Code refers to "serious impropriety". Criminal behaviour is still covered, but a much more relaxed view is taken to sexual misdemeanour. Commercial abuses can also be included and courts have accepted there is a public interest in the affairs of corporations. Shareholders have a right to know if they are being misled about the company they part-own but football, music or movie fans have no corresponding right to know about those they pay to watch perform.

Under the right to correct misleading public utterances, there was a worrying aside from Baroness Hale in *Campbell*. Although she accepts the newspaper's right to put the record straight in this instance, she says: "It might be questioned why, if a role model has adopted a stance which all would agree is beneficial rather than detrimental to society, it is so important to reveal that she has feet of clay."[94]

Why is it important? Because it would be a stance based on a deception. It is important to reveal what is true and the public should not be deceived even where it might be a convenient deception. The public are not there to be fed a line and kept in compliant ignorance. Healthy public discourse has to be based on honest, rational foundations; anchored in reality not pretence.

---

[92] ibid., para.149.
[93] PCC Code of Practice, *www.pcc.org.uk*.
[94] ibid., para.151.

The latter is particularly worrying for journalists as the PCC Code refers to correcting any false impression given to the public by any individual or organisation. It would be of great concern if the courts took the view that it doesn't really matter if the public are misled as long as it isn't about anything the courts consider important. That is dangerous territory to enter. There is enough that is phoney about the public sphere already without providing the pedlars of myths with the protection of the law. No-one has to lie to the media; they can always decline to comment.

Wherever public interest is relied upon as justification for making public material considered defamatory or in breach of confidence, the degree of damage done has to be in proportion to the importance of the matter. So in *Campbell*, readers were entitled to know that Campbell had made misleading statements about drug use, but the newspaper should not have gone so far as to run a photograph of her outside Narcotics Anonymous which is by the nature of the organisation a private activity.

Judgments examined in the emerging appeals to uphold Art.8 rights, suggest a move to define public interest in predominantly political terms. So infringements may be justified affecting the lives of those holding public office or involved in the implementation of public policy, but footballers, actors and other celebrities would be off-limits. This comes through strongly in *McKennitt* where a woman who makes a living from performing publicly is judged not even to be a public figure.

Accusations of any impropriety have to be judged against what claims that person has made of themselves and what expectations there are of them. If a cabinet minister is caught committing adultery, abusing position or lying to the public, then an intrusion into an intimate area of his life and in greater detail could be acceptable. The cabinet minister claims to be a fine, upstanding family man in his election material so he has misled the public who can reasonably expect him to live up to his claims, behave within the law and meet the required standards of public life. His abuse of power undermines the political system and there is a clear public interest in exposing him. He may even resign.

If a pop singer has an extra-marital affair what justification do we have to publish? There is no criminality, hardly an impropriety in this day and age and he won't necessarily have said much on public record about his family life. The public has no particular expectations of him and no obvious harm has come of his fling. Even if the "other woman" or the wronged wife wants to tell their story, in the weighing of their Art.10 rights against his Art.8, very little personal or public benefit can be claimed in the name of freedom of expression to counterbalance the damage to him from the intrusion into his privacy.

Given the way the law has developed, that is broadly how the courts would see it now.

When it comes to putting the record straight, the PCC Code includes any attempt to mislead by anyone. There is no threshold regarding the type of person doing the misleading. The public is entitled to honesty across the board. Lying should be challenged—there is a public interest in honesty and in challenging dishonest versions of events.

Perhaps media lawyers in time will be able to establish a series of sliding scales with a points system. Take one backbench MP worth eight points times a cocaine habit worth nine points times fronting up a "Just Say No" drugs campaign worth eight points, making a total of 576 points. Victory to Art.10 possible.

Take one minor league footballer worth one point times an extra-marital affair (barely worth anything in the courts these days) times no media profile worth speaking of, worth one point making a total of one, heading towards zero. Defeat for Art.10. As of 2007, injunction granted.

This is somewhat fanciful, but is not that much of a stretch from the principles being laid down by the higher courts in 21st century privacy cases. Journalists might prefer some greater clarity but we would not want that much rigidity. News organisations want some "wriggle room" too to reflect the unique circumstances of each case. But rough, rule-of-thumb calculations along the lines given above are not that far fetched.

Certainly the news media can expect to have to work a great deal harder to justify its rights to run intrusive stories and be clearer about why a story matters and why it needs to be in the public domain. We will return to this in greater detail in Chapter 4 on privacy.

There is one further concern in the great proportionality debate over competing human rights. Apart from all the caveats and the accent being on the right to express, rather than the right to know, there is also a downside from the central, albeit understandable, focus on the rights of the individual rather than the collective. This opens up the risk that general, shared "public interest" may be downplayed.

Sir Christopher Meyer, chairman of the Press Complaints Commission, made the point well with regard to moves to restrict coverage of inquests.

He said:

"There will surely be a temptation for coroners, when faced with applications for anonymity from the bereaved, to side with those vulnerable individuals who appear before them against the interests of the general public—who will of course be absent and anonymous."[95]

The very suggestion of anonymity entirely negates the purpose of an inquest—which is to uphold the rights of those who die in unusual circumstances to have a public investigation into the circumstances of their death.

Sir Christopher went on:

"The right of journalists to report on inquests is not to be defended solely in terms of press freedom, although that is of course important. Such a right is also a key feature of an open society in which the public

[95] Sir Christopher Meyer, from 'PCC in plea against Coroner gagging powers', Press Gazette, September 5, 2006.

as a whole has a right to know what is going on and be reassured that there are no cover-ups of unusual or premature deaths.

"As with evidence given in other courts, the possibility of public scrutiny also focuses the minds of those appearing before the coroner on the importance of giving accurate evidence."[96]

These are the kinds of other "public interest" benefits which need to be accounted for in demonstrating why freedom of expression should prevail in any particular circumstance.

9. Prior Restraint in Practice

Publish and be damned has always been a potentially expensive option but it is vital that it remains an option. In less inflammatory terms, it means journalists retain the freedom to run any story, as long as we are prepared to accept the consequences. Anticipation of those consequences can for ethical, or purely financial, reasons lead to a story being spiked but at least that is the journalist's decision.

To intervene to prevent the story being run at all is the most draconian infringement of freedom of expression and yet we can expect to see more of it thanks to the Human Rights Act.

The recent debacle over the attempt to injunct an email in the cash for honours inquiry demonstrates the practical difficulty of restraining media across the board. If an injunction is sought against one news organisation, as it was against the BBC here, other media may not even be aware as there may well be a bar even on reporting the existence of the injunction. In this case, as the BBC fought to ease the scope of the injunction, its battle came to dominate the television news and details were gradually released. Meanwhile, the Guardian went ahead with a fuller version of the claims and attempts to impose an injunction failed because, by the time restraint was sought, the edition carrying the story was already in circulation.

Once a story begins to emerge it can be difficult to put the brakes on. Even though a police inquiry was held to be at stake, the central involvement of leading Government figures made it almost impossible to keep the lid on the information, which ended up in the public domain despite the best efforts of the Attorney General.[97]

As more cases are being fought on Art.8 privacy grounds, the demand for injunctions will inevitably rise. No-one wants defamatory material to run, but at least it can be corrected after publication if untrue. Where the

---

[96] ibid.
[97] *Attorney General v BBC* [2007] EWCA Civ 280.

main concern is secrecy, logically prior restraint will be to the fore as the whole purpose is to stop information entering the public domain.

10. Forum Shopping in Practice

The transfer to journalism online has moved the question of forum shopping up the agenda. Although jurisdictional issues are technically platform-neutral, online material is more likely to offer claimants a choice of where to sue. The physical separation of publisher and audience accentuated by the web makes it even easier to demonstrate that, although material may be generated in one country, it is consumed all around the world. In defamation terms, if the subject has a reputation in a particular country where the relevant material has been accessed, a writ may be issued.

Lawyers assessing the chances of success may decide one forum is likely to be more sympathetic than another in terms of win or lose, higher damages awards higher and/or lower costs.

Northern Ireland is emerging as a popular option. Film actor Jennifer Lopez, for instance, suing over drugs allegations, issued writs in Northern Ireland against the US tabloid the National Enquirer and against distributors based in Dublin and Edinburgh. For privacy, the Barclay Brothers chose the French courts for a planned action against the Times, since dropped.

Thanks to the American constitution, journalists are generally seen to be in a stronger position in the US courts, so European jurisdictions are becoming more popular.

Significantly, action can be taken in multiple jurisdictions, although the costs and risks obviously multiply too. While this could be seen to deter the actions, the rich and famous may be prepared to take their chances, meaning the potential costs to news organisations which fight and lose would be even more daunting.

11. Conditional Fee Arrangements in Practice

Despite the noble sentiments of "justice for all" behind the introduction of CFAs they don't appear to have widened the range of media litigants particularly beyond the usual suspects among the rich and powerful. In practice CFAs have just upped the bill for media defendants. At least in the days of outrageously high damages awards, news organisations only got stung if they lost. Now defending a claim for libel or breach of confidence is potentially a prohibitively expensive undertaking, win or lose. Damages may have been capped but costs have soared, making them the prime consideration in whether to proceed with any action.

A losing defendant pays all costs plus success fee, but if the media wins, even if costs are awarded these can be claimed only from the claimant, who may not have the assets and is not required to take out "after the event" insurance. The main gainers would appear to be the lawyers.

At least there is some recognition of the dilemma within the judiciary. In *Tierney v News Group Newspapers Ltd* [2006],[98] Eady J. cites Brooke L.J. in *Musa King v Telegraph Group Ltd* [2005]:

"It cannot be just to submit the defendant in these cases where their right to freedom of expression is at stake, to a costs regime where the costs they will have to pay if they lose are neither reasonable nor proportionate and they have no reasonable prospect of recovering their reasonable and proportionate costs if they win."[99]

So is any relief in prospect? In *Tierney*, a legislative solution was seen as the appropriate route. However cost-capping procedures are very much to the fore. The judicial reluctance to cap costs is that it would make it harder for a claimant without the resource for other than a CFA-funded action to attract lawyers to take a case. With damages awards reduced, the costs and success fees are what make the risk worth their while.

It would also not be fair under the principle of "equality of arms" for the media defendant to weigh in with top-notch counsel and the CFA claimant not to be able to match it. It is clear from the judgment that horse-trading can take place where both sides agree to deals such as to instruct only junior counsel to keep costs down.

In *Tierney*, Eady J. queries the entire costs-capping procedure with the question:

"Does it have to be shown that there is reason to anticipate extravagance, or that retrospective assessment would not be adequate to exclude the paying party from having to meet unnecessary or disproportionate costs?"[100]

And he speaks favourably of the tendency, not shown in *Tierney*, to impose costs-capping on both sides rather than just the CFA claimant, which does indeed seem to be fair and would uphold the "equality of arms" principle.

Forum shopping impacts here too, as it is cheaper to run a case from Belfast than from London which can influence the choice of forum for any action.

[98] [2006] EWHC 3275 (QB).
[99] [2005] 1 W.L.R. 2282 para.101.
[100] ibid.

It cannot be healthy for media organisations to throw in the towel and fail to defend their rights to freedom of expression because the costs of fighting their corner are so high. The government has considered a proposal to bar CFAs in defamation actions to avoid the chilling effect on the media. But, to date, it has been rejected. The Department for Constitutions Affairs did say:

"The DCA does not propose to legislate to restrict the use of CFAs in these actions. However it supports the vigorous use of the existing and extensive case management and cost control powers contained in the civil procedure rules to ensure reasonably and proportionate behaviour and costs on both sides."[101]

But yet another development in the area of media law is adding to the "freeze" factor facing journalists when the handling of civil actions becomes driven even more by issues of cost rather than principle. The worst-case scenario becomes so nightmarish that the pressure mounts for publishers to opt, quite literally, for damage limitation and settle cases where they are in the right. One of the most galling experiences for any editor is to pay out under advice from insurers who play safe and would rather accept a dent to the news organisation's reputation by admitting fault than a dip in the bank balance of paying to fight. Indeed, the temptation grows not to run contentious stories in the first place, especially when the outcome seems so unpredictable.

What it definitely means is that the cost of making legal mistakes is rising. Consequently it becomes even more important for journalists to understand how to tell stories in legally-safe ways—and for organisations to have the courage to stand up for their freedom to tell them.

12. Freedom of Expression Around the World

Our discussion on Freedom of Expression should end with a reminder of the appalling price many journalists pay for exercising that right. Journalists don't just suffer embarrassment or upset by upholding their Art.10 rights. They die for them.

And it isn't just the state that suppresses news and deprives the public of information. BBC Gaza correspondent Alan Johnston survived his kidnapping ordeal. Many journalists have not!

Gangsterism is rife, especially in countries where the traditional forces of law and order are disrupted, as they were in Northern Ireland and as

---

[101] Reported in "Ministers investigate no win no fee libel suits", Guardian July 7, 2004.

they are in many countries of the world, including Russia and the Philippines. In too many countries, the restraint on a journalist's freedom of expression is a bullet in the head. Masked gunmen executed 11 employees of a fledgling TV channel in Baghdad in October 2006, the year of the murder of Russian journalist Anna Politkovskaya, who exposed human rights abuses in Chechnya. Barely one in ten murders of a journalist has led to a prosecution.[102]

Significantly, an Asian editor, forced recently to operate with soldiers in his newsroom, came up with an interesting answer to the question: What is the greatest threat to press freedom?

"Self-censorship" was his reply. He likened freedom of speech to an elastic band—it only fulfils its purpose when in use; when stretched. Journalists must exercise their freedom, investigate its limits or it withers. His greatest fear was of journalists playing safe; not asking the awkward questions, not running stories that ruffle feathers within the corridors of power and thereby selling the public short.

Journalists must stand up for our Art.10 rights, pushing the boundaries of freedom of expression and pursuing the cause of a free press. The greater our knowledge of the law, the greater our chances of success. But we cannot afford to stand idly by as celebrities, officials and politicians look to the law to gag us.

---

[102] What price world press freedom when journalists die? International News Safety Institute, May 2007, *www.newssafety.com*.

CHAPTER 2
DEFAMATION

In late October 2005, a libel jury awarded Rupert Lowe, the then chairman of Southampton Football Club, damages amounting to £250,000 (finally settled "behind the scenes" for £50,000). This was way off the scale as the maximum had been assumed to be £200,000. (See *Lillie & Reed v Newcastle City Council* [2002]).[1] One would assume that, for an award so high, the defamatory remarks must have been very serious. After all, when George Galloway MP "defeated" the Daily Telegraph, not once but twice in 2004 and 2006, he was awarded £150,000 for what amounted to a huge slight on his character. Being accused by the newspaper of being traitorous was only one aspect of the libel. So what had the Times said? Its chief sports writer had the audacity to accuse Mr Lowe, in his capacity of chairman, of treating his then manager "shabbily." The background to the story was that the manager, David Jones, had been accused of being the perpetrator of a number of sexual assaults on young people in his care when he had worked, years before, as a social worker in Liverpool. The Southampton Board did not dismiss its manager but sent him on "gardening leave" on full pay and appointed Glenn Hoddle to manage the club in the interim.

So what exactly was said?

Martin Samuel, the chief sports writer, stated that Mr Lowe was:

"... a chairman whose idea of crisis management was to remove his manager over a court case that collapsed within 24 hours ... How would Lowe approach the issue of an England player accused of breaking the law, when he so shabbily handled the case of David Jones, his manager?"

We have commenced this section with this case to highlight the fact that a journalist does not have to use seemingly strong or abusive words to be found "guilty" of defamation. Yet readers must appreciate that we are not advocating that you should practise "defensive" journalism because of any potential legal consequences that may result from your outpourings.

This section attempts to provide our best legal and practical advice on how, hopefully, you will be able to exercise your rights under Art.10 of the European Convention on Human Rights (freedom of expression)

---

[1] [2002] EWHC 1600 Q.B.

to carry out the legally recognised functions of the Fourth Estate to be both watchdog and bloodhound in pursuit of information in which the public has a legitimate interest. Your role as a journalist is to pursue what is true and that simple fact will also provide the major defence of justification if you happen to be accused of defaming someone in what you publish or broadcast. For example on July 11, 2006, Mr Justice Eady gave his decision in the case of *Veliu v Mazrekaj and Bucpapaj*.[2] Some libel cases are heard by a jury others by a single judge depending on the complexity of the case. In this case, the first defendant was the owner and publisher of a Kosovan daily newspaper entitled Bota Sot which is available to the Albanian community in London of whom there are approximately 20,000. The second defendant was its editor. The claimant is a young journalist living in London who took exception to the following:

"An Albanian called Mohamed Veliu who claims to be one of the most prominent journalists of his country, who resides in London, and is known by his close relations with the Pakistani Islamic Community, has become one of the latest protagonists relating to the terrorist bombing attacks on the British capital's underground system . . . The terrorist Mohammed Sidique Khan, the worst of the four killers who bombed the London underground, was a close friend of the Albanian, who claims to be one of the most prominent journalists in Albania."

The judge said:

"There is no doubt that the allegation made against the claimant in this article was one of the gravest imaginable . . . [he became] anxious for his physical safety."

The defendants grudgingly issued an unqualified offer of amends admitting there was no truth in what the newspaper had published. The court ordered the defendants to pay compensation (damages) amounting to £175,000 and that of course does not take into account the legal costs in bringing the case to court. We cite this case to illustrate the principle that if a journalist cannot *prove* that any assertion that adversely impacts on the claimant's character is substantially true then the case is lost (in the absence of a defence of fair comment or privilege of which more later) and damages are likely to be high always depending of course on the nature and extent of the slur.

Later in this section we give examples of the way stories might be approached so as to avoid potential claims for defamation. But first it is our belief that any self-respecting journalist should have some knowledge of the legal context in which he or she will operate.

---

[2] [2006] EWHC 1710 Q.B. . . .

1. Freedom of Expression

We made the point in the introductory chapter that freedom of expression as defined in Art.10 of the European Convention on Human Rights is the foundation upon which all journalists operate. The general principles are not in doubt and a neat summary is to be found in the case of *Selisto v Finland* [2004][3]

"General Principles
According to the court's well-established case-law, freedom of expression constitutes one of the essential foundations of a democratic society and one of the basic conditions for its progress and each individual's self-fulfilment. Subject to paragraph 2 of article 10, it is applicable not only to "information" or "ideas" that are favourably received or regarded as inoffensive or as a matter of indifference, but also to those that offend, shock or disturb. Such are the demands of pluralism, tolerance and broadmindedness, without which there is no "democratic society.". . . This freedom is subject to the exceptions set out in Article 10(2) which must, however, be construed strictly. The need for any restrictions must be established convincingly.

The Court further recalls the essential function the press fulfils in a democratic society. Although the press must not overstep certain bounds, particularly as regards the reputation and rights of others and the need to prevent disclosure of confidential information, its duty is nevertheless to impart—in a manner consistent with its obligations and responsibilities— information and ideas on all matters of public interest. Not only does it have the task of imparting such information and ideas: the public also has a right to receive them. In addition, the Court is mindful of the fact that journalistic freedom also covers possible recourse to a degree of exaggeration, or even provocation . . . "

This "theme" is also reflected in statements of the UK judiciary at the highest level. Thus in the key House of Lords decision of *Reynolds v Times Newspapers Ltd* [1999][4] Lord Nicholls said:

"My starting point is freedom of expression . . . At a pragmatic level freedom to disseminate and receive information on political matters is essential to the proper functioning of the system of parliamentary democracy cherished in this country . . . The common law is to be developed and applied in a manner consistent with article 10 . . . and the court must take account of relevant decisions of the European Court of Human Rights.

---

[3] [2004] ECHR 634; [2005] EMLR 178.
[4] [1999] UKHL 44.

Likewise, there is no need to elaborate on the importance of the role discharged by the media in the expression and communication of information and comment on political matters . . . Without freedom of expression by the media, freedom of expression would be a hollow concept. The interest of a democratic society in ensuring a free press weighs heavily in the balance in deciding whether any curtailment of this freedom bears a reasonable relationship to the purpose of the curtailment. In this regard it should be kept in mind that one of the contemporary functions of the media is investigative journalism. This activity, as much as the traditional activities of reporting and commenting, is part of the vital role of the press and the media generally."

We make no apology for quoting at length because with these words you have the explicit support of the highest court in England and Wales and the European Court of Human Rights. There is no need to be reticent; just a need to be wary. There is a need to know that your role is "vital" to the proper functioning of a democratic society. There is no need to be defensive.

The above statements refer to the media's role in respect of public interest matters. A nation waits to be enlightened about what our government is doing in our name as well as what those who hold public office are doing or shouldn't be doing in carrying out their public functions.

2. Public Interest

The first chapter made reference to the overriding importance of the concept of the public interest to the media. It outlined the approaches advocated by the Press Complaints Commission Code of Practice and the Broadcasting Code. It would be helpful to take a moment out to revisit chapter one and reacquaint yourself with the legal and industry context to public interest. Please bear in mind that certain restrictions or prohibitions in the Codes can be ignored if to do so would be deemed to be in the public interest. For example we mentioned in chapter one that it was in the public interest to "put the record straight" as illustrated by the Daily Mirror's article relating to Naomi Campbell's use of drugs after she had publicly denied taking drugs.

There are those who might cynically say the definition in the PCC Code gives the print media a wide margin of appreciation and that it is the industry making a judgment upon itself when a complaint is made to the PCC. This is examined further in Chapter 6.

3. Reputation

On this voyage of initial discovery, we now come to reputation. Even journalists have reputations to lose I hear you say and that is in fact a correct statement of the law in this country. If what you publish or broadcast amounts to an attack upon reputation then you are at risk of being sued for defamation. The risk is always there. However, the success rate will be massively lower than the risk might suggest. Please remember it is not only individuals who have reputations to lose. A company has the right to sue for defamation and therefore attacks upon a company, its products and performance should always be underpinned by accurate and verifiable information. The other vital piece of information to bear in mind is that, as the law stands, there is an automatic presumption of damage to reputation. In other words if the words are proved to have been defamatory then the claimant will succeed without any need to prove that he or she has actually suffered a negative consequence as a result of the "sting." This fairly contentious position was recently reviewed by the House of Lords in the case of *Jameel v Wall Street Journal Europe Ltd* [2006].[5] The current law was upheld, but only by a 3:2 majority, and this holds out the prospect of the presumption being re-examined at some future stage.

As Lord Bingham succinctly put it:

"The first (question raised by the appeal) concerns the entitlement of a trading corporation . . . to sue and recover damages without pleading or proving special damage."[6]

The majority were of the opinion that the good name of a company is a valuable commodity. The loss of reputation can have damaging consequences for a company that may not be apparent immediately after the alleged defamatory material is published or when proceedings are commenced. The minority were represented by Lord Hoffmann and Baroness Hale. It could be argued that their approach is the more enlightened and reflects the view that the press should be free to challenge the actions of large corporations just as much as they have a duty to criticise the actions of government.

As Baroness Hale points out:

"These days the dividing line between governmental and non-governmental organisations is increasingly difficult to draw. The power wielded by the major multi national corporations is enormous and growing. The freedom to criticise them may be at least as important in a democratic society as the freedom to criticise the government."[7]

[5] [2006] UKHL 44.
[6] ibid., para.1.
[7] ibid., para.158.

To be fair Lord Bingham did state that, if it could be shown that a corporation had suffered no financial loss, then the measure of damages should be kept "strictly within modest bounds."

The decision of the majority in *Jameel* on the damages point should be regarded as somewhat conservative. The Faulks Committee, in considering the future of the defamation laws way back in 1975, proposed:

"That no action in defamation should lie at the suit of any trading corporation unless such corporation can establish either: (i) that it has suffered special damage, or (ii) that the words were likely to cause it pecuniary damage."

In 1964, Lord Reid had expressed the view that "a company cannot be injured in its feelings, it can only be injured in its pocket."[8]

Yet as a consequence of the *Jameel* decision, at least for the foreseeable future, that issue is settled in favour of the presumption of damage to reputation irrespective of whether the claimant is an individual or trading corporation.

We now refer you to a number of judicial statements to establish the importance of reputation in the eyes of the law.

In the landmark *Reynolds* case Lord Nicholls said this:

"Reputation is an integral and important part of the dignity of the individual. It also forms the basis of many decisions in a democratic society which are fundamental to its well being: who to employ or work for, whom to promote, whom to do business with or to vote for. Once besmirched by an unfounded allegation in a national newspaper, a reputation can be damaged for ever, especially if there is no opportunity to vindicate one's reputation . . . Protection of reputation is conducive to the public good. It is in the public interest that the reputation of public figures should not be debased falsely."

Indeed, Lord Nicholls began his speech in *Reynolds* this way:

"This appeal concerns the interaction between two fundamental rights: freedom of expression and protection of reputation."

Of more recent ilk is this statement by Mr Justice Gray in *Charman v Orion Publishing Group Ltd (No 3)* [2006]

". . . there is a clear public interest in the promotion of (a) free and vigorous press to keep the public informed and journalists should be permitted a good deal of latitude in how they present the material; but reputation is an integral and important part of the dignity of the individual, the protection of which is conducive to the public good. In

---

[8] *Lewis v Daily Telegraph* [1964] A.C. 234, at p.262.

some cases the reputations of other individuals than the claimant may
be engaged."[9]

So to summarise reputations are worth protecting in law. That process is
for the public good. The preservation and encouragement of freedom of
expression is also deemed to be before the the public good. There, in a
nutshell, you have the journalists' dilemma. Which will take precedence?
According to Gray J., a journalist will be allowed a fair measure of latitude when presenting a story but in so doing he or she must not exceed
the bounds of what a responsible journalist would do. Unless, of course,
the journalist is fully aware that the story is untrue and it is his intention
to attack the individual and his reputation regardless of the likely consequences.

4. General Principles of Defamation

In our opinion, if a journalist is aware of the basic legal principles of
defamation then that knowledge should assist in making informed
choices about what to publish with minimal risk of a defamation action
resulting. Initially, consider the matter from any claimant's viewpoint.
    The first stage is that the claimant has taken umbrage at what has been
published. It has been regarded as an unwarranted attack on reputation.
Every person is presumed to have a reputation. The claimant doesn't
need to prove damage has resulted from the "sting."
    Reputation is assumed in law to have a value. A key factor to remem-
ber is that the claimant *doesn't* have to prove that what you have written
is untrue. In legal terms, the burden of proof is on the publisher. So the
onus is upon the publisher (really your organisation providing you are
working within the course of your employment) to justify what you have
written. Section 5 of the Defamation Act 1952 demands only that what
has been written or broadcast is *substantially* true. *The standard of proof is
on the balance of probabilities.*

Publication

The next point is a pretty obvious one. A claimant will need to prove that
the material about which he complains has been published. This means
that the communication has been seen, as lawyers say by a "third party."
This clearly is not going to cause a problem where the material forms
part of a newspaper or broadcast irrespective of whether it is locally,
regionally or nationally targeted. If the circulation of a newspaper is
15,000 then there has been a publication. If it is 15 then there has still

[9] [2006] EWHC 1756 Q.B., at para.108.

been a publication in law providing at least one of those 15 subscribers will have linked the content to an individual, group or organisation. In the *Jameel v Dow Jones & Co Inc*,[10] case it will be recalled it was held that where only five people were known to have accessed a website containing alleged defamatory material it was an abuse of process to allow the case to continue because it was most unlikely that the complainant's reputation would have been affected. However (and this is not meant to worry you) the Court of Appeal endorsed a view that where a person was identifiable then in principle it could still lead to an action being brought even though a reasonable reader had no prior knowledge of the claimant. The assumption here is that a newspaper or broadcasting company can create and then besmirch at reputation at one and the same time.

The words complained of must be capable of being regarded as defamatory. In the absence of agreement to that effect between the parties then a judge will have to decide this issue of capability. If the judge agrees that the words are capable of being defamatory then the final decision in the case will rest with the jury. There are cases where a jury may be dispensed with because the judge decides that the case is too complex for the matter to be fully understood by them.

We will not discuss the matter here but later in this chapter when we look at specific examples of what has been held to be capable of having a defamatory meaning. We have already mentioned the Rupert Lowe case and the use of the word "shabbily." It is fair to say that it is rarely one single word to which a claimant takes exception but the meaning of a paragraph or of the piece as a whole.

The "sting"

So one is entitled to ask how a judge will decide this issue and also how a jury will make its final decision on meaning. The initial answer is to be found in the case of *Gillick v BBC* [1996][11] and subsequent decisions that have endorsed the approach namely *Gillick v Brook Advisory Centres* [2001][12] *Jameel v Times Newspapers* [2004][13] and *Charman v Orion Publishing (No 2)* [2005].[14]

The onus is cast upon the "hypothetical reader or viewer" to make that important decision. The Court of Appeal expressed it in these terms:

[10] [2005] EWCA Civ. 75.
[11] [1996] E.M.L.R. 267.
[12] [2001] EWCA Civ. 1263.
[13] [2004] EWCA Civ. 983.
[14] [2005] EWHC 2187.

1 The courts must give to the material complained of the natural and ordinary meaning that it would have conveyed to the ordinary reasonable reader.

2 The hypothetical reasonable reader is not naïve but he is not unduly suspicious. He can read between the lines. He can read in an implication more readily than a lawyer and may indulge in a certain amount of loose thinking. But he must be treated as being a man who is not avid for scandal and someone who does not, and should not, select one bad meaning where other non-defamatory meanings are available.

3 While limiting its attention to what the defendant has actually said or written the court should be cautious of an over-elaborate analysis of the material in issue.

4 The court should not be too literal in its approach: (see *Lewis v Daily Telegraph Limited* [1964] A.C. 234 at 277 *per* Lord Devlin and in particular "the lawyer's rule is that the implication must be necessary as well as reasonable. The layman reads in an implication much more freely; and unfortunately, as the law of defamation has to take into account, is especially prone to do so when derogatory").

5 A statement should be taken to be defamatory if it would tend to lower the claimant in the estimation of right-thinking members of society generally or affect a person adversely in the estimation of reasonable people generally.

6 In determining the meaning of the material complained of the court is not limited by the meanings which either the claimant or the defendant seeks to place upon the words.

Look closely at point 5, above. That is the standard test to apply. Has the claimant's reputation been lowered in the estimation of right-thinking members of society generally or affected a person adversely in the estimation of reasonable people? Our advice is that when a journalist is writing his story then he should put himself in the position of the hypothetical viewer or reader and once it is completed ask whether you genuinely believe that the piece can be construed in such a way as to prompt the subject matter to seek legal advice. One assumes that journalists can be included in the phrases "right-thinking members of society" and "reasonable people." If journalists get into the habit of reflecting on what they have written and making all allowances for the time pressures that they may well be under, then they may end their careers without having crossed the threshold of the High Court as a participant rather than reporter.

It should not be assumed that just because a journalist fails to name the claimant in the publication then there is no possibility of a writ landing on the doorstep. The crucial question is whether or not from the information that has been published the "hypothetical reader or viewer" will understand that the "sting" relates to or includes the claimant. You do not need to name the members of a premiership soccer team for people to conclude that your story is about those players who regularly appear in the first team. To comment on the activities of a vicar of a church in the village of X who it is alleged is having sexual relationships with parishioners hardly obscures identity if there are only two churches in the village. While we are on the subject it should be made absolutely clear that the simple device of using the word allegedly when revealing information about an individual that he or she would rather wasn't in the public domain will not necessarily protect the writer from a defamation action. The legal authority for that proposition is *Lewis v Daily Telegraph* [1964].[15]

> **"I agree, of course, that you cannot escape liability for defamation by putting the libel behind a prefix such as "I have been told that . . .' or "It is rumoured that . . .' and then asserting that it was true that you had been told or that it was in fact being rumoured. You have . . .'to prove that the subject matter of the rumour was true'."**

The answer will ultimately be determined by reference to what the ordinary or hypothetical reader or viewer would conclude in the particular circumstances of the publication or broadcast. The courts have long recognised the so called "repetition rule." The only thing that can be assumed to be true is that the person told you something.

A journalist cannot without further questioning accept that what has been said is true. That further action may be to persuade the individual to sign a statement that it is true. The difficulty in this approach is that the person signing might believe what has been said to be true but it is not incontrovertible evidence that it is true. Running stories that are based on information received "secondhand" will always fraught with danger and be a matter of judgment based upon the best evidence available.

5. The Defamation Defences

The best time to think about the working of the legal defences to defamation is when the story is being constructed. One should ask:"If this piece were to be challenged on the basis that it is potentially defamatory would I have a reasonable prospect of succeeding by pleading an established defence?" In practice, the more likely outcome is that the claimant will not pursue the case if his or her lawyers are of the opinion that, on the basis of information supplied to them, the media will win your case. We now discuss the legal principles underpinning the standard defences of privilege, justification and fair comment.

---

[15] [1964] A.C. 234 at p.283–284.

Responsible journalism and privilege

The law provides a "defence" for journalists who have inadvertently defamed someone while delivering a public interest story. That defence is referred to as common law qualified privilege or Reynolds privilege after the House of Lords case in 1999 that developed the existing common law principles at the time. Journalists have long enjoyed protection from defamation actions because Parliament has recognised that in certain circumstances the right to free expression prevails over protection of reputation. The situations are however limited. All journalists will be acquainted with the terms of s.14 of the Defamation Act 1996 entitled Absolute Privilege. This section of the Act bestows total protection upon a journalist when reporting court proceedings *providing* the report is a "fair and accurate report of proceedings in public before a court to which the section applies, if published contemporaneously with the proceedings . . .".

Contemporaneous means as soon as possible after the proceedings for the day have finished or even while they are going on if you are reporting, for example, on the lunchtime news or in an edition of a newspaper.

Section 14(3) applies this absolute privilege to:

a   any court in the United Kingdom;
b   the European Court of Justice or any court attached to that court;
c   the European Court of Human Rights; and
d   any international criminal tribunal established by the Security Council of the United Nations or by international agreement to which the United Kingdom is a party.

That is absolute privilege . . . total protection providing the reports are fair, accurate and contemporaneous. Yet there is still more protection on offer from s.15 of the Defamation Act 1996. This section deals with so-called statutory qualified privilege. Sch.1 of the Act identifies a number of reporting situations where journalists can expect to be protected from inadvertent defamation in the report. The protection is offered providing the publication can be shown to be made without malice. The other major point to remember is that this protection only applies if the publication relates to something of public concern and the assumption is that the publication is "for the public benefit." There are eight different situations identified in Sch.1, Pt 1. They cover fair and accurate reports of legislatures anywhere in the word, courts anywhere in the world, public inquiries and so on. You should become familiar with these situations and the list can be found by accessing the *www.opsi.gov.uk* website and clicking on "legislation."

Part II of the Schedule offers protection for fair and accurate reports of proceedings at any meeting in the UK of a local authority so "cutting your teeth" at local council meetings can be done safe in the knowledge that, providing your report is a fair and accurate reflection of the proceedings, then you need have no particular worries about the laws on defamation. This second part also covers reports of public meetings and according to a House of Lords decision in 2000 this also covers press conferences and press releases. (*McCarten, Turkington & Breen v Times Newspapers* [2000])[16]

Finally note that in the situations mentioned in Pt 1 of the Schedule the protection is offered without the media outlet having to offer the opportunity to a "claimant" to explain or contradict what has been published. However in the second part the statements made by the journalist are subject to explanation or contradiction.

Reynolds, Jameel and responsible journalism

The House of Lords decision in Reynolds is often heralded as a landmark ruling in that the court took the opportunity to emphasise the importance of freedom of expression in light of the Human Rights Act 1998 having received royal assent immediately prior to the case being heard. (It was not to come into effect until October 2000). It will be recalled that parliament had expressly included s.12 in the Act intended to stress the importance of freedom of expression. The House was therefore balancing two fundamental rights: freedom of expression against protection of reputation.

According to the House, common law qualified privilege protection was dependent upon the report and reporter meeting a number of criteria. The first related to the story. This had to be one of public interest in the sense that the media organisation is under a social, moral or legal duty to publish and the audience has a corresponding interest in receiving the information. In simple terms the story must be clearly one of public interest as distinct from being of interest to the public. It will usually be fairly evident if that is the case. The subject matter may concern corruption in high places, misinformation of a public nature, politicians abusing power or conflict of interest situations.

The most familiar of recent times is the reporting by the Daily Telegraph alleging links between George Galloway MP and the Saddam Hussein regime in Iraq in 2003. Such a story relating to a sitting MP when the country had just participated in the invasion of Iraq, was without a shadow of doubt one of public interest.

Gray J. said in *Charman* (No.3):

"in order to determine whether publication was in the public interest, it is first necessary carefully to analyse the information which has been provided to the public and to pose and answer the question whether the public had a right to know or a legitimate interest in knowing the facts alleged, even if they cannot be shown to be true".

If the first "hurdle" was cleared, then the second one related directly to journalistic conduct.

[16] [2000] UKHL 57.

The question was whether the journalism that went into creating the story was "responsible." In *Reynolds*, Lord Nicholls identified ten "non-exhaustive" factors to help judges to decide whether the journalism passed muster. The common law said Lord Nicholls:

"... does not seek to set a higher standard than that of responsible journalism, a standard the media themselves espouse. An incursion into press freedom which goes no further than this would not seem to be excessive or disproportionate. The investigative journalist has adequate protection."

It was the practice of judges to take into account all ten factors when deciding the issue of responsible journalism. That approach has more recently relaxed and *Reynolds* is treated more as a broad approach. However it is worth journalists familiarising themselves with the ten factors because their professionalism is still likely to be judged by reference to them. The factors are:

i.   The seriousness of the allegation. The more serious the charge, the more the public is misinformed and the individual harmed, if the allegation is not true.
ii.   The nature of the information, and the extent to which the subject matter is of public concern.
iii.   The source of the information. Some informants have no direct knowledge of the events. Some have their own axes to grind, or are being paid for their stories.
iv.   The steps taken to verify the allegation.
v.   The status of the information. The allegation may have already been the subject of an investigation which commands respect.
vi.   The urgency of the matter. News is often a perishable commodity.
vii.   Whether comment was sought from the claimant. He may have information others do not possess or have not disclosed. An approach to the claimant will not always be necessary.
viii. Whether [the book] contained the gist of the claimant's side of the story.
ix.   The tone of the [book] and [author] can raise queries or call for an investigation. It need not adopt allegations as statement of fact.
x.   The circumstances of the publication, including its timing.

The media's difficulty with these factors related not to their existence but the fact that it was alleged that trial judges had turned them into ten "tests" to be passed or "hurdles' which all had to be jumped before the defence could succeed. This was not what Lord Nicholls had intended when he established the factors. Gray J., in the *Charman (No.3)* case [2006] made that clear at paras 107 and 108 which deserve to be quoted at length:

"The requirements of responsible journalism will vary according to the particular circumstances. Depending on the circumstances, factors other than those identified by Lord Nicholls may come into play. It is necessary always to bear in mind that the publication is defamatory and cannot be shown to be true. The standard of conduct by which the responsibility of the journalism is judged must be applied in a practical, fact-sensitive and elastic manner.

"This will be determined by reference to the information which is known to the publisher at the time of publication."

Therefore melding the two concepts we come to the following conclusion as articulated by Gray J:

"the touchstone being that of the public interest and responsible journalism, it is then necessary to ask whether in the particular circumstances of the case the publisher has demonstrated that he was acting responsibly in communicating the information to the public. For that exercise the starting point is to consider such of the factors set out by Lord Nicholls in Reynolds at [208] as are applicable."

In summary then the claimant will lose the action if a judge determines (and it is a question for the judge not a jury) that both the duty/interest test and the responsible journalist "test" have been established. To put it another way if the journalism is palpably "responsible" the legal advice received by a claimant is likely to suggest that the chances of success are not great and the claim is unlikely to be pursued. The less responsible the journalism, the more cause for optimism from the claimant. There have been a number of cases since the *Reynolds* decision in which the "defence" has failed. The key to understanding these cases and consequently the criticisms of the media is to identify why the journalists were not able to convince the judge that they had been responsible in the legal sense of the word and whether the judge was too "rigid" in assessing the impact of the 10 factors. It has been said that of 15 cases that went to trial only three have succeeded when using the defence.[17] One of these was *GKR Karate v The Yorkshire Post* [2000].[18] The defence of qualified privilege was used by the defendants in respect of articles in a Leeds "freesheet" owned by them that alleged the karate club was "ripping off" its members. The judge was asked at the pre-trial stage to rule on whether the defence was applicable. It was held that the journalist concerned had acted honestly and despite there being some inaccuracies these did not defeat the purpose of allowing reliance upon the defence.

However, the defence was lost in the *Galloway v Telegraph Group Ltd* [2004][19] case and arguably rightly so. The claimant was a Member of Parliament and had been accused by the Daily Telegraph of being in the pay of Saddam Hussein's regime. The first rule of course is that the media should be able to plead justification especially when making such serious

---

[17] Richard Rampton Q.C., The Times, November 24, 2006.
[18] [2000] 2 All E.R. 931.
[19] [2004] EWHC 2786 (QB) and [2006] EWCA Civ 17.

allegations against a serving member of Parliament. The Telegraph did not. Instead it relied upon *Reynolds* privilege. Eady J. had no hesitation in deciding that the defence should not succeed. Looked at from the Telegraph's point of view the newspaper had a public interest story particularly as the story broke within weeks of the invasion of Iraq. However the judge held that the newspaper failed the duty/interest test because it was not under a social or moral duty to publish the story at that time. If the newspaper had held the story for a few more days that would have allowed further investigation to have occurred and possibly then a defence of justification might had been used. The Telegraph had rushed to publish when there was no need. No other media outlet was aware of the story.

The judge reserved his major criticisms for when asked to decide whether the Telegraph's journalism had been responsible. He was not impressed. The Telegraph had not taken any steps to verify the information it was putting into the public domain. Remember there is deemed to be no public interest in receiving misinformation. Secondly, the tone of the coverage was "dramatic and condemnatory." Allegations had been adopted as statements of fact. Instead of simply adopting a neutral tone (what is known as reportage) the Telegraph had chosen to sensationalise the material. If it had simply raised queries or called for an investigation by the appropriate authorities it would have been on firmer ground. Galloway was awarded £150,000 in damages. The Telegraph's subsequent appeal to the Court of Appeal was emphatically dismissed, the court agreeing with virtually every conclusion reached by the trial judge. If there is a better case study on how not to comply with the responsible journalism test we have yet to come across it.

It is worth contrasting the Galloway case with one where the journalism was deemed to have failed to have met the responsible journalism "test" but was not as blatantly irresponsible as that in the Galloway case. In *Henry v BBC (No.2)* [2005],[20] the claimant, Mrs Henry, had alleged that she had been defamed by the regional BBC Points West news programme. The programme had used unedited footage of a press conference in which the speaker had named the claimant as a manager who had instructed her to manipulate waiting list figures when she had worked at a local hospital. The BBC relied on *Reynolds* privilege arguing that this was a local news story that had to be broadcast to coincide with the release of an official report into the allegations.

The Judge ruled against the BBC. Once again, a key question was whether the public needed to be informed at that time with that particular piece of information. In addition the BBC had not had time to put the allegations to Mrs Henry with the consequence that the judge believed there was not a proper "balance" in the news item.

This decision may seem a little harsh. The time scale from recording the press conference to going on air was something like three hours. The reporter had to travel more than 20 miles to go back to the studio before

[20] [2005] EWHC 2787 (QB).

he could start to assemble his piece. In between, he also had to present a "slot" on local radio. Could it not have been argued that just like the reporter in the *GKR* case he was doing his best to be as professional as possible in the time-limited circumstances he found himself in?

Look also at *Loutchansky v Times Newspapers* [2001].[21] Here the Times had published an article which suggested the claimant was involved in criminal activities. The allegations were published in both the print and online editions of the newspaper. The newspaper relied on *Reynolds* privilege in that it maintained that it was in the public interest to publish the story. This argument was accepted for the print edition but not the online edition. The matter that concerned the Court of Appeal, was the presence of the alleged defamatory material in the newspapers online archive. This was available to the public and the court took the view that this was "stale news" and could not therefore enjoy the same protection as contemporary news material.

What will have become apparent is that despite trial judges applying the 10 criteria in almost a "checklist" manner there will always be a certain amount of subjectivity in the decision-making process. This subjectivity will embrace the circumstances of the case and a consideration of whether the journalist has done his best to act in a professional manner.

One can also imagine the frustration of the media. The pro-media comments of the judges in *Reynolds* would by 2006 seem hollow and a distant memory. The media believed that its Art.10 rights were being restricted as a result of the approach adopted by trial judges. There was need to reconsider the workings of the *Reynolds* defence to ascertain whether the initial aspirations were being subverted. That opportunity arose with the case of *Jameel v. Wall Street Journal Europe Ltd* [2006].[22]

The Journal had pleaded the *Reynolds* defence in response to the claimant's allegation that he had been named and therefore defamed as a result of an article entitled "Saudi Officials Monitor Certain Bank Accounts. Focus Is On Those With Potential Terrorist Ties."

The High Court rejected the defence and this was subsequently confirmed by the Court of Appeal. There were two major grounds supporting the rejection. The first was the questionable reliability of the sources relied upon by the author and secondly the fact that Jameel had not been given sufficient opportunity to comment on the allegations. The Journal appealed to the House of Lords.

Lord Hoffmann said that the *Reynolds* decision was intended to provide ". . . greater freedom for the press to publish stories of genuine public interest." However he went on to state:

"But this case suggests that Reynolds has had little impact on the way the law is applied at first instance. It is therefore necessary to restate the principles."[23]

---

[21] [2001] EWCA Civ 1805.
[22] [2006] UKHL 44.
[23] ibid., para.38.

The lack of success of the *Reynolds* defence was of major concern because of the potential to inhibit good investigative journalism carried out in the public interest. In such circumstances, any story or report might well contain defamatory statements but that should not of itself prevent the publication of a story that was clearly justified by reference to the public interest. Lord Hoffmann and Baroness Hale were of the opinion that the defence should no longer be referred to as *Reynolds* privilege. It was, said the latter, "a defence of publication in the public interest." In assessing whether the report was in the public interest there was no reason to dispense with the reference to the duty/interest test but essentially the task will be to distinguish that which is of public interest from that which is of interest to the public. The assessment of the public interest will encompass the elements of reciprocal duty and interest. As Baroness Hale commented, ". . . the most vapid tittle-tattle about the activities of footballers' wives and girlfriends . . ." might interest the public but". . . no-one would claim there is any real public interest in being told all about it."[24]

The House took the opportunity to emphasise the key role of the editor in the publishing process. Even though the story may prove to be of public interest, the editor will still have to justify the inclusion of the alleged defamatory material. The approach, said Lord Hoffmann, was to consider the article as a whole and not isolate the defamatory statement. If the public interest test is passed, then one moves on to an assessment of whether the journalism underpinning the story was responsible. That, said Lord Hoffmann, may be divided into three topics:

- The steps taken to verify the story.
- The opportunity given to the claimant to comment.
- The propriety of the publication at that particular time.

So what of the ten hurdles or non-exhaustive factors to use Lord Nicholls' words? The House was of the opinion that they had been applied too strictly. A more liberal or flexible approach was needed. The trial judge said Lord Hoffmann had assumed that ". . . the defence can only be sustained after "the closest and most rigorous scrutiny" by the application of what he called "'Lord Nicholls' ten tests." He went on:

"... That is not what Lord Nicholls meant. As he said in Bonnick[25] (at page 309) the standard of conduct required of a newspaper must be applied in a practical and flexible manner. It must have regard to practical realities."[26]

In conclusion, it is fair to assume that trial judges should in the future take a more "relaxed" approach in assessing whether journalists have acted in a legally responsible manner. However, as Richard Rampton Q.C. said in October 2006:

---

[24] ibid., para.147.
[25] [2003] UKPC 31.
[26] ibid., para.56.

"So, for editors, lawyers and judges, the future looks interesting but not necessarily easier. Flexibility is no doubt a good thing. But so is certainty."[27]

Justification

The simplest way to view this defence is that, if one can prove that what has been published is substantially true, then it will succeed. The critical issue is to remember that it may be up to two years before attending the court hearing, where journalists and witnesses experience cross examination and try to convince a judge or jury that what was published about the claimant is true. It is not something that any journalist should underestimate. In fact, it is an experience which one would do well to avoid.

However here are the basic principles:

1　　The burden of proving the defence of justification rests upon the defendants on the balance of probabilities.

2　　The "quality" of the evidence to be adduced will depend on the nature and gravity of the "sting." The law generally seeks to put the publication into one of three categories know as the Lucas-Box[28] "levels" from the case of that name in 1986. Do not think that they are dated because the High Court has recently confirmed their appropriateness in the case of *Fallon v Mirror Group Newspapers [No.2][2006]*:[29]

"This case requires consideration of the disciplines imposed in the context of pleading a Lucas-Box meaning which is pitched at Level 2 or Level 3 on the scale identified in *Chase v News Group Newspapers Ltd [2003]* EMLR 11 at [45] and *Musa King v Telegraph Ltd [2005]* 1 WLR 2282 at [21]-[22]. It may be a somewhat artificial scale in the sense that defamatory words are capable of bearing an infinite variety of meanings and implications and, correspondingly, a range of levels of gravity which do not necessarily lend themselves to classification in one or other of these three categories. 'It is not perhaps an entirely satisfactory distinction': *per* Simon Brown *Jameel v Wall Street Journal Sprl [2004]* EMLR 6 at [19]; see also *Armstrong v Times Newspapers Ltd [2006]* EMLR 9 at [23]-[25]. Nevertheless, the categorisation is currently found useful primarily because it represents a convenient way of identifying what should be pleaded if it is sought to advance a defence of justification to some defamatory allegation falling short of a direct attribution of guilt. Moreover, it appears to have had the imprimatur of AC 234, 282 Lord Devlin in *Lewis v Daily Telegraph Ltd [1964]*, 285."

---

[27]　The Times October 24, 2006.
[28]　[1986] 1 W.L.R 147.
[29]　[2006] EWHC 783 (QB).

In our opinion the best and probably the most succinct statement in respect of the Levels is to be found in the case of *Elaine Chase v News Group Newspapers* [2002]:[30]

"The sting of a libel may be capable of meaning that a claimant has in fact committed some serious act, such as murder. Alternatively it may be suggested that the words mean that there are reasonable grounds to suspect that he/she has committed such an act. A third possibility is that they may mean that there are grounds for investigating whether he/she has been responsible for such an act." (*per* Brooke L.J.)

Therefore, when composing a story, a good journalist will make a mental note to decide whether or not it is a Level One, Two or Three story. It sounds easy but as Eady J. said in *Fallon* (above), the sting is "capable of bearing an infinite variety of meanings and implications and, correspondingly, a range of levels of gravity which do not necessarily lend themselves to classification in one or other of these three categories . . .".

The first issue is whether it is a Level One story. Is it being stated that something is definitely true? There is little or no room for doubt. To take Brooke L.J.'s example: Does the story make it clear that the public are being told that Mr X has committed murder? This is clearly a massive attack on his character and reputation. Can it be proved to be true? What evidence is there for making that statement? Remember a Level One statement is not an allegation. It purports to be a statement of fact. Take this recent example from *Purnell v Business F1 Magazine* [2006][31]: "Purnell bribed top journalist to puff achievements."

No-one would doubt that those words constituted a Level One statement. There is no ambiguity in the wording. There is no suggestion of any reasonable doubt or that the author of those words merely suspected that was the case. Therefore, the evidence to support the claim would have to be impeccable in order to succeed with the defence of justification. It wasn't and the case was lost with damages set at £75,000.

A Level Two story is one in which the wording used conveys to the reader or viewer that there are reasonable grounds to suspect that what is stated is true. You might look at the *Fallon* case cited above and read in full the article published by the Racing Post. The claimant pleaded that the words used meant that he had agreed with another person (MR) to "throw" races and thereby engaged in behaviour that would amount to a criminal conspiracy. The judge held, after considering all the evidence, that the words were consistent with a Level Two meaning. It follows from this that the higher the "level", with One being the highest, the stronger the evidence needed to support the defendant's case. No attempt should be made to move the burden of proof onto the claimant. In this case the evidence of the defendants would have had to establish a "bridge" between the claimant and MR. In the telling words of Eady J.:

---

[30] [2002] EWCA Civ. 1772.
[31] [2006] EWHC (QB), unreported.

"It need not be a particularly robust construction at this stage, but it must at least be strong enough to support 'reasonable grounds.'"

The conclusion was that the evidence relied on by the defendants was insufficient to support the case of reasonable grounds to suspect. To put it simply, the words published suggested to the ordinary reader that there were reasonable grounds to suspect that the claimant had been involved in race fixing, but MGN Ltd's evidence could not support the claim.

Level Three is where a report states there are grounds for investigating allegations relating to the claimant. The media organisation is stating that it has enough evidence to suspect the claimant has been involved in certain activities, e.g. race fixing, and is calling upon the relevant authorities to investigate. It will be evident that, while the "sting" will still need to be supported by the best available evidence, that does not have to be of the same "quality" as that required to back up a Level One or Two assertion.

An analysis of the final case in the *Henry v BBC* litigation will serve as an excellent example of how the defence of justification works in practice and its potential inter-relationship with the *Reynolds*/public interest defence. (See p. 82.)

Fair Comment

The premise underpinning the defence of fair comment is straightforward. Journalists are permitted to exercise their right to comment on matters of public interest and if in so doing they inadvertently defame someone then the defence is available to the media organisation. The current judicial view is that the defence is better described as "honest opinion." This would appear to be consistent with the principles of freedom of expression. As Lord Nicholls said in the leading case of *Tse Wai Chun Paul v Albert Cheng [2001]*:

"The purpose for which the defence of fair comment exists is to facilitate freedom of expression by commenting upon matters of public interest. This accords with the constitutional guarantee of freedom of expression."[32]

The basic ground rules for running a defence of fair comment are contained in this judgment. Lord Nicholls regarded the following as "non-controversial." They are:

- The comment must be on a matter of public interest. Public interest is not to be confined within "narrow limits."
- The comment must be recognisable as comment and distinct from imputations of fact. Clearly the context of what is written or spoken will be all important in reaching a conclusion as to whether

---

[32] [2001] E.M.L.R. 777.

the reasonable reader or viewer would regard the information as comment.
- Any comment must be based upon facts which are either true or have the protection of privilege.
- The reader or viewer should be able to glean the facts from what has been published. In other words, the reader or hearer will be able to establish a causal connection between the facts and the comment upon which he can base a conclusion.
- The comment must be one which an 'honest person' could hold however 'prejudiced he might be and however exaggerated or obstinate his views'. As Lord Nicholls emphasised, the comment:

> "must be germane to the subject matter criticised. Dislike of an artist's style would not justify an attack upon his morals or manners. But a critic need not be mealy mouthed in denouncing what he disagrees with. He is entitled to dip his pen in gall for the purposes of legitimate criticism."

So there you have it. These are the rules upon which the judiciary will decide whether or not what has been published is amenable to the defence of fair comment. However, remember that the "burden of establishing that a comment falls within these limits and hence within the scope of the defence, lies upon the defendant who wishes to rely upon the defence." (*per* Lord Nicholls).

The *Galloway* case study analysis later in the chapter provides a good example of how these rules were applied in practice. You may also care to peruse the recent decision of the High Court in *Lowe v Associated Newspapers Ltd* [2006].[33] This case decides that to sustain a successful fair comment defence the words used must be assessed objectively and not subjectively. This echoes what we said earlier that journalists should place themselves in the position of the reasonable (objective) reader or viewer. You may have meant to say one thing, but looked at objectively that may not be the impression given. The case also decides that, while comments should be based upon facts, all the facts do not need to be explicit in the piece. Clearly facts not mentioned in an article must exist and be known to the journalist at the time of writing. Eady J. summarised the position by identifying the following nine statements of principle in respect of the commentator's state of knowledge at the time of publication. The argument is centred on the assumption that there cannot be "fair comment" in respect of facts that are unknown to or not at the forefront of the commentator's mind at the time of writing:

1. Any fact pleaded to support fair comment must have existed at the time of the publication.
2. Any such facts must have been known, at least in general terms, at the time the comment was made, although it is not necessary

---

[33] [2006] EWHC 320.

that they should all have been in the forefront of the commentator's mind.

3 Any general fact within the commentator's knowledge (as opposed to comment itself) may be supported by specific examples even if the commentator had not been aware of them.

4 Facts may not be pleaded of which the commentator was unaware (even in general terms) on the basis that the defamatory comment is one he would have made if he had known them.

5 A commentator may rely upon a specific or a general fact (and, it follows, provide examples to illustrate it) even if he has forgotten it, because it may have contributed to the formation of his opinion.

6 The purpose of the defence of fair comment is to protect honest expressions of opinion upon, or inferences honestly drawn from, specific facts.

7 The ultimate test is the objective one of whether someone could have expressed the commentator's defamatory opinion (or drawn the inference) upon the facts known to the commentator, at least in general terms, and upon which he was purporting to comment.

8 A defendant who is responsible for publishing the defamatory opinions or inferences of an identified commentator (such as a newspaper column or letters page) does not have to show that he, she or it also knew the facts relied upon provided they were known to the commentator.

9 It is not permitted to plead fair comment if the commentator was doing no more than regurgitating the opinions of others without any knowledge of the underlying facts—still less if he was simply echoing rumours.

As a final point, Mr Justice Eady went on to state:

"It would plainly be unacceptable to dredge up a "welter" of factual allegations after the event of which he knew nothing at the time and upon which he might have written a different article—if only it had been drawn to his attention. Nor, as a matter of principle, can it be right to find the material for one's comment ex post facto by interrogating the Claimant or by obtaining order for disclosure, whether from him or third parties."[34]

Offer of Amends

This is a popular way to bring defamation proceedings to a reasonably speedy conclusion. The basis of the defence is found in ss.2–4 of the Defamation Act 1996. A person who has published an alleged defamatory statement may make an offer of amends. The offer must be in

[34] ibid., para.74–75.

writing and make it clear whether the offer relates to the statement "generally" or in relation to a specific defamatory meaning that the offeror accepts the statement conveys. This latter situation is referred to as a "qualified offer".

The purpose of the offer is to:

a   make a suitable correction of the statement complained of and make a sufficient apology to the aggrieved party;

b   to publish the correction and apology in a manner that is reasonable and practicable in the circumstances; and

c   to pay to the aggrieved party such compensation (if any) and such costs, as may be agreed or determined to be payable.

The media organisation should have in place a robust system to determine complaints as quickly as possible. Many correspondents will simply wish to correct something that is inaccurate and most newspapers will remedy an inaccuracy within hours. However, as the case of *Campbell-James v Guardian Media Group* [2005][35] illustrates, there can be severe penalties for a failure to respond quickly enough. In this case, the claimant was a serving Army officer who had been accused by the newspaper of being involved in the Abu Ghraib prison scandal in Iraq where prisoners were, according to the report, "systematically abused and humiliated." Colonel Campbell-James responded by stating: "I was not even in Iraq until two months after the abuses had been exposed."

The Guardian eventually published an apology some three months after the original piece by which time the allegations had been reprinted in the French newspaper Le Matin. The Guardian considered defending its position by reference to all three established defences. The judge Mr Justice Eady was plainly unimpressed by the Guardian's stance. He had the task of assessing damages and as is normal in these circumstances was prepared to make a discount for "the belated offer of amends and apology". There is no standard percentage discount and therefore each case must be assessed on its own facts. The 35 per cent discount was towards the lower end of the discount range. The judge awarded the claimant £58,500 and his costs.

6. Defamation in Practice

Few working journalists will have spent much time reading formal court judgments unless directly involved in the case. Yet these daunting-looking documents are very informative about far more than the specific

[35]   [2005] EWHC 893 (QB).

details of each case and indeed about more than pure media law. Developments in defamation cases, particularly the emergence of the *Reynolds* defence in qualified privilege, raise key issues about what it means to be a responsible journalist. Judges are discussing and defining acceptable investigative methods in at least as much detail as most journalism textbooks.

The chilling effect of libel decisions which go against media outlets cannot be ignored but there are encouraging features of recent developments which can help the working journalist. Understanding the risks and responsibilities imposed by defamation law is not just about staying out of court; it is about having the confidence and expertise not to be frightened of running stories which should rightly be put in the public domain.

The number of libel cases which actually go to trial represents the tip of an iceberg. Few journalists will be directly involved in a court room clash. However, nearly all will find their work subject to claims of defamation at some point in their career. Every journalist has to bear that threat in mind in every story covered, however innocuous it may appear. A good journalist will know enough about the law to be aware of those risks and to take advice on how to avoid them. Only very rarely should that have to mean abandoning the story. The skill is in crafting a story which avoids being defamatory or proceeding in such a manner as to construct a robust defence to any subsequent action. Many people threaten to sue for libel. Few proceed if met with a convincing defence. Most discussion here focuses on procedures before publication which will protect you against claims.

Many complaints are resolved without recourse to the courts, including by offer of amends. If the newspaper has made a mistake, it is best corrected. Apologising may stick in the craw of many editors but some defamation claims result from an error which is obvious after the event. Doing the decent thing means correcting it. If legal action is a possibility, making this a formal offer of amends is advisable. (It is then necessary to find better ways of spotting errors before publication.) Trying to defend the indefensible is pointless and potentially very costly.

If the journalist's newsgathering procedure or sources cannot be relied upon, the advice will be to settle as cheaply as possible. If a defence is in place with evidence and procedural probity, the complaint may well be withdrawn. The lack of certainty in defamation cases may increase the caution on journalists, but it also weighs against claimants. They can also lose and face considerable costs.

To pursue a defence of justification, a journalist will have to produce evidence that the sting of the libel is substantially true.

It may be true, but proving it can be very demanding. A journalist has to consider what would be available if a claim went to court. A reassuring combination for any defence lawyer is a credible source backed by some documentary evidence. Working in anticipation of a libel action, a journalist will secure a sworn affidavit from any source who may later have to stand up to be counted in court.

Seeking a sworn affidavit may seem overly elaborate but it can be vital and is an effective way of weeding out poor sources. A refusal to sign at best means a source cannot be relied upon in court but it should also ring alarm bells for a journalist. Is the source genuine? Are they who they say they are? Do they have evidence for their claim? Are they in a position to know what they claim to know? These are the questions any journalist should ask themselves about a source but where a story is potentially defamatory they become essential.

A signed statement, or better still signed draft article, is no guarantee that a source will go to court but most who have made the commitment have followed through when required. There is, however, little point in persuading a source to sign a statement only to run a story that goes way beyond its contents, especially if the way beyond includes the sting of the libel. An overblown story makes it easy for the source to wriggle out of giving evidence and, even if they are still prepared to go to court, their evidence is unlikely to go far enough.

The mundane matter of record keeping can make or break a defence too. Documents and tapes must be stored so they can be easily retrieved, if called upon to mount a defence. Key interviews should be transcribed, partly for security but also to guard against journalists hearing what they want to hear. Sources can seem more convincing and categorical in the heat of the moment than when their words are scrutinised later. Only rely on the actual quotes. It should go without saying, but a refusal to comment is not an admission. Never treat it as such.

Paid sources can still provide evidence, but the payment will always be an issue in court and can easily undermine credibility. A source will be asked if payment was offered in such a way that changing or exaggerating their evidence earned them more. It doesn't help either if they haggled. Juries don't like the idea that someone made a fortune from their revelations.

The other key requirement on good journalists protecting themselves against the threat of libel action is that the methods they employ in chasing and presenting the story stand up to scrutiny. As one in-house media lawyer put it, pursue and write every story as if you were having to defend your actions to a judge.

The *Reynolds* defence, which many working journalists may not have caught up with yet, is hugely influential and has great potential. However, it comes with a health warning. Some media organisations, believing it offered more protection than it does, have gone to trial relying on a *Reynolds* defence of common law qualified privilege which has failed. It is worth remembering too that despite Lord Nicholls helpfully expanding upon the legal onus on a journalist, he found in favour of the claimant. The newspaper lost.

The law remains highly protective of individual reputations. Qualified privilege under common law will tend to be complex and unpredictable to rely on. In the absence of a justification defence, the *Reynolds* defence specifically does not provide carte blanche for any stories in the public interest to be run whatever their defamatory content. The public interest must be there in terms of the right to know test but there must be evidence too of journalistic rigour and an open mind. Here the emerging definition of reportage is highly significant for the working journalist. Simon Brown L.J. described it as "neutral reporting of attributed allegations rather than their adoption by the newspaper" (Al Faghi v HH Saudi Research & Marketing (UK) Ltd [2001]).[36] Or as media lawyers have been known to put it: "In a Reynolds defence, the person on trial is the journalist."

Online journalism

Broadly speaking, websites are subject to the same laws as any other media, but the explosion of web-based journalism, message boards and other public contributions has thrown up a welter of new questions as to how the law is applied to these platforms.

These include, for defamation purposes, where internet service providers sit within the definition of "publisher", where the "audience" now is, where actions are taken in terms of forum shopping, and any difference made by the easy availability of electronic news archives to the general public.

One of the other key considerations is of the effective removal of a time limit to action. Journalists had benefited from the limitation on defamation actions being reduced from six years from publication to just one. This helps for stories in print but any material on a website will never reach the limitation as every time it is accessed counts as a new "publication" for the purposes of a defamation action.

Loutchansky is one of the few cases where this has mattered and a judgment has been platform-specific. A print version of a story was cleared of defamation, but the action was upheld against the online version because it persisted so much longer than a single edition of the newspaper which was also given more leeway for having been published under considerable time pressure. This judgment has caused headaches for the industry which must now establish how news organisations are to protect themselves against similar actions in future.

In principle, the situation has not changed, as newspapers have generally always allowed public access to their dusty, bound volumes of newspapers dating back, in some cases, for centuries. Actionable material would not have been ripped from their covers but may have had a warning note attached. But in practice, making these archives electronic and searchable has made the level of access much higher and the chances of the public re-accessing defamatory material so much greater. However, a similar principle may well be acceptable and is certainly encouraged for correcting inaccuracies, whereby material remains in the archive, but is tagged with the changes made after first publication.

[36] [2001] EWCA Civ 1634.

Where material is defamatory, the court may demand its removal from the archive.

A further headache arises from message boards. To date, if a member of the public has posted defamatory material, the "host" has generally been thought likely to avoid an action as long as the offending material is removed as soon as it is brought to the host's attention. Newspapers, for instance, wanting to encourage interaction with and between readers, have created all kinds of avenues for public comment. But are they responsible for anything that appears online under the banner of the newspaper? If so, everything would have to be moderated which would impose severe restrictions on the volume and speed of the exchanges. The attitude to date of trying to limit the responsibility of the host effectively encourages a much more hands-off approach. It is far easier for the host to limit liability if the off-shoot sites are not moderated than if they are. Yet this, in practice, is more likely to allow defamatory material to be published. What is a "responsible" newspaper to do?

This is certainly what one could call an "emerging" area of the law. To date, the courts have tended to treat websites as minor adjuncts to mainstream news organisations or as low-level irritants. The rapid expansion of traffic to the web makes many of the existing positions untenable.

This expansion has potential implications for internet service providers. Complainants who find it is not worth suing members of the public who have contributed defamatory material to message boards or blogs, say, may turn their attention to the facilitators. The High Court decision in *Bunt v Tilley* [2006][37] has now offered ISPs a reasonable degree of protection against such claims. ISPs will be viewed as 'secondary publishers' within the terms of s.1 of the Defamation Act 1996. However ISPs should not become complacent because the protection could be lost if the ISP has reason to believe that defamatory material has been posted and does not take steps within a reasonable time to remove the offending content.

Fair Comment in practice

Fair comment is involved in several of the key cases considered in defamation and the defence was clarified considerably in *Lowe*. It had been considered an "easier" defence than justification or *Reynolds* privilege but in *Galloway*, for example, it failed as a defence too. The court was not prepared to protect comment based on allegations rather than fact and the Daily Telegraph never attempted to prove that the claims were true.

There was also considerable debate on the distinction between fact and comment. Our attitude to freedom of expression is such that claimants tend to be less likely to challenge a story which is clearly opinion, such as a newspaper's leader column. It is therefore tempting

[37] [2006] EWHC 407 (QB).

for a publisher to claim material falls under comment rather than fact in attempting to defend it against defamation actions. Judges are well aware of this and will thus give very careful scrutiny to which is which.

Just as comment frequently creeps into news stories, so not everything in an opinion column will be accepted as comment. The judge in *Galloway* decided the sting of the leaders was fact not comment. Talk of treason, for instance, relates to fact. Treason is a crime; it is not a matter of opinion. The leader also referred to the discovery of prima facie evidence. As the judge said: "That is not comment."

Recent judicial opinion in the area of fair comment provides both greater clarity and a greater challenge to journalists. Judges are, seemingly intentionally, in particular cases providing frameworks for their judgments to set out general principles in those areas which are ECHR-compliant. These have some potential to act as guidelines for journalists working on other stories and lend at least a degree of predictability to the likely outcome in other cases. The principle of deciding each case on its merits is clearly vital for the interests of justice, but it can create a quagmire for journalists seeking to reveal the strongest, fullest possible story without falling foul of the law. While even those frameworks are subject to reinterpretation in subsequent cases, they can provide some help to the journalist in determining the legal boundaries and in outlining what will be required to mount a successful defence to any claim.

Comment is a growth area in UK media, particularly in print, but effectively in broadcast too, where specialist reporters are increasingly being called upon to "interpret" events which can raise the question of where analysis ends and comment begins. Some newspapers are actively adopting a policy whereby, given the preponderance of "breaking news" in 24/7 broadcast and online platforms, their role is predominantly to provide considered analysis and place events in perspective. What that means in practice, is an explosion of punditry which goes well beyond analysis and clearly into the realms of opinion and advocacy.

That alone is likely to bring fair comment defences to the fore. Prior to the Human Rights Act, fair comment tended to feature less than justification in key libel judgments. Claims for defamation arising from opinion pieces were often not brought because it was felt the fair comment defence would be too strong. Even before Art.10, it was harder to censure a journalist for expressing a genuinely held opinion based on fact than it was for getting their facts wrong in a news story. So we might have expected the defence to have been strengthened by UK adoption of the EHCR.

Yet there are various pointers in the *Lowe* judgment referred to earlier in the chapter that ring alarm bells or at least underline a need for caution. There are certainly massive risks in assuming that anything goes as long as we run it under the banner of comment. The judgment also highlights the ways in which the legal waters are muddied further by the growing tendency in UK media, particularly print, not to separate news from comment. This is exemplified by the editor of the relaunched tabloid Independent, Simon Kelner, branding his own publication a "viewspaper" not a newspaper.

Both in *Lowe* and *Galloway*, it is clear judges are certainly not following him down that road. They are determined to separate the two. Defamation defences demand it and any defendant seeking to use them must be able to demonstrate that both the journalist and the audience could tell the difference.

There is also the argument that, because the defence of freedom of expression in areas of public interest is now so strong, as outlined in Chapter One, judges fear any sort of carte blanche for journalists and are determined to rein us in, partly by generous interpretation of Art.8 privacy rights, but also, within libel, by making those freedoms subject to evidence of "responsible" journalism. So the framework emerging for fair comment has much in common with the *Reynolds* approach to the privilege defence.

At one level, this is to be welcomed with open arms for strengthening "serious" journalism genuinely driven by the public right to know but, at another, one cannot help feeling more than a faint whiff of judicial disapproval, particularly for the "popular" press. Journalists may have to be "responsible" but they will never be entirely respectable, and nor should they be. Only those with an unhealthy devotion to the status quo would ever achieve that standing. So perhaps we are destined always to cause judges, and the rest of the establishment, some degree of offence.

Moreover, the very fact that we use the term "popular" as one of the range of pejorative labels attached to newspapers sneered at by the establishment and academics, masks a deeper dilemma for the UK, which is that far more of the population choose to buy those papers, despite having a wide range of weightier alternatives.

Also, being from a regional newspaper background, where tabloids have dominated for decades, I refuse to use the generic word 'tabloid' as indicating a paper devoted to trivia and sensationalism. While it is arguably not even a reasonable shorthand to describe the mass-market national newspapers, it is certainly not applicable regionally. There is no simple association between the format of a newspaper, per se, and its core values and approach to content; nor its commitment to "responsible" journalism.

Offer of amends in practice

The introduction of offer of amends in the 1996 Act has proved a useful avenue either to avoid going to court or to act as a defence to reduce eventual damages.

It makes sense where the publisher is not going to contest the libel for whatever reason. Sometimes stories are run which put the author clearly in the wrong, say where a libel has been run by mistake or through failure to spot the risk. It can also be useful where the author is unable to mount a defence because the evidence is weak or unwilling to pursue a defence because of the worst case scenario on costs. Sometimes editors have to cut their losses.

Certainly, where the defamation was unintentional or due to a mistake—which happens more times than editors would like to admit— it can be worth instigating an offer of amends. There is no point pro- longing the agony and seeing costs mount pursuing a lost cause. Drafting an offer of amends which is suitably generous generally puts the publication in a stronger negotiating position than having to respond to an overblown draft from the claimant. Typically the text first acknowledges that the claim was wrong then apologises for having published it. In print, this is usually taken to be an article of agreed wording headlined "Claimant name: an apology." There will probably also be negotiations over positioning so that reasonable prominence is given relative to the prominence given to the material complained of. (See Case Study Two: *Henry v BBC (No. 2)* [2005].[38]) Having to bite the bullet and make offers, not just of correction but usually apology too, plus probably some compensation and costs makes this by no means penalty free.

The defence was born out of a desire not just to settle more such matters without recourse to the court but also to avoid the impasse whereby if a libel claim was threatened or even conceivable, the last thing a newspaper would do was run any sort of follow-up which was tantamount to an admission of guilt.

Issuing an offer of amends commensurate with the seriousness of any initial complaint will generally now be seen as working in the defendant's favour although the negotiations will be conducted "without prejudice."

However, reaching an agreement on an offer of amends can be fraught. A potential claimant may demand far more than an editor is comfortable about conceding or paying. In these instances, the court expects some negotiation to take place. The advice from *Henry (No.2)* was that the BBC should not have rejected the claimaint's suggested correction and apology out of hand. The judge said it was incumbent on the BBC to raise objections and try to reach agreement on the wording proposed.

If an offer of amends cannot be negotiated and the matter goes to trial, the defendant will be credited for having attempted to agree an offer of amends and any damages can be discounted by a third or more. The degree of discount will depend on how any such negotiations were handled.

The *Guardian* suffered for being both grudging and tardy in its apology over Abu Ghraib so it was given less credit for what it ran.

If an offer of amends is accepted, the party accepting the offer cannot bring or continue defamation proceedings.

However, as in the Guardian case, even where agreement is reached, the parties may end up in court if there is a dispute over the implementation

---

[38] [2005] EWHC 2787 (QB).

of the offer. Similarly the court may be called upon to settle the appropriate level of compensation, which will be affected by the court's assessment of how reasonably the defendant has behaved over the offer of amends.

If the offer is not accepted, the fact that the offer was made is a defence to defamation. The defence cannot be advanced if the person making the offer knew or had reason to believe that the material referred to the claimant and were both false and defamatory, although that would have to be demonstrated to the court.

The restriction is a warning shot for journalists against running blatant false stories then expecting to limit the damage by claiming to be really sorry.

If the offer is used as a defence it can be the only defence but whatever the defence pursued the offer can be used to mitigate damages.

The Guardian's response to the judgment against it is illuminating and in true Guardian style much of it is on the record. It ran the judgment across eight columns with the headline "British colonel wrongly linked to Iraqi jail abuse awarded damages." The newspaper also records and discussed the judgment against it both on the website and in a column by its then readers' editor Ian Mayes.

It did seem almost perverse that a national newspaper which pioneered a daily Corrections & Clarifications column should lose out for being slow to resolve a complaint.

However as Ian Mayes made clear:

"I do not touch complaints in which lawyers are involved. I do not deal with complaints once the Press Complaints Commission is involved. I never represent the Guardian in disputes. When people come to me without the threat of legal action I deal with their complaints impartially."[39]

In this sense, the readers' editor is the first avenue of recourse for complainants. Often grievances which could have ended up with legal action are resolved by his intervention, promptly and to the satisfaction of the complainant. A few dissatisfied parties subsequently take their complaint to the next stage. But, if complainants make it clear from the outset that they want to by-pass the readers' editor then he doesn't get involved.

Once solicitors' letters start flying, the Guardian deals lawyer to lawyer, as most newspapers do. Then negotiations take place on a much more formal basis, without prejudice, as both sides explore ways to resolve the dispute. This may account for the time taken which the judge found unacceptable.

The Guardian initially contemplated a *Reynolds* defence to the action, probably because the offending article was born out of a series of

---

[39] A costly lesson in libel, Guardian June 4, 2005.

Parliamentary questions, which themselves were prompted by testimony to the Abu Ghraib inquiry itself.

However it did belatedly run an apology in its Corrections & Clarifications column, which the judge considered inappropriate. Here, the Guardian fell victim perhaps to Ian Mayes' renowned ability to make the column immensely readable, embracing as it does sarcasm and the more humorous Homophones. The judge was not amused.

Indeed the Guardian has responded to the criticism by accepting such juxtaposition is not appropriate to the more significant corrections required. In the wake of the *Col Campbell-James* ruling, the newspaper made an immediate settlement for a similar amount with the second named officer Col Christopher Terrington. The apology to him appeared as the only item in the corrections column that day.

It is worth noting that, despite the scathing remarks of the judge, damages were still discounted by 35 per cent, less than the ball park 50 per cent, but still enough so as not to deter parties from contemplating that route which the courts are seeking to encourage.

Evaluation

Those concerned about escalating costs in defamation actions are eager to encourage parties to consider avenues more akin to conciliation which it is hoped would resolve 'sticking points' in actions without them having to set foot in court.

Sir Henry Brooke, who retired as vice-president of the Court of Appeal, Civil Division, in 2006 agreed in early 2007 to give an evaluation as to the meaning of words used in a defamation dispute between snooker player Peter Ebdon and the Times as to whether they were fact or comment.

Key players in the field of defamation representing both newspapers and leading law firms now seem interested in moving in this direction which may prove a useful way of resolving defamation claims relatively cheaply and speedily.

7. Defamation Case Studies

Case Study One: Galloway v Telegraph Group Ltd [2004] EWHC 2786 (QB)

We have chosen the Galloway case to illustrate the pitfalls facing journalists when material that has been published is alleged to have been defamatory. One can never predict with absolute certainty the outcome of any proceedings but by drawing attention to journalistic practices that failed to impress the judges and courts of this country we hope that your decision making will be better informed and 'defamation free'. Although this case was decided prior to the recent decision in *Jameel* there is no reason to assume that the analysis and indeed the outcome would have been any different if the case had been heard today.

The *Galloway* case is fascinating and relevant for the working journalist. The media, in this case the Daily Telegraph, lost the case in which it had hoped to rely on a *Reynolds* (now public interest) defence of qualified privilege for its news reports. It also lost a fair comment defence.

MP George Galloway received libel damages of £150,000 over claims he received money from Saddam Hussein's regime in Iraq. Coverage variously talked of:

- him receiving at least £375,000 a year from Saddam;
- "damning" new evidence;
- "bluster" in his responses; and
- him being Saddam's little helper.

One leader column began: "It doesn't get much worse than this." It later said: "There is a word for taking money from enemy regimes: treason." And "The alleged payments did not come from some personal bank account of Saddam's but out of the revenue intended to pay for food and medicines for Iraqi civilians; the very people whom Mr Galloway has been so fond of invoking."

The story was prompted by the contents of documents said to have been found in Iraqi intelligence files after the fall of Baghdad which also referred to Fawaz Abdullah Zureikat, who acted in Iraq for the Mariam Campaign, an appeal launched by Galloway to pay for medical treatment for a particular Iraqi child but also to campaign against the war.

Galloway complained that the coverage in April 2003 accused him of being in the pay of Saddam; of making profits personally and secretly from the oil-for-food programme; of asking Iraqi intelligence to "up" his payments and of using his Mariam Appeal as a front to obtain money for himself.

The outcome in his favour is certainly further evidence that the *Reynolds* defence is not the panacea some hoped it would be in running stories of public interest where reputations are at stake but where material is not easily susceptible to proof.

The importance of the story is not enough. The judgment made it very clear that a story covering claims about a British MP in a secret service dossier in Iraq would pass the duty/interest or public right to know test. The Daily Telegraph lost because it fell down on the 'responsible journalism' test in several ways. Its *Reynolds* defence failed because the judge deemed that it had:

- rushed to print;
- not approached obvious third parties for verification;

- not put the "sting" of the libel to Galloway in advance of publication; and
- rubbished his other responses.

In terms of the *Reynolds* ten-point but non-exhaustive list, several key elements were:

Under i: The seriousness of the allegation. The allegation was very serious so if it were wrong the public would be badly misinformed as well as Galloway being defamed. It's a double-edged sword as a media defence.

Under iv: the steps taken to verify the allegation. These were deemed inadequate, particularly as no approaches were made to third parties. In this case the Daily Telegraph journalists were expected to have talked at least to Zureikat who featured prominently in the source documents and was Galloway's representative for the Mariam Campaign in Iraq. It didn't help that, as the court noted, Channel 4 had managed to interview Zureikat on the day the Daily Telegraph began its coverage.

Under vi: the urgency of the matter. The judge was not convinced of the urgency of running the story without further investigation. The urgency must extend beyond the desire for a scoop. A quest for competitive advantage is not sufficient.

Under vii: comment from the claimant. Galloway was interviewed, but the judge was particularly dissatisfied with how this element was handled on various levels. Primarily, although the documents were discussed, the "sting" of the libel was not put to him. Galloway was told that the documents claimed money had gone from the oil-for-food programme to the Mariam Campaign but not that the Daily Telegraph was going to say he had gained personally; that he was "in the pay" of Saddam. Galloway denied that any money had been paid to the Mariam Campaign. The Daily Telegraph later tried to argue that Galloway, having denied that any monies were paid by Iraq, was effectively denying having received any personally as well as denying any had gone to the campaign. The judge deemed this disingenuous.

Under viii: giving the gist of the claimant's side. The defence fell down here because Galloway wasn't invited to reply to the "sting" of the libel. What he did say was presented as "bluster". The transcript of the reporter's conversation with Galloway was pored over by the court in forensic detail.

This is part of their exchange quoted word for word in the judgment:

> Mr Sparrow said: "Just to recap. You've sort of made this clear before, but I just want to be sort of crystal clear on this, because I mean it's quite serious. You say the Mariam Campaign sort of never to your

knowledge sort of received money or solicited money from the Iraq regime?"

Mr Galloway said "No" and Mr Sparrow persisted: "Did they ever—did they ever sort of try to give you money? It must have been very tempting for them."

The judge was not impressed.
How would your records stand up to such scrutiny?

Under ix: the tone. This applies at every stage in the story; the investigation, the story content and its presentation. The tone as well as the substance of the reporter's conversation was commented upon. There was particular concern that the reporter had invited Galloway to "explain away" the claims in the documents. The tone of the headlines was also criticised for presenting Galloway as guilty rather than under investigation. This even extended to scrutiny of story lists at editorial conferences—not known for their restrained descriptions of stories. All this was used as evidence that the Daily Telegraph had made its mind up about the allegations—that it had gone beyond reportage and "adopted" the allegations.

The choice of words such as "damning" and "bluster" did particular damage here. Journalists must choose their words carefully during the investigation as well as the reporting of a story. For instance, don't talk of "shocking revelations". Tell it to readers straight and let them decide to be shocked or not. The language required for a *Reynolds* defence may seem bland but is a smattering of flamboyant adjectives really worth losing a libel case with damages and say £1 million in costs? Any whiff of trial by media is particularly offensive to judges who believe questions of guilt should be established by due process. It is considered acceptable, even in some cases desirable, for the media to reveal matters and to call for and report on official inquiries into them, but judges, and often juries too, decide the media is overstepping the mark if it dispenses its own verdict.

Building a Reynolds/public interest defence

So how could the Daily Telegraph have run the story in such a way as to have a defence against defamation?

Some of this should now become obvious in that it needed not to do those things which cost it a *Reynolds* defence of common law qualified privilege. In the *Galloway* case, these related to various aspects of journalistic procedure and behaviour.

The Daily Telegraph tried to argue that readers were told, in the introduction to the first story and at various other times, that these were allegations. This failed to convince the judge. Stating that the defamatory "sting" is based on a claim or allegation is never enough of a defence on its own. Repeating someone else's libellous statement is, in principle, unsafe. This is the repetition rule. Journalists can only escape its restriction where they can demonstrate a high standard, not just of their sources, but of the way in which a story has been handled and projected.

If, as in this case, other elements of the article, and comment on it, go on to discuss the claims as proven fact, journalists will struggle to sustain the defence. Thinking the insertion of "alleged" makes a story safe is a dangerous rule of thumb. Judges require genuine balance not a disingenuous "nod" in the direction of avoiding action.

Put all allegations to Galloway. What wasn't put to him included what the court deemed to be the "sting" of the libel that monies said to be paid had benefited him personally rather than going to the Mariam Campaign. The judge couldn't understand why the Daily Telegraph had not gone to Galloway in Portugal and showed him the documents. In practice putting allegations to a potential claimant is made more complex when several reporters are working on the same story. The interview with Galloway was based on early notes rather than copy produced with a view to publication. If the story has moved on and the content changed, the subject must be re-interviewed, especially if the claims have become more serious. Otherwise a *Reynolds* defence will not stand up.

How reliable were the documents? There is a quandary for the journalist here. A balanced story requires acknowledgment at very least that Galloway claimed the documents must be forged. So if we are alerting readers that there is question mark over the authenticity of the documents or the accuracy of the contents, what are we doing using them as a single source for very serious allegations?

Question third parties. Galloway's agent Zureikat was an obvious omission but there were many potential sources who could have helped say about the oil-for-food programme. Security sources, for which the Daily Telegraph is renowned, could have shed some light on authenticity.

Don't go beyond the information in the documents. The right to know in this case was based on the defence that the public should be told of the claims about a British MP. These documents, whether genuine or forged, accurate or inaccurate, did not say Galloway was receiving money personally.

The courts may have been prepared to live with a little journalistic exaggeration but not reporting which creates new allegations. So where it might not have been fatal to the defence to exaggerate how much money was involved; it was fatal to suggest it had gone to Galloway himself rather than to the Mariam Campaign. The Daily Telegraph records and reports treated the Mariam Campaign and Galloway's personal gain as equivalents; a blurring of the situation which weakened its position. The court was not prepared to accept that the two were inter-changeable.

Don't revel in the revelation. The Daily Telegraph was criticised for treating the accusations with "relish". This is a particular difficulty for newspapers with a perceived political stance. The Daily Telegraph's pro-establishment tendencies put it on the back foot when trying to claim neutrality in reporting a provocative figure such as Galloway.

All journalists cross swords with people, politically and/or personally, and the challenge of proving fairness is much greater if you can be accused of initiating and pursuing inquiries "against" someone from a pre-existing hostile position. This leads to another key piece of advice, not just for legal protection. Journalists love to expose wrongdoing but such enthusiasm can cloud the judgement. The more useful information is to your story; the more it is what you want to hear; the more sceptical you must be of it. Battle-hardened investigative reporters sum up the risk as: "If it sounds too good to be true, it probably is." Beware.

Claiming qualified privilege requires a demonstrable fairness and neutrality. A reporter is not assembling and presenting the case for the prosecution. Balance extends to tone as well as content. Don't present a potential claimant's responses as excuses, or worse, lies.

Keep an open mind and look back over the facts from all sides. What other explanations could there be? Journalists can right wrongs but need to take tremendous care ethically and legally. It is easy to get caught up in a crusade where you decide who the good and bad guys are in advance and then seek the evidence to prove it. Legally that can lead into high-risk territory. Like a "bent" copper, you decide someone is guilty and warp the evidence to fit. That is not good journalism and, significantly, it will lay you wide open to successful defamation actions. Only journalism of impeccable procedure and approach will be able to claim the protection of the law. Let the facts speak for themselves.

If journalists want to claim protection under a broader *Reynolds* public interest defence they must employ procedures which demonstrate proficiency as responsible journalists. Whether we like it or not, journalists are now reliant on judges for a broad brush definition of what is expected from us to sustain a *Reynolds* public interest defence and for their individual decisions in any case that goes the distance.

Case Study Two: Henry v BBC (No.2) [2005] EWHC 2787 (QB) & Henry v BBC (No.3) [2006] EWHC 386 (QB)

The claim arose from a report on BBC Points West responding to an inquiry vindicating a whistleblower who had quit her job at a hospital in the region after claiming she was instructed to manipulate waiting lists to meet Government targets. Two earlier inquiries had dismissed her allegations; the third upheld them.

The broadcast named three of the senior managers in the relevant hierarchy including Marion Henry who sued.

The BBC rejected a request to air a retraction which might have served as an offer of amends because it objected to the wording which it said was more emphatic than the findings of the inquiry.

The BBC claimed privilege; both statutory and *Reynolds*. It kept a defence of justification in reserve. Typically, a defence of justification is seen as extremely difficult to sustain. Also, where justification is one of multiple defences, if it is lost, the case as a whole has been considered to be lost. Only if it lost on *Reynolds* privilege, did the BBC wish to countenance the justification defence.

In the privilege hearing, Henry (No.2), the judge accepted that reporting on the executive summary of the inquiry issued by the hospital was covered by statutory privilege as outlined in s.15 of the Defamation Act 1996 but that the item as a whole forfeited that privilege by moving beyond the facts of the report into "editorialising" and into naming Mrs Henry. He ruled that neither statutory privilege nor *Reynolds* common law privilege extended to identifying Mrs Henry. She was not named in the privileged executive summary of the inquiry report nor was it in the public interest to identify her.

He did, however, accept that a press conference called in a car park by the whistleblower constituted a public meeting for the purposes of s.15 of the 1996 Act which could help future reports of relatively informal gatherings.

And he accepted that although the source could be considered to have an axe to grind—she had mixed motives for being a whistleblower—the journalist was entitled to treat her as a credible source.

As was the norm in libel cases at the time, the judge dealt with each of the ten points of the *Reynolds* defence, although he did express caution saying they were not definitive criteria and that focusing on them too closely created a danger "of missing the wood for the trees." This further emphasises that mounting a successful *Reynolds* defence required far more than a tick-box exercise.

A further element was considered in this case, namely the claim for greater freedom of expression for the whistleblower because she was replying to attack, having been criticised in press releases relating to earlier inquiries into her claims. However the judge was adamant that any attack on the whistleblower came from the hospital, not from Mrs Henry, so again it was not reasonable to identify her.

The BBC went on to mount a justification defence in Henry (No.3) which it won. The judge ruled that on the evidence of the whistleblower, reports of conversations and partial email records, the damaging comments of which Mrs Henry complained were substantially true. A lot hinged on his assessment of the credibility of various witnesses. Remember in a libel case the standard of proof is that it is more probable than not that the words are true; not that they are proved beyond reasonable doubt. Also, although he ruled the BBC had not justified one of the accusations against Mrs Henry, because the criticisms it had proved were more serious, overall the defence of justification was sound.

The case ended in victory for the story and the BBC certainly felt vindicated overall. However, few organisations have the persistence and resources of the BBC. Many would have settled after the first defeat or even earlier. There are pointers, particularly from the defeat on privilege, which can help a journalist make a similar action less likely to be mounted and certainly easier to defend on either front.

The two judgments contrast sharply, not only because the BBC lost one and won the other. The journalist and the coverage are central to the judgment on the privilege defence; whereas the justification defence focuses on the hospital, the evidence of waiting list manipulation and who was complicit in it. It certainly bears out the earlier observation that in a *Reynolds* defence, the person on trial was the journalist.

The result in *Henry (No.3)* may cause libel lawyers to re-evaluate the chances of success as between justification and privilege. Justification puts the focus on substance. If a journalist basically gets the facts right and can prove they are substantially true, the defence succeeds. In privilege, the journalist can be right but if the judge takes some exception to the methods or language used, the defence may fail.

The judgment also included some very interesting commentary on the nature of the hospital's waiting list manipulation. The judge said it seemed plain to him that incriminating documents had been deliberately removed, although it was not suggested that Mrs Henry removed them. He also commented on the behaviour of managers senior to Mrs Henry by name, including those who had ordered manipulation of the lists. This was very helpful in establishing what had gone on at the hospital; a matter of considerable public interest.

How to sustain a privilege defence

Who is, or needs to be, identified? The judge ruled that privilege did not extend beyond the executive summary of the inquiry report into identifying any individual. It was not safe to be specific about individual responsibility because the report essentially covered collective responsibility.

On first reading this seems to be at odds with the advice not to blur questions of identity in potential libel cases. Too general a description can lay the journalist open to claims from innocent members of the group and a specific description, which fights shy of naming someone but effectively identifies them, will be liable anyway. However in this case there was a collective rather than individual responsibility.

The Points West piece actually followed up an interview with the whistleblower in the Sun which didn't name names. Technically various senior managers at the hospital could have tried to claim the article defamed them but the Sun, by being more in line with the executive summary, could have mounted a stronger privilege defence than the BBC.

Consider what can be deemed to be in the public interest. While the substance of the story—exposure of wrongdoing at the hospital—passed the test as did the executive summary of the official investigation into it, additional elements, such as exactly who might be to blame, were not deemed to be covered particularly as there was the prospect of future and separate disciplinary action against individuals.

Be sure of what you are being told. Being told that someone "must have known" isn't enough to prove that they did. Being aware of something is not the same as authorising it. Both may be reprehensible depending on circumstances, but indicate very different levels of responsibility for an event or practice. Although the reporter sensibly sought documentary evidence to back up the whistleblower's claims, the judge questioned the implications drawn from the emails produced and also agreed with the defence that an email being sent is not evidence of an email being read.

Allow those whose reputation is at stake to respond. The reporter had requested an interview with Mrs Henry through the press office and been refused. This is no substitute for putting allegations directly to the subject and is unlikely to be deemed adequate for a Reynolds/public interest defence. Making a general request for an interview via a press office and being fobbed off won't cover it. One option is to put in writing to the subject the exact nature of the allegations under investigation.

Let the facts speak for themselves. Don't try to dramatise a report by peppering it with loaded adjectives. Don't over-egg it. Exaggeration is not always fatal to a defamation defence, but it will weaken it and is one of the most common reasons a lawyer will advise a publisher to settle. The language used in the waiting lists report led the judge to rule that the BBC had "adopted" the whistleblower's claims which puts it outside the protection of reportage. Statutory privilege attached only to the inquiry report and he said the Points West broadcast was "far from a detached account" of its findings. He, for instance, objected to the report calling the whistleblower "brave" and the description of what took place as a "scandal". Most journalists wouldn't think twice about using such language but it can fatally undermine a privilege defence.

The media's natural instinct to side explicitly with the underdog—in this case a vindicated whistleblower—must be suppressed if a *Reynolds/* public interest defence against any defamatory content involved is to succeed.

Be prepared to negotiate the wording of an offer of amends. Don't reject a claimaint's suggested correction and apology out of hand. The judge in Henry (No.2) said it was incumbent on the BBC to raise objections and try to reach agreement on the wording proposed.

A defendant will generally be credited for any attempt to resolve matters without resort to the court. If the case goes to court despite what the judge deems to have been a reasonable offer of amends, any damages can be discounted by around a third, or more.

More generally, if the defamation is unintentional, it can be worth instigating an offer of amends. Drafting an offer of amends which is suitably generous generally puts the publication in a stronger negotiating position than having to respond to an overblown draft from the claimant. Typically the text first acknowledges that the claim was wrong then apologises for having published it. In print this is usually taken to be an article of agreed wording headlined "Claimant name: an apology".

Prominence is another issue to be negotiated. In print, claimants will often demand the front page, especially if this is where the article at issue appeared. However, the requirement doesn't mean it has to be in the same position, just that it is used with reasonable prominence. Equivalent negotiations take place in broadcast media over the appropriate time to air the agreed correction and apology.

Cost is a powerful consideration. The process of resolving a defamation complaint can be expensive in itself without going anywhere near court. Offers of amends will also be recommended where defences are weak but also where a publisher isn't prepared to risk the cost of wrangling let alone losing in court.

Journalists should not expect to rely on libel insurance, favoured by book publishers, magazines and some regional newspapers. If anything, insurance adds to the pressure to settle as the risk assessment by insurers tends to be even more cautious than that of legal advisers and, as in any insurance, as you claim the premiums rise.

Case Study Three: *Jameel v Wall Street Journal Europe Sprl* [2006] UKHL 44

Jameel was about getting the balance right in defence of responsible journalism on matters of public concern.

Lord Hoffmann makes explicit at [38] the new balance sought by the courts.

"Until very recently, the law of defamation was weighted in favour of claimants and the law of privacy weighted against them. True but trivial intrusions into private life were safe. Reports of investigations by the newspaper into matters of public concern which could be construed as reflecting badly on public figures, domestic or foreign, were risky. "

Campbell v MGN Ltd [2004] was designed to redress the balance in favour of privacy and *Reynolds v Times Newspapers Ltd* [2001] in favour of greater freedom for the press to publish stories of genuine public interest.

The gist of *Jameel* was that *Reynolds* had not made enough difference to achieving this balance. Judges were still clinging to older interpretations of privilege and interpreting *Reynolds* too narrowly, thereby placing an unreasonable restriction on freedom of expression and of public debate. A House of Lords judgment was required to achieve the necessary rebalancing.

A major legal element was whether a company's reputation should be treated differently from an individual's by requiring evidence of actual financial damage to distinguish it from a more personal approach where evidence is not required. Upholding the level of protection for a corporation is annoying for journalists but the reservations expressed within the overall judgment on this issue give some room for optimism that the position, still relying in part on a judgment from 1894, could ultimately be challenged successfully in the light of the ECHR.

The encouragement came from Baroness Hale who favours requiring corporations to produce at least some evidence that financial loss was likely. She said at [157]:

"In my view such a requirement would achieve a proper balance between the right of a company to protect its reputation and the right of the press and public to be critical of it. These days, the dividing line between governmental and non-governmental organisations is increasingly difficult to draw. The power wielded by the major multinational corporations is enormous and growing. The freedom to criticise them may be at least as important in a democratic society as the freedom to criticise the government."

However we will concentrate here on the implications for a *Reynolds/* public interest defence.

Jameel may not rely on a point-by-point application of the *Reynolds* defence but it very much reinforces the spirit of it: that there is a defamation defence for responsible journalism on a matter of public interest.

It also emphasises the divide over the types of story that could claim to be in the public interest, particularly with regard to remarks by Baroness Hale quoted earlier.

The Journal lost in the Court of Appeal over *Reynolds* considerations of right to reply. The Court of Appeal ruled that the claimant should have been given longer to respond. This was overruled partly because of the move away from the *Reynolds* "ten-hurdle" approach, but also because of the particular nature of the alleged libel and what might have been achieved by waiting.

Under iii) The source of the information. The Journal claimed five sources for its story from within the American and Saudi establishments but the jury was not convinced, perhaps because the judge directed that in the absence of a plea of justification the jury should assume the fact of the surveillance to be untrue. Not surprisingly the jury doubted whether sources would have been so wrong about what was going on.

Under iv) The steps taken to verify the allegation. Reporter James Dorsey was able to provide very detailed evidence of the processes he and colleagues followed to verify his story. These included the time of his calls, the questions asked and answers given. There is also a lovely line in his own account of the case which would put many journalists to shame in that he apparently withheld one name because it had been authenticated by only four of his five sources. Not all of the Journal evidence of the process of verification was accepted by the original jury but the thoroughness shown and the meticulous records kept did put Dorsey in a strong position to claim the title of responsible journalist whose work was professional and appropriate under the circumstances.

He had a more sympathetic hearing in the final judgment. Lord Hoffmann was even prepared to accept the kind of horse-trading that goes on between journalists and official sources of the "you might say that, I couldn't possibly comment" variety. The reality of day-to-day dealings is that a code can develop with regular contacts and that, in some cases, the absence of a denial is effectively a confirmation. It also establishes that an off-the-record response can be an official response rather than an unofficial leak. It is perhaps an extreme variant on the principle in libel actions that the meaning of any word is significantly dependent on the context in which it is used.

Under vii) Whether comment was sought from the claimant. He may have information others do not possess or have not disclosed. An approach to the claimant will not always be necessary. The claimant objected to being included in a list of companies believed to be under surveillance by the Saudi government at the behest of the Americans post 9/11 seeking to track terrorist funds. The company was not in a position to confirm or deny that the surveillance was taking place. Whether it was or was not, the company would not know of the surveillance. All the company could have said would have been to claim that any such surveillance would uncover nothing untoward but the story did not say it would. So the key assertion, unlike the accusation against Galloway, was not something the claimant was in a position to verify or deny. This is particularly helpful in hopefully deterring respondents from thinking that failure to reply can put an effective block on a story.

Lord Hoffmann also challenged the naïvety of the assumption that a denial from the Saudi agency, SAMA, would have killed the story. As he put it in typically succinct manner:

"There was no way in which SAMA would admit to monitoring the accounts of well-known Saudi businesses at the request of the US Treasury."

Where a delay would not have made any difference, the decision to publish before responses were obtained was not enough to lose the Journal its *Reynolds* privilege, he ruled. This is hinted at in the original point.

The newspaper had also been admonished for publishing information that the US government had agreed not to publish. Thank goodness Lord Hoffmann challenged and rejected this. Any undertaking the US government gave was not binding on a newspaper and was not enough to deprive the matter of designation in the public interest.

The US Treasury had not tried to claim that national security or interest was at risk, so it was for the newspaper to decide whether it was right to run or not.

Under ix) The tone can raise queries or call for an investigation. It need not adopt allegations as statement of fact. The Journal played it straight. It never suggested that wrongdoing by the companies had been found, or indeed that it might be. The whole point of the story was the action of the Saudis; not of the companies mentioned. What was in the public interest was the behaviour of the Saudi government; not the behaviour of the companies about which nothing was claimed. The names of the companies were used to give the story credibility not to lay accusations at their door.

As Lord Bingham of Cornhill said at [35]:

"The subject matter was of great public interest, in the strictest sense. The article was written by an experienced, specialist reporter and approved by senior staff on the newspaper and the Wall Street Journal who themselves sought to verify its contents. The article was unsensational in tone and (apparently) factual in content. The respondents' response was sought, although at a late stage, and the newspaper's inability to obtain a comment recorded. It is very unlikely that a comment, if obtained, would have been revealing, since even if the respondent's accounts were being monitored it was unlikely that they would know.

"It might have been thought that this was the sort of neutral, investigative journalism which the Reynolds privilege exists to protect."

Elsewhere in the appeal judgment are various useful pointers of a more general nature.

Lord Hoffmann exhibited some "real world" appreciation of how sources are to be assessed and also understood why a plea of justification could not have been mounted. As he said at [42]:

"In the nature of things, the existence of covert surveillance by the highly secretive Saudi authorities would be impossible to prove by evidence in open court. That does not necessarily mean that it did not happen. Nor, on the other hand, does it follow that even if it did happen, the Jameel group had any connection with terrorism. The US intelligence agencies sometimes get things badly wrong."

Indeed it does. The Journal article was written on that basis and asserted no more, no less than its evidence that the monitoring was taking place.

Lord Hoffmann went on to describe the article as "a serious contribution in a measured tone to a subject of very considerable importance". He also provided support for journalists when it comes to deciding how much detail is reasonable to include to justify the thrust of the story. An argument is often advanced that detail is not necessary, yet Lord Hoffmann here recognises the contribution it makes to lending the story credibility with its audience.

He said at [52]:

"The inclusion of the names of large and respectable Saudi businesses was an important part of the story. It showed that co-operation with the US Treasury's requests was not confined to a few companies on the fringe of Saudi society but extended to companies which were by any test within the heartland of the Saudi business world. To convey this message, inclusion of the names was necessary. Generalisation such as "prominent Saudi companies", which can mean anything or nothing, would not have served the same purpose."

And Baroness Hale said at [148]:

> "This was in effect a pro-Saudi story, but one which, for internal reasons, the Saudi authorities were bound to deny. Without names, its impact would be much reduced."

And she went on at [150]: "*We need more such serious journalism in this country and our defamation law should encourage rather than discourage it.*"

Precisely. Providing specific detail is part of what it takes to stand up a story and it needs to be included. And, of the Reynolds ten matters, Lord Hoffmann says at [56]:

> "They are not tests which the publication has to pass. In the hands of a judge hostile to the spirit of Reynolds, they can become ten hurdles at any of which the defence may fail. That is how Eady J treated them."

Lord Scott of Foscote pointed out that the only response *Jameel* could have given was to deny any involvement in terrorist funding and that there was no reason for its accounts to be monitored. The company could have requested, or demanded, publication of such as response in the next edition of the Wall Street Journal Europe but never did so. This was raised as part of the opinion that the delay was not enough to demolish the *Reynolds* defence.

So, a judgment designed to draw something of a line in the sand regarding the definition of what constitutes responsible journalism on a matter of public interest, certainly sets down a range of markers for the future. The scrutiny of journalists' methods will remain key but perhaps be assessed more generously than in the early stages of *Jameel*.

What is also clear is that there will be greater focus on editorial decision-making. Evidence of supervision of the reporting process, of extra checks being made further up the hierarchy and of an explicit consideration of what it is reasonable to run in the public interest were all influential in *Jameel*.

Case Study Four: Lowe v Associated Newspapers Ltd [2006] EWHC 320 (QB)

To sustain a fair comment defence, journalists could do well to take into account various of the principles outlined here. Eady J. returns to the five points provided by Lord Nicholls in the *Chang* case.

1. The comment must be on a matter of public interest. Public interest is not to be confined within "narrow" limits. To date, this suggests judges are prepared to accept a public realm wider than formal politics.

Commerce, certainly so far as it involves public companies, is also likely to be covered. The running of football clubs appears to be included but fame itself is not enough.

2. The comment must be recognisable as comment as distinct from imputations of fact. This is a challenging one. The focus is clearly on whether the audience, not the journalist, can differentiate between the two. It will certainly help if a journalist aids that distinction, by clear labelling and separation of news and comment within the publication or programme. However that is not necessarily enough. Even where material appears clearly under the banner of opinion, it may not be accepted as such by the court. Sport is an area where coverage relies heavily on comment, often vehemently expressed and that has often been shrugged off as being in the nature of the beast. Eady J. draws no such distinction in his expectation of the calibre of debate required to satisfy a fair comment defence. The widespread use of "celebrity" columnists, again prevalent in sport, may come into play given that the disputed piece was written by former MP turned commentator David Mellor. He may not be such an obvious case, as he has acquired credentials as a pundit that have arguably eclipsed his political career, but this could be another warning shot across sports commentators' bows. The legal expectations of a celebrity columnist are just as high as of any other commentator. The concept of 'responsible journalist' may raise interesting questions about such contributors. They may need to argue that their sporting experience makes them better informed and provides a wealth of "facts" to draw upon to justify their opinions.

3. Any comment must be based upon facts which are either true or have the protection of privilege. No change there. Not all the facts supporting the opinion need to be included in the piece. The defendant does not have to prove every fact mentioned, just sufficient to support the comment to the satisfaction of the jury (para.38). But that does still mean the comment cannot rely on facts that are wrong.

4. The reader or viewer should be able to glean the facts from what has been published. Defamatory opinion, to be defensible, must not just rely on fact, but those facts must be transparent. There is debate in *Lowe* over the degree to which those facts have to be included in the article defended under fair comment. Eady J. allows that facts on which the opinion is based may range from being used in great detail in the piece to being already of common knowledge, of which more later.

However, a telling point to emerge in these considerations relates to the rigour of argument advanced and that the audience should be able to follow that argument, as well as being presented with the opinion. The significant requirement seems to be that an argument must be advanced.

Whether the facts are stated or not, the reasons why the facts lead to a particular opinion must be explained. Readers must be able to assess the situation for themselves. So in a successful fair comment defence, the rights of the defamed claimant are sacrificed, not so much to the commentator's freedom of expression but to the reasonable requirement for public debate on matters of public interest. The judgment is spelling out that the pursuit of enlightened public opinion can only be served by the audience being brought into the debate so as to be able to draw conclusions for themselves. There is no right to bombard the audience with opinion in isolation.

So the interpretation of fair comment has clearly moved on and in many ways puts a greater onus on the journalist. Fair comment has always had to be based on fact or privileged information. The facts have always been at issue but here the focus is the "based on" element. The route from the facts to the opinion must be clear, and to the audience not just to the journalist.

This again places demands on the journalist and puts their abilities under scrutiny.

5. The comment must be one which an "honest person" could hold, however prejudiced he might be and however exaggerated or obstinate his views. This is of some assistance, in that the journalist isn't required to come up with the sort of mathematical proof that makes an opinion indisputable. The whole audience does not have to be won over to that view; it just has to be one of many possible opinions capable of being drawn from the facts. Again this supports the principles of healthy public debate in defending a plurality of opinion. However the scope to exaggerate or be obstinate would not remove the requirement to provide a rationale for the view being held, even where it is expressed flamboyantly. Indeed the more emphatic and damaging the opinion, the more important it will be to back it up with a strong, clear argument.

How to sustain a Fair Comment defence

Focus on the audience. Provide enough information and argument for them to make up their own minds on the issue. Provide them with an opinion piece that is coherent, evidence-based and well-argued.

Do not fudge the facts or argument. Lack of clarity makes it worse. The article at issue in *Lowe* written by David Mellor comes in for criticism for its lack of clarity. As Eady J. states in para.3:

> "One of the difficulties about the present case is that the article is written in such an obscure way that it is difficult to divine its message or messages."

He goes on to make it clear that such obscurity will not aid a defendant's position. He allows the claim to proceed on the basis of any imputation which the words complained of are capable of bearing and states:

> "It follows that an author or publisher may sometimes take advantage of the lack of clarity in his writing to prolong and complicate the issues, should there be a claim for libel. That is unavoidable, although I am conscious that close scrutiny is required of any defence in order to ensure that impermissible advantage is not being taken."

So precious little wriggle room there, then.

Be sure of the facts upon which you are basing your opinion and make that obvious to the audience. Eady J.'s nine-point framework goes into considerable detail about the requirements on the commentator before the piece is written. Again, as in the *Reynolds* defence, the argument is not just over what was aired, it places demands on the processes which underpin the formulation that is put in the public domain. So for Mellor it is not just about what he wrote; it is about whether he was in a reasonable position to write what he wrote in terms of what he—and his audience—knew at the time.

There is some acceptance that not every fact relied upon needs to be included in the item, but this does not allow for the kind of cavalier reasoning so often heard in common conversation: "Everybody knew that . . .". Such reasoning will not suffice in a fair comment defence. There not only have to be facts; there have to be "specific" facts.

There is also allowance for fair comment defence to rely on a "general" fact known at the time which is fleshed out later, but the commentator cannot trawl around for supporting evidence after publication.

Eady J. also allows for a fact to be in the back of a commentator's mind rather than in the forefront but it needs have been there somewhere. This, to me, reflects rather well the ways in which a journalist's mind works. Many aspects of a situation are just sort of out there and accepted as "known". Recall may be hazy but some incident or story from long before will be lodged in the memory and feed in to subsequent coverage.

There are, however, two major stumbling blocks in attempting to argue such a defence. How is a commentator able to convince a judge as to the extent of any "hazy" background knowledge she did or did not possess to underpin her piece at the time of writing? It is quite a big ask given the onus is on the defendant to establish such matters. Where a defence is required, this allows some chance of justifying how a defamatory opinion was advanced but if we are looking at ways of avoiding claims, the advice would certainly be to avoid having to go down that road in court.

It also still leaves open the question, very likely to be asked by the courts these days, why weren't the facts checked? If expressing an opinion involves the inclusion of potentially defamatory material, it is worth the extra effort required to dredge up those hazy memories. If writing a news story which needed to recap on background material, a journalist would not rely on memory. Checks would be made and information verified. That has to be the sensible course when putting together a comment piece too. For comment to be valuable to the audience, and to attract the protection of the courts, it clearly needs to be well-informed.

Make a reasoned case for your opinion and make that reasoning clear. How exactly do those facts justify your opinion? Spell it out and present an argument to establish how the opinion is based on the facts. Colourful language and harsh criticism can still be defended but reason and fairness have also to be in evidence to justify them. A defamatory comment cannot be made carelessly nor as part of an indulgent tirade. Avoid off-hand, throwaway remarks or innuendo. Commentary becomes legally risky where a journalist is simply venting spleen.

It is also crucial to learn the lesson of point 9:

"It is not permitted to plead fair comment if the commentator was doing no more than regurgitating the opinions of others without any knowledge of the underlying facts—still less if he was simply echoing rumours."

A journalist seeking to rely on a fair comment defence has to build a case for the opinion. An opinion on its own without the supporting facts is likely to be treated as a statement of fact and therefore requiring a defence of justification. It is the linking of the opinion to the fact that makes it fair comment. Any journalist who doesn't provide the link may lose the defence.

CHAPTER 3
CONTEMPT OF COURT

Article 6 of the European Convention on Human Rights establishes that everyone is entitled to a fair and public hearing within a reasonable time by an independent and impartial tribunal established by law if deemed to have contravened the criminal law. It goes on to state that:

"Judgment shall be pronounced publicly but the press and public may be excluded from all or part of the trial . . . or to the extent strictly necessary in the opinion of the court in special circumstances where *publicity would prejudice the interests of justice.*"

Open access to our courts has been a long-standing principle. Lord Chief Justice Hewart said in the *R. v Sussex Justices* that "justice should not only be done, but should manifestly and undoubtedly be seen to be done."[1]

The Contempt of Court Act 1981, therefore, has a strong legal and principled underpinning. In truth, the Act is something of a ragbag of provisions each well intentioned but by now the Act is beginning to show its age. This is especially true of the provisions designed to deter the media from publishing anything that "*creates a substantial risk that the course of justice in the proceedings in question will be seriously impeded or prejudiced.*"[2]

The Act was passed in an era that did not possess the rolling news environment that we have today. Nor did we have the internet. Judges may advise jurors that during the course of a trial they must not access the internet in order to discover information about the defendant such as previous convictions. Yet how is this to be policed? Given the enormous amount of information that we are subjected to by radio, television, internet, and mobile phones it is somewhat disingenuous to assume that jurors, who are often regarded as the weak link in the criminal justice system, come into a trial in total ignorance of what is at stake in the trial.

The main provisions of the 1981 Act are undoubtedly a restriction on freedom of expression and work against the principle of open justice. Parliament determined that any breach of s.2(2) is to be regarded as a *strict liability* offence. In practice that means that a publication or series of publications that creates a substantial risk of prejudice to the criminal justice process will breach the section without proof of any intent on the part of the publisher. It is the same approach that results in the speeding motorist being convicted without the need to prove that he intended

---

[1] [1923] All E.R. 233, [1924] 1 K.B. 256.
[2] Contempt of Court Act 1981, s.2(2).

to break the law or was reckless as to whether the speed limit was breached. The objective of strict liability is to raise standards by conveying the message that dropping below the legal expectations in respect of a particular activity will be certain to result in conviction.

Therefore, the expectation running through the Act is that the media will be restrained with pre-trial and in-trial reporting. This will not be a consideration in the overwhelming majority of cases because the media will show little or no interest in the upcoming trial. It does become important if the trial is deemed to be high profile or notorious because of the identity of the defendant(s) or because of the nature of the offence with which he is charged or both. Two of the alleged second wave of London bombers were arrested in late July 2005. The final moments prior to their arrest were captured on videotape by a member of the public who lived in the block of flats where the arrests took place. Within minutes the media had secured the rights to the tape and broadcast the images around the world. The following day the headline in the Sun newspaper screamed "Got The Bastards". This type of publicity led to calls for the media to show more restraint and much debate as to whether the actions had indeed contravened the 1981 Act.

Their trial commenced at Woolwich Crown Court some eighteen months after their arrest. Nevertheless, it would be naïve to assume that at least some members of the jury would not still remember the television footage or the Sun's headline. But the key question is whether or not those memories will influence a jury in its decision making. Will they be able to decide the case purely by reference to all the evidence they have seen and heard throughout the duration of the trial?

Prior to the commencement of the trials of Ian Huntley and Maxine Carr at the Old Bailey in November 2003, the press were issued with a stark warning by the trial judge Mr Justice Moses. He told the press:

"The detection and suppression of crime depends to an important degree on a fair trial with safe verdicts. The press plays its part in that fairness by ensuring balanced and fair reporting. I cannot imagine that any journalist wants to face the families and friends of the victims, whose interests they so loudly seek to defend, and confess that their work, their articles, their stories, their photographs have prevented a trial taking place at all or continuing. In short the important right of the press to report on public trials carries with it a responsibility to protect the fairness of a trial not just for the defendants but for the victims, their families and the community."

It appeared the press were not listening because some six weeks later the judge had to make a postponement order under s.4(2) of the 1981 Act "prohibiting publication of any report revealing or tending to reveal the detail of the evidence against [Huntley and Carr] until such time as proceedings against [them] are concluded." The judge later issued a clarification because the order as written would have prevented the press from reporting the trial.

So the question is: how real is the threat to the criminal justice process from pre-trial and in-trial reporting? Parliament believed in 1981 that certain types of background reporting could produce a substantial risk that a defendant may not receive a fair trial. What is the current view?

The Act has not been amended but judicial thinking would appear to downplay the threat. In *R. v Abu Hamza* [2006],[3] Lord Phillips, the Lord Chief Justice, offered the following statement of principle:

> "The fact, however, that adverse publicity may have risked prejudic-
> ing a fair trial is no reason for not proceeding with the trial if the judge
> concludes that, with his assistance, it will be possible to have a fair
> trial."[4]

In reaching this conclusion, the court took into account the following statements from other relevant cases:

R v West [1996]. "... however lurid the reporting, there can scarcely ever have been a case more calculated to shock the public who were entitled to know the facts. The question raised on behalf of the defence is whether a fair trial could be held after such intensive publicity adverse to the accused. In our view it could. To hold otherwise would mean that if allegations of murder are sufficiently horrendous so as inevitably to shock the nation, the accused cannot be tried. That would be absurd. Moreover, providing the judge effectively warns the jury to act only on the evidence given in the court, there is no reason to suppose that they would do otherwise."[5]

Montgomery v HM Advocate [2003]. "Recent research conducted for the New Zealand Law Commission suggests that the impact of pre-trial publicity and of prejudicial media coverage during the trial, even in high profile cases, is minimal . . . The actions of seeing and hearing the witnesses may be expected to have a far greater impact on their minds than such residual recollections as may exist about reports about the case in the media. This impact can be expected to be reinforced on the other hand by such warnings and directions as the trial judge may think appropriate to give them as the trial proceeds, in particular when he delivers his charge before they retire to consider their verdicts."[6]

---

3 [2006] EWCA Crim 2918.
4 ibid., para.93.
5 [1996] 2 Cr. App. R. 374 at pp.385–6.
6 [2003] 1 A.C. 641.

In the Matter of B [2006]. "... juries up and down the country have a passionate and profound belief in, and a commitment to, the right of a defendant to be given a fair trial. They know that it is integral to their responsibility ... The integrity of the jury is an essential feature of our trial process.

Juries follow the directions that the trial judge will give them to focus exclusively on the evidence and to ignore anything they may have heard or read out of court . . . We cannot too strongly emphasise that the jury will follow them [appropriate directions], not only because they will loyally abide by the directions of law which they will be given by the judge, but also because the directions themselves will appeal directly to their own instinctive and fundamental belief in the need for the trial process to be fair. "[7]

In the *Abu Hamza* case, the trial judge had rejected an application to stay the proceeding on no fewer than three occasions. The defence submission was that the defendant could not possibly have had a fair trial in light of the general and specific pre-trial reporting. The "general" issue was the media's response to the July 2005 bombings and the judge postponed the trial for some six months in recognition that there would be a fair amount of anti-Muslim feeling generated in the print and broadcast media. The "specific" matters related to the defendant and his regular appearance in UK broadcast new bulletins and the print media because of his association with the discredited Finsbury Park mosque and the Home Secretary's withdrawal of his British citizenship.

It was held by the Court of Appeal that, in light of the admirable summing up by the trial judge to the jury, there was ". . . no reason to believe that the jury were not able to consider and resolve the relevant issues objectively and impartially."[8]

So it would appear that the threat to a fair trial envisaged by Parliament in 1981 is more apparent than real. In the *Huntley and Carr* case, the judge proceeded to trial despite having been told by defence counsel that the pre-trial reporting was the worst in 15 years, because he said the jury would only have a "general recollection" of what had been reported in the media. The murders were perpetrated in August 2002 and the trial did not commence until late 2003. It will also be recalled that an embargo was placed upon the media in June 2003 preventing any reference to any matter pertinent to the defendants up to the date of trial. We can conclude from all of this that trial judges will not wish to stay proceedings unless there is absolutely no prospect of a fair trial being held.

However, the media should take note. The fact that a trial proceeds is not the final determinant of whether the media has breached the provisions of the Contempt of Court Act. As the wording of the legislation has

---

[7] [2006] EWCA Crim 2692.
[8] [2006] EWCA Crim 2918 at para.106 *per* Lord Phillips C.J.

it the media simply has to create a "substantial risk" of impediment or prejudice to the course of justice. In other words, there can still be both a trial and a prosecution for contempt. The impact of any pre-trial publicity is going to be a factor that the defence will take into account when determining its strategy in respect of any appeal against conviction.

In December 2003, the High Court in Northern Ireland found the Belfast Telegraph Group and Martin Lindsay, the editor of the Sunday Life newspaper, guilty of contempt and fined them a total of £5,000. The defendant, one Sean Toner, was to face trial at Belfast Crown Court on September 22, 2002 on serious drugs charges. One week before the trial the newspaper published an article that repeatedly linked Toner to drugs. The headline was "Fugitive Dealer Busted." Toner was named and was referred to as "A drug dealer," "the fugitive dealer," and the readership was informed that he had "escaped from a drugs raid on his south Belfast home."

Proceedings for contempt under the 1981 Act must be approved by the Attorney General or "on the motion of a court having jurisdiction to deal with it."[9] The strict liability provisions of the 1981 Act apply once proceedings are *active*. The "initial steps" are:

- Arrest without warrant
- The issue of a warrant for arrest
- The issue of a summons to appear
- The service of an indictment or other document specifying a charge
- Oral charge

Proceedings cease to be *active*:

- By acquittal or sentence
- By any other verdict or order putting an end to the proceedings
- By discontinuance or by operation of law[10]

In "sensitive" cases, the Attorney General may issue advice notices (legal advisories) to the media informing them to respect the underlying principles of the legislation. This was done in December 2006 when the Attorney General had concerns over the reporting of the murders of five Ipswich prostitutes. Two suspects were arrested and the second, Steven Wright was subsequently charged with all five murders. In a BBC radio interview the Attorney General said:

> "I think the time has come to ask the media, to urge the media, to exercise restraint in the reporting of these events, though . . . it is for them to take their own legal advice."[11]

---

[9] Section 7.
[10] Section 2(3).
[11] December 21, 2006.

He had two major concerns. The first related to reports that the press were interviewing witnesses or potential witnesses. The second that he did not wish to see the possibility of a subsequent trial being aborted because of a high degree of prejudicial reporting. The intensity and volume of media reporting could have a lasting effect upon the minds of potential jurors. Against that there is no certainty that the trial will be held in Ipswich in which case potential jurors, while being aware of the background, might not take such an "intimate" interest in the detail. Local news stations and newspapers would in all probability have a more intense focus on the story than the national media organisations.

It should be stressed that the Attorney General will simply give his opinion. It is for the media to take their own legal advice and make their decisions in light of the strict liability provisions of the 1981 Act. The media will also be aware that despite the criticism surrounding the *Huntley and Carr* reporting no newspaper or broadcasting organisation was ever prosecuted for contempt. The media may feel with some justification that they can push the limits without being overly concerned with the prospect of contempt proceedings following.

The major concern from a police point of view is the collection of evidence and issues of identification. Powerful images in newspapers or on television may play tricks with the memory when, months later, a witness is asked to testify at the trial. Did he or she really see the defendant at that spot at that time or was he recognisable simply because the witness had seen photographs in the newspapers? Identification evidence, particularly a victim's testimony, can be critical to a successful prosecution. This was never more evident than in the aftermath of the "Premiership Footballers Rape Allegations" in September 2003. It may be recalled that a young woman made allegations of rape against a number of Premiership footballers. She claimed to have consented to sex with one of them but not to others who were present in the hotel room. The Attorney General and the Metropolitan Police made numerous requests to the newspapers not to name the players who had been questioned.

The Daily Star broke ranks and in its edition of October 23 identified two players. There was also a pixilated photograph of one of them. Both according to the report had answered bail at the London police station in connection with a gang rape. The Attorney General brought contempt proceedings against the newspaper. The court, in *Her Majesty's Attorney General v Express Newspapers* [2004],[12] emphasised that the report was the "culmination of a series of media pieces published . . . by newspapers and television, on an almost daily basis, from September 30, 2003 until October 23, 2003."[13] The court went on to emphasise that the newspaper "did not heed the guidelines, requests and advice repeatedly issued in relation to this case from September 30 to October 22."

---

[12] [2004] EWHC 2859 (Admin).
[13] ibid., para.3 *per* Lord Justice Rose.

The guidelines had stated that identification was an issue and requested that the suspects should not be named nor any photograph or likeness of them published. The newspaper for its part admitted that the guidelines had been "overlooked" and admitted the story should not have been published.

Early the following year, the Crown Prosecution Service decided there was insufficient evidence upon which to proceed to charge the players. We shall probably never know how influential the publication was in the CPS deciding not to progress the case to trial.

The Court concluded that the newspaper had clearly contravened the provisions of the Contempt of Court Act 1981 and fined the newspaper £60,000. In so doing the court identified certain points of law in relation to the application of the strict liability provisions. As Lord Justice Rose said:

"There is no material issue between the parties as to the relevant legal principles to be applied in relation to the statutory test."

They are:

- The risk of impediment or prejudice has to be assessed at the date of publication per Lord Diplock in *Attorney General v English*.[14]
- "Substantial risk" means a risk that is more than remote[15] or "not insubstantial"[16] or "real."
- The risk must be "practical rather than theoretical or illusory."[17]

A key factor in all of this is to assess the degree of likelihood in the publication(s) coming to the attention of potential jurors and critically, if it does so, whether it is likely to remain in their memories. The "fade factor" is the label attached by judges to the length of time between the publication(s) and the date of the trial. It will be obvious that each case will depend on its own particular facts.

So, given the criteria mentioned above, it will be obvious to the media that potentially all but trivial risk will be covered by the adjective "substantial" and the adverb "seriously." Sir John Donaldson, the Master of the Rolls, explained in the News Group case[18] that the tests of "substantial risk" and "serious prejudice" are separate but overlapping concepts. One has to consider the likely impact of the risk upon a trial together with the extent of any impact. Judges are then asked to make value judgements taking into account all the circumstances. What the courts do seem to be clear about is that the facts of other cases are of little value nor will the solution necessarily be provided by the decision in the trial.

---

[14] [1982] 2 All E.R. 903, at p.918 (j).
[15] [1982] 2 All E.R. 903, at p.919 (b).
[16] *Attorney General v News Group* [1987] Q.B. 1 at p.15C.
[17] *Attorney General v Guardian Newspaper Ltd (No.3)* [1992] 1 W.L.R. 874, at p.881C.
[18] See n.16.

The question to pose is whether a publication would have to render a conviction unsafe before there could be a finding of contempt against the media responsible for the publication(s). In *Attorney General v Unger* [1998],[19] Simon Brown L.J. was of the view that, before contempt could be established it had to be shown that the"publication materially affects the course of the trial . . . requires directions from a court well beyond those ordinarily required or routinely given to juries . . . or creates at the very least a seriously arguable ground for an appeal on the basis of prejudice."[20] He reiterated that view in *Attorney General v Birmingham Post and Mail* [1999].[21] He said:

". . . one and the same publication may well constitute contempt and yet, not so prejudice the trial as to undermine the safety of any subsequent conviction."

However, a different view was taken by Collins J. in *Attorney General v Guardian Newspapers Ltd* [1999].[22] He said:

"To establish contempt it needs only be shown that there was a substantial risk that serious prejudice, which must in my view mean such prejudice as would justify a stay or appeal against conviction, would result from the publication. That such prejudice does not in the event result is nothing to the point."

What appears to have been a contentious point in the late 1990s does not appear since to have troubled the courts. The judge in the Belfast Telegraph case did not "find it necessary to choose between these differing positions in order to reach a decision . . ." and the court in the Express case had no need to take on board the precedents as there was not to be a trial of the issue. The point remains to be decided but Lord Diplock's view in the only House of Lords case dealing with the strict liability rule was unambiguous:

"That the risk that was created by the publication when it was actually published does not ultimately affect the outcome of the proceedings is . . . neither here nor there . . . the true course of justice must not at any stage be put at risk."[23]

Criminal proceedings for contempt are rare, but the Attorney General indicated in February 2007 that he was to bring proceedings against Associated Newspapers, the Mail on Sunday editor and a journalist after the newspaper published an interview with a witness in a forthcoming murder trial.

[19] [1998] 1 Cr. App. R. 309.
[20] ibid., at pp.318–9.
[21] [1999] 1 W.L.R. 361 at p.369H.
[22] [1999] All E.R. (D) 856.
[23] *Attorney General v English* [1982] 2 All E.R. 903, at pp.918–919.

What is at issue of course with this constant jousting between the media and the Law Officers of the Crown is the objective of avoiding trial by media. Lord Diplock was blunt and to the point:

"The public policy that underlies the strict liability rule in contempt of court is deterrence. Trial by newspaper or, as it should be more comprehensively expressed today, trial by media, is not to be permitted in this country."[24]

So what is the current legal position? The expectation is for the media to be measured in its reporting particularly in high profile cases both before and during the course of the trial. There have been some examples of good practice when the media has arguably *not* said enough to keep the public informed. For example very little was published in the run up to the trial of the alleged "second wave" of London bombers prior to the commencement of their trial at Woolwich Crown Court in early 2007. Yet it is suggested that the combination of the Lord Chief Justice's strong support for the objectivity of juries and the Attorney General's decisions not to prosecute any media organisation for the *Huntley and Carr* reporting leads to the conclusion that the media is on reasonably safe ground. It is hard to imagine that if the facts of the *Attorney General v BBC & Hat Trick Productions* [1997][25] were to arise today the result would be the same. In a broadcast of the popular programme Have I Got News for You, Robert Maxwell's sons were referred to as ". . . heartless, scheming bastards." Six months later, they were due to face trial on fraud charges. The court found the respondents to be in contempt. The words used were, said the judge, ". . . strikingly prejudicial and go to the heart of the case." The broadcast apparently created such a risk that any juror who had seen the programme (and of course was able to recollect what was said) would not approach the matter with an open mind. As a result there was a substantial risk that the trial would be seriously prejudiced. Compare this decision with that of the Attorney General not to proceed with contempt charges in the *Huntley and Carr* case. Compare the degree and extent of the publicity in that case with this single isolated comment in the *Hat Trick* case. Not even in the same league.

Material that contradicts what the judge has said to the jury when summing up at the conclusion of the trial is also more likely to provoke action. The Sunday Mirror was fined £75,000 for contempt in 2001 when a trial at Hull Crown Court collapsed as a result of a story, seen by jurors, that informed readers that the attack on the victim was racially motivated when the judge had said the exact opposite to the jury. A retrial was ordered at great expense to the public purse. With the advent of the Courts Act 2003, such "serious misconduct" could escalate that penalty considerably by making the publisher liable for the money wasted on the collapsed trial.

[24] ibid., *per* Lord Diplock at p.918.
[25] [1997] E.M.L.R. 76.

1. Section 4

This section establishes that fair and accurate reports of legal proceedings held in public and published contemporaneously and in good faith will never result in a finding of contempt under the strict liability provisions.[26] Clearly this provision relates to reporting during the course of the trial. There are a number of points to raise but the section gives rise to very little legal difficulty. The key words of warning relate to the word *proceedings*. It is possible and from a media perspective occasionally desirable to detail other matters which have been observed while in court, for example the demeanour of the friends or relatives of the victim who are sitting in the public gallery. Any such report would *not* be covered by these provisions even though they are fair, accurate and published in good faith. Who is seated in the public gallery and how they react is no part of criminal justice proceedings. However, what is written or broadcast could in fact influence the jury and the newspaper and the reporter could be found guilty of contempt. In the *Huntley and Carr* case, an article by Brian Reade a writer for the Daily Mirror was referred to the Attorney General for possible contempt proceedings. In the article he used emotive and emotional language to describe the pain and suffering etched on the faces of young victims' parents as the defendants gave evidence. It is not difficult to comprehend that not only critical and openly damaging material could influence a jury.

The words *fair and accurate* echo the words used by Parliament in ss.14 and 15 of the Defamation Act 1996. This public interest defence in the 1996 Act means that the publisher of defamatory material when for example reporting on court proceedings will not be "guilty" of libel. The recent case of *Curistan v Times Newspapers Ltd* [2007][27] provides invaluable guidance on the meaning of "fair and accurate" as the words refer to reporting of judicial proceedings albeit, in this case, in the context of the Defamation Act rather than the Contempt of Court Act. Gray J. cited with approval statements contained in *Gatley on Libel and Slander*[28] to the effect that what is required is "*substantial fairness and substantial accuracy.*"[29]

Section 4(2) relates to postponement orders. A court has the power under this subsection to order that a report of the proceedings should be postponed for such a period as the judge thinks necessary. This is obviously a restriction on freedom of expression but Parliament must be assumed to have considered this when the Bill was passing through Parliament.

It should be emphasised that the restriction can also be imposed in relation to one trial in order to avoid a ". . . substantial risk of prejudice

---

[26] Section 4 (1).
[27] [2007] EWHC 926.
[28] Sweet and Maxwell,10th edn., November 2005: London.
[29] [2007] EWHC 926 at para.48.

to the administration of justice in . . . any other proceedings pending or imminent."

The postponement will normally be only for a short period but everything will depend on the circumstances of the particular case and of any pending litigation. One of the longest embargos imposed under this section ran from January 2001 until October 2004 as other members of an alleged criminal conspiracy were tried after the alleged mastermind was convicted. In October 2006, the Court of Appeal overturned a postponement order after the convicted terrorist Dhiren Barot was sentenced to 40 years' imprisonment. The judge sought to prevent the press from reporting the severity of the sentence because he believed that it could influence jurors at upcoming terrorist trials involving a number of men with whom Barot had been expected to stand trial. This had not occurred because he changed his plea to guilty. The Appeal Court overturned the order.

The risk with this type of order when it relates to the sentencing hearing is that the media often fear that the order will prevent *any* discussion or analysis of the case on the assumption that such reporting might prejudice the trial of other defendants. The Court accepted that the media could report a "sensational" case without the words "sensational" and "prejudicial" being synonymous.[30] Judges should exercise their discretion very carefully and in light of all the circumstances given that any such order is a restriction on the freedom of the press to report, often, on matters of great public concern and interest. In a case such as this the judge at the subsequent trial of the other alleged participants in the conspiracy to murder would be well aware of the reporting of the previous sentencing hearing. As such it would be a simple task to bring this to the jury's attention with a warning that whatever happened in the previous case should not be taken into account in assessing the guilt or innocence of these defendants.

2. Discussion of Public Affairs

Section 5 of the 1981 Act provides that it is not a contempt of court for the media to publish, in good faith, material that forms part of a discussion "of public affairs or other matters of general public interest." This is subject to the proviso that the ". . . risk of impediment or prejudice to *particular* legal proceedings is merely incidental to the discussion." It would appear that, in light of the Lord Chief Justice's comments in *Abu Hamza*, this section is unlikely to be called upon by the media in the way that it was in the case of *Attorney General v English* [1982].[31] In this case, the

---

[30] [2006] EWCA Crim 2692.
[31] [1982] 2 All E.R. 903.

Daily Mail published an article in support of a pro-life candidate in local elections in London. The publication coincided with the highly publicised trial of a well-known paediatrician being held in the East Midlands. The article stated that it was common practice among paediatricians to let severely handicapped babies die of starvation. Proceedings against the newspaper were instituted by the Attorney General with the newspaper relying on the s.5 defence. The House of Lords found in the newspaper's favour. There was no reference in the article to the trial. The reporting of the election address would have been meaningless without reference to such allegations.

As Lord Diplock said:

> "The gagging of bona fide public discussion in the press of controversial matters of general public interest, merely because there are in existence contemporaneous legal proceedings in which some particular instance of those controversial matters may be in issue, is what s.5 . . . was in my view intended to prevent."[32]

3. Juries

We stated earlier that the jury is perceived to be the potential weak link in the criminal justice system in the sense that members could be influenced by potentially prejudicial reporting. Lord Phillips C.J. has affirmed the belief that whatever pressure upon juries from the media, members will carry out their task in a professional way and decide the case only on the basis of the evidence presented in court. Views should be exchanged in the jury room with members convinced that they can speak openly and with the knowledge that what is said will remain confidential.

Section 8 of the Contempt of Court Act is designed to support this principle and provides that it will be a contempt of court for the media to:

> ". . . obtain, disclose or solicit any particular statement made, opinions expressed, arguments advanced or votes cast by members of a jury in the course of their deliberations in any legal proceedings."

Any action for alleged breach of s.8 must be made with the consent of the Attorney General or the court.

It may well be that journalists are approached by members of the jury expressing dissatisfaction at the process by which the decision was reached. While jury members may believe that they are acting in good

---

[32] ibid., at p.920.

faith and after all due consideration, the media is still in breach of their s.8 obligations if such concerns are published. In *R. v Connor and Mizra* [2004],[33] the House of Lords made it clear that if jurors had concerns about what was occurring once they had retired then they should be brought to the attention of the trial judge at that time not after the trial has been concluded. The principles to be applied in respect of s.8 are to be found in the decision of the House of Lords in *Attorney General v Associated Newspapers* [1994].[34] In this case, a newspaper revealed information about the jury's deliberations in the aftermath of a much publicised fraud trial. Some members of the jury, believing that they were contributing to a legitimate research exercise, had passed on their views and opinions. The transcripts of the "research" formed the basis of the publication. Jury members had not spoken directly to the newspaper. It was held that the newspaper was in breach of the "plain and unambiguous" wording of s.8. The newspaper, its editor and the journalist concerned were fined a total of £60,000 for the "disclosure."

The legal message therefore to journalists is to stay away from juries. What, however, is permitted is for the press to speak with jury members about their "general" experience without the media referring specifically to any aspect of the particular case in which the individual participated.

4. Section 11 Orders

Providing that the name of a witness or defendant has not been mentioned in open court, then it is possible for a court to place a permanent embargo upon the media to prevent disclosure. As may be expected the use of s.11 is not widespread because it runs counter to the presumption in favour of freedom of expression and open justice. The section says that if a court has power to withhold a name from the public it:

"... may give such directions prohibiting the publication of that name or matter in connection with the proceedings as appear to the court to be necessary for the purpose for which it was so withheld".

Section 11 orders may be used when members of the security services are called as witnesses if their lives may be put at risk because of public exposure. They may be used to persuade key witnesses to come forward to give evidence in circumstances where they fear for their safety if identified. The Court of Appeal in the *R. v Davis* [2006][35] paints a graphic

---

[33] [2004] UKHL 2.
[34] [1994] 1 All E.R. 556.
[35] [2006] EWCA (Crim) 1155.

picture of the dangers faced by those who seek to assist the police to bring ruthless criminals to justice. The President of the Queen's Bench Divisional Court quoted from Hughes J. in *R. v Bola* [2003][36]:

> "... the experience of police is that after an incident of this kind (fatal shooting) witnesses are frequently content to come confidentially to the investigators to tell them what they know, what they saw, to give them leads and help them about what the background may be and sometimes to name names but that such witnesses are to a very large extent frightened to be identified as co-operating with the police ... they fear similar incidents ...."[37]

Section 11 orders can help to allay such fears but should not be used in such a way as to stifle freedom of expression, without good cause. The terms of any such order should be very specific and be in writing.

5. Contempt in Practice

The freedom of journalists to put legal proceedings in the public domain relies on the long-standing commitment to open justice and the recognition of its benefits to a democratic society. Having said that, the core commitment is to the publication of judgments. The public access to, and airing of, any particular proceedings have long been seen as sacrificeable to the broader interests of justice, particularly to protect the jury system itself. The principle is now further circumscribed by the requirement to uphold the art.6 rights of any defendant to a fair trial.

These various limitations on the freedom to provide a public account of legal dealings are mainly outlined in a variety of provisions within the Contempt of Court Act. Contempt under the Act becomes a criminal offence which is daunting for journalists but does require a case to be proven beyond all reasonable doubt as well as meeting the more particular requirements of the Act.

The legal restrictions designed to protect the right to a fair trial have a wide variety of repercussions for journalists and impact on far more than straightforward court reporting.

Day-to-day crime coverage and any stories relating to issues which could end up in court require an understanding by the reporter of the basic principles at stake and of the specific restrictions which apply at each stage. In practical terms a useful distinction can be made between pre-trial and in-trial reporting as outlined earlier.

On paper, the UK provides considerable protection for the defendant and for the process of trial by jury by imposing limits on any reporting

---

[36] Unreported, June 18, 2003.
[37] Op. cit, para.8.

which creates a substantial risk of serious prejudice—and those limits kick in very early in the process. This is in stark contrast to the sort of reporting allowed in the United States both before and even during a trial.

Historically journalists had free rein to report on crime, for instance, until a suspect was charged. Now proceedings are active from the point of arrest or the issuing of a warrant. As soon as the finger points at a particular individual, restraint is demanded under strict liability provision.

Avoiding contempt according to the letter of the law imposes considerable restrictions on the manner in which crime is reported. In practice, the absence of enforcement has led to risky material being run routinely. In many cases this custom and practice has merely allowed reasonable latitude for the public right to know about such incidents and suggests the judicial interpretations of "substantial" and "serious" have put the bar high for establishing contempt.

Certainly journalists are far less cautious now than they were in the early days of the Act. The danger for any novice, and indeed for more experienced journalists, is that we are behaving almost as if the law does not exist and that could tempt us to be too cavalier. The process of assessing the risk of being held in contempt must be gone through even where the likelihood of being prosecuted seems remote enough to take that risk.

Journalists should also consider their moral position. Personally, being responsible for coverage which set the foundation for an innocent person to be wrongfully convicted would prey on my conscience far more than falling foul of a privacy complaint from a celebrity with a punctured ego. Any journalist concerned about being fair to all, high and low, needs to move beyond a simple assessment of the chances of being called to account into how we impact upon the vital principle that any suspect is innocent unless proven guilty.

On the other hand there is the risk that, if a contempt involves a trial being abandoned, a journalist could be responsible for a "guilty" defendant being freed and the victims forever being denied justice.

Where proceedings are active, it is important to recognise the degrees of latitude being exercised.

6. Crucial Questions to Avoid Contempt

Are proceedings active?

Remember the restrictions apply from the time of arrest; the issue of a warrant or summons, the service of an indictment or an oral charge. They also continue to apply until acquittal or sentence.

In practice, it can be difficult to establish whether proceedings are active, but reporters are expected at least to attempt to find out. Police still talk of people "helping with inquiries" which may, or may not, involve arrest. If someone being questioned is not free to leave, proceedings are definitely active. The same is true if they are released on police bail. However if they are simply released without charge and not bailed, there are no proceedings to be active in relation to them.

Alert newsdesk if proceedings are active—this ensures the risk is weighed by those with the responsibility to assess any legal risks and it covers your back if the worst should happen.

Will a report create a substantial risk of serious prejudice?

This is a tough test with a high threshold and proceedings for contempt by publication under the Act have to be authorised by the Attorney General. But journalists should not be complacent about creating coverage that could be held in contempt.

Is the report written as if the person arrested is definitely the person who committed the crime?

The risk of being held in contempt rises considerably if a report is worded so as to leave no doubt that the suspect is guilty. Police cannot have definitely caught the guilty person: that is for the courts to decide. To be safe there needs to be enough wriggle room in any report to allow for the suspect to be innocent. It must at very least be possible for someone other than the suspect to be guilty. This need not prevent a pretty full account of the nature of the crime, but it does restrict coverage of who is responsible for it. A report needs to be about the crime and the victim, rather than a whodunnit. This, logically, tends to push reports into focussing on the victim rather than the perpetrator. To cover an incident by the book where proceedings are active, it is best to focus on common ground—a sequence of events which is not disputed, such as who the victim was, how the body was found, the cause of death, items removed by police. The aim is to exclude material that is likely to be disputed at trial. In practice, it is rarely possible to be certain what exactly that includes. But, in the current more lax climate, a reasonable amount of detail could be given on the basis that judges have defended the entitlement of the public to know the facts of major criminal incidents. A degree of care not to incriminate the suspect should be sufficient but reporters should always bear in mind that the risk exists.

Does it place the suspect at the scene?

Problematic cases are where suspects are "caught red-handed", arrested on the spot, after a chase or in a citizen's arrest or other dramatic, newsworthy way. The account of the crime needs to be separated from the arrest in such a way that the police could have detained the wrong person.

How is the suspect described?

Be as neutral as possible about the suspect's character. *A* man was arrested; not *the* man was arrested. Some reservations could be expressed (libel allowing) but the more closely these relate to the accusation at issue the riskier they become. Be cautious with any damning quotes from neighbours or colleagues suggesting guilt and do *not* introduce previous convictions. The presumption of innocence, which is said to be a foundation of the criminal justice system, used to mean that these were never made known to the jury during the trial. Even though they now can be under bad character provisions, this is only at the judge's discretion so including them in any pre-trial report would deprive the judge of this power so still be at risk of being deemed in contempt.

Is it safe to include eyewitness accounts?

Witness accounts can easily be seen to risk prejudicing a fair trial. The concern here is that once an eyewitness goes on the record in the media, there could be an argument that the evidence is tainted. If, say, the witness or the reporter exaggerates the account, there is a danger the witness may feel obliged to live up to the initial media statement when it comes to giving evidence in court or, even sooner, when giving a statement to police.

The closer the source was to witnessing the crime itself rather than say its aftermath, the greater the risk and nothing should be used which points to the guilt of any particular individual.

However, the main threat to the integrity of witnesses was the old habit, previously prevalent among the national mass market tabloids, to "buy up" witnesses for the backgrounder at the end of the trial. Some payments were even conditional on conviction. That made sense for the newspaper as there would nearly always be far more interest in the background of a mass murderer than the ordeal of an acquitted defendant. Yet effectively the payment gave the witness a significant incentive to provide damning evidence. This practice was frowned upon by the judiciary as tending to pervert the course of justice. It was ruled out in the Press Complaints Commission code in the wake of the Rosemary West trial. Care still needs to be taken to make a proper assessment of the witness's reliability.

Is it safe to interview the victim?

It can be with care. Again the focus needs to be on the ordeal with the inclusion of verifiable facts which will not be at issue at trial and which do not point to any particular guilty party.

Is it safe to run a confession?

If someone confesses to a crime, it might be tempting to think it would be safe to run because there would be no trial and therefore no jury to prejudice. However, a confession made to a journalist carries no legal weight, is not binding on the confessor, and is certainly not the equivalent of a guilty plea in court. Also such coverage would certainly provoke the wrath of the judiciary as being in the realms of "trial by media." Confessions can only properly be made through legal channels and otherwise would be inadmissible and could actually make conviction impossible.

It is generally considered safe to report claims of innocence although technically these are potentially prejudicial, especially if the defendant effectively introduces evidence, as again this would stray into trial by media.

Is identity going to be an issue?

Identity very often is an issue and it will certainly be difficult to rule it out in the immediate aftermath of an incident. The printing of photographs of those accused is particularly frowned upon and is likely to provoke a warning if not full-blown proceedings. The fear is of a kind of auto-suggestion that by running a photograph, witnesses may convince themselves they saw the suspect when they didn't. This would particularly taint any identity parade evidence.

However an exception is made for the publication of e-fit images where the police are actively appealing for witnesses or warning the public to protect themselves against a suspect. This is a typical balancing act area of compromise where the public interest is seen to be sufficient to outweigh concerns for the suspect's rights. Usually this is justified on the grounds that a suspect is violent and a potential threat even though a warrant is out for arrest and therefore proceedings active for contempt.

In the case of the footballers, used earlier, even using the names was seen as provoking a risk because where the suspect is a celebrity that can be enough to raise a doubt because their image may be seen as sufficiently familiar even if it is not run with the item.

Will it be tried by jury?

The vast majority of incidents that attract major coverage will involve an indictable offence, namely one that is likely to end up at jury trial and remember it is primarily the jury process the Act is designed to protect.

If the nature of the crime means it will be tried by magistrates, the risk of contempt is very low as magistrates are not to be swayed by media reports. Given that they decide questions of innocence and guilt in full knowledge of a defendant's previous convictions and that, for instance, other reporting restrictions such as those of the Magistrates' Court Act, do not apply to trial before magistrates, it would be difficult to sustain an argument that they were influenced by media coverage.

The fact that the jury is central to issues of contempt and that the jury is drawn from the area close to the crime means that local newspapers are more likely than the nationals to face action. Their coverage is literally closer to home and can be considered more likely in the first instance to be read by jurors and also to be more meaningful and thereby to persist in their minds. Trials can be moved to a different area to reduce the risk, but that could increase the irritation with the author of the local coverage that made the switch necessary.

How long will the case take to come to trial?

The public interest in reporting crime helps provide the extra latitude when covering the crime itself and it can easily be 18 months before a major case comes to trial. The fade factor may help with coverage of a crime at the time it comes to light but, as the trial date nears, there comes a point where there may not be time for memories to lapse. What is not clear is when that point is. Often, the bigger the case, the longer it takes to get to trial and some can take 18 months to come to court. But is three months long enough? Is three weeks? Certainly the closer to trial the harder it would be to use the fade factor defence and the public interest in disclosure may be harder to argue too. Generally a more cautious approach is usually adopted from the first court appearance before magistrates.

The media's ability to rely on the fade factor does however depend on the sense of transience. In this regard a newspaper's role as tomorrow's catlit liner works in its favour and judges have previously deemed broadcast news to be even more forgettable. However that argument is potentially seriously undermined by the 21st century availability of online archives. In defamation, every "hit" on an article is treated as a fresh publication which creates a fresh liability. The same general principle is likely to make it much harder for the media to rely on fade factor if the material accused of being claimed to be contemptuous is still on the website for jurors to see.

Is the trial incidental to discussion of an issue of general public interest?

This can be useful, but journalists can't afford to be disingenuous. A s.5 defence is harder, although not impossible, to sustain if the upcoming trial is what makes debate of the issue timely. Don't mention it!

How can I describe the crime?

Technically, it is not for a crime reporter to determine the nature of the offence committed, particularly to distinguish between murder and manslaughter. So, if someone has been arrested on suspicion of murder, a report should stick to the physical events, at least referring to a stabbing, say, or even more cautiously to the victim being found with knife wounds.

Judges are also very sensitive to anything that smacks of trial by media so reports in that vein are much more susceptible to action. Coroners have been known to challenge incident reports referring to suicide, arguing that it is for their inquest to reach a verdict as to how a victim came to be found hanging or dead from a drugs overdose. How cautious a newspaper is may depend on how protective a particular coroner is of the procedure. A good rule of thumb in deciding what to include is to ask yourself: will it annoy the judge or coroner? Will it be seen as treading on the judge's toes? That may still not absolutely rule out particular content, but the likelihood of action is significantly increased.

One further note of caution is that the sort of report that could provoke action under the Contempt of Court Act is also likely to be defamatory and there could be a serious libel risk if a suspect is identified and subsequently charges are dropped or never even brought. So, although the contempt risk may be dismissed, the chances of a libel action need to be considered too.

7. Trends in Contempt

The discernible trend, as remarked upon in the examples given on *Huntley and Carr*, is of greater risks being taken pre-trial. Perhaps it is reasonable not to wring our hands over this. Even judges recognise the fade factor.

Also, given the proliferation of material online and the relative difficulty of closing the jury off to outside, and certainly, historical influences, the protection envisaged in the Contempt of Court Act is simply not achievable. Moreover, if we trust the jury to recognise their personal prejudices and put those aside, is it really that unreasonable to require them to ignore any preconceived ideas generated by banner headlines in the Sun months before?

Where a case has received considerable media attention, the judge can step up the force of the reminder to the jury that they must swayed only by the evidence heard in court.

For contempt cases to be successful, the judge would have to concede not only that the jury would struggle to weigh the case on the facts but also that his own powers of persuasion with them were limited.

Also, despite the caveat that coverage can be contempt without necessitating the abandonment of the trial, the very rarity of prosecutions would make it very difficult in practice to proceed with any case where reports had been held in contempt, whether pre-trial or in-trial.

Similarly, there are broader reasons why the Attorney General is loathe to instigate contempt proceedings, preferring the warning shot across the bows. The Attorney General has a political as well as a legal role and whatever UK Governments do behind the scenes, they are ultimately reluctant to be seen to be acting overtly to curb the press.

Politically too, there are few Brownie points to be won with the public by standing up for the rights of suspects to a fair trial, especially where terrorism is allegedly involved. If the case against a defendant collapses as a result, perhaps the Attorney General would end up taking a share of the blame along with the media.

For all these reasons, it would appear that the judges and the Attorney General would have a lot to lose by clamping down, particularly on pre-trial contempt.

That is further grounds for journalists themselves to pause for thought. Journalists could well celebrate the ineffectiveness of the Contempt of Court Act as a victory for freedom of expression and a sign of a more reasonable balance between the right to record what is going on in the world. It would also suggest the jury system is more robust than the Act presumes.

However, is the Attorney General's reticence good enough reason to report an arrest in such a way as to undermine the chances of a fair trial? Just because we might get away with something does not make it reasonable to do it anyway. In many other contexts, journalists have established a noble tradition of upholding the rights of the individual against an oppressive State machinery. Should we really be applauding the use of pre-trial headlines which damn a defendant, especially an "unfashionable" one such as a terror or paedophile suspect?

It is also worth bearing in mind that the position of Attorney General may be set to change to separate the legal and political aspects of the role. A purely "legal" arbiter may well find it easier to bring actions than under the existing regime. The Procurator Fiscal in Scotland, responsible for bringing contempt proceedings there under the same legislation, is held to have fewer qualms about bringing an action and the news media are more restrained as a result.

Perhaps the increased latitude allowed in practice pre-trial has intentionally, or otherwise, developed as a counterbalance to a more draconian system for reporting during the trial.

Contempt at trial

A court report that is not both fair and accurate, or is run with malice can be held in contempt. Coverage independent of the trial but run during it may also be in contempt.

Information given in the absence of the jury can also not safely be reported during the trial because of the risk of contempt. Common sense dictates that is should not be used at that stage given that the jury is absent only because it is deemed jurors should not be privy to it lest it prejudice their deliberations.

What has made media operators sit up and take notice is the provision in the Courts Act 2003 whereby in cases of "serious misconduct"—effectively where reporting is so prejudicial that it triggers the collapse of a trial, the publisher can be held liable for costs of the trial to date, which can run into millions of pounds.

The Act also firms up the position on reporting of material in the absence of the jury. It had been argued that it was for the court to issue a postponing order to delay use of such information and that, in the absence of an order, a journalist could go ahead without risk of being held in contempt. However the Act raises the prospect of treating such revelations as 'serious misconduct' which could prove even more costly.

Even for organisations driven by financial rather than ethical considerations, this tips the balance firmly towards extra caution during trial. Magistrates and judges are likely to be less reticent than the Attorney General in making the media pay for overstepping the mark.

Backgrounders

Technically proceedings are active for contempt until sentence. But the Act is designed to protect the jury from undue influence and once jurors have returned their verdict, their role is over. The judge is the one determining sentence and the received wisdom is that a judge is not susceptible to media influence or, at least, would never admit to being so. Many backgrounders are now run immediately after verdict rather than waiting until sentence which can be months later.

8. Section 4(2) Orders in Practice

These orders are proving popular with judges and magistrates and as a consequence they are throwing up difficulties for reporters and giving rise to a growing number of challenges. Reporters in court should be aware of the requirements of the orders and the likely erroneous justifications used in making them, which can be challenged.

Lack of clarity can be an issue. The court should make clear the scope of the order—exactly what information needs to be postponed or withheld. It should also give the grounds for making the order. Reporters should always request this information in writing. This is partly to protect the journalist to ensure compliance with the order; so that neither too much nor too little information is withheld. The mere act of requesting clarification may help to ensure any order receives appropriately detailed consideration and is no broader than it need be. It will also highlight possible grounds to challenge the order, or at least its scope.

Two key judgments worth remembering are *R v Horsham Justices, Ex p. Farquharson* 1982[38] which requires judges and juries to act according to the evidence put in front of them and not what they read in the papers. *Ex p. HTV Ltd v Rhuddlan Justices* 1986[39] established that s.4 orders cannot be used to postpone reports of matters outside the court.

Section 4(2) postponing orders tend to be used where a sequence of related trials is taking place and is again based on the desire not to prejudice a jury by knowing the outcome of these other trials. But there is a growing inconsistency with their application given the general trends to treat juries as more impervious to influence than previously. If we trust juries to come to a verdict based solely on the evidence given, and if we trust them, in some instances, to come to a verdict in the knowledge of the defendant's previous convictions, could we not also trust them to ignore the guilt or innocence of another defendant in a different aspect of the overall case.

This aspect came to the fore in the *Barot* case mentioned earlier in the judgment of Sir Igor Judge. He said:

"The freedom of the press to report the proceedings provides one of the essential safeguards against closed justice. In our view, broadcasting authorities and newspaper editors should be trusted to fulfil their responsibilities accurately to inform the public of court proceedings and to exercise sensible judgment about the publication of comment which may interfere with the administration of justice."[40]

This was a victory in the specific case and a welcome reiteration of the "precious principle" of open justice. However there is, as usual, a caveat. The judgment is not giving carte blanche for the material to be printed; rather it is saying it is not for the court to ban coverage. It puts the onus on the media to make its own decision about what to include/exclude but reminds them of the broader restrictions of contempt. This effectively undermines the notion that any report of court proceedings, in the absence of a ban, is protected against contempt.

Significantly, it was also an "important consideration" that Barot's conviction would be admissible at the forthcoming trial and that the jury would be told details of his activities. What then is the purpose of contempt which is designed to shield the jury from information they are now going to be given? The introduction of the bad character provisions basically calls into question the whole underpinning of the Contempt Act which assumes juries need a great deal of protection from information which could undermine the defendant's chances of a fair trial. If they can have his previous convictions put to them at trial, most other potentially damaging facts pale into insignificance.

---

[38] [1982] Q.B. 762.
[39] [1986] Crim L.R. p.329.
[40] Quoted by Tony Jaffa and Nigel Hanson, of Foot Anstey Solicitors on *www. holdthefrontpage.co.uk*.

9. Section 11 in practice

Section 11 was designed to protect vulnerable witnesses and was seen as a justifiable retreat from openness in the interests of justice so as to encourage witnesses to come forward. However, this is no guarantee that it will be employed to those ends.

There is a tendency for Section 11 to be used out of some kind of sympathy for the defendant so reporters should be in a position to remind the court that "it was not enacted for the comfort of defendants and so cannot be used to exclude, for instance, the address". (*R v Evesham Justices, Ex p. McDonagh* [1988][41]). Any perceived misuse should not go unchallenged.

The Judicial Studies Board guidelines, Reporting Restrictions in the Magistrates' Courts, advise:

> "Consistent with the general requirement of open justice, the Court's prime consideration should be the administration of justice and whether it is satisfied that failure to make an order would frustrate or impede it (sympathy for the accused or protection of his business interests against economic damage are not good enough)."[42]

But it would appear that sympathy for the defendant's family is being considered by the courts. Various news organisations, as of May 2007, were challenging an order by a judge to protect the identity of an alleged paedophile because of the upset coverage would cause to his child. While one can have every sympathy for the innocent relatives of criminals, this is a route the courts can simply not be allowed to go down unchallenged.

The logic would be that any defendant with a family could be protected from being held publicly accountable for his crimes. This would be a massive retreat from the principles of open justice. Moreover, one of the serious issues underlying criminal behaviour is that many people end up in the dock precisely because they have not considered the consequences of their actions, either for themselves or other people. Allowing them to evade them further by granting anonymity would not be fair but would also not do anything to get them to face up to the reality of their offending.

Any court contemplating a s.11 order is also invited in the guidelines to consider if a lesser order, such as a postponement order under s.4(2) might suffice. Also, in accordance with *R v Arundel Justices Ex p. Westminster Press* [1985],[43] a s.11 order cannot make secret a name that has already been spoken in open court or put on the court list.

---

[41] [1988] Q.B. 553.
[42] Reporting Restrictions in the Magistrates' Court, Judicial Studies Board. To view this extract in context, full guidance can be found on the Judicial Studies Board website at: *www.jsboard.co.uk.*
[43] [1985] 2 All E.R., at p.390.

CHAPTER 4
PRIVACY & CONFIDENTIALITY

When Princess Caroline of Monaco took her grievances against the German media to the European Court of Human Rights in 2004 it could not have been envisaged what a profound impact it would have on the English courts' approach to the protection of "privacy" rights. English common law has never recognised a tort of privacy. This was never more graphically illustrated than when the Court of Appeal failed to identify a "privacy" remedy for Gorden Kaye in his dispute with the Sport Newspaper over being ambushed in his hospital bed.[1] Lord Justice Gildwell left no room for doubt as to the current position within this jurisdiction:

"It is well known that in English law there is no right to privacy and accordingly there is no right of action for breach of a person's privacy. The facts of the present case are a graphic illustration of the desirability of Parliament considering whether and in what circumstances statutory provision can be made to protect the privacy of individuals."

Other judges supported this assessment of the law. Bingham L.J. said that the case highlighted the failure of both the common law and statute to "protect in an effective way the personal privacy of individual citizens."

The Court of Appeal reiterated the message in 2000 in the first of the many cases in the long running dispute between Michael Douglas, Catherine Zeta Jones, OK! Magazine and Hello Magazine.[2] It is worth reading this passage from Lord Justice Sedley's judgment in full as it emphasises the problem at the heart of the *Kaye* case:

"Lawyers in this country have learned to accept that English law recognises no right of privacy. It was for this express reason that counsel for the actor Gordon Kaye instead put his case against the Sunday Sport, whose reporter and photographer had shamefully invaded the hospital room where Mr Kaye was recovering from serious head injuries, not as a breach of privacy, which it plainly was, but as a case of libel, malicious falsehood, trespass to the person and passing off. He managed only to hold an injunction to stop the paper claiming, by way of malicious falsehood, that Mr Kaye had voluntarily given an interview. But, this court . . . did not affirmatively consider

---

[1] [1991] F.S.R. 62.
[2] *Douglas v Northern & Shell Plc* [2000] EWCA Civ 353.

and decide whether there was a right to privacy in English law. The court adopted—for it plainly shared—counsel's assumption that there was none."[3]

The popular tabloids' obsession with prurience at every level has become the staple fare in British homes not just on Sundays but every day of the week. The Mail on Sunday has the story of the former chairman of British Petroleum's one-time gay lover who, it has been claimed, was paid a substantial sum of money for his revelations. If one searches hard, it is possible to detect a public interest element in the story as it alleges that there was a misuse of company funds by Lord Browne.[4] Yet three years ago after the *Caroline* decision, it was envisaged that "kiss and tell" stories would disappear from our newspapers and celebrity magazines. Leading media lawyer, Matthew Nicklin, wrote:

"It is difficult to imagine that revelations about the sexual conquests and prowess of celebrities and similar trivialities, which have so entertained newspaper readers in the UK for many years, will be found to be anything other than unjustifiable invasions of privacy from now on."[5]

So where does the law currently stand in respect of protecting personal privacy? When does an individual have a "reasonable expectation of privacy?" This latter question is critical because if answered positively then the claimant's Art.8 rights are engaged. Article 8 of the European Convention on Human Rights states:

1 Everyone has the right to respect for his private and family life, his home and his correspondence.
2 There shall be no interference by a public authority with the exercise of this right except such as is in accordance with the law and is necessary in a democratic society in the interests of national security, public safety or the economic wellbeing of the country, for the prevention of disorder or crime, for the protection of health or morals, or for the protection of the rights and freedoms of others.

It then becomes obvious that the exercise of any rights under Art.8 is inevitably going to result in conflict with the exercise by the press of its Art.10 rights to freedom of expression. One is then entering into the realms of "parallel analysis" to decide which right should prevail over the other. One of the key issues from the media's viewpoint is whether there is a public interest justification that will override the claimant's attempt to keep information private. On occasions, the more lurid revelations of

---

[3] ibid., para.113.
[4] Sunday May 6, 2007.
[5] The Princess, the Paparazzi and the Press: *www.5rb.co.uk*, July 2004.

a personal nature will go hand in hand with revelations about abuse of position or resources and a conflict of interest.

The most obvious example is when a senior politician is exposed having an affair. David Blunkett, when Home Secretary, was revealed to have had an affair with Kimberly Fortier, a married woman. The press were able to justify bringing the relationship to the public's attention because it was alleged that he had abused his position in helping Ms Fortier to obtain a visa for her nanny and using taxpayers' money on train travel for his mistress. If there is an obvious public interest element then the press is in a strong position.

However, this kind of situation raises the question: Should personal details remain secret and only the "public interest" element be reported? This may appear the obvious solution but of course, the story would be virtually meaningless unless the press could provide the full context. And, of course, it would not sell as many newspapers if the identity of the participants were to be kept secret.

Also of importance is the answer to the question: Is any or all of the information that the press wishes to publish already in the public domain? If so then there will be little or nothing to protect by way of injunction.

Another issue to ponder at this preliminary stage is that, in stark contrast to the failure to recognise a tort of privacy, English law has since 1849 provided an *equitable* remedy for breach of confidence. It will be obvious that much of any "kiss and tell" content will be derived from a relationship that from the very outset the parties wished to keep secret, usually from their partners. It follows that if a relationship were to break down and one party wished to sell their story to a newspaper the other may resort to an action for breach of confidence in order to prevent intimate details entering the public domain. Therefore Art.10 rights of the press may be pitted not only against the claimant's Art.8 rights but also against any right to confidence.

1. The Law on Confidence

In *Prince Albert v Strange* [1849] the court granted an injunction to the Queen's husband after sketches they had produced found their way onto the open market as a result of a breach of trust. It was said that the

"... maker and owner of etchings which have never been exhibited or published, and of which no impressions have been made except for ... private use, but impressions whereof have, by improper and surreptitious means come in to the possession of others, is entitled to an injunction ..."[6]

[6] [1849] EWHC Ch J20.

So began the long and distinguished history of the action for breach of confidence. In its current guise, there is no need to establish an *initial* confidential relationship between the parties as a precursor to making a claim. That requirement was abandoned as a result of the decision in the case of *Stephens v Avery* [1988],[7] confirmed by Lord Nicholls in *Campbell v MGN* [2004][8] and cited with approval by the Court of Appeal in *Lord Browne v Associated Newspapers* [2007]:

"The best known statement of principle in recent times is perhaps that of Lord Nicholls in Campbell v. MGN [2004]. He observed that the 'confidence' in the phrase 'breach of confidence' is the confidence arising out of a confidential relationship. He said that the cause of action has now firmly shaken off the limiting constraint of the need for an initial confidential relationship."[9]

Lord Nicholls could not have been clearer:

"This cause of action has now firmly shaken off the limiting constraint of the need for an initial confidential relationship. In so doing it has changed in nature . . . Now the law imposes a 'duty of confidence' whenever a person receives information he knows or ought to know is fairly and reasonably to be regarded as confidential. Even this formulation is awkward. The continuing use of the phrase 'duty of confidence' and the description of the information as 'confidential' is not altogether comfortable. Information about an individual's private life would not, in ordinary usage, be called 'confidential'. The more natural description today is that such information is private. The essence of the tort is better encapsulated now as misuse of private information."[10]

In *Douglas v Hello! Ltd* [2007][11] Lord Hoffmann cited with approval the "well-known" criteria from Megarry J.'s judgment in *Coco v AN Clark (Engineers) Ltd* [1969][12]:

"First the information itself . . . must have the necessary quality of confidence about it. Secondly, that information must have been imparted in circumstances importing an obligation of confidence. Thirdly, there must be an unauthorised use of that information to the detriment of the party communicating it."

Information will also include photographs. In the *Douglas* case the wedding photographs contractually committed to OK! magazine were

---

7   [1988] 2 All E.R. 477.
8   [2004] UKHL 22.
9   [2007] EWCA Civ 295, at para.19 *per* Sir Anthony Clarke M.R.
10 [2004] UKHL 22, at para.14.
11 [2007] UKHL 21.
12 [1969] RPC 41, at 47.

held to be confidential information. The guests at the wedding were made aware that no photographs were to be taken. The third criteria, that the illicit photographs were used to the detriment of OK!, was "plainly satisfied."

In the same case, Lord Walker of Gestingthorpe made the following important statement of principle in respect of the law of confidentiality:

> "This House has quite recently reaffirmed that English law knows no common law tort of invasion of privacy: Wainwright v. Home Office [2004] 2 AC 406. But the law of confidentiality has been, and is being developed in such a way as to protect private information . . . The most important single step in the course of the law's recent development has been the speech of Lord Goff of Chieveley in *Attorney-General v Guardian Newspapers Ltd (No 2)* [1990] 1 AC 109, 280."

Lord Walker was referring to Lord Goff's three "limiting" criteria in respect of breach of confidence. The first is that confidentiality only applies to information to the extent that it is confidential. Secondly it applies to "neither useless information, nor to trivia." The third point is that the pubic interest in protecting confidence may be outweighed by some other countervailing public interest that favours disclosure.

The conclusion thus far is that the law on confidence has been adapted or extended to provide the opportunity for a remedy where one would not otherwise be provided because of the absence of a statutory or common law tort of privacy. Judges have shown themselves unwilling to create such a tort despite the occasional statement to the effect that we have such a remedy in all but name. Lindsay J., in the Douglas litigation, thought that it should be Parliament and not the judges who should decide if a new tort should be recognised.

The problem comes about because judges often use the words "confidence" and "privacy" as synonymous. Lords Carswell and Hope concluded that the Daily Mirror's publication of the photograph of Naomi Campbell exiting Narcotics Anonymous amounted to an infringement of her "right to privacy." Lord Nicholls in the quotation mentioned above speaks of ". . . misuse of private information." Lord Phillips in *Douglas* [2005][13] expressed concern:

> "We conclude that, in so far as private information is concerned, we are required to adopt, as a vehicle for performing such a duty as falls to the courts in relation to convention rights, the form of action formerly described as breach of confidence . . . . The court should, insofar as it can, develop the action for breach of confidence in such manner as will give effect to both Article 8 and Article 10 rights . . . . it is right to have regard to the decisions of the European Court of Human Rights. *We cannot pretend that we find it satisfactory to be required to shoe-horn within the cause of action of breach of confidence claims for pub-*

---

[13] [2005] EWCA Civ 595, at para.53.

lication of unauthorised photographs of a private occasion." (Emphasis added).

Whatever the doubts expressed by Lord Phillips, recent examples to have come before the courts have all been treated as confidence cases. In December 2006, the Court of Appeal delivered its decisions in two significant cases, *McKennitt v Ash*[14] and *The Prince of Wales v Associated Newspapers*.[15] In the former case Ms Ash, a long-time friend of McKennitt, wished to publish a book in which elements of the claimant's private life were to be revealed. McKennitt was a successful folk singer with an international following, had recording contracts and toured the world giving concerts. The relationship between the two women was essentially based upon friendship but on occasions Ash had worked for McKennitt in a business capacity and was exposed to commercially sensitive material. McKennitt sought injunctions to prevent elements of her private life appearing in the book.

In the latter case, the Prince of Wales was known to send correspondence to a circle of friends offering his opinions and giving his impression about official visits abroad and other activities undertaken in his capacity as Prince of Wales. He had been present at the ceremony when Hong Kong was handed back to China in 1997. He wrote a diary of the events including a less-than-flattering assessment of the Chinese leadership. The correspondence was "leaked" by a member of his private office to the Mail on Sunday. The Prince brought an action for an injunction to prevent the newspaper publishing the material.

2. Current Legal Principles

In each case, the High Court granted injunctions for breach of confidence and the decisions were upheld by the Court of Appeal. The cases are significant not only for their recognition of breach of confidence as the appropriate action but because they explain the foundation upon which the current legal principles are based.

In *Browne v Associated Newspapers* [2007], the Court of Appeal acknowledged there had been "considerable" development of the principles applicable to cases of this kind in recent years. In *McKennitt*, the Court of Appeal had agreed the following five propositions:

> **1** There is no English domestic tort of invasion of privacy the authority cited being the House of Lords decision in *Wainwright v Home Office* [2004][16]

---

[14] [2006] EWCA Civ 1714 on appeal from [2005] EWHC (QB) 3003.
[15] [2006] EWCA Civ1776 on appeal from [2006] EWHC (Ch) 522.
[16] [2004] 2 A.C. 406.

2   As a result in order to protect private information the courts have to proceed through the tort of breach of confidence. Articles 8 and 10 jurisprudence has to be "shoe-horned" into this action.

3   However there was a "feeling of discomfort" when the action for breach of confidence is used where there is no existing relationship between the parties. For example, when unlawful or surreptitious means are used to acquire information which the person knows he is not free to use. A good example is the *Campbell* case where, the photographs were taken without Campbell's knowledge and where the photographer was in breach of his own industry code of practice.

4   To avoid the confusion of using the word confidence when dealing with private information the tort has been rechristened the "misuse of private information." (per Lord Nicholls in *Campbell*).

5   "Old-fashioned breach of confidence" applies when there has been conduct that is inconsistent with a pre-existing relationship, rather than simply the purloining of private information.

It will be evident that, in each of the cases, there was a breach of trust. In the *McKennitt* case they were long-standing friends and also engaged in a business relationship. The information that Ash sought to use in her book had been obtained only as a result of being a party to that relationship. The information had not been put into the public domain by McKennitt. The court acknowledged that, even though she was in the public eye, she had always sought to divorce her private from her public life.

In the *Prince of Wales* case, the private correspondence had been leaked by a member of his private office in clear breach of her terms of contract. She was well aware that the information contained in the letters were not for public consumption. Here was a gross breach of trust. Never before, nor for that matter since, has any of the private correspondence of the Prince entered the public domain.

In undertaking a legal analysis of whether or not to publish private information will constitute a breach of confidence, one has first to carry out the "parallel analysis" of balancing Art.8 rights with the Art.10 rights of the media defendant. If the application is for an interlocutory injunction, then a judge will have to consider s.12 of the Human Rights Act 1998. As we know there is a rule against prior restraint. In defamation cases it is referred to as the rule in *Bonnard v Perryman* [1891].[17] In respect of breach of confidence application, the court has to consider the wording of s.12. Under s.12(3), it has to be determined, in respect of each piece of information that is the subject matter of the application whether, if the case were to go forward to a full trial, the applicant is *likely* to establish that the publication will be allowed.

[17] [1891] 2 Ch. 269.

There is no one legal definition of the word"likely". Lord Nicholls considered the matter in *Cream Holdings v Banerjee* [2004].[18] The word should be given a"flexible"meaning depending on the circumstances. There can be "no single, rigid standard governing all applications for interim restraint orders." The threshold test would appear to be whether the applicant's prospects of success are"sufficiently favourable"to justify the order being made. Courts should be"exceedingly slow"to make interim restraint orders if the applicant"has not satisfied the court he will probably (more likely than not) succeed at the trial."[19]

The Court of Appeal in *Browne* suggested the following approach:

1. Is Art.8 engaged? In other words is there a reasonable expectation of privacy from the claimant's viewpoint?
2. Is Art.10 engaged?
3. Has the applicant satisfied the court that if the case went to trial he is likely to establish that publication should not be allowed?

3. Article 8

There is no need for an initial confidential relationship between the parties. The question first to be asked is whether the information is"obviously private."The information in the Prince of Wales case was considered to be so.

If there is no pre-existing relationship, then the"primary focus"must be on the *nature* of the information. It does not follow that just because there is a relationship that all information passed between the parties should be regarded as confidential. However the basis of any relationship between the parties must be of considerable importance when trying to decide whether there is a reasonable expectation of privacy. One would need to question the recipient of the information and decide whether it was obvious that the information was"fairly and reasonably to be regarded as confidential or private." That question must be applied to each and every piece of information that the claimant regards as confidential. A further feature will be the *circumstances* in which any information is imparted to the recipient.

An interesting question is whether *business* information imparted to another because of a relationship or via a domestic situation can be regarded as private. The Court of Appeal in *Browne* accepted that it would all depend on the circumstances and in fact endorsed the trial judge's view that the expression of opinions by the chairman to his partner about BP colleagues should be regarded as private. Eady J. said:

---

[18] [2004] UKHL 44.
[19] ibid., at para.22.

"Those views are entitled to the protection of privacy because of the circumstances of communication and the nature of the relationship. Moreover, there is . . . nothing to override the duty of confidentiality. There is no particular public interest in knowing how the Claimant may have described his personal feelings about colleagues. It would rank simply as a bit of gossip."

However, the court was not prepared to accept that stories about the alleged misuse of BP resources that Browne's former lover wished to put into the public domain should be regarded as private. That approach is consistent with the recognition of the important role of the press under Art.10 in acting as public watchdog and bloodhound. This information, whether true or false, should be communicated to the shareholders and board members to consider. So in essence each case must be decided on its own facts and circumstances and from these a decision reached as to whether there is a reasonable expectation of privacy.

4. Article 10

The media will wish to exercise their Art.10 rights. It is obvious that in doing so there is always the potential for a clash with Art.8 rights. Which takes precedence will be determined by an exercise of the so-called"new methodology". That is simply a reference to comments made by Lord Steyn in *Re S (A child)*[20] outlining four propositions that he said "emerged"from the *Campbell* case. It will be recalled that neither Article has precedence over the other and that when they are in conflict an "intense focus" on the comparative importance of the specific rights being claimed is called for. There must be good reasons for interfering with the exercise of either right and finally the proportionality test must be invoked. In practice the question is often resolved by asking where the public interest lies.

In carrying out this type of balancing exercise different trial judges may come to different conclusions. That is not a matter for appeal. The Court of Appeal in *Browne* stressed that it is only likely to interfere with a trial judge's decision if he or she erred in principle or reached a conclusion that was plainly wrong. The court used the phrase:"outside the ambit of conclusions which a judge could reasonably reach."[21]

In considering the impact of the European jurisprudence, one should not ignore the contribution of the Court of Human Rights through its judgment in *Von Hannover v Germany* [2004].[22] Princess Caroline of Monaco, the wife of Prince Ernst Von Hannover, had taken exception

[20] [2004] UKHL 47.
[21] [2007] EWCA Civ 295, para.45, *per* Sir Anthony Clarke M.R.
[22] [2004] E.M.L.R 379.

over a number of years to appearing in German "celebrity" magazines. She was not concerned about photographs of her attending functions and galas at which she expected to be photographed, but drew the line at photographs of her undertaking "everyday" activities with her family and friends. She tried unsuccessfully to rein in the paparazzi's activities by taking action in the German courts. From there her only recourse was to the European Court of Human Rights.

The question for the court was whether German laws provided adequate protection for her Art.8 rights to be upheld. The answer was an emphatic no. It should be remembered that Princess Caroline had no "official" status. She did not represent Monaco and would not succeed as Head of State on the death of her father Prince Rainier. The court had no doubt that the taking and publishing of such photographs meant that her Art.8 rights were engaged, i.e. she had a reasonable expectation of privacy. It was noted that the taking of such photographs created a climate of "continual harassment leaving a strong sense of intrusion into private life or even a feeling of persecution."

The taking of such photographs did not contribute to "a debate of general interest." In simple terms, there was no public interest reason to justify such intrusion into her private life. The public had no legitimate interest in knowing anything about her lifestyle, which restaurants she frequented or her whereabouts in general. Individuals deserved protection under Art.8 as a means of helping to develop every human being's personality. Even well known people had a legitimate expectation that their private lives would be protected from unwarranted media intrusion.

As a result of the Human Rights Act, judges in England and Wales have to have regard to the decisions of the European Court of Human Rights. "Passing reference" was made to the *Von Hannover* decision in the *Douglas* case in 2005, but Eady J. grasped the nettle and applied the principles at first instance in the *McKennitt v Ash* case. He said:

> "It is clear that there is a significant shift taking place as between, on the one hand, freedom of expression for the media and the corresponding interest of the public to receive information, and on the other hand, the legitimate expectation of citizens to have their private lives protected ... even where there is a genuine public interest, alongside a commercial interest in the media in publishing articles or photographs, sometimes such interests would have to yield to the individual citizen's right to the effective protection of private life ... private life ... includes a social dimension."[23]

And, indeed, it is quite apparent that the courts are more prepared than ever before to grant injunctions to protect Art.8 rights.

Two cases decided in the latter part of 2006 give credence to that last statement. In *X & Y v Person or Person's Unknown* [2006][24] the court was

---

[23] [2005] EWHC 3003, at para.57.
[24] [2006] EWHC 2783 (QB).

faced with the relatively familiar situation of newspapers being touted with information regarding the alleged marital difficulties facing a well-known model and her husband. Eady J. had granted an ex parte injunction against "those persons unknown" (a John Doe injunction). It was granted on the basis that the information being touted for sale was known to be "inherently confidential in character." As such, those seeking to sell the information would be aware that it was subject to a duty of confidence. Newspapers were then informed of the existence of the injunction so that if those "persons unknown" approached any particular newspaper it would be apparent that the information was subject to injunction.

This action was brought by the Mirror Group and News Group Newspapers seeking the discharge of the injunction. The defendants argued two things. Firstly, that the claimant's Art.8 rights were not engaged. In other words, that there was no reasonable expectation that information of this kind should be protected by law. Secondly, that if Art.8 were engaged that after carrying out the balancing exercise (Art.8 v. Art.10) the court would be unlikely to find in favour of the claimants. This is what a court would regard as the proportionality argument.

From an analytical perspective the first issue to be determined is whether Art.8 rights are engaged. It should be noted at this point that the "trump card", (Freedom of expression) the favoured adage of a few years ago no longer has relevance after Lord Steyn's comments in *Re S (A Child)* [2004].

In seeking to answer this question, there has to be a major focus on the circumstances of the individuals and in particular whether by their own conduct they have:

"... exhibited a willingness to forego privacy to which they would be prima facie entitled; that they have, in effect drawn public attention to their relationship and through interviews and comments made in the public domain offered a running commentary upon it."[25]

This could pose a potential difficulty for "celebrity" couples because much of their business lives involves interacting with (possibly) an adoring public during which images and some details of their private lives may become public. However it does not automatically follow that it is true in every case. The court accepted in the *McKennitt v Ash* case that McKennitt was essentially a private person and when making public appearances made it clear to reporters that she would not discuss any aspect of her private life.

In *X v Y* the judge warned that information in the public domain about celebrities may not always be factually correct. There will inevitably be much speculation about who they are seeing and what they are doing. The fact that a female celebrity is taking lunch with a younger man when

---

[25] ibid., para.24, *per* Eady J.

her husband is out of the country is not in any sense to be regarded as the precursor of a passionate affair or for that matter evidence that the affair has been consummated ... but try telling the mass-market tabloids that!

Eady J. suggested there should be a distinction between those who are in the public eye and those who may be classed as *publicity seekers* while recognising that occasionally the two will overlap. Someone in the public eye does not necessarily"waive entitlement to privacy with regard to, say, intimate personal relationships or the conduct of a private life generally."[26] In this case, the judge concluded that X, the model, was not a person who"willingly sets out for self promotion to live her private life in the public eye."

Eady J. is a most experienced media law judge. He states in *X v Y* that there ought to be a distinction drawn between "... matters which are naturally accessible to outsiders and those which are known only to the protagonists."The fact, for example, that the parties are living separate lives or are regarded by friends as"no longer an item"is hardly likely to result in Art.8 being engaged in respect of those particular pieces of information.

The information that a claimant wishes to protect should be specifically defined. At this early stage in proceedings, a court will also wish to consider the s.12 issue of whether it is likely that, if the case were to proceed to a full trial, the claimant would be successful. Newspapers for their part will no doubt resort to their electronic archives to"dredge up" everything possible to endeavour to prove to a court that"he or she has indeed become public property."From the claimant's point of view there should be a full and frank disclosure. That is not to say that every possible item discovered in the newspaper archives must be addressed. It is suggested that the claimant's lawyers should engage in a search of the internet as a means of second-guessing what the defendant's lawyers are likely to rely upon. In this way the claimant's lawyers should be able to defeat a claim of non-disclosure by the defendants.

The judge should then decide whether, in light of all the circumstances there has been a"genuine waiver"of privacy on the part of the applicant.

At this point, the court should also consider whether the public have in any way been misled by the applicant in such a way as to permit the defendants to invoke the public interest defence of"putting the record straight."It will be recalled that this was used to good effect by the defendants in the *Campbell* case. Naomi Campbell had publicly denied taking drugs. Why then, asked the Daily Mirror, did she need to visit Narcotics Anonymous? Despite ultimately winning her claim for breach of privacy in relation to the photograph all five Law Lords upheld the Mirror's right to tell the story on the basis it was correcting the record. A similar approach was taken in March 2005, when David and Victoria Beckham sought to obtain an injunction to prevent the News of the World from revealing details of their private life based upon information obtained

---

[26] ibid., para.28.

from the couple's ex-nanny. There seemed to be a clear breach of trust on the part of the nanny, but that was not enough to convince Langley J. that an injunction should be granted. "Putting the record straight" was invoked on the basis that the couple had portrayed themselves as being the "golden couple" whereas in fact the nanny's information suggested that there were in fact stresses and strains upon the marriage.

In the case of *X v Y*, Eady J., while acknowledging there had been some non-disclosure, did *not* regard it as sufficient evidence from which to conclude that the media should be permitted to exercise their Art.10 rights.

A month later, in December 2006, Eady J. was faced with another application for an injunction in the case of *CC v AB* [2006].[27] The claimant had conducted an adulterous relationship with the defendant's wife. The affair was discovered and the defendant wished, it appeared for purposes of revenge and to make some money from the media, to use the press to put his side of the story. The claim was based upon an action for breach of confidence because as the judge said ". . . it is not yet recognised that English domestic law offers an enforceable right to privacy." The case is unique, being as it is based upon the proposition that the defendant, i.e. the cuckolded husband owed a duty of confidentiality to the man who has committed adultery with his wife.

Neither party to the relationship wished it to be made public, and therefore, it follows that a reasonable expectation of privacy must exist. In other words, the Art.8 rights of the parties are engaged. Taking the logic one-step further, unless the media could find a public interest reason for disclosing the information then an injunction should be granted. The court was also invited to consider the Art.8 rights of the claimant's wife and children who clearly would be adversely affected should there be media publicity. They of course were not parties to the proceedings. A final point was that the claimant's wife was suffering from stress and anxiety and there was a risk of self-harm and possibly even suicide.

In a case such as this, the courts have to engage in what has become referred to as "parallel analysis" as defined by Sir Mark Potter the President of the Family Division of the High Court in the case of *A Local Authority v W* [2005][28] reflecting the approach determined by the House of Lords in *Re S (A Child)* [2005]. It is perhaps worth quoting in full as a statement of principle to be adopted in such cases:

"The exercise to be performed is one of parallel analysis in which the starting point is presumptive parity, in that neither Article has precedence over or 'trumps' the other. The exercise of parallel analysis requires the court to examine the justification for interfering with each right and the issue of proportionality is to be considered in respect of each. It is not a mechanical exercise to be decided upon the basis of rival generalities. An intense focus upon the comparative importance

---

[27] [2006] EWHC 3083.
[28] [2005] EWHC 1564 (Fam), at para.53.

of the specific rights being claimed in the individual case is necessary before the ultimate balancing test in terms of proportionality is
carried out."

In most of these "privacy" cases, there will be no doubts about the
media's Art.10 rights being engaged. Therefore, the focus will be on the
claimant's rights under Art.8 and in particular, whether they are
engaged. The court *refused* to accept the proposition that there". . . is no
legitimate expectation of privacy for a person who conducts a relationship with another person's wife." The court also acknowledged that it
might be necessary to have regard to the"nature of the relationship." The
judge suggested, but no more, that a "one-night stand" might deserve
less protection than a long-term relationship.

Eady J. also made it clear that, in deciding cases such as this, the judge
should be extremely careful to ensure that one"guards against allowing
legal judgments to be coloured by personal attitudes."

This case is important because of the judge's reflections on the position
of the media in cases involving the sexual peccadilloes of celebrities. To
purvey what the House of Lords in *Jameel v Wall Street Journal Europe*
[2006] referred to as the". . . most vapid tittle-tattle about the activities of
footballers' wives and girlfriends"[29] may be of interest to the public but
would not be an element of any legal definition of public interest.

The judge concluded that"the communication of material to the world
at large in which there is a genuine public interest is naturally to be rated
more highly than the right to sell what is mere 'tittle-tattle.' "[30] Those
involved in illicit relationships will invariably wish to keep them secret
and"secret"for these purposes may also include a"public element." The
parties may on occasions "take a risk." They will meet in a hotel or in a
restaurant or club. They may travel to other cities or go abroad in each
other's company. They run the risk of being identified or 'show' themselves to generate speculation from those who may see them together
and put one and one together to make two. The decision in *Von Hannover
v Germany* [2004] recognises that the law is capable of". . . extending its
protection to public places and also to a social dimension, that is to say,
to the relationships which people conduct with others."

In this case the parties to the relationship wished to put the past
behind them and move on without the full glare of a national tabloid
exclusive to hinder their remedial endeavours. The injunction was
granted and, in February 2007, was made permanent by consent.
Whether this case should be viewed as setting a precedent is debatable.
There were special circumstances concerning the health of the
claimant's wife that are unlikely to figure in future cases. Yet it can still
be said that in this case the court held that a third party owed a duty of
confidence to the man who was committing adultery with his wife.

[29] [2006] UKHL 44, *per* Baroness Hale of Richmond at para.147.
[30] [2006] EWHC 3083, at para.36, *per* Eady J.

5. Public Domain Proviso

As alluded to earlier, if a person is in the public eye, then it is more than likely that the media will have a plethora of information, both recent and from the past, stored away for future use. Therefore, if information is in the public domain, the press need to know exactly what they are not permitted to publish. Any injunction should therefore include what has become known as a Public Domain Proviso. As Eady J. said in *A v B* [2005][31]:

> "An important consideration when assessing the background . . . . is that the claimant has himself made public through the media a great deal of information that might usually be considered as falling within the protection afforded to private or personal information . . . ."[32]

From the media's perspective, knowing what is or is not in the public domain is crucial when deciding what to publish without fear of breaching any injunction that may exist.

Hence, a court must make it absolutely clear by including such a proviso in the injunction. That had been one problem stemming from the interim injunction granted on an *ex parte* basis in the *X v Y* case. It may be that certain pieces of information have reached the public domain but the court believes that its confidentiality has not been lost. This may be true when the internet is used as the medium to disseminate information. Given the vast scale and reach of the internet it may be that the particular information has passed relatively unnoticed. In these circumstances, the court should make it clear that the information is not to be included within the proviso.

In the *X v Y* case, the injunction was against persons unknown. It was argued that this was not "sufficiently certain to identify those who are, and those who are not included within the restrictions." However, the court was prepared to follow the reasoning adopted in *Bloomsbury Publishing Group v News Group Newspapers Ltd* [2003][33] to the effect:

> "I can see no injustice to anyone if I make the order . . . but considerable potential for injustice to the claimants if I do not."[34]

Summary

We need to ask where the law stands at the time of writing. It is abundantly clear that this jurisdiction does not have a tort of privacy.

---

[31] [2005] EWHC 1651 (QB).
[32] ibid., para.16.
[33] [2003] EWHC 1205 (Ch).
[34] ibid., para.22, *per* Sir Andrew Morritt VC.

Parliament, or to be more pertinent the government, has shown no inclination whatsoever to draft legislation for Parliament's consideration. The
government has occasionally engaged in a bout of sabre rattling and
warned the press that it is drinking in the last chance saloon after some
loathsome media activity of the type seen in the *Gorden Kaye* case. Self-
regulation is the order of the day for the print media but not so for the
broadcast media that is subject to a statutory regime and an industry
regulator, Ofcom.

The Culture, Media Sport and Culture Select Committee recommended to the government in 2003 that Parliament should have the
opportunity to consider whether "privacy" legislation be introduced only
to have the recommendation thrown back at them within weeks.[35]

"On balance we firmly recommend that the government reconsider
its position and bring forward legislative proposals to clarify the protection that individuals can expect from unwarranted intrusion by
anyone—not the press alone—into their private lives. This is necessary
to fully satisfy the obligations upon the UK under the European
Convention on Human Rights. There should be full and wide consultation but in the end Parliament should be allowed to undertake its
proper legislative role."[36]

This approach, of course, is consistent with the line taken by Lindsay J.
in the *Douglas* privacy case in 2003 when he declined to lay down new
privacy principles on the basis that it was Parliament's responsibility to
act if thought appropriate.

What has become evident over the past few months is that the House
of Lords in its judicial capacity is showing no inclination to grasp the
nettle. Niema Ash and Lord Browne's appeals were both rejected on the
grounds there was no point of law of general public importance that
needed to be considered. In all three cases to have reached the Court of
Appeal since November 2006 the court has treated "private information"
issues in the context of breach of confidence actions. For the moment at
least that is where the law stands.

Injunctions may well be granted to prevent the dissemination of
private information including photographs via the law of confidentiality
that only two years ago Lord Phillips hinted at being an inappropriate
vehicle. Privacy was being "shoe-horned" into the action for breach of
confidence. European jurisprudence has already had an impact on how
unwarranted media intrusion should be dealt with via Art.8 and the *Von
Hannover* decision has proved to be the catalyst for developing the protection on offer. However there has been a further judgment which has
not received anything like as much scrutiny as the *Von Hannover* case. In
September 2006, the European Court of Human Rights handed down its

---

[35] 5th Report 2003, Available on UK Parliament website.
[36] ibid., para.111.

decision in *Wainwright v United Kingdom* [2006][37] The precursor to this case was the House of Lords decision in *Wainwright v Home Office* [2003].[38] When visiting a jail in Leeds, Mrs Wainwright and her son were strip-searched in a way that did not comply with prison rules. Both parties suffered a stress-related reaction to something that clearly caused great embarrassment. There was a great deal of discussion in the various courts about whether the parties' privacy had been breached. Despite support from the High Court neither the Court of Appeal nor House of Lords was prepared to countenance the creation of a new tort of privacy. It was appreciated that in particular circumstances the courts might have to provide a remedy for the breach of a person's privacy.[39] However, the House was not prepared to go as far as to create a new *general* tort of privacy.

The European Court of Human Rights accepted that Art.8 provides protection of "moral and physical integrity under the respect for private life"[40] and went on to hold that "the searches carried out on the applicants cannot be regarded as 'necessary in a democratic society' within the meaning of Article 8 paragraph 2 of the Convention. There has accordingly been a breach of Article 8 . . ."

This is not a "media" case and may be thought of as superfluous to the general matters that have been discussed. However, that would be a mistake because the European Court of Human Rights is continuing to put pressure on the UK government by pointing out the deficiencies in its Art.8 protection. The *Peck* case was another example of where the European Court found against the United Kingdom. Peck had attempted to commit suicide and his actions had been caught by CCTV cameras in Brentwood High Street. Some of the images were subsequently transmitted by the BBC. The European Court decided in the applicant's favour. English law had not provided appropriate remedies to protect his privacy.

The United Kingdom therefore has two European Court rulings against it on matters relating to personal privacy. There was no response from the government to the *Peck* decision and certainly nothing in response to *Wainwright*. Surely, the time has come for the thorough review of the law relating to personal privacy, taking full account of the media's rights to freedom of expression. There are clearly important issues other than those affecting the media and a free press. There are those within the media who would also like the law to be clarified in order to provide a modicum of protection for the media in knowing what they can or cannot publish. There was some disappointment expressed when the *McKennitt* case did not find its way to the House of Lords. Media Lawyer quoted Gill Phillips, head of litigation at Times Newspapers, as saying:

---

[37] [2006] ECHR 807.
[38] [2003] UKHL 53.
[39] For an example of what Lord Hoffmann had in mind see *Peck v United Kingdom* [2003] ECHR 44.
[40] [2006] ECHR 807, at para.43.

"It is extremely disappointing that the House of Lords has not taken the opportunity to explore what the media regard as some of the crucial matters on where the law on privacy is going."[41]

In the same article, Hugh Tomlinson Q.C., a leading media law barrister, concluded:

"The House of Lords decision means that the very strong privacy protection given in the Court in McKennitt is now firmly established in English law."

Perhaps the final words should be given to Lord Hoffmann in *Campbell v MGN Ltd* [2004] and Lord Justice Sedley, a judge who has been a major advocate for the establishment of new privacy laws. The law of confidentiality said Lord Hoffmann:

"focuses upon the protection of human autonomy and dignity—the right to control the dissemination of information about one's private life and the right to the esteem and respect of other people."

That is the wake-up call for the media and nothing that has occurred in the courts since 2004 suggests that the media will be able to indulge with the court's support, in the sort of "kiss and tell" stories illustrated by the Gary Flitcroft case.

In *A v B&C* [2002][42] a relatively well-known footballer with a Premiership football team had engaged in concurrent adulterous relationships with two women. The People newspaper wanted to publish their stories in a classic case of a women spurned seeking revenge through the media. He obtained an injunction from the High Court but that was lifted on appeal.

The court accepted that the women's rights to freedom of expression should prevail. If this case were to come before the court today, the outcome might be different. Lord Justice Sedley in a speech at Oxford University in May 2006 said that in light of the *Von Hannover* decision "it is extremely doubtful whether the *Flitcroft* case could now be decided as it was."[43] He said that the story when published had no news value whatsoever. He concluded with these words:

"Britain has a press which is among the world's leaders in serious investigative journalism . . . It also has a press which is the undisputed world leader in prurience and vulgar abuse. Nothing in my suggestions or in the developing privacy jurisprudence threatens serious investigation of issues of public concern: rather the reverse. If the long

---

[41] Media Lawyer, March 30, 2007.
[42] [2002] EWCA Civ 337.
[43] "Sex, Libels and Video-surveillance", Blackstone Lecture, Pembroke College, Oxford 13/05/06.

field-day of those who live and prosper by unwarranted intrusion into private lives is now drawing to a close, it will not be necessarily be a bad thing, even if it is the end of civilisation as we have come to know it. It will never, one fervently hopes, inhibit the ability of the press to confront us with questions of the kind with which the Daily Express not long ago stunned its readers: Did Diana's driver have bird flu? "

6. Protection from Harassment

Lawyers representing celebrity clients are increasingly resorting to the Protection from Harassment Act 1997 (as amended by s.125 of the Serious Organised Crime and Police Act 2005) as a means of putting pressure on the media to stop photographers from following their clients in a hope of getting cash-generating photographs. The Act was never intended to be used for this purpose rather as a means of offering protection to those at risk from "stalkers."

In order to gain a conviction or injunction, the Act requires evidence of a course of conduct which amounts to harassment of another, and which he knows or ought to know amounts to harassment. The test therefore combines both subjective and objective factors. In assessing whether the person ought to have known a reasonable person test will apply bestowing upon the reasonable person the same information as known to the accused. The remedies available to the applicant are both criminal and civil. In the latter case an injunction can be obtained and in the former a person can be imprisoned for up to five years for breaches of the injunction.

The Act requires a "course of conduct" and that must mean there must be at least two instances of the behaviour that is the subject of complaint. The two most obvious examples are the persistent encroachment of photographers into a person's private life and the "doorstepping" techniques much practised by journalists to achieve a useful soundbite.

Cases actually initiated against the media are rare. The one notable case is *Thomas v News Group Newspapers* [2002].[44] It is an important decision because it reminds editors that it would be wrong to "target" particular individuals, for example, as part of a smear campaign, if it was apparent that the individual would be subject to abuse or possibly violence. A clear distinction though must be drawn between this type of journalism and "normal" press criticism. As Lord Phillips M.R. said:

"In general, press criticism, even if robust, does not constitute unreasonable conduct and does not fall within the natural meaning of harassment . . . It is common ground . . . that before press publications are capable of constituting harassment, they must be attended by

---

[44] [2001] EWCA Civ 1233.

some exceptional circumstance which justifies sanctions and the restriction on the freedom of expression that they involve."[45]

The court held that, in three articles, the newspaper had harassed Ms Thomas by "publishing racist criticism of her which was foreseeably likely to stimulate a racist reaction on the part of their readers and cause her distress."[46]

The recent hounding of Kate Middleton, the former girlfriend of Prince William, generated much comment on the role of the paparazzi. It is a useful case study from which to examine the options available to a complainant other than seeking an injunction for breach of Art.8 rights. The Press Complaints Commission Code of Practice states "Journalists must not engage in intimidation, harassment or persistent pursuit."[47] Those who saw television pictures of the press camped outside her house and then chasing her down the street might wonder whether cl.4 is worth the paper on which it is written. The Code though is ineffective if there is international interest in the subject as in this case. The foreign press will not be subject to the Code and photo agencies and photographers do not necessarily adhere to the Code, although they should if commissioned by a UK media outlet.

Action could clearly be taken under the 1997 Act against a particular photographer, but that is likely to be ineffective because an agency would simply employ someone else. Action could perhaps be taken against an agency and that might prove to be more effective. Recent legislation could also be used. The Serious Organised Crime and Police Act 2005 amended the Criminal Justice Act 2001. Section 126 of the 2005 Act inserts a new section—42A—into the 2001 Act. It states:

"Offence of harassment etc of a person in his home.

1. A person commits an offence if—
    a. that person is present outside or in the vicinity of any premises that are used by any individual (the resident) as his dwelling;
    b. that person is present there for the purpose (by his presence or otherwise) of representing to the resident or another individual (whether or not one who uses the premises as his dwelling) or of persuading the resident or such another individual—
        i. that he should not do something that he is entitled or required to do; or
        ii. that he should do something that he is not under any obligation to do;
    c. that person—
        i. intends his presence to amount to the harassment of, or to cause alarm or distress to, the resident; or

---

[45] ibid., para.34.
[46] ibid., para.49.
[47] cl.4.

ii. knows or ought to know that his presence is likely to result in the harassment of; or to cause alarm or distress to, the resident . . ."

Although it is envisaged that this section will rarely be used against the media, in legal terms, it is not outside the bounds of possibility. If the continuing presence of the paparazzi causes distress to celebrity residents to the extent that they are afraid to come out of their house then it is possible an offence has been committed. The inclusion of the word *vicinity* also means that photographers waiting to apprehend a celebrity a few hundred yards away from their residence could also be caught by the provision. A constable in uniform may arrest without warrant any person he reasonably suspects is committing or has committed an offence under s.42A.

Section 127 of the 2005 Act amends s.42 of the 2001 Act and gives the police powers to order that a person may be required to leave the vicinity of any premises in which the "resident" feels harassed and not return for a period not exceeding three months.

Conclusion

It is probably fair to say that people affected by unwarranted media intrusion into their lives have never been in a stronger legal position. As a result of the recognition by the Court of Appeal that the law on confidence can now provide an effective remedy through which to protect private information, and the statutory provisions centred on the prevention of harassment the media will have to rethink its strategy about how "personal" stories are put into the public domain. A clear public interest justification for publication will invariably override privacy protection. Yet the media would welcome a modern interpretation of what exactly constitutes the definition of *public interest*. It is reasonable to suggest that there may yet be further mileage in the race to protect privacy.

In 2006, Ireland introduced a Privacy Bill that received a predictably cool response from the media. The Bill, if brought into law, will create a new tort of violation of privacy and as with defamation in England and Wales, there will be no need to prove special damage. A person who wilfully and without lawful authority violates the privacy of an individual commits a tort.[48] Individuals will have a statutory entitlement to privacy defined as:

"... that which is reasonable in all the circumstances having regard to the rights of others and to the requirements of public order, public morality and the common good."[49]

---

[48] cl.2.
[49] cl.3(1).

The following will amount to a violation of privacy:

- To subject an individual to surveillance.
- To disclose information, documentation or material discovered as a result of surveillance.
- To pass oneself off as someone else by using their name or likeness of voice with a view to commercial or financial gain.
- To disclose letters, diaries, medical records or other documentation.

The factors to be considered in an assessment of whether the law has been breached include:

- Place where and the occasion on which the act was committed
- Age of the individual
- Any office or position
- The purpose for which the information or documentation was going to be used
- Whether there was any trespass by the person accused of violation of privacy
- Whether in so doing that person committed an offence
- Whether the disclosure consisted of sensitive or intimate private facts
- Whether the disclosure concerns the individual's private life
- Whether the disclosure is in contravention of a public duty
- The manner of the disclosure
- The extent of the disclosure[50]

The Bill provides defences, as may be expected, based mainly upon the violation of privacy being in the public interest or in accordance with the law. If the breach was occasioned during an "act of newsgathering" then it is a defence to show the act was done in good faith, for the purpose of discussing a subject of public importance, for the public benefit and was fair and reasonable in all the circumstances.

If the Bill eventually becomes law in its current form it will be a nightmare for the media and a source of income for lawyers. However, at least the Irish government has attempted to put developing privacy principles onto the statute book. The fact that very little has happened to this Bill since it was introduced in mid-2006 would suggest it may just quietly disappear.

7. Privacy in Practice

In the light of the advice on the latest position on privacy, it is worth examining the *Browne* judgment in detail before looking at how

[50] cl. 4 (1) and (2).

journalists can develop a privacy checklist which can be applied to other key cases.

Lord Browne of Madingley and Asssociated Newspapers Limited [2007] EWCA Civ 295. The *Browne* case provoked mixed reaction in the media itself. It has been derided in some quarters as primarily concerned with cheap revelations driven by his sexuality, for which the alleged abuse of his position within a public corporation provided a public interest justification for avoiding injunction.

However, it can be argued that there was a proper story to be run about revealing the allegations of abuse of position for which identification of the source and how he came by the information underpinning the accusation was required to lend authenticity to the claims. This ultimately was the argument the courts recognised.

The manner in which the combination of information is revealed is not for the judges to determine, as a concession to free speech and the need for plurality, especially where those creating the climate of public discourse are partisan. So the prominence given by the media to the different elements of the story could not be controlled by the courts.

We should ask ourselves why Lord Browne resigned. It wasn't because of revelations of his homosexuality; it doesn't appear even to be about whether the accusations of misuses of BP resources were true or not; it was because in the process of trying to stop the matters being aired he lied to the court.

The lie to the court is arguably also why the partial lifting of the injunction was granted—enough to do the damage and enough to reveal the lie. Yes, he could decline to answer media questions about his private life, but he could not lie to a court about them and expect sympathetic treatment. There was, of course, also a legal justification for this lack of sympathy in that, by undermining his own credibility, he lessened the chances of success in a subsequent legal claim to a level where success could be deemed not "likely" and therefore the injunction could be lifted. We can only speculate whether, in the absence of the lie, the public interest in the accusations would have been sufficient to lift the injunction. The newspaper cannot entirely claim victory as various elements of its story from his ex-lover, Jeff Chevalier, remained subject to injunction.

The Court of Appeal judgment in the case pulls together strands from various of the cases outlined earlier in the chapter and provides a useful summary in itself of where the law stands as of 2007. We can usefully look at how it answers the key concerns for future actions. Setting aside the particular requirements of an injunction, the questions the court considers are whether Art.8 rights are engaged and whether Art.10 rights are engaged.

The Art.8 consideration centres on the question: Is there a reasonable expectation of privacy from the claimant's viewpoint?

Chevalier had a pre-existing relationship of confidence which gave Lord Browne a reasonable expectation of privacy for much of what passed between them. However, the court accepted that a previous contractual or intimate relationship does not create a reasonable expectation of privacy in relation to *all* information learned or activities witnessed during the relationship. (The exemptions granted were enough to give the Mail on Sunday its story.)

More generally, what guidance does the judgment provide for journalists regarding the nature of private information?

There are some worrying definitions cited. Lord Phillips C.J. in *Douglas v Hello!* (No.3) [2005] EWCA Civ 595; [2006] Q.B.125 at [83] answered the question thus:

> "It seems to us that it must include information that is personal to the person who possesses it and that he does not intend shall be imparted to the general public. The nature of the information, or the form in which it is kept, may suffice to make it plain that the information satisfies these criteria."

The definition is of little help to defendants in that any claimant attempting to keep secrets clearly does not intend them to be imparted to the general public so would effectively be calling the shots over the definition. Information would be private if the claimant wanted it to be.

Also, the use of the words general public would seem to allow for a pretty wide circle of people to be "in the know" as so many were about Lord Browne's homosexuality, before it will be considered to be already in the public domain.

The Court of Appeal challenged the original acceptance that the relationship between Lord Browne and Chevalier was already in the public domain. Although it didn't affect the outcome, there was an ominous statement at [61]:

> "It appears to us that there is potentially an important distinction between information which is made available to a person's circle of friends or work colleagues and information which is widely published in a newspaper."

So large sections of the establishment and the oil industry can know of a relationship and the couple can dine with the Prime Minister but that still does not put the relationship in the public domain.

Similarly, call something a diary or journal and it is "obviously" private even if it is copied and circulated by civil servants to a range of people including journalists rather than hidden under the bed.

Looking at *Browne*, and other recent privacy rulings, including the *Prince of Wales* case, it would appear likely that journalists will be forced to rely on public interest justification rather than trying to argue that the information is not private, although it worked to a limited extent in *Browne*.

Where there is a pre-existing relationship, even trivial information may be regarded as subject to an expectation of privacy. So the relationship does raise the barrier. The expectations can be higher. The law seeks to uphold confidential relationships so the onus will be on the defendant to demonstrate how breaches of that trust would be justified. On the other hand that does not mean that anything said within a confidential relationship is private.

In *McKennitt v Ash*, seemingly trivial matters were not allowed, partly because they related to the home, which Eady J. considered "sacrosanct", but also because there had been a relationship which created a general expectation of privacy. Not everything that happened during the course of it would be deemed private but where the relationship exists it seems the onus is on the party wanting to exercise freedom of expression to demonstrate that the facts to be disclosed can be exempted from that general expectation.

When it comes to sex, the issue is pretty clear cut. Personal sexuality is considered "extremely intimate" by the courts and the more intimate the aspect of private life that is being interfered with the more serious must be the reasons for interference before the disclosure can be legitimate. Which explains why the Mail on Sunday did not seek to go into detail, of which more later.

Business dealings

Also in *Browne*, it was not accepted that business information necessarily fell outside the definition of private. Sir Anthony Clarke said at [34]:

"It seems to us that business information passed by a company director to his sexual partner could readily be held to be information which the latter knew or ought reasonably to have known was fairly and reasonably to be regarded as confidential or private and in respect of which the former had a reasonable expectation of privacy."

A section of the disclosures was allowed not only because it related to misuse of BP assets; the matters also related to Lord Browne's actions, mainly in the outside world, taken as a result of the relationship rather than "secrets" passed on in the course of the relationship. Although the Court of Appeal questioned this distinction it did endorse the reasoning outlined by Eady J. at [43]:

"One may ask whether there can be a reasonable expectation that the law will protect the privacy of a senior executive, in relation to the use of corporate information and resources, when the effect would be to keep such allegations from those who might ordinarily be expected to make the relevant judgments or exercise supervision; that is to say, shareholders and colleagues on the board of directors."

He also said it was for the company not the judiciary to assess the extent and gravity of any such behaviour and it was not for a judge to keep the relevant information from them.

The Court of Appeal judged that Art.8 was engaged. The question was whether interference with those rights could be justified under art.8.2 which in cases of protecting private information would usually be found in the rights and freedoms created by Art.10. Similarly, where Art.10 rights are engaged, the court has to consider whether interference with those rights can be justified under art.10.2 to prevent the disclosure of information received in confidence. Then, at trial, it is a question of proportionality. Where rights clash, something has to give, and the court will consider the nature and degree of sacrifice involved on either side.

Supporting detail

There is further good news in the *Browne* judgment over the revelation of the relationship. The motives of the Mail on Sunday for wanting to reveal it can be questioned, but in practice it does reinforce a key consideration for journalists in terms of the need to provide supporting evidence for a story as was allowed, under different circumstances, in *Jameel*. Various elements of helpful definition emerged.

The newspaper did not seek to publish "intimate details of the relationship such as sexual matters or minutiae of domestic life" (and wouldn't have been allowed to), but sought to refer just to the fact that the relationship took place "not least because it may be important background in authenticating in readers' minds the other allegations they wish to publish. That is, of course, a legitimate consideration," Eady J. said.

The Court of Appeal endorsed that view in [59]:

"In our judgment, that is sufficient reason to permit publication of the bare fact of the relationship. Publication of the information in categories b) and d) would make no sense without publication of the nature of the relationship between the claimant and JC."

Mary Riddell, commentating in the Observer , concluded:

"Today, readers of the Mail on Sunday may learn more than most people could wish to know about Browne. The squeamish may recoil from the account of his remaindered 'rent boy' but, in the end, this is all about freedom and liberties. Without the freedom of the muckraking and imperfect British media, we should know nothing of the liberties Lord Browne has taken with truth and justice."[51]

It should be remembered that some material was injuncted and that reportedly included accounts of dinners with Blair and Mandelson. Here there would at least be an argument that, if the views expressed privately differed markedly from their public utterances, a public interest exists in voters having a fuller account of their position to weigh against their

---

[51] Observer, 6 May, 2007.

reasonable expectation of privacy at a private dinner. Evidently this was weighed and the freedom of expression case found wanting.

8. Privacy Checklist

Analysis of the judgments to date suggests a range of questions journalists need to ask themselves when considering running stories which may require revelation of personal information.

Is the information private?

Does the subject of the story have a reasonable expectation of privacy in regard to the information to be used? The answer will depend on the information itself and the circumstances in which it has been imparted or obtained.

Lord Hoffmann in *Campbell v MGN* [2004] said at para.21:

> "Essentially the touchstone of private life is whether in respect of the disclosed facts the person in question had a reasonable expectation of privacy."

Judicial interpretation has broadened considerably since *Von Hannover*, and *Peck* influences the definition too. Court battles have frequently boiled down to issues of the images used alongside stories. In various cases, such as *Campbell*, the facts in the story have been allowed; it was the accompanying image that offended.

The old PCC rule of thumb was that, if someone was clearly visible in a public place, permission was not needed to take and use a photograph of them, whether they were aware of the photograph being snapped or not. There were issues over use of long lens but they now seem almost out-of-date. Even where someone is on clear public view, without any suggestion of the need for a long lens, they can be deemed to enjoy a "reasonable expectation of privacy." The photographer should certainly not be hiding but even if they and the subject are in full public view, an intrusion of privacy may be claimed.

All is not lost. It will depend what the subjects are doing when the photograph is taken. If what they are doing has a private or embarrassing quality to it, such as attending Narcotics Anonymous, judges may consider this a private matter.

However, even in *Von Hannover* which is considered as setting a draconian benchmark in press terms, there were extra requirements established to claim a reasonable expectation of privacy in a public place. The *Von Hannover* ruling was influenced by the fact that the whole catalogue of images involved in the action was held to be part of a campaign of harassment of Princess Caroline as she went about her daily life and that she was entitled at times to be considered "off-duty."

This is the kind of principle behind the deals brokered by our British royal family, say, when they go ski-ing. Prince Charles and his sons, for example, agreed to a formal, official photocall in return for being left alone in an otherwise public place to have some time to themselves. This was the kind of relief from permanent paparazzi presence that the *Von Hannover* ruling was designed to provide.

There was also mention of one photograph of her tripping up which also suggested that any embarrassing shots of the subject off-guard would earn more protection than those of her looking good.

The court also took into account the massive audience reach of paparazzi shots so that behaviour that, although in public, might be witnessed only by a handful of people could end up being shared with millions.

The conclusion of the judgment is worryingly emphatic about the lack of public interest in her and the extent of her right to privacy, but in the arguments which precede it there is more recognition of the special circumstances involved and the sense that the court, put simply, essentially believed she deserved a break.

Baroness Hale in *Campbell* made a useful distinction to help define "reasonable expectation of privacy" in a public place. She says in para.154:

> "We have not so far held that the mere fact of covert photography is sufficient to make the information contained in the photograph confidential. The activity photographed must be private. If this had been, and had been presented as, a picture of Naomi Campbell going about her business in a public street, there could have been no complaint. She makes a substantial part of her living out of being photographed looking stunning in designer clothing. Readers will obviously be interested to see how she looks if and when she pops out to the shops for a bottle of milk. There is nothing essentially private about that information nor can it be expected to damage her private life. It may not be a high order of freedom of speech but there is nothing to justify interfering with it."

Based on this line of reasoning, Elton John failed to secure an injunction to prevent publication of photographs of him in the driveway of his home.

It is no coincidence that photographs have been at the centre of so many privacy disputes. In part this emphasises how often the real issue at stake is more about image rights than personal concerns of privacy. But it is also because photographs are seen as more damning and intrusive than words to the same effect. Photographs can be more memorable, less easy for readers to brush off, less transient, but that is why newspapers want to run them, to stand the story up and give it credibility with the reader. The photograph is the evidence. The suggestion now is that journalists should take the photographs to back up a story, but not necessarily seek to run them.

Historically, the more visual broadcast media tended to be seen as more transient and forgettable compared with the printed word in defamation terms. But for privacy, images loom large.

What were the expectations of any pre-existing relationship?

A former confidential relationship necessitates an assessment of whether the party disclosing the information had reason to believe it was to be kept secret. This is a complex matter relating to states of mind. The closer, especially sexually, the relationship the harder it is likely to be to justify infringement of privacy rights of any parties.

The public interest in protecting confidential relationships is weighed by the court. There is a value in upholding the expectations of trust in commercial and personal relationships. In freedom of expression terms, those wanting to exercise Art.10 rights but "guilty" of breach of trust will lose out. Article 10 rights can be overridden by the need to protect confidential arrangements as in a marriage, as in *CC v AB*. In the eyes of the law, someone who has breached a trust has done wrong. Yet, the gross breach of trust involved in adultery is no longer treated as wrongdoing or a serious impropriety when it comes to establishing a public interest in divulging private information about that breach.

Is the information already in the public domain?

This may seem obvious but judgments in *Browne*, *Prince Charles* and others make it difficult to determine how many people need to know a "secret" before it is considered secret no more. The "amalgam" of considerations come into play relating to how the information was gleaned, in what circles it has been disseminated previously and in what form.

Courts tend to focus on the specific information and, as in *Browne* and the *Prince of Wales*, are becoming generous about the number and range of people who may already be privy to the "private" information before it is considered to be in the public domain. In the realm of "open secrets" a journalist would say the "open" is the clue that the privacy has already been breached whereas the courts are ignoring the tautology and treating the information as remaining "secret". Even inclusion on websites is not enough to put material in the public domain, so here again proportionality goes against the mainstream media players. A complainant would struggle to gain redress against a website read by a few hundred people; but can claim against or injunct operators with larger audiences. By happy coincidence for the claimants, they also tend to be the defendants with assets to claim against.

What is the claimant's history of prior revelations?

Has material on a par with the story in question been placed in the public domain previously with the claimant's full consent or indeed at their behest? Have they sought publicity and what level of intrusion have they allowed? A celebrity may have effectively put most of their "private"life on show. Can those who have bared all literally and figuratively then decide to cover up? They may not only have put specific information in to the public eye; they have put every sordid detail of their lives out there. This gives some room for manoeuvre but is not a reliable protection.

The general stance is that previous behaviour does not prevent the new material being considered private but it can have a bearing on proportionality. Yes, the more exposed a celebrity has been previously, the harder it will be to justify secrecy further down the line but, as ever, it depends. If the intrusion is great enough, previous exposure, even of similar sorts of information, may still mean judges uphold Art.8 rights over Art.10.

9. Infringing the Subject's Right to Privacy

What exactly is the public interest and how serious are the consequences of the public remaining in ignorance?

The PCC definition can be useful here. The public interest includes, but is not confined to:

- Detecting or exposing crime or serious impropriety
- Protecting public health and safety
- Preventing the public from being misled by an action or statement of an individual or organisation

Serious impropriety can be called upon where there is alleged misuse of public or corporate resources.

The third element has been much to the fore in say *Campbell* where the Mirror's justification was to "put the record" straight over Campbell's drug involvement. Campbell was accepted as a role model so it was reasonable for the public to know they were being misled.

Putting the record straight can rely on provoking a celebrity into denial then revealing their lie, as in *Campbell*.

The courts are tending to a view that it doesn't matter whether a celebrity is telling the truth about their private life or not. The public realm is shrinking. There is also a pecking order as established by Baroness Hale on which most "celebrities" are in danger of dropping off the bottom such that the answer to whether the image they present to the public is real or not is none of our business.

How serious an invasion is it?

Think like a judge, not a journalist. Sex is very private; medical treatment and health concerns are private and in *McKennitt* "home" is sacrosanct. So the subject matter will influence the degree of public interest required to justify the intrusion. Some material may be considered sufficiently "anodyne" to be published but the range is broad and, as ever, is assessed case by case.

Who is it about?

An Art.10 case will depend on the target; the position held in society as well as the prior approach to publicity. An adulterous MP would do it but only if promoting family values.

What rights can be claimed under Article 10?

The focus tends to be on whether Art.8 rights are involved and whether the infringement of them can be justified. But technically the parallel weighting must also take place. The claimant is requesting an infringement of the journalist's Art.10 rights and the "damage" caused in so doing must be considered by the court. So it is important that journalists can argue what is being lost for them and more particularly the public by the infringement. This tends to be less emotive than the damage claimed of an Art.8 infringement so it is important to ensure it is not overlooked or discounted during the "proportionality" test.

Case Study One: Associated Newspapers Ltd v Prince of Wales [2006] EWCA Civ 1776

Associated was appealing against Prince Charles' successful claim for breach of confidence and infringement of copyright over publication of extracts from his journals. The copyright ownership was not disputed, but the newspaper argued that the journal content was not confidential.

The case on the face of it appears pretty blatant. The material was from diaries, traditionally private material and the source was an assistant who had signed up in her contract to protect the Prince's confidences.

She had been dismissed for unrelated reasons and she had sought money from the press in return for copies of the journals.

The Prince's solicitors threatened proceedings if the journals were published, but appear not to have sought an injunction.

So how did the newspaper hope to succeed in justifying publication? First that the material wasn't actually private. Any of us would expect our diary to be private but these are not ordinary journals. The journals are hand-written, photocopied and distributed to various people, albeit marked Private and Confidential, but they are circulated to between 21 and 75 people depending on whose evidence was accurate. The extent of availability to royal staff was also disputed. Also journalist Jonathan Dimbleby had been given free access to the journals in 1994 during his work on a biography of Prince Charles which would have included some of the journals at issue.

The Court of Appeal decided the matter could be perfectly well handled under the "old" breach of confidence as there was an explicit contractual duty of confidence but did also consider the Art.8 and Art.10 issues. They judged that, even in the absence of a confidential relationship, the journals would be treated as private.

The judges even used the Mail on Sunday's own promotional material against it. The newspaper had tried to argue that the material was already in the public domain, not just because it was made available including to a biographer, but because it described public events. In para.39, the response is cutting:

"That newspaper's headline that it 'reveals the extraordinary and historic journal' gives lie to the suggestion that what was being published was already in the public domain."

The Court of Appeal said the Dimbleby access was clearly confined to him and that giving one person permission to use material did not allow for a free for all.

So it went on to consider whether the breach was sufficient to deprive the Mail on Sunday of its Art.10 rights to publish material which was clearly of significance to political debate in that it concerned the views of the heir to the throne on issues deriving from his official duties abroad. Where was the "pressing social need" to stop them?

Part of that consideration of what is necessary in a democratic society is the public interest in upholding duties of confidence, which weighed heavily with the judges in comparison to the public interest of us knowing more about the political views of the heir to the throne, particularly as they agreed that the contribution of the journals to these matters was "minimal." No contest.

Case Study Two: Niema Ash v Loreena McKennitt [2006] EWCA Civ 1714

The frustrating aspect of this case is that, in journalistic terms, it is not a strong one, yet it led to some unhelpful definitions which have effectively become a precedent which the media fear will be used to curb stories which would otherwise be more obviously in the public interest.The case is not helped because there was at times a contractual obligation which creates a requirement for an even more significant public interest defence if the infringement of Art.8 rights is to be accepted. McKennitt's public role was sufficiently vague to allow for a very unwelcome definition of what constitutes a public figure. And, in PCC Code terms, there was no wrongdoing claimed (other than that already dismissed in another court) nor any need to set the record straight. For this to become a "test" case is most unfortunate for mainstream media which cannot choose its battles when it comes to legal restrictions emerging through ad hoc judgments from the higher courts which are entirely dependent upon which cases go the distance. These are not necessarily the ones which prove most helpful either in helping to clarify key issues at the margin or in representing an opportunity to the Law Lords to be more sympathetic to freedom of expression and more generous in their definition of public interest.

The only hope is that given that it was a weak case that failed; a stronger one with a more significant public interest could allow Art.10 to prevail.

Applying the checklist

Is the information private? Eady J. refused protection for some "anodyne" information, but allowed as private broadly:

- Ms McKennitt's personal and sexual relationships.
- Her personal feelings and, in particular, in relation to her deceased fiancé and the circumstances of his death in a boating accident—although she had spoken publicly about these issues in the context of her water safety campaign.
- Matters relating to her health and diet—broader again than a restriction on straightforward medical records.
- Matters relating to her emotional vulnerability.
- Details of work done on her cottage in Ireland.
- Details of a recording contract.
- Details of a property dispute between them which was resolved separately.

What were the expectations of any pre-existing relationship? Again, this reverts to a fairly traditional duty of confidence arising from a transaction or relationship, so any public interest or Art.10 assertion is weakened by the commitment to sanctions against breach of trust. Use of the phrase"confided to me"is used as evidence that Ash knew she was expected to keep the secret. The closer the relationship, the more important it becomes to honour its obligations and the more serious any revelation would need to be in public interest terms to justify it.

The Court of Appeal stated at [23]:

"A person's health is in any event a private matter, as the Campbell case demonstrated. It is doubly private when information about it is imparted in the context of a relationship of confidence."

Is the information already in the public domain? In most incidences the answer was no.

What is the claimant s history of prior revelations? McKennitt had shared some intimate issues in her campaign for water safety but in a controlled way and was otherwise unforthcoming. The fact that some disclosure had taken place as part of the campaign did not justify a detailed account of her grieving process. Despite a challenge to a view that a person can limit publication to what he wishes to be published, the Court of Appeal was adamant that to the extent information was private it was for the individual to decide how much of it to reveal.

If it is private, is there a public interest in revealing it? and how serious an invasion is it? McKennitt's "home" was deemed sacrosanct in Art.8 terms influencing the degree of public interest required to justify the intrusion.

Who is it about? McKennitt is famous as a performer but otherwise had kept a relatively low public profile apart from the safety campaign. This is the area of real concern for the media in the Ash appeal. Being in the public eye has generally put subjects of media interest into a separate category from average, relatively unknown individuals. Fame has been enough to justify an expectation of greater scrutiny by the media. The declaration that McKennitt is "not a public figure" suggests there is little scope for mounting a public interest justification for running any private information about her. What other subjects of extensive media coverage would fall into the same category? Gary Flitcroft, the footballer in *A v B & C*, as Lord Sedley opined, probably would.

What exactly is the public interest and how serious are the consequences of the public remaining in ignorance? Treating McKennitt as a public figure, which journalists would automatically have done, means there is also a public interest in exposing misbehaviour or hypocrisy, a freedom to put the record straight. In the PCC code, these public interest justifications can be invoked for any individual or organisation; no particular profile and certainly no public office is required.

This is where the media is losing out considerably through a narrow definition of public discourse related to a narrow definition of democratic processes which in turn relies on a narrow definition of matters of public interest which are pursued by those narrowly defined as public figures exercising official functions.

The Court of Appeal questioned whether McKennitt was a public figure in the terms of *A v B & C*. She was not a particular role model and had generally kept a low profile. Even if she were a role model, there was no misbehaviour, hypocrisy or deceit to uncover. Some of the revelations treated as private did attack McKennitt's "probity and honesty" but these were considered to be unfounded removing any parallel with *Campbell*.

What rights can be claimed under Article 10? Shared experience poses a challenge to privacy. In a shared experience, if one party wants to discuss it can the other prevent them? Traditionally, say with kiss and tell, as long as the story was true, one party could not stop the other from divulging it. Now they can.

In *A v B & C*, the fact that two women were prepared to divulge their relationship with A meant their rights to freedom of expression more or less outnumbered his right to protection.

> "The fact that the confidence was a shared confidence which only one of the parties wishes to preserve does not extinguish the other party's right to have that confidence respected, but it does undermine that right."

The key difference relied upon by Eady J. was that casual sex does not constitute a relationship of confidence; a close friendship over 20 years does.

But also sex, even casual sex, is a shared experience in a way that listening to and repeating the confidences of a friend is not. Ash's appeal to exercise her Art.10 rights was diminished for Mr Justice Eady because the book in dispute was not the story of Ash's life, with incidental reference to McKennitt. It was pitched—and marketed—as a story about McKennitt who is the central character. This was a key issue at appeal but it was decided emphatically that Ms Ash had no story to tell that was her own.

Regarding the long OK!/Hello spat over pictures of the *Douglas* wedding, journalists would do well to familiarise themselves with the case from a privacy perspective, even though at heart it is a classic breach of confidence action. The response of leading media commentator Simon Jenkins can stand as a journalist's "take" on the whole saga. He said:

> "Nobody can stage a wedding, sell the publicity rights for £1m and then claim that they were trying to remain private. Managed publicity is not privacy. As for the 'obligations of confidence' on newspapers not to scoop rivals who have paid for so-called exclusives, this is

censorship born of madness. Newspapers must guard their exclusives as best they can, not call on law lords to act as their bouncers and heavies. Either way, this is a blatant case of one law for the rich and one for the poor."[52]

10. Privacy in Practice—General Conclusions

Sections of the media appear to be busy tying themselves up in knots to justify continuing to run the juicy gossip on celebrities and even the kiss and tell exposés by coming up with a public interest justification. They are not giving up without a fight.

Sexual behaviour, per se, whether involving adultery, homosexuality or any other non-criminal activity, is now heavily protected. It is very private on the one hand; yet will rarely qualify as wrongdoing in public interest terms. For some time running such material has required the media to identify public interest grounds for the invasion beyond say the breach of the marriage vows in itself. Even with Government ministers, revealing the fact of an affair might not be enough, so misuse of public funds and serious impropriety are brought into the equation as referred to in *Blunkett*, but also applied when revealing John Prescott's infidelity with a subordinate.

This could be seen as disingenuous and in print used incidentally to the main revelation but it does not make it wrong to allow it. Just because a popular tabloid and/or its readers may not focus primarily on the public interest element of a story does not mean it is not proper for the courts to recognise it. Indeed it is vital that they do.

More serious investigative journalism relies on these elements to justify exposure. Distaste among the upper echelons of society for the scandalmongering of the popular tabloids must not become the basis of stricter controls on the media. The danger is there and that is part of the dilemma for supposedly more high-minded journalists. It is not just about reining in the excessive methods of the popular tabloids; it becomes about changing their priorities and that appears to be the main driver of the argument of a privacy law.

Do we condemn the froth of the popular tabloids because it is goading the powers-that-be into more draconian controls which would affect serious journalism too or do we defend their right, as we defend ours, to decide what to cover and how to cover it with the minimum intervention by the state as required under Art.10?

---

[52] Quoted by Peter Preston, Observer, May 6, 2007.

Injunctions

If privacy is the new libel, then the media can expect far more battles between Art.8 and Art.10 rights and they are very likely to involve applications for injunctions.

Any attempt to keep secrets is going to involve issues of prior restraint. Damages may be sought after the event, but a breach of privacy cannot be rectified after the event in the same way as a defamatory statement can be retracted. The secret is already out.

So the media need to be prepared to have to fight it out over injunctions. The threat of injunction makes it tempting not to approach the subject of the story at all, or only immediately prior to publication when lack of time would make it difficult to trigger effective legal action. However the courts would tend to take a dim view of this approach. An approach that may not be as crucial as it is in defamation actions, but it would still be considered an essential feature of journalism wanting to claim the protection of the law to assert its freedom of expression over another's privacy. Arguably, it is also potentially cheaper to fight it out at injunction stage. If there is going to be a dispute, better to know before publication. The hurdles for achieving an injunction are still fairly high. The onus will tend to be on the complainant to justify the use of prior restraint, which does retain a vestige of special pleading for freedom of expression within the Human Rights Act. If the case is not clear cut and deemed not likely to succeed at trial, the newspaper may still be allowed to run at least part of its story, as it did in *Browne*.

The Court of Appeal decision in *McKennitt* weakens the limits of prior restraint by deciding that information can be deemed private, without having to decide if it is true or not. Previously disputes over the truth or otherwise of allegations were in the realm of defamation. Privacy issues were used where information was true but secret. Significantly for the media, under *Bonnard v Perryman*, an injunction can not be granted on publication of material claimed to be defamatory if the defendant intends to plead justification. So where a claimant seeks to prevent false information being run, a privacy route and thereby most likely an injunction could be pursued to circumvent Bonnard.

Perhaps the news media should be pleased *McKennitt* didn't go all the way, because it isn't the strongest of cases. Dare we hope that the Law Lords are waiting for a case where the claims to freedom of expression and public interest are actually stronger and more finely balanced with the right to privacy before they set down a more definitive framework for demonstrating where journalists can expect the balance to be struck.

11. Privacy is the new libel

Privacy is an uncomfortable subject for a journalist. Editors used to rail about libel actions—now we have privacy to contend with. Now defamation issues are a relative doddle and the legislation appears positively fair and reasonable. Now we have the legal quagmire surrounding issues of privacy. And of course that switch has been engineered intentionally by the judiciary in response to the ECHR.

For most people privacy is considered a "good." The expression "a right to privacy" is bandied about even though breach of privacy does not exist as a tort in its own right, although arguably it may as well given the way breach of confidence judgments are going.

For a journalist there is something unhealthy about the concept. That may be difficult for some to understand. But consider one of the most famous definitions of news (Randolph Hearst's actually):

"News is something someone, somewhere doesn't want to see published."

Privacy plays into the hands of those with something to hide. And the more they have to hide the harder they will work to keep facts hidden and the more expensive they will make it for a journalist to expose them.

The starting point for journalists is that everything should be out in the open. The public right to know demands it. It is then up to a society to determine what the exceptions should be; what information can reasonably be withheld.

A full-blown privacy law as applied in France, say, could make some information sacrosanct; it could effectively sanction not only secrecy but deception too. Statute there is seen by journalists as a major curb on investigative journalism because it is so protective of reputation and confidentiality, being at least as much about image rights as genuine individual privacy. Yet some UK media players feel statute would be preferable to the creeping restrictions of case law and more may now be in that camp in the wake of *McKennitt v Ash*.

Why is the threat of privacy legislation worse than other restraints such as libel? For me it must be that truth is a defence to libel. It is not to claims of privacy invasion. Exposing the truth is an essential part of being a good journalist. The public needs to know what is really going on. Society is ultimately the healthier for it. We can thank John Stuart Mill for asserting that truth should never be denied a platform.[53]

The majority of cases to date concern celebrities, and often C-list ones at that. This creates complacency, and even approval, because courts upholding Art.8 rights threaten to put an end to paparazzi hounding celebrities and to the "tittle-tattle" of kiss and tell.

Apart from the slippery slope argument, it is reasonable to ask why so many cases are brought by celebrities. It is not just because they make the headlines while Jo Bloggs's plight is ignored; it is not just because newspapers consider them fair game and it is not just because the popular tabloids have moved to a celeb-driven agenda.

---

[53] Mill, J.S., *On Liberty*.

It is because maintaining privacy can be worth a fortune to celebrities because it protects their image; even where that image is false. What media commentators so often fail to acknowledge in the rush of sympathy for the claimant is that, for some, this is business. Lucrative endorsements depend on maintaining the squeaky clean public image which makes it well worth taking even costly action to protect it. There is also money to be made if an infringement is spotted and claimants are certainly not immune from seizing upon claims against the media purely as money-making ventures. Let's not be naïve about this.

Surely, it cannot be wrong for a newspaper to reveal the truth about someone who is peddling a lie, even if that lie concerns their private life. The more significant that lie is, the more the liar has resting on it, the more public reputation rests on perpetuating the lie —the more important it is for it to be exposed *and* the greater the lengths to which the mythmaker will go to keep it secret. The tension is there.

Take the thorny issue of an elected politician's sexuality. Is it private or not? A voter may not care what her MP's sexual orientation is—but it would concern her if he/she were lying about it. It is the pretence and potential hypocrisy that matters. In a representative democracy it is vital to trust those we elect. They should be who they appear to be. Any legislation which makes it easier for them to act covertly has to be a retrograde step in an elected democracy.

There is a balance to be struck. In the EHCR, as well as the English Courts, it emerges as Art.8 v Art.10.

The Press Complaints Commission Code of Practice also upholds privacy entitlements but these are, if not exactly trumped, at least more explicitly circumscribed when the public interest is at stake. Editors will be expected to justify intrusion into any individual's private life without consent but the door is opened to such arguments.

Under the code, it is unacceptable to photograph individuals in private places without their consent. Private places are defined as public or private property where there is a "reasonable expectation" of privacy. This begins to confront the difficult grey area within privacy. Superficially, logically how can something that takes place in public be private? However, at least within the PCC code, the public interest exemption challenges the privacy entitlement by including the justification of *preventing the public from being misled by an action of statement of an individual or organisation.*

Outing the phoney is OK and no distinction is made between different categories of individual or organisation. Certainly, the more significant a role someone plays in public life, the more likely it is to matter if they are misleading the public, but anyone could fall within the definition.

Elected politicians and public servants should not be allowed to mislead the public, even where otherwise private information has to be revealed to prevent it. But what about other public figures, such as TV personalities. There the PCC is working hard to strike an appropriate balance. Celebrities who court press coverage to promote their careers do not lose all protection but they do become in a sense public property. And they should not have a right to mislead.

Too many celebrities rely on being phoney and have a great deal to lose from exposure of the truth about them. And too often newspapers play along. There are more grounds for newspapers being censured for perpetuating myths than for debunking them. Far too many titles collude in the celebrity pretences where it suits agents to raise the profile of their clients and newspapers to sell copies. The deals struck there are far more unethical than occasional intrusive photographs. Journalists and editors who knowingly present false information to the public are the real villains of the piece.

Is it about the money?

Weighing up whether or not to print a controversial—and potentially actionable—story is complex. Different editors will have different elements in the equation—and lend very different weight to them. Watching the popular tabloids, there can appear still to be a cavalier attitude. Who cares about falling foul of the law as long as the money from extra sales outweighs any penalty?

Apart from the fact that a reliable calculation is hard to come by few editors are that unsophisticated. Newspapers want to be right—for their reputation, for their readers, for their professional pride. Losing a libel action, in those terms, is generally very damaging for an editor. If you cannot prove a defamatory statement, you shouldn't make it (although there are occasional honourable defeats).

A journalist wouldn't necessarily feel that bad about invading the privacy of the great and the good—by revealing that they are neither as great nor as good as they would have us believe.

Because truth is no defence to an invasion of privacy, it would not necessarily be that damaging to an editor's reputation to lose a case. Editors might therefore be inclined to push the boundaries, dare I say it, on a point of principle.

Would that it were otherwise but that often leads us back to celebrities. The fabrication that surrounds many celebrities leaves them wide open to the media delivering a reality check. Many celebrities want a legal remedy to compensate them for the possible damage done to their earning power. In those cases our existing laws of confidentiality—borne from a business model — seem much more appropriate and adequate.

Genuine cases of infringement of privacy where a real personal hurt has been caused can be dealt with appropriately by the PCC. The "back off" message is getting through (see Chapter 6).

The privacy debate has thrown up some broader and questionable assumptions. One is that the media is more intrusive now than previously. The reality is more complex. The language used to discuss more intimate issues has become more explicit, coarser too. Yet journalists' behaviour is, if anything, more restrained as media commentator Roy

Greenslade outlined in a memorandum to the Commons Select Committee on Culture, Media and Sport.[54] There are also changes in what is deemed the public realm. People live their lives behind closed doors far more than they used to.

Take the matter of funerals. In local and national papers, funerals used to be a regular source of lengthy stories, complete with lists of mourners. A reporter would stand at the gate taking all the names. The longer the report and list of mourners the more important the person clearly had been. Attendance by the newspaper was a mark of respect. Suggest attending a funeral now and many people are highly offended. Funerals are seen as private events. In the spirit of the PCC code we would seek permission, especially for photographs, and would often be denied.

The public realm is shrinking and in sociological terms there is increasing paranoia over privacy is alarming. Human Rights legislation was supposed to be about protecting individuals from the excesses of public authorities. The use of those safeguards against the media are part of a broader trend whereby individuals feel the need to protect themselves from each other. This is part of a withdrawal from society driven by the fear that participation in the public sphere makes one vulnerable; that other people are a threat. That raises issues far wider than whether or not a newspaper gets to run a photograph of a drunken prince.

The judges who wanted to strike a new balance of less draconian libel restraints but more restrictive privacy protection have certainly succeeded in the latter endeavour. We need to think long and hard about the implications this has not just for the media but for society as a whole.

Why do people guard their privacy so jealously? For many celebrities, it is more about controlling image for commercial purposes and for those not enjoying their 15 minutes of fame, the fear of disclosure seems disproportionate. Each of us should have a degree of choice as to whether to share our lives with the public but it is not necessarily a bad thing. The public does not have a right to know Lord Browne's sexual orientation but surely one of the big questions we should be asking ourselves is why, in this day and age, was he so bothered about people finding out?

The supposed trade-off between more relaxed libel laws and more restrictive privacy doesn't in practice deliver a benefit on balance to journalism; it just changes the line of attack for those who want to keep things quiet. Where a claimant has a grievance against the media, instead of bringing a defamation action, the option will be taken to couch the complaint in terms of invasion of privacy, which now includes the protection of false private information, and grants much greater injunctive powers.

How exactly has the public right to know and freedom of expression been advanced here?

---

[54] Commons Select Committee on Culture, Media and Sport, 5th report, June 2003.

12. Data Protection Act

The Data Protection Act 1998 is supposed to protect the public against the abuse of all-seeing, all-knowing computerised Big Brother data-bases, primarily created by the powers-that-be. It was born out of an EC directive and effectively is designed to embody in statute the requirement on public authorities to safeguard the individual's Art.8 rights.

There are eight principles outlined in the Act:

PART I—THE PRINCIPLES

1. Personal data shall be processed fairly and lawfully and, in particular, shall not be processed unless—
   a. at least one of the conditions in Schedule 2 is met, and
   b. in the case of sensitive personal data, at least one of the conditions in Schedule 3 is also met.
2. Personal data shall be obtained only for one or more specified and lawful purposes, and shall not be further processed in any manner incompatible with that purpose or those purposes.
3. Personal data shall be adequate, relevant and not excessive in relation to the purpose or purposes for which they are processed.
4. Personal data shall be accurate and, where necessary, kept up to date.
5. Personal data processed for any purpose or purposes shall not be kept for longer than is necessary for that purpose or those purposes.
6. Personal data shall be processed in accordance with the rights of data subjects under this Act.
7. Appropriate technical and organisational measures shall be taken against unauthorised or unlawful processing of personal data and against accidental loss or destruction of, or damage to, personal data.
8. Personal data shall not be transferred to a country or territory outside the European Economic Area unless that country or territory ensures an adequate level of protection for the rights and freedoms of data subjects in relation to the processing of personal data.

The Act is relatively rare in making special provision for "journalistic" data. Section 32 describes this protection.

1. Personal data which are processed only for the special purposes are exempt from any provision to which this subsection relates if—
   a. the processing is undertaken with a view to the publication by any person of any journalistic, literary or artistic material,
   b. the data controller reasonably believes that, having regard in particular to the special importance of the public interest in freedom of expression, publication would be in the public interest, and
   c. the data controller reasonably believes that, in all the circumstances, compliance with that provision is incompatible with the special purposes.

2. Subsection (1) relates to the provisions of—
   a. the data protection principles except the seventh data protection principle,
   b. section 7,
   c. section 10,
   d. section 12, and
   e. section 14(1) to (3).
3. In considering for the purposes of subsection (1)(b) whether the belief of a data controller that publication would be in the public interest was or is a reasonable one, regard may be had to his compliance with any code of practice which—
   a. is relevant to the publication in question, and
   b. is designated by the Secretary of State by order for the purposes of this subsection.
4. Where at any time ("the relevant time") in any proceedings against a data controller under section 7(9), 10(4), 12(8) or 14 or by virtue of section 13 the data controller claims, or it appears to the court, that any personal data to which the proceedings relate are being processed—
   a. only for the special purposes, and
   b. with a view to the publication by any person of any journalistic, literary or artistic material which, at the time 24 hours immediately before the relevant time, had not previously been published by the data controller, the court shall stay the proceedings until either of the conditions in subsection (5) is met.
5. Those conditions are—
   a. that a determination of the Commissioner under section 45 with respect to the data in question takes effect, or
   b. in a case where the proceedings were stayed on the making of a claim, that the claim is withdrawn.
6. For the purposes of this Act"publish", in relation to journalistic, literary or artistic material, means make available to the public or any section of the public.

It is an offence under s.55 of the Act unlawfully to obtain, disclose or sell personal information without the consent of the data controller.

Its implications have been many and varied for working journalists. The most obvious impact was a clamming up on the part of organisations, particularly the emergency services, which had previously been the mainstay of daily news reports. The introduction of the Act saw a massive shift to "anonymised" information to the extent that most of it became of little value.

One of the saddest repercussions is that many schools have taken the view that the Act prevents them from allowing their pupils to be identified or even photographed by the local newspaper. This overly-protective stance is such a shame. Schools are such an important part of a local community it is ridiculous if that cannot be reflected in the columns of the local newspaper. Also, local press photographers turn up at schools on almost every occasion to take happy pictures of children playing sport or music, creating tremendously imaginative art work, raising money for charity or excelling in exams. The media is accused, particularly by young people themselves, of presenting only a negative view of youth—of its anti-social behaviour, drug habits and binge drinking. Reporting their achievement in school provides endless opportunities to strike a balance which local newspapers had done for decades—until the Data Protection Act.

The Act is pretty demanding in itself, but the situation was made worse by the caution exercised by public bodies through fear of litigation that, played safe so as to limit any risk of challenge under its authority. Rather than make an informed judgment on what it was reasonable to release to the public, organisations found it easier to say nothing. Where there was discretion to justify degrees of openness in the organisation's schedule of disclosure, this was rarely exercised.

The police are allowed to release information for "policing purposes" but there is a continuing debate over what this means in practice; about what information can properly be placed in the public domain via the media. Part of that purpose is to raise awareness of crime, alert the public to dangers and appeal for help in particular cases but again, in most instances, it is felt this can be done without revealing identities of those involved. The police had little stomach for pushing the boundaries to maintain the flow of information in press calls. The gains to be had from meaningful coverage of accidents and crime were vague and unquantifiable compared with the threatened cost of legal action by an aggrieved party, annoyed about being identified and claiming redress under the Act.

Not everything that happens to an individual is private information, especially if it happens in a public place and involves public agencies. The famous proportionality test was rarely applied so that the degree of public interest in knowing what was happening to real people in real situations was not acknowledged.

The public relates to the familiar, especially to people they know. Anonymity is the bane of journalists because it hinders engagement; it hinders the ability to make the information relevant to readers. Take the attitude of the Data Protection Act to road crashes. Accidents that happen in full public view, affect perhaps thousands of motorists, occur on the public highway and are dealt with by publicly-funded emergency services are deemed to be private matters. If any party, whether famous or not, asks for details to be withheld they will be. It is supposedly enough for us to know there has been an accident and that one male person was injured. Few people appear to appreciate what is being lost.

Apart from the capacity to cover up significant information—if a public person is somewhere they shouldn't be, for instance, this disembodied information hinders a response, makes it less likely that witnesses will come forward and also means the victim may not receive expressions of concern, outpourings of sympathy and assistance. The public is denied the opportunity to respond in a meaningful way.

The attitude is not only that individuals will desire privacy; there is almost a presumption that putting information in the public domain is damaging, even dangerous, in just about any circumstance. Police assume a victim will not want to talk to the media.

Yet this can be very cathartic, it can generate support and be a catalyst for witnesses to come forward. The presumption that disclosure is automatically bad for the victim means much information is never released. Instead of a sophisticated assessment, the balance of public right to know and privacy is reduced to a standard formula that the media want information purely to satisfy self-interest and that any benefit to them is necessarily at a cost to the victim. This is very often nonsense.

Not passing on "data" has appeared to be a risk-free strategy but, as well as significantly reducing the flow of information to the media, it has triggered some ridiculous situations, most famously the belief by police that they were prevented by the Act from retaining information on Ian Huntley who went on to murder two girls in Soham.

Journalists should also appreciate that not all sources are covered by the Act. The clamming up by official channels does not mean a journalist can't obtain and run the information wanted if it can be confirmed from other sources. There is often less resistance, even from those directly involved. Often officials assume publicity is not wanted, say by victims of crime, when in fact they or their family are happy to speak. However the journalist will face general privacy issues if the information is acquired without consent of its subject.

A perverse impact of the Act—in that it frees up information—was that it also provides rights to the individual about whom the information is held. For many, the Act has not been about preventing disclosure of their private information to the world at large. It has been about gaining access to their own private information and exercising their rights to find out what details are held about them by organisations. Public authorities and employers in the UK previously enjoyed remarkable rights to keep information secret even from those it described. So our own health, work and financial records were suddenly available to us, with the usual caveats and not in every instance. This provoked a flurry of shredding in some quarters but has engineered greater accountability and the right to challenge the content of much private information held about us.

This can be useful to journalists, partly because they can find out information about themselves to show how the system works, or doesn't. But more importantly it means that where a journalist is investigating a complaint on behalf of an individual, whereas the journalist would be denied access to "private" information, the individual may well be able to find out for themselves if pointed in the right direction by the reporter.

Information Commissioner

The Data Protection Act is overseen by the Information Commissioner who has become active of late in various areas.

The positive actions for journalists are a variety of pronouncements where it is felt authorities have been too protective of information and overplayed the restrictions. There is at least a sense of proportionality being introduced and the recognition that withholding information can be more dangerous than releasing it.

The danger of withholding has been acknowledged in the *Huntley* case and where British Gas failed to inform social services that the heating supply to an elderly couple's home had been cut off. Both these cases involved people dying which is how, by backtracking over the circumstances which led up to the deaths, they came to be revealed. The proportionality test is clear.

The Information Commissioner did also provide some reassurance to schools that pictures of activities were not necessarily covered by the Act. Some schools had even banned parents from taking photographs of nativity plays and sports day and the Office of Information Commissioner issued guidance in 2005 that pictures taken purely for personal use were exempt and that most pictures taken by the media were also "usually exempt". The message isn't unequivocal and many schools remain cautious, but at least it suggests that the commissioner may help to restore a balance where there is overzealous interpretation of the Act.

In less dramatic instances, in the relative minutiae of daily life, it is much harder for the news media to demonstrate the dangers of restricting the flow of information to the public, so there is a long way to go in the proportionality battle if the restrictive side-effects of the Act are to be challenged.

The other main area of activity of the Information Commissioner has been a significant tightening up on improper disclosure, mainly by those making a business out of trading information.

The maximum sentence for people unlawfully trading in, or misusing, personal data will be increased from a £5,000 fine to two years' imprisonment from Crown Court and 12 months' imprisonment from Magistrates' Courts once s.154 of the Criminal Justice Act 2003 comes into force.

The work of private investigation firms has come under the spotlight, not least as an off-shoot to the jailing of News of the World royal reporter Clive Goodman in 2007 for hacking in to the mobile phone calls of various people. Although his offence was not under the Data Protection Act, it did uncover the extensive use made by his newspaper and other media of investigation agencies.

The allegation was that some newspapers were attempting to conduct investigations at arm's length to evade PCC Code obligations without sufficient scrutiny of the methods being employed by the agencies providing them with personal information. The PCC launched its own investigation into these related matters and published its findings and advice in May 2007. See the final section of this Chapter.

The Information Commissioner's Office regulatory action division head Mick Gorrill, as reported in Media Lawyer, said:

"Personal information must be properly protected by those organisations which hold and process it, and we will investigate where there are failures to do so.

"The ICO will not hesitate to prosecute those involved in this illegal trade. We are currently investigating other organisations which buy this information."[55]

The Information Commissioner Richard Thomas' 2006 report, What Price Privacy? said of personal information:

"Among the 'buyers' are many journalists looking for a story. In one major case investigated by the ICO, the evidence included records of information supplied to 305 named journalists working for a range of newspapers.

"The 'suppliers' almost invariably work within the private investigation industry: private investigators, tracing agents, and their operatives, often working loosely in chains that may include several intermediaries between ultimate customer and the person who actually obtains the information."[56]

A private investigation firm was fined £3,200 in April 2007 under the DPA for "blagging" information about more than 250 individuals from the Department for Work and Pensions by pretending to be colleagues. And a husband and wife were fined £3,300 and £4,200 respectively in November 2006 for "blagging" personal information from organisations including Customs, British Telecom and banks.

Under the Act news organisations running what turns out to be "blagged" material could face prosecution. Although the "buyers" may not know if some of that information has been obtained illegally, they cannot afford to be disingenuous about how it has been obtained, particularly where it is clearly very personal.

The jailing of Clive Goodman obviously made journalists sit up and take notice. Whether this is the forerunner to a whole flurry of DPA-related prosecutions of reporters and news organisations remains to be seen. At very least, news organisations which trade in private information are now aware that their relationships are under very close scrutiny and they have the new PCC guidance to go by.

The Information Commissioner also took enforcement action in 2006 to order removal of data from a website which was offering searches for individuals by making mis-use under the Act of certain electoral roll information.

The experience of the Data Protection Act provokes many of the misgivings felt by the news media about privacy generally. The Act is part of

[55] Media Lawyer.
[56] Information Commissioner Richard Thomas, What Price Privacy?, 2006.

that broader trend whereby individuals feel the need to protect themselves from each other. This is part of a withdrawal from society driven
by the fear that participation in the public sphere makes one vulnerable;
that other people are a threat.

This is another statute designed to protect the individual against the
power of the state which is in practice being used to stem the flow of
information via the media into the public domain. It is about more
than the right to freedom of expression against the right to privacy;
there is a general public interest in knowing as much as possible about
anything going on in the word that affects them. There is a common
good in disclosure which carries less and less weight. Journalists need
to work hard to ensure that in these days of the weighing of proportionality, that the benefits of a free flow of information are not discounted.

There is always a danger that legislation designed to protect the
private individual will in practice be perverted for the purposes of public
cover-up. Civil servants and public bodies can attempt to hide behind
the Data Protection Act, just like they do other restrictive statutes such
as the Official Secrets Act and the Human Rights Act.

Journalists need to avoid falling foul of the Act themselves but they
also need to discover enough about its workings to ensure its restrictions
extend no further than required and be prepared to challenge the
Information Commissioner if organisations are taking its protections too
far, especially if it is for their own benefit rather than to defend those it
is designed to protect.

The PCC report on subterfuge and newsgathering is given in full
because it provides such a timely reminder of so many of the issues
raised in this chapter:

PCC Report on Subterfuge and Newsgathering

1.0 Introduction

The Press Complaints Commission has conducted an investigation into the use
of subterfuge by the British newspaper and magazine industry, with particular
reference to phone message tapping and compliance with the Editors' Code of
Practice and the Data Protection Act.

1.2 The inquiry followed the convictions in January 2007 of News of the World
journalist Clive Goodman and inquiry agent Glenn Mulcaire for offences
under the Regulation of Investigatory Powers Act 2000 (RIPA) and Criminal
Law Act (1977). They had speculatively tapped into private mobile phone messages and used the information they discovered for stories in the News of the
World.

1.3 This type of snooping has no place in journalism, and the Chairman of the Commission has publicly deplored it on a number of occasions. The Commission as a whole condemns such behaviour.

1.4 Despite the police inquiry, court case and convictions, the Commission considered that there were a number of outstanding questions that arose under the Code of Practice, which sets out the required professional standards for UK journalists and, as such, supplements the law. Last November, before the verdict was reached, the Chairman of the PCC had already put the then editor of the News of the World, Mr Andy Coulson, on notice that, depending on the outcome of the trial, the PCC might wish to pursue matters with him.

1.5 On January 26 2007, Mulcaire and Goodman were sentenced to 6 and 4 months in prison. Mr Coulson resigned his post, saying that he had "decided that the time has come for me to take ultimate responsibility for the events around the Clive Goodman case". Mr Colin Myler was appointed editor in his place.

1.6 Despite Mr Myler's appointment, the question arose whether the PCC should ask Mr Coulson to give an account of what had gone wrong. The PCC decided not to do so. Given that the PCC does not—and should not—have statutory powers of investigation and prosecution, there could be no question of trying to duplicate the lengthy police investigation. Furthermore, Mr Coulson was, following his resignation, no longer answerable to the PCC, whose jurisdiction covers journalists working for publications that subscribe to the self-regulatory system through the Press Standards Board of Finance.

1.7 As a result, that part of the investigation involving the News of the World was conducted by the Director of the PCC with Mr Myler. The Chairman of the Commission also discussed the matter on a number of occasions with the Chief Executive of News International, Mr Les Hinton.

1.8 In a statement on 1st February 2007, the Commission said that "the public has a right to know that lessons have been learned from this episode, both at the newspaper and more generally". It announced that it would be:

- Writing to the new editor of the newspaper for detailed information on what had gone wrong and to find out what steps would be taken to ensure that the situation did not recur;
- Conducting a broad inquiry across the whole of the press to find out the extent of internal controls aimed at preventing similar abuses;
- Publishing its findings.

1.9 There was a further point for consideration. The arrests and conviction of Mulcaire and Goodman coincided with a campaign by the Information Commissioner to raise awareness of the terms of the Data Protection Act, which applies to journalists but which also contains an exemption for some journalistic activity. The Information Commissioner was concerned that information provided to journalists by inquiry agents had been obtained by "blagging" or bribery in breach of the Act.

1.10 As part of its inquiry, the Commission therefore also asked the industry what was being done to raise awareness of the Data Protection Act, including its public interest defences.

1.11 In its approach to this matter, the Commission has also been concerned not to obscure or undermine the legitimate role of subterfuge in journalism that is in the public interest.

1.12 This report is therefore concerned with two main subjects: events at the News of the World in relation to Clive Goodman and Glenn Mulcaire, how the situation developed and how repetition will be avoided; and what the industry as a whole is doing to ensure that lessons have been learned from this incident so that British journalism is not brought into similar disrepute in the future.

2.0 The News of the World inquiry

2.1 Clive Goodman was a full time member of staff at the News of the World. The court heard that Glenn Mulcaire was an inquiry agent who was paid a retainer of £104,988 per annum by the newspaper. The court also heard that he had received £12,300 in cash from Clive Goodman.

2.2 The Director of the Commission wrote to the new editor of the News of the World, Colin Myler, on 7th February 2007. He said that the Commission had been especially concerned whether the employment of Mr Mulcaire represented an attempt to circumvent the provisions of the Code by sub-contracting investigative work to a third party. There are no loopholes in the Code in this regard, which says that "editors should take care to ensure it is observed rigorously by all editorial staff and external contributors, including non-journalists".

2.3 The Commission asked a number of questions with regard to the Mulcaire and Goodman situation and also what the newspaper proposed to do to ensure that it would not happen again.

2.4 With regard to Goodman specifically, the PCC said that it seemed from the evidence submitted to the court that he had repeatedly breached the Code as well as the law. The Commission therefore required the clearest reassurance that the paper made its staff journalists fully aware of the requirements of the Code and the law with regard to subterfuge, including when it would be justified.

2.5 The Commission informed the newspaper that it would be broadening its inquiry to involve the industry at large. It invited the News of the World to make any points, based on its experience and understanding of what went wrong, that might be helpful in this context.

3.0 The News of the World response

3.1 The editor, Mr Myler, replied to the Commission on the 22nd February. He described how the situation with Goodman and Mulcaire had developed and detailed what action was now being taken to minimise the chances of repetition. He urged the Commission to see the episode in perspective as it represented "an exceptional and unhappy event in the 163 year history of the News of the World, involving one journalist". Moreover, two people had been sent to prison, Goodman had been dismissed from the paper and the previous editor had resigned.

3.2 He emphasised the newspaper's commitment to the Code of Practice, drawing attention, by way of example, to an episode where a reporter had been dismissed for breaching its terms. He said that "every single News of the World journalist is conversant with the Code and appreciates fully the necessity of total compliance".

4.0 Goodman and Mulcaire

4.1 The editor told the Commission that it was important to distinguish between the aberrational Goodman/Mulcaire episode which resulted in the prosecutions and the paper's day to day contract with Mulcaire. It had emerged during the trial that Mulcaire had been paid a retainer by the newspaper. The editor confirmed to the Commission that this had been for £2,019 per week. Cash payments of £12,300 from Goodman to Mulcaire were in addition to this.

4.2 Because of the convictions, questions had been raised about the nature of the services provided by Mulcaire for which he was paid almost £105k per annum. The editor told the Commission that there had been a "great deal of inaccurate media speculation" concerning this contract. In fact, the work was entirely "legal and legitimate". The police had thoroughly investigated the retainer, and the prosecution had made clear to the judge that they were not suggesting that the retainer agreement involved anything illegal. This had been accepted by the judge.

4.3 The editor accepted that the retainer paid to Mulcaire may have seemed "substantial", but argued that the cost to the paper would have been much greater had the work been contracted out on an ad hoc basis. He contended that Mulcaire's hourly rate probably averaged less than £50. The editor added that there was nothing unusual about the employment of outside investigators; and that the practice was shared by solicitors, insurance companies, banks and many commercial organisations as well as newspapers.

4.4 The editor told the Commission what services Mulcaire provided. They were: gathering facts for stories and analysing the extent of the paper's proof before publication; confirming facts and suggesting strategies; credit status checks; Land Registry checks; directorship searches and analysis of businesses and individuals; tracing individuals from virtually no biographical details, including date of birth searches, electoral roll searches and checks through databases; County Court searches and analysis of court records; surveillance; specialist crime advice; professional football knowledge (Mulcaire was a former professional footballer); contacts in the sports and show business worlds; and analysis of documents and handwriting.

4.5 The editor hoped that it would be clear from this evidence that Mulcaire was not employed by the newspaper in order to circumvent the provisions of the Code, but to carry out legitimate investigative work.

4.6 But Mulcaire had a second, clandestine relationship with the paper through Clive Goodman. This was described to the Commission as a "direct and personal" relationship, and involved cash payments amounting to £12,300 between November 2005 and August 2006, when the arrests took place.

4.7 Questions have been raised about how the newspaper could have allowed such payments to have been made, and whether anyone else at the newspaper was aware of Mulcaire and Goodman's illegal activities, which also breached the terms of the Code. The editor told the Commission that the paper has a standing policy on cash payments and transparency, something that was reiterated in a written memo to department heads and senior staff in 2005, and repeated at the start of 2006. Goodman was aware of this.

4.8 Despite this, the Commission was told that Goodman deceived his employers by disguising Mulcaire's identity and hiding the true origin of the information. Goodman claimed that the payments were for a confidential source on royal stories, identified only as "Alexander".

4.9 The Commission heard that "the identity of that source and the fact that the arrangement involved illegally accessing telephone voice mails was completely unknown and, indeed, deliberately concealed from all at the News of the World". The editor added in his submission that "it was made clear at the sentencing hearing that both the prosecution and the judge accepted that".

5.0 Action to prevent repetition

5.1 As to the Commission's questions about what would be done to avoid a repetition of the incident, the editor said that a number of steps were being taken.

5.2 With regard to external contributors, he had written to them to emphasise the absolute requirement that they abide by the Code and the law. The editor supplied the Commission with a sample copy of the letter that had been sent. In it, the editor set out to contributors that their contracts would now include "a clause robustly reflecting [the paper's] fundamental commitment to the letter and spirit of the Code".

5.3 The clause reads:
"The Contributor agrees that it is the Contributor's responsibility to review the Standards [the News Corporation Standards of Business], details of applicable rules, policies and procedures and the Code of Practice. The Contributor acknowledges that the Standards, such rules, policies and procedures and the Code of Practice may change or be updated from time to time and that these changes or updates will be notified to him or her by the Company from time to time. The Contributor agrees that, having been so notified by the Company, it is the Contributor's absolute responsibility to ensure that he or she is conversant with any such changes and updates and to observe them fully." The Contributor understands and accepts that failure to comply with the requirements of this clause may lead to termination of the contract".

5.4 With regard to staff journalists, the editor told the Commission that it had long been the practice of the paper "to make clear to staff the importance of fundamental observance of the Code, with emphasis on the fact that the use of third parties to circumvent the Code is unacceptable and may be illegal". The editor told the Commission that, in light of this, the Goodman case appeared to have been a "rogue exception".

5.5 The editor said that, following Goodman's conviction, he had e-mailed every member of staff individually, and written to them at home, with the Code of Practice. Staff had been informed of a new clause in their contracts, replacing a long-standing one which had said that "the employer endorses the Press Complaints Commission Code of Practice and requires the employee to observe the terms of the Code as a condition of his employment".

5.6 The new clause states:
"The employee agrees to comply in full with the News Corporation Standards of Business Conduct (the 'Standards') and all other applicable rules, policies and procedures of the Company and its Associated Companies including News Group Newspapers, and the Press Complaints Commission Code of Practice (the 'Code of Practice') which are included herewith and are available on the News International intranet and on the PCC website." The employee agrees that it is the employee's responsibility to review the Standards, details of applicable rules, policies and procedures and the Code of Practice. The employee acknowledges that the Standards, such rules, policies and procedures and the Code of Practice may change or be updated from time to time and further agrees that it is the employee's absolute responsibility to ensure that he or she is aware of any such changes or updates. The employer is responsible for notifying the employee of any such changes and/or updates. The employee agrees that having been notified by the employer it is the employee's absolute responsibility to ensure that he or she is conversant with any such changes and updates and undertakes to observe them fully. "The employee understands and accepts that failure to comply with the requirements of this clause will lead to Disciplinary Proceedings which may result in summary dismissal".

5.7 With regard to cash payments, the editor had written to all members of staff to reiterate the paper's clear policy on cash payments: "they are only permitted in exceptional circumstances. Every such payment requires a compelling justification and must be fully recorded".

5.8 In response to questions from the Commission about what further controls on cash payments were being developed, the editor said that the following protocol and policy was now in place:

- Cash payments are to be kept to a minimum and regarded as the exception;
- Requests for cash payments must be accompanied by a compelling and detailed justification signed off by the relevant department head;
- Information supplied on Cash Payment Request documents must be accurate and comprehensive;
- In the exceptional event of a requirement for a cash payment to a confidential source, the following would apply:
1. If the department head/staff member requesting the payment asserts that the identity of the source must be withheld, he/she is required to demonstrate clear and convincing justification for such confidentiality;
2. A memo detailing the reason for making the payment to a confidential source has to be provided to the Managing Editor's office.
- Every cash payment request must be signed off by the relevant Department Head;
- Details of the intended recipient's name and address are then verified via the electoral register/other checks to establish that they are genuine;
- Any journalist requesting a cash payment is required personally to endorse, with their signature, each page of the relevant documentation;
- Each request for a cash payment must be accompanied by the appropriate supporting documentation with a copy of the relevant story attached.

5.9 Turning then to the question of continuous professional training for his staff, the editor told the Commission that the paper had conducted a regular training programme in legal and PCC issues for some time. The latest series, starting on 20th February 2007, would focus on undercover journalism and its ethical and legal dimensions in light of the Goodman case; and highlight the requirements of the Regulation of Investigatory Powers Act, the Data Protection Act, the Computer Misuse Act and the PCC Code. For the first time, a representative of the PCC would attend and address each seminar. Attendance by staff would be mandatory.

6.0 The Commission's findings

6.1 The offences for which Goodman and Mulcaire were convicted were deplorable. Members of the Commission deprecated what had happened. The Commission has always made clear that subterfuge is justifiable only when there are grounds in the public interest for using it. Undercover investigative work has an honourable tradition and plays a vital role in exposing wrongdoing. It is part of an open society. But it risks being devalued if its use cannot be justified in the public interest.

6.2 In this case Mulcaire and Goodman paid a high price for their breach of the law (and in Goodman's case of the Code of Practice as well). They were sent to prison. Goodman, who had compliance with the Code written into his contract of employment, was dismissed from the News of the World. The editor left his post. The case attracted a large amount of negative publicity.

6.3 No evidence has emerged either from the legal proceedings or the Commission's questions to Mr Myler and Mr Hinton of a conspiracy at the news-paper going beyond Messrs Goodman and Mulcaire to subvert the law and the PCC's Code of Practice. There is no evidence to challenge Mr Myler's assertion that: Goodman had deceived his employer in order to obtain cash to pay Mulcaire; that he had concealed the identity of the source of information on royal stories; and that no-one else at the News of the World knew that Messrs Goodman and Mulcaire were tapping phone messages for stories.

6.4 However, internal controls at the newspaper were clearly inadequate for the purpose of identifying the deception.

6.5 It was therefore right for the new editor to introduce a series of measures aimed at preventing repetition. These included: a revised contractual relation-ship with external contributors and staff members, with a new and robust refer-ence to the Code, including a reminder that failure to comply with it could result in dismissal; a review of the policy on cash payments, and a reminder to staff about the current approach; and a renewed programme of mandatory training seminars aimed at raising awareness of the Code and the law. Commission offi-cials have now completed seven 2 1/2 hour seminars on undercover investiga-tions and the Code of Practice at the paper.

6.6 The Commission endorses this approach and welcomes the seriousness with which the editor and the company evidently take this matter. The review that the newspaper carried out has, in the Commission's view, thrown up examples of good practice—in particular in relation to the new reference in contracts to compliance with the Code of Practice, the new arrangements with external contributors, and the initiative of inviting Commission staff to help with the training seminars. The Commission also welcomed the tighter internal controls on cash payments.

6.7 The Commission's role here has been additional to the law, which has already investigated, prosecuted and punished the people responsible for the phone message tapping. The Commission has a duty to promote high professional standards and to hold editors responsible for the implementation of the Code on their publications by editorial staff and external contributors. It has ensured that the background to the episode, and the solutions that the newspaper proposed, would be ventilated publicly and be subject to scrutiny. Journalists and contributors to the newspaper can now be in no doubt of the serious consequences that will arise if there is any repeat of this highly regrettable incident.

7.0 Wider inquiry

7.1 The convictions of Mulcaire and Goodman raised questions about press practice in this area generally, and threatened to undermine confidence in journalism. The Commission believes that the public has a right to be reassured that this behaviour is not tolerated and that other publications have learned the lessons from what went on and have sufficient internal controls to prevent something similar happening elsewhere.

7.2 The Director of the Commission wrote to newspaper and magazine editors, with copies to their managements, to inquire about the extent of internal controls and what they did with regard to educating journalists about the requirements both of the Code and the law. The Data Protection Act was highlighted. The Commission wrote directly to national newspapers and to magazine companies. It was grateful to the Newspaper Society for disseminating the questions through the regional press.

7.3 The Commission received a large number of responses, which contained a varying degree of detail. Some simply told the Commission that they did not and would not engage in telephone message tapping. Others went into some detail about the various measures that were in place at their publications to ensure compliance with the Code and the law. Perhaps understandably, the Commission received greater detail from the national press than the regional press.

8.0 Current practice

8.1 There were a number of instances of good practice. Contractual compliance with the Code of Practice is widespread, with further references to the necessity to abide by its requirements to be found in staff handbooks, and in regular internal reminders to journalists—both written and during meetings with heads of departments. Many newspapers told the Commission that the Code of Practice was available on the company's intranet or that the editor wrote to journalists with copies when they joined the company or when the Code was updated.

8.2 Some publications also provided formal legal training for journalists or had updated their contracts with journalists to make explicit reference to the Data Protection Act.

8.3 There was a reference to the PCC's own series of training seminars for journalists which have, among other things, raised awareness of when the Commission considers subterfuge to be appropriate. Some publications had had, or planned, internal "master classes" on particular issues to achieve similar results and update journalists on the legal position.

8.4 One company had a "Review Group" of editors which reported to the Chief Executive on matters of editorial policy and which was responsible for raising awareness of the Code and the law among journalists across the company.

8.5 There was less specific feedback about the circumstances when subterfuge might be acceptable or how journalists would know when the public interest exceptions to the Data Protection Act might apply. There was an assumption that such occasions would be rare, and when it was referred to in the responses the Commission was told that journalists would be expected to consult with the publication's lawyers, editor or managing editor.

8.6 One newspaper told the Commission that, in addition to the internal controls that were in place, the threat of negative publicity along the lines of that experienced during the Goodman case would be a sufficient deterrent.

9.0 Data Protection Act

9.1 The Commission had specifically highlighted the DPA in its letter to the industry following the publication by the Information Commissioner of two reports titled *What price privacy?* and *What price privacy now?*

9.2 In those reports, the Information Commissioner published details of newspapers and magazines that had been paying inquiry agents for information. There was a suspicion that some of the information may have been obtained in breach of the Data Protection Act. The Information Commissioner called on the industry to bring forward proposals to clamp down on the illegal trade in information. He also called on the government to increase penalties for breaching the Act to two years' imprisonment. There would be no exemption from such a penalty for journalists.

9.3 The Commission condemns breaches of the DPA—or any law—when there are no grounds in the public interest for committing them. However, it has said before that it does not consider that the case for stronger penalties has been made out. Jailing—or threatening to jail—journalists for gathering information in the course of their professional duties is not a step to be taken lightly, and would send out a worrying message about the status of press freedom in the United Kingdom.

9.4 It seems to the Commission from the exercise it has just carried out that the DPA is taken seriously across the industry. As highlighted above, some companies have rewritten their journalists' contracts specifically to make reference to the DPA. Others had specific training on the Act. There were numerous references to the Information Commissioner's work.

9.5 The industry has also been working together to draw up a practical note for journalists on how the DPA works and applies to them.

10.0 Conclusions and recommendations

10.1 It is essential that the type of snooping revealed by the phone message tapping incidents at the News of the World is not repeated at any other newspaper or magazine. Such events threaten public confidence in the industry, despite the considerable change in culture and practice that has undoubtedly occurred over the last decade and a half, leading to greater accountability and respect by the press for the privacy of individuals.

10.2 But it is similarly important that the industry guards against overreaction. There is a legitimate place for the use of subterfuge when there are grounds in the public interest to use it and it is not possible to obtain information through other means. It would not be in the broader public interest for journalists to restrain themselves unnecessarily from using undercover means because of a false assumption that it is never acceptable.

10.3 This balance will be achieved when journalists are confident about where the line is drawn. The Commission welcomes the numerous initiatives that are under way to raise awareness of the Code's requirements on subterfuge and the law; and it endorses the decision by the industry to draw up guidelines on compliance with the Data Protection Act. These will complement those drawn up by the PCC itself in 2005.

10.4 The Commission believes very strongly that the impact of these initiatives should be assessed before the government proceeds with its proposals to increase the penalties for journalists who breach the DPA to two years in prison. Such a move would be difficult to reconcile with notions of press freedom. The mere threat of a custodial sentence could be enough to deter journalists from embarking on legitimate investigations, despite reassurances about the public interest exemption from the Information Commissioner.

10.5 As a result of this inquiry, the Commission has a number of specific recommendations, drawn from the News of the World episode and best practice around the UK. In particular:

- Contracts with external contributors should contain an explicit requirement to abide by the Code of Practice;
- A similar reference to the Data Protection Act should be included in contracts of employment;
- Publications should review internal practice to ensure that they have an effective and fully understood "subterfuge protocol" for staff journalists, which includes who should be consulted for advice about whether the public interest is sufficient to justify subterfuge;
- Although contractual compliance with the Code for staff journalists is widespread, it should without delay become universal across the industry (the PCC will be pursuing this further);
- There should be regular internal training and briefing on developments on privacy cases and compliance with the law;
- There should be rigorous audit controls for cash payments, where these are unavoidable.

10.6 The PCC recognises that it has a key role to play in assuring the high journalistic standards that are the cornerstone of a free press and a credible system of self-regulation. To that end, the Commission will continue to offer free training

seminars to UK publications. It will invite all national newspapers to attend a
seminar in July 2007 specifically on subterfuge and the public interest. It will continue its training courses for budding journalists around the UK. It will, increasingly, take part in and promote seminars and debates on the great issues
surrounding freedom of expression and journalists' responsibilities in a digital
age.

10.7 Finally, the industry, and the general public, should be in no doubt that the
Commission will continue to take the severest view of any publication which
uses inquiry agents to gather news in a manner that would otherwise breach the
Code.

CHAPTER 5
JOURNALISTS' SOURCES

The Press Complaints Commission Code of Practice is unambiguous. Journalists have a *moral* duty to protect their confidential sources.[1] So what is the legal position? Section 10 of the Contempt of Court Act 1981:

> "No court may require a person to disclose, nor is any person guilty of contempt of court for refusing to disclose, the source of information contained in a publication for which he is responsible, unless it is established to the satisfaction of the court that disclosure is necessary in the interests of justice or national security or for the prevention of disorder or crime."

The PCC Code acknowledges, albeit by implication, that no journalist is above the law. There is no absolute legal protection for journalists who have given a guarantee of confidentiality to a source. Yet the journalist who endeavours to adhere to his or her professional code of practice is set upon an immediate collision course with the courts should action be commenced to seek a disclosure order from the courts.

If journalists comply with court orders to disclose sources then their professional credibility will immediately disappear. How many sources are likely to provide information in return for a guarantee of confidentiality once it is known that the particular journalist cannot be relied upon to adhere to the commitment?

In discussing the legal interpretation of s.10, the reader should consider whether litigation in this area of law is really worth the effort, not to mention the cost. In July 2007, the House of Lords refused Mersey Care NHS Trust leave to appeal. This finally put an end to attempts to obtain the name of the person who revealed the Moors murderer, Ian Brady's medical records to a journalist who forwarded them to the Daily Mirror for publication. The litigation commenced in late 1999. Reference will be made to the *Interbrew* litigation that ended in 2002. On the face of it, Interbrew was successful in that it persuaded the High Court and Court of Appeal to order disclosure but in the end "threw in the towel" when the newspapers involved were contemplating taking the case, on a point of principle, to the European Court of Human Rights.

The European Court of Human Rights has been far from silent in supporting journalists in their endeavours to resist compliance with orders

---

[1] cl.14 of the Press Complaints Commission Code of Practice.

made under s.10. In the well-known case of *Goodwin v United Kingdom* [1996][2] the Court went on record to say:

"Protection of sources is one of the basic conditions for press freedom . . . without such protection, sources may be deterred from assisting the press in informing the public on matters of public interest. As a result the vital public watchdog role of the press may be undermined and the ability of the press to provide accurate and reliable information may be adversely affected. Having regard to the importance of the protection of journalistic sources for press freedom in a democratic society and the potentially chilling effect an order of source disclosure has on the exercise of that freedom, such a measure cannot be compatible with Article 10 of the Convention unless it is justified by an overriding requirement in the public interest."[3]

The case became something of a cause celebre in light of the fact that the European Court found that the order for Goodwin to release his notes of a telephone conversation with his source breached Art.10 of the European Convention on Human Rights. The report of the English decision is to be found at *X v Morgan Grampian* [1990].[4] A company had prepared a business plan based upon which it intended to apply for a substantial loan. A copy was stolen from its premises and details were then telephoned to a magazine. The journalist was William Goodwin and his contact with the firm to verify the story resulted in an application to the High Court for a disclosure order. The Claimant believed the identity of the source could probably be gleaned from the notes of the telephone conversation between the source and Goodwin. As a general principle, there is a public interest in preserving commercial confidentiality. It was accepted by the court that releasing this information into the public domain would be likely to cause severe damage to the company's business and may even result in job losses.

The House of Lords ordered the documents to be released. The reasons are are as follows:

1   The information had been obtained through unlawful means and there was clearly a breach of confidence. The publishers had "received" this information and wished to publish an article based upon it. In so doing, they were "mixed up in the tortuous acts of the source from the moment they received the confidential information."[5] Consequently the publishers were under a duty to assist the company in an attempt to redress the wrong perpetrated against it.[6] An injunction against the company prevented

[2] [1996] ECHR 16.
[3] ibid., para.39.
[4] [1990] 2 All E.R. 1.
[5] ibid., p.2.
[6] The dictum of Lord Reid in *Norwich Pharmacal Co v Customs & Excise Commissioners* [1973] 2 All ER. 943, at p.948 applied.

the dissemination of the story but that did not prevent a court from ordering discovery in such circumstances.

2   Having established the preliminary point the House then considered the matter in light of Section 10 of the 1981 Act. The House acknowledged that the protection of the identity of a source was a matter of "high necessity" and "nothing less than necessity would suffice to override it."[7]

The reference in s.10 to the interests of justice did not merely encompass the administration of justice through court proceedings but also in the broader sense of allowing people to exercise important legal rights. Equally, they should be able to protect themselves against serious legal wrongs. The House could find no legitimate public interest that the publication was "calculated to serve." In fact, just the opposite would be true as failure to obtain increased working capital might mean the closure of the company and in consequence significant unemployment. The appeals of the publisher and the journalist were dismissed.

What is interesting about the two judgments is that the principle of upholding press freedom through protecting sources was acknowledged by each court. The difference was in the conclusion. This suggests that everything will ultimately depend on the facts of each case. Judges are expected to engage in a "balancing exercise" starting with the assumption nothing less than necessity will override the protection offered to journalists by Parliament through the medium of s.10. So what factors will tip the balance one way or the other? Lord Bridge offered the following while at the same time emphasising that they did not amount to "comprehensive" guidance:

1   Does the claimant's livelihood depend upon disclosure?
2   Is the claimant seeking only to protect a "minor interest?"
3   The greater the public interest in the nature of the information the greater the need to protect the source.
4   How was the information obtained? If it was obtained legitimately then that will "enhance the importance of protecting the source."
5   If the information is obtained illegally this will "diminish the importance of protecting the source" unless there is a clear public interest in the information being revealed.[8]

The judicial approach would appear to be supportive of the right to protection of sources and lawyers may wonder why journalists such as Goodwin are prepared to risk fines and imprisonment for failing to comply with a court order. As Lord Bridge said:

"I have not heard of any campaign in the media suggesting that the law itself is unjust or that the exceptions to the protections are too

---

[7] ibid., p. 2 (j).
[8] ibid., pp. 9(h)–10(b), *per* Lord Bridge.

widely drawn. But if there were such a campaign, it should be fought in a democratic society by persuasion, not by disobedience to the law ... The journalist cannot be left to be a judge in his own cause and decide whether or not to make disclosure. This would be an abdication of the role of Parliament and the courts in the matter and in practice would be tantamount to conferring an absolute privilege."[9]

There we have the nub of the problem. However reasonable that interpretation may be as a vindication of parliamentary supremacy and the rule of law, individual journalists are most unlikely ever to comply with a disclosure order. The critical period for the journalist is when it is being decided whether to offer a guarantee to the source. If the journalist has doubts about the veracity of the source or the quality of the information or whether the source is seeking to manipulate the journalist then a guarantee should *not* be given. Only when satisfied that the source and the information to be imparted are credible should a commitment to anonymity be given. Once that is done the journalist is on a road of no return.

The legal position in this country is no different to other democratic nations. For example in the recent Australian case of *Harvey v County Court of Victoria* [2006],[10] Hollingworth J. said:

"Although the journalists' code of ethics may preclude them from naming a source, that code has no legal status. The law does not currently recognise any "journalists' privilege." If a journalist chooses not to reveal a source and thereby to commit an act of contempt that is a matter of personal choice."[11]

The fact that a journalist is unlikely to divulge the identity of a source is not a factor that the court should take into account in carrying out the balancing exercise. To do so would mean only one conclusion and that is that self-determination would be invoked on each and every occasion. Citizens cannot select which laws are to apply to them without being aware of the legal consequences of such actions. There is no reason why journalists should not be given greater protection in the form of a genuine public interest defence akin to that of *Reynolds/Jameel* defence in respect of the law on defamation. In Australia, the Commonwealth Attorney General is considering instituting a new "confidential relationship privilege" where journalists receive information that may be of evidential value in a court case. In practice, this would mean that the courts would have to balance the likely harm to the source if the evidence is adduced against the probative value to the case in question and presumably achieving justice in the particular case. Even if this were to be introduced it would be simply another form of balancing exercise of the

[9] ibid., p.13(c), *per* Lord Bridge.
[10] [2006] V.S.C.293.
[11] ibid., at para.90.

type currently carried out by the UK courts. Journalists would not be above the law.

Claimants when considering legal action for disclosure must take detailed legal advice on the prospects of achieving their objectives. Such proceedings are invariably going to be defended. The time spent, effort expended and the costs accumulated are likely to weigh heavily when making that assessment.

Let us now consider the two pieces of litigation referred to above whilst bearing in mind the question "What has been achieved? Does it justify the time and cost of such litigation?

Ashworth Security Hospital Authority v MGN Ltd [2002][12]

This litigation commenced in January 2000. Ian Brady, was, and still, is incarcerated in a secure mental hospital in the North West of England. His notoriety stemmed from the "Moors Murders" that he and Myra Hindley committed in the mid 1960s. Hindley died in 2002. Details of his medical records from Ashworth High Security Hospital were published by the Daily Mirror. The hospital responded by publishing a statement to the effect that the Mirror's story was a flagrant breach of patient confidentiality. The question for the authorities at Ashworth was: Who was responsible from the leak of Brady's medical records?

It proved to be, as the Court of Appeal said in early 2007 ". . . a most unusual case."[13] The hospital was successful in obtaining a disclosure order from the trial judge in April 2000. Subsequently, MGN appealed and the Court of Appeal and then the House of Lords dismissed the newspaper's appeals. These two courts, unlike the High Court, took into account that the Human Rights Act had come into force. In coming to their decisions, the courts adopted the established view that s.10 of the 1981 Act and Art.10 of the Convention had a "common purpose" in seeking to enhance "the freedom of the press by protecting journalistic sources." Lord Woolf said in the House of Lords:

"The important protections which both section 10 and article 10 provide for freedom of expression is that they require the court stringently to scrutinise any request for relief which will result in the court interfering with freedom of expression including ordering the disclosure of journalists' sources. Both section 10 and article 10 are one in making it clear that the court has to be sure that a sufficiently strong positive case has been made out in favour of disclosure before disclosure will be ordered."[14]

---

[12] [2002] UKHL 29.
[13] [2007] EWCA Civ 101, at para.1.
[14] [2002] UKHL 29, at para.49, *per* Lord Woolf.

The consequence of applying Art.10 said Lord Woolf was that any disclosure order had to be not only *necessary* but also proportionate to achieving the aim in question, i.e. which of the two public interest arguments should prevail. The "necessity for any restriction of freedom of expression must be convincingly established." Adopting the terminology of Art.10, the jurisdiction should only be exercised if there was a "pressing social need" and that any restriction upon freedom of expression should be *proportionate* to the "legitimate aim being pursued."[15]

In summing up the "new" post-Human Rights Act approach one can do no better than quote from Lord Justice Laws' judgment in *Ashworth v MGN* in the Court of Appeal. He said:

"... in any given case the debate which follows will be conducted upon the question whether there is an overriding public interest, amounting to a pressing social need, to which the need to keep press sources confidential should give way. That debate will arise under section 10 in the municipal legislation; it will arise more broadly by reference to article 10 of the Convention, and in the light of the Strasburg jurisprudence on article 10."[16]

However, there was a "curious feature" to this series of cases. Mirror Group Newspapers was not aware of the identity of the principal source of the information. The medical information had been passed to a local journalist Robin Ackroyd who in turn passed the information to the Daily Mirror. It appears that no one ever thought to ask over the two years of litigation whether MGN knew the name of the original source. As the Court of Appeal said in its most recent judgment, *"That Rougier J, this court and the House of Lords should consider the matter on the basis of a false assumption is disturbing."*[17] Some might argue that it was more than just disturbing; it was an utter waste of time and money.

Mersey Care NHS Trust had by then assumed managerial responsibility for Ashworth. It had a decision to take. To continue the quest for a name through embarking upon further litigation or to throw in the towel. After all there had been no further leaks of information from the hospital and the number of staff having access to the medical records had been dramatically reduced. Unsurprisingly Ackroyd refused the hospital's request to reveal the source of his information. Proceedings were then issued against him. Gray J. granted summary judgment to the Trust based upon the decision of the House of Lords in the Trust's favour. Ackroyd appealed that decision and the court accepted that there were potentially important differences between the *MGN* issues and the issues in this case. There should be a trial.

---

[15] ibid., at paras61–62.
[16] [2000] EWCA 334, at para.101.
[17] [2007] EWCA Civ 101, at para.87.

That trial commenced in January 2006 and judgment was lodged in Ackroyd's favour in February 2006.[18] In his judgment, Mr Justice Tugendhat acknowledged the importance of European jurisprudence and not only in the context of Art.10. Confidential medical records fall within the ambit and protection of Art.8 of the Convention as determined by Lord Woolf in the House of Lords. Personal data including medical information was deemed "of fundamental importance to a person's enjoyment of his or her right to respect for private and family life as guaranteed by article 8 of the Convention."[19]

None of this should come as a surprise. Many employees will find in that their contracts contain a clause against revealing sensitive or confidential information. That was certainly the case at Ashworth.

The judge went on to consider the approach to resolving conflicting rights based upon the well-known speech of Lord Steyn in *Re S (A child) (Identification: Restrictions on Publication)* [2004].[20] He identified four important points of principle:

1 Neither article had precedence over the other.
2 There must be a detailed examination of the "comparative importance of the specific rights being claimed."
3 Judges should identify the reasons for interfering with or restricting each right.
4 The ultimate balancing test was determined by reference to proportionality.

In reaching his decision not to order disclosure the judge first considered the value of freedom of expression. The court acknowledged that not all types of speech have equal value. The public interest elements must then be considered. Was it in the public interest to disclose Brady's medical records? Certainly one can envisage occasions when it may be in the public interest to divulge some or all of a person's medical history although that must be kept within very narrow limits and therefore would be a rare occurrence. *X v Y* [1988][21] concluded that the public interest in preserving confidentiality of hospital records identifying Aids victims "outweighed the public interest in the freedom of the press to publish such information." The reasoning was that such publicity would act as a potential deterrent to those with the disease from seeking appropriate medical treatment.[22] However, in this case, the court refused to order disclosure of a source who had provided the newspaper with information about two doctors who were alleged to be suffering from Aids.

A court has then to consider whether there has been "wrongdoing" by the source, his duty towards this employer and whether there was

---

[18] [2006] EWHC 107 (QB).
[19] [2002] UKHL 29, at para.95, *per* Lord Woolf.
[20] [2004] UKHL 47.
[21] [1988] 2 All E.R. 648.
[22] ibid., at p.648 (h).

justification in doing what he did. There had been a number of concerns about the way the security hospital was being managed. Serious allegations had surfaced giving real cause for concern. Brady, for instance, had been on hunger strike for a month over plans to move him from one ward to another and other issues connected with his personal safety. Ackroyd had taken a particular journalistic interest in the issue and, given the number of dangerous patients incarcerated, it was clearly a public interest matter to know what was going on inside the hospital.

The judge went on to find that the source was probably someone working at the hospital but he could not determine from the evidence available whether the person was actually employed at the hospital. As such, the judge found that the source, irrespective of whether he or she was employed there, owed a duty of confidentiality to both Brady and the hospital.

Was there a justification for the disclosure? It was accepted that the source did not receive payment for the information that was provided. Ian Brady may well have encouraged the leak because he was in dispute with the hospital authorities and possibly felt this would draw the public's attention to his grievances. No harm may have accrued to Brady, but a wrong had been perpetrated against the hospital because of the breach of confidence.

The next question to consider was whether there was a public interest defence available to the source. Brady had claimed to have been assaulted and mistreated by nurses. That was a matter of general public interest that warranted investigation. However, the judge found that on the balance of probabilities there was no public interest justification for revealing Brady's medical records. The information contained in the records would be of little value when investigating the wider claims of mistreatment and mismanagement at the hospital. A wrong therefore had been perpetrated against the hospital for which there was no public interest defence. The "threshold" test for disclosure based upon the *Norwich Pharmacal* case (see footnote 6) had been passed.

Having taken the above matters into account the judge decided there was no pressing social need to make a disclosure order. This was clearly at odds with the decision in the *MGN* case but that was justified on the basis that the facts were somewhat different from those in the previous case. The judgment appears to be entirely pragmatic and all the better for it. Six years had passed since the records were released to Ackroyd. If the Health Authority were to discover who was the source, what action could it take? The first huge assumption is that the source was still employed by the hospital. In fact, he may never have been an employee. The court was told that over 50 per cent of the hospital employees had left since 1999. The individual could be dead. In either situation, the health authority would have no remedy against the individual.

The court accepted that the numbers having access to medical records had been substantially reduced. If a leak were to occur today then it would be much easier to identify potential culprits. There had been no further leaks from the hospital in the intervening period.

Thus taking into account the *proportionality* argument for interfering with the concept of freedom of expression, it was clear that the hospital had little to gain from discovering the source of the leak. Even if the person were still an employee, all that the Authority could do would be to discipline the person or dismiss him. All other effective remedies to ensure the confidentiality of medical records had been instigated without the identity of the source being known. Practical and effective remedies to prevent breaches of confidence can be put in place without the necessity of costly litigation. Perhaps the best example of that is the advice given by the Court of Appeal in the case of *John v Express Newspapers* [2000].[23]

Draft documents had been taken from a barrister's chambers. It was assumed someone working for outside cleaning contractors had removed the documents relating to the financial affairs of Sir Elton John. The information found its way to Express Newspapers. Legal action was instigated in an attempt to discover the source of the leaked information. The High Court made a disclosure order on the basis that support needed to be given to ensure that the lawyer/client relationship remained as confidential as possible. The Court of Appeal saw this as an over reaction. The most efficacious way of ensuring confidentiality in such circumstances, thought the Master of the Rolls, was to invest in a shredding machine and to make staff more security conscious rather than engaging in expensive litigation! By that simple expedient, the right to freedom of expression need not be challenged.

The court spoke of the devastating consequences to their careers that can be suffered by journalists who get involved in such litigation. After the Court of Appeal's decision in 2007 confirming the High Court Robin Ackroyd "confessed" that the past decade had not been the most auspicious in his life. His career was essentially placed on hold as the litigation continued to roll.

The Court, and subsequently the Court of Appeal, emphasised that nothing in the judgments should be taken "as providing any encouragement to those who would disclose medical records."[24] All the judges associated themselves with the remarks of the House of Lords in the *MGN* case.

The judge also paid tribute to Robin Ackroyd concluding that he was "a responsible journalist whose purpose was to act in the public interest." It should however be noted that whether the actions taken by a journalist are deemed legally to be in the public interest will be determined *objectively* not *subjectively*.

It is respectfully submitted that the approach of the courts in *Ackroyd* has been the correct one. There has to be a realistic possibility at the outset of litigation that the objective is attainable. The objective surely is not simply to obtain a court order but to obtain a court order safe in the knowledge that there will be compliance with the order. The initial

---

[23] [2000] EWCA Civ 135.
[24] [2006] EWHC 107, at para.196 and [2007] EWCA Civ 101 at para.86.

litigation could *never* have led to the naming of the source. The Court of Appeal said in 2007 that it is:

> ". . . almost inconceivable that this court or the House of Lords would have given permission to appeal the decision of Rougier J. had it been appreciated that far from disclosing the ultimate source, all that would be disclosed was the journalist who provided the story and who would have had his own right to maintain the confidence of his source . . ."[25]

The Court of Appeal also referred to the:

> ". . . enormous amount of money and, perhaps more significantly, energy on the part of the hospital (that) would have been saved and better directed to other activities."[26]

How might the problem be solved in the future? The Court of Appeal offered two solutions:

1. That the "underlying principles are now reasonably clear, so it should not be necessary for cases of this kind to come to this court or go to the House of Lords in the future. It should be possible for any dispute to be resolved by the judge carrying out the balancing exercise."

2. To ask the editor to confirm that the source of an article or programme is not a journalist "whose own article 10 and section 10 rights would fall to be considered if his or her identity were disclosed." If the editor failed to disclose that information then there should be request for summary disposal of the application.

Disputes of this sort should be "resolved as soon as possible after the relevant incident has occurred." Having said all that it still does not answer the question of whether it is even remotely possible that a journalist will comply with a court order. That of course is not a matter for a court but for "individual" conscience, but what we are dealing with here is a "collective" conscience as hinted at by cl.14 of the PCC Code. In other words the outcome will be known in advance.

Financial Times v Interbrew SA [2002][27]

Interbrew SA, the largest brewing group in Europe, was considering making a bid for South African Breweries. It was receiving confidential advice from its merchant bankers. The Financial Times and a number of other prestigious newspapers received copies of a leaked and (as it turned out) partially forged document containing details of the contemplated

---

[25] [2007] EWCA Civ 101, at para.88.
[26] ibid., para.88.
[27] [2002] EWCA Civ 274.

takeover. The newspapers ran with the story causing an immediate negative impact on Interbrew's share price. Interbrew commenced litigation against the newspapers seeking a disclosure order in an attempt to identify the source of the "leak" from the document they each had received.

The issue was succinctly described by the High Court in these terms:

"The essential issue on this application is whether the Claimant's interest in obtaining the Documents and its (and I would add the public) interest in identifying the Source is sufficiently compelling to override the defendant's and the public interest in protecting the media's sources of information."[28]

The major discursive points can be summarised as follows:

- Has crime been committed? Was the document stolen?
- Has a civil wrong been perpetrated against the company?
- Has there been a breach of confidence?
- Is the entitlement to disclosure blocked by s.10 of the Contempt of Court Act?
- If the "shield" of s.10 is to be removed then the "interests of justice" ground would appear to be the most appropriate. This could include the right to bring legal action against the miscreant, the detection of crime and the exercise of any civil rights the company has against the source.
- In determining whether disclosure is *necessary* there is a ". . . close regard to be had to the relationship between the mischief and the measure. If the mischief is a civil wrong, the measure which needs to be justified as relevant and proportionate is one which will right the wrong."
- The source's motive and purpose in revealing the information.
- Is the court exercising discretion when considering s.10? The Court of Appeal was emphatic in answering that in the negative. It was said Lord Justice Sedley ". . . a matter of hard-edged judgment, albeit one of both fact and law, and one the less so for having to respect the principles of proportionality."[29]

The Court of Appeal concluded "though not without misgiving" that the order for disclosure should stand. Such evidence as the newspapers held could be vital in identifying the source and permitting the company to bring an action for breach of confidence against the source. The court thought that the right to free expression is not negated, only limited, on prescribed grounds and in a particular situation.

---

[28] *Interbrew SA v Financial Times* [2001] EWHC (Chan) 480, at para.4.
[29] *Financial Times v Interbrew SA* [2002] EWCA Civ 274, at para.45.

"Whether production is then a proportionate response is a value
judgement which further analysis cannot assist. It requires a synthe-
sis of what has been established as legally relevant in fact and law."[30]

A determining factor seemed to be the source's evident purpose
described by the judge as ". . . a maleficent one calculated to do
harm . . ."Sedley L.J. went on:

"The public interest in protecting the source of such a leak is in my
judgment not sufficient to withstand the countervailing public interest in letting Interbrew seek justice in the courts against the source."[31]

So, armed with victories in the High Court and Court of Appeal, one
would assume Interbrew would have made sure the story ended there
and the documents were handed over. The assumption may have been
correct; the reality though was somewhat different.

In July 2002, the editors of the four newspapers and the head of
Reuters news agency refused to comply with the court order claiming
that there were fundamental issues of press freedom at stake. The five
organisations were refused leave to appeal by the House of Lords against
the Court of Appeal judgment. There was an indication that, with no
further legal avenue open to the five, they would be prepared to take an
action to the European Court of Human Rights in Strasbourg.

Of major concern was the relationship between financial journalists
and their sources. A key role of the press is to bring to the public's attention any hint of corporate fraud or wrongdoing. This task would be made
all the harder as a result of this decision because potential whistleblowers would think twice about revealing information unless there was an
absolute guarantee against disclosure. In the light of Enron, the biggest
scandal in US corporate history in December 2001, one can easily understand the position adopted by the organisations in response to the
Interbrew decision. The stakes were raised when Interbrew applied to the
High Court for an order to seize the Guardian's assets on the basis that
the newspaper was in contempt for failing to comply with the court
order. Fortunately, reason prevailed and Interbrew handed the whole
matter over to the Financial Services Authority to carry out an investigation. The FSA has search and seizure powers, yet a nine-month investigation came to nothing. In September 2003, the FSA terminated the
investigation. At the time of writing the matter has not been taken before
the European Court of Human Rights. The source has not been revealed.

In February 2004, Lord Saville, the chairman of the Bloody Sunday
inquiry in Northern Ireland, confirmed that he was not to take contempt
proceedings against three journalists who had refused to reveal the
names of their sources to the inquiry. The threat of legal action had been
hanging over them for 18 months. Lord Saville concluded that, even if he

---

[30] ibid., para.53.
[31] ibid., para.55.

knew the names, it would not result in the inquiry gaining any information that it didn't already possess.

So the first decade of the millennium has been a reasonably good one for the media. We are hopefully unlikely ever to see again a litigation saga to parallel the *Ashworth* case. The legal principles we are told by the Court of Appeal are reasonably clear. The courts in *Ackroyd* have taken a pragmatic approach that doesn't challenge the right of free expression.

The test for the future though is likely to occur when the claimant is the government and the ground relied upon is national security. It is hoped that the reasoning adopted by the House of Lords in *Secretary of State for Defence v Guardian Newspapers* [1984][32] will be consigned to the dustbin of history and civil servant whistleblowers will feel they can reveal information, of clear public interest to the media, without threat of exposure.

1. Access to Journalistic Material

In the normal course of business, media organisations accumulate a tremendous amount of material. It may be that the media is invited to assist the police and, as part of an investigation, there may be potentially helpful material held by a newspaper or broadcasting organisation. In many situations, the media will take on the role of "good citizen" and hand over material to the police for analysis. However, a media organisation that *appears* to be working too closely with the authorities may well lose its credibility and to some extent its objectivity. If handing material to the police becomes a regular occurrence then reporters and particularly photographers may be at risk when covering stories. That in turn may have a potentially negative effect on the free flow of information and the withdrawal of co-operation from sources.

We again find that a balancing act is required between two competing public interest issues. The first, in helping the police with their inquiries, and the second, freedom of expression.

That fact was recognised by Parliament in the Police and Criminal Evidence Act 1984. As Bingham L.J. said in *R. v Crown Court at Lewes, Ex Parte Hill* (1991)[33]:

"The Police and Criminal Evidence Act governs a field in which there are two very obvious public interests. There is, first of all, a public interest in the effective investigation and prosecution of crime. Secondly, there is the public interest in protecting the personal and property rights of citizens against infringement and invasion. There

---

[32] [1984] 3 All E.R. 601. The Guardian complied with a disclosure order and the source Sarah Tisdall was prosecuted under the Official Secrets Act and sentenced to six months' imprisonment.

[33] (1991) 93 Crim. App. R. 60 at pp.65–66.

is an obvious tension between these two public interests because crime could be more effectively investigated and prosecuted if the personal and property rights of citizens could be freely overridden and total protection of the personal and property rights of citizens would make the investigation and prosecution of crime impossible or virtually so."

Police intent upon obtaining a production order will have to satisfy the relevant provisions of the Police and Criminal Evidence Act. Material held by media organisations falls into one of two categories—Excluded Material or Special Procedure Material. The former is journalistic material that a person holds in confidence. For these purposes "confidence" is defined as:

"a. [Holding material] . . . subject to an express or implied undertaking to hold it in confidence or subject to restriction on disclosure or an obligation of secrecy contained in any Act or Parliament, and

b. it has been continuously held subject to such an undertaking, restriction or obligation since it was first acquired or created for the purposes of journalism."

This means all journalistic material that does not comply with the above definition becomes subject to the special procedure. This material can be accessed by the police but only after convincing a circuit judge that the relevant provisions of the Act have been fulfilled. As Lord Justice Maurice Kay put it in *R. v Bright, Alton and Rusbridger* [2000][34]:

"Journalistic material was either special procedure material or excluded material and, in either case, was beyond the reach of the police under the general provisions relating to search warrants to search and enter premises."

The legislation refers to the "access" provisions that have to be satisfied. A judge has to be convinced that a serious arrestable offence has been committed and if so the following criteria proved:

• The journalistic material is likely to have substantial value to the investigation.
• That the material is likely to constitute relevant evidence at any subsequent trial.
• That other methods of obtaining the "evidence" have been tried without success or that the police have not even tried to because there was no realistic prospect of success.
• It is in the public interest that the material should be handed over.

[34] [2001] 1 W.L.R. 662.

The legislation may be perceived as supporting the concept of freedom of expression and the approach adopted by Parliament is consistent with Art.10(2) of the European Convention on Human Rights.

The *public interest* in respect of special procedure material was identified in *R v Bristol Crown Court Ex p. Bristol Press and Picture Agency Ltd* (1987)[35] as :

"... The balancing exercise which has to be carried out is between the public interest in the investigation and the prevention of crime and the public interest in the press being able to report and to photograph as much as they can of what is going on in our great cities . . . there is also public interest in the press being able to go about that activity in safety."

The Home Office announced in March 2007 that it was to undertake a review of police powers including the procedures relating to search and seizure of journalistic material. The government wishes to examine:

"whether the special provisions to access under sections 9-14 of the Police and Criminal Evidence Act 1984 require updating to meet the 21st century challenges in tackling crime."

2. Official Secrets

The Official Secrets Act 1989 is of importance to the media as potential sources of public interest information will be bound by its provisions. This legislation makes it an offence for those working for the Crown to reveal information relating to national security, defence, international relations and criminal investigations. Therefore, journalists utilising such information will find they are committing a criminal offence under the terms of s.5 of the Act.

However, not all is lost, because the legislation provides a comprehensive defence for the media in such circumstances. The defence centres on the word "damaging." In relation to "sensitive" information identified in ss.1–3 of the Act[36] an offence is committed only if:

a   the disclosure by him is damaging; and
b   he makes it knowing, or having reasonable cause to believe, that it would be damaging.

To date no journalist had been prosecuted so the courts have not had the opportunity to determine the legal meaning of the word damaging.

---

[35] (1987) 85 Cr. App. R. 190.
[36] Security and intelligence (s.1); defence (s.2); international relations (s.3).

For the offence to be established it appears that the prosecution will have to establish a causal connection between the release of the information into the public domain and a particular consequence such as an attack on our armed forces or military buildings. Even then a jury may acquit on the basis that the journalist did not know or have reasonable cause to believe that it would be damaging.

We saw earlier in this chapter that the government may seek to recover names, information or documentation that helps to identify "whistle-blowers" inside government.[37] The consequence was that Sarah Tisdall, a clerk at the Ministry of Defence, received a six months prison sentence for breaching the Act. The policy seems to be to "go after" the person leaking rather than the journalist who is exercising his or her Art.10 rights and publishing the information.

The government's enthusiasm for prosecutions remains undiminished. In May 2007, David Keogh, a Whitehall communications officer, was jailed for six months after disclosing a "highly sensitive" document which detailed discussion between George Bush and Tony Blair at the White House in 2004. The document was sent to Leo O'Connor a researcher for a Member of Parliament. O'Connor was sentenced to three months in prison. Mr Justice Atkins acknowledged that the disclosure had not resulted in any actual damage.

Nevertheless the judge was of the opinion that his action in releasing the document "could have cost the lives of British citizens." It was, said the judge, a gross breach of trust. In this case journalists were not involved in receiving the information. It had been Keogh's intention that the information be disclosed in Parliament. Would a journalist have been guilty of an offence under the 1989 Act if he had published the information? In light of the judge's comments that no actual damage was done then it is difficult to see how an offence would have been committed by a journalist.

This does not mean that journalists should be complacent. Also in May 2007, a member of the Metropolitan Police's Specialist Operations unit was charged with breaching the Official Secrets Act and misconduct in office for allegedly disclosing secret documents to a Sunday Times reporter knowing that the information would be published. He was remanded in custody for trial at the Old Bailey later in the year. Once again it would appear that the policy is not to charge journalists with involvement in breaching the Act but to target crown servants in an attempt to deter them from speaking to the media.

3. Legislation

It is not the purpose of this chapter to engage in a polemic about the growing number of statutes that increase the powers of the authorities

---

[37] *Secretary of State for Defence v Guardian Newspapers* [1984].

to access information and to engage in covert surveillance. Attention should be paid to the Police Act 1997, the Regulation of Investigatory Powers Act 2000 and the Terrorism Acts of 2000 and 2006. The terrorism legislation places obligations upon all citizens to reveal information about terrorist-related activity including money laundering. There are no statutory exceptions for journalists. This may cause members of the media real difficulties if they acquire such information as a result of their investigations. The Terrorism Act 2000 is clear. The legal obligation is to reveal the information to the police . . . not publish it.

4. Sources in Practice

S.10 Contempt of Court Act 1981 in practice

This classic clause appears to protect journalists but the exemptions pretty much cancel out that protection in practice. Journalists can be made to give up their source in *the interests of justice, national security or for the prevention of disorder or crime*. The protection is likely to disappear if the name is wanted by the courts, the government or the police, and that embraces most of the agents who are going to demand a source be revealed.

The contentious confidential sources themselves are likely to be accused of committing a crime such as breach of the Official Secrets Act or the Data Protection Act so it would be simple to argue an exemption.

Given that the interest of justice can also encompass the exercising of rights by others to claim, for example, breach of confidence, there would appear to be few s.10 situations where the exemptions would not apply.

Effectively the only way to protect a source is to be prepared to be held in contempt and accept the penalty, including a jail term if need be. Every time a journalist agrees to protect a source that is the deal being entered into. This needs to be appreciated by every working journalist so the implications of this in practice will be examined later.

The courts are uncomfortable with a stance that effectively means journalists will uphold their right to protect a source, even in defiance of the law. In other respects, journalists and news organisations will fight their corner but ultimately fall in line with a judgment, such as an injunction. So the courts' disquiet is understandable, but journalists have no choice. A journalist who doesn't protect a source will not be a journalist for long. Some things are worth going to jail for.

But first we need to consider whether the Human Rights Act has strengthened the position of journalists in this regard. The ECHR comment in *Goodwin* is encouraging and the judgments in the *Ashworth* and *Ackroyd* litigation would suggest this to be time.

Ashworth Security Hospital Authority v MGN Ltd [2002]

In terms of the s.10 exemptions, it is important to appreciate that, although the action was billed as protecting patient confidentiality, the hospital was acting to protect the confidentiality of its own procedures. The issue at stake was not the protection of Brady's privacy. The medical records were wanted to corroborate Brady's own claims of poor treatment. The wrong weighed against Art.10 rights was the wrong done to the hospital, not to Brady, who claimed to have been assaulted and mistreated by nurses. He went on hunger strike and is being force fed.

The judges accepted there was a public interest in investigating the claims but argued that Brady's medical records would be of little value in investigating the allegations. To a journalist, this seems perverse given the nature of the allegations Brady was making. Investigation was most certainly called for and corroboration was needed. Brady and the other patients deserve fair treatment whatever their crimes but Brady's background clearly detracts from his value as a credible single source.

So, in journalistic terms, the judgment is not particularly sympathetic. There was no public interest defence to justify the wrong to the hospital. A disclosure order was not made because it would not have helped the hospital put right the wrong.

This mirrors other key 21st century cases which have hinged on the extent of detail required, or deemed reasonable, to be included by a journalist to corroborate a story for the audience. Judges vary enormously in their approach to this. It is established that there should be discretion for editorial judgment of the news organisation that has obviously come to its own view on proportionality in deciding what to run. Where that involves, say, private material or breach of confidence, the assessment of proportionality is effectively assumed by the judge.

Lord Hoffmann has been one of the more understanding by both allowing editors some leeway to make a different decision from a judge, but also by appreciating that extra evidence, such as confidential material, extra details or a photograph, can be needed to make a story convincing. The broader package is a mark of a job well done and usually demonstrates responsible, rather than prurient, journalism. However, even with the more liberal judges, journalists have to find a more convincing way of making that distinction. This appears to be easier for a journalist from the Wall Street Journal than from the News of the World.

One of the most helpful principles for the journalist who steadfastly maintains a right to protect a confidential source is the *Spycatcher*-derived axiom that *a futile measure cannot be a necessary one*. In the other classic case of *Interbrew*, despite the judgment against the media, the source was not revealed. In *Ashworth*, the fact that the case dragged on for so long helped too. But still the introduction of effectiveness into the proportionality issues is useful when asking the question: What would be gained by ordering a journalist to sacrifice a confidential source? If the answer is not a lot, there is some hope.

The effectiveness approach chimes with journalists too to the extent that it encourages organisations subject to breaches of confidentiality to focus on improving their management procedures rather than pursuing the person who exploited the gaps in them.

Taking that logic one step further, maybe such organisations could also make it a priority to investigate the allegations which were the catalyst for the leak in the first place and ask itself some tough questions about why someone felt obliged to leak them.

The framework of the debate in the *Ashworth* judgment seems different too. In privacy cases, for example, the weighing process is debated mainly in terms of Art.8 rights and whether there is sufficient public interest under 8(2) to impinge upon them. Art.10 rights are included in the equation but receive less explicit attention.

In *Ashworth*, under s.10, because the judges have to justify any disclosure order, the Art.10 rights are to the fore and the language of 10(2) is brought into play concerning the existence of a pressing social need to override them. This different perspective certainly means the judgment reads as if Art.10 rights loom large, which many judgments do not.

Lord Saville took a similar line over sources relevant to the Bloody Sunday inquiry which is encouraging but the experience of *Interbrew* and some of the reasoning in *Ashworth* demonstrate that judges are adamant that journalists are not off the hook.

The question of a "confidential relationship" privilege is interesting in that it might provide a basis for lending more weight to protection of the relationship but the weighing will always be conducted by judges and journalists will always have to fight hard to demonstrate that the right is worth protecting.

A further thorny question is where this leaves the news organisation as opposed to the individual journalist. The sanction against an individual journalist is likely to be jail; the sanction against a publisher for contempt is seizure of assets. So although individual journalists see it as a moral duty to protect a source come what may, the companies tend ultimately to cave in as they did in the first round of *Ashworth*. Their shareholders may take a dim view of them defying the court; would be very likely to object to the seizure of assets, and demand capitulation.

Using the effectiveness argument and the debacle in *Ashworth*, it could be safest if the company simply does not know the source. There are difficulties here in practice to be discussed later but this would seem to be the rational response to the judgments.

5. Confidential Sources Checklist

The most useful lesson a journalist can learn from this chapter is not to enter into a confidentiality agreement lightly because the ramifications can be enormous for reporter and employer. This is a very damning area in which to be found wanting. The 21st century judgments analysed reinforce some fundamentals of good journalistic practice but they also generate some new advice for those wanting to pursue effective investigations which may involve dealing with confidential sources.

Exercise extreme caution before giving any undertaking to protect the identity of a source. Once an assurance is given it has to be honoured and this may become more uncomfortable and costly than it first appears. The information has to be worth risking a career for and going to jail for. As in other cases, know the legal ramifications of any journalistic activity and enter into it with eyes open.

Define your terms. As soon as a source even hints at a degree of confidentiality, be very explicit about what exactly each of you is committing to and establish the ground rules at the beginning of an interview even where nothing momentous seems to be at stake.

What is meant by "off the record", "in confidence" or "don't quote me"? Even journalists don't agree on what these terms mean so it is very easy to get at cross-purposes with sources. The definitions have to be spelt out with each source.

There is a fascinating section on sources in the *Jameel* judgment beginning at para.59 particularly the account of exchanges between the Wall Street Journal and the US Treasury which at face value makes no sense but which reflects an established "code" operated by journalists and officials to negotiate this awkward territory of deniability. Clarity is the aim and lack of it can lead to the downfall of journalist and source.

Assess the source.

- Are they who they say they are? Have a telephone number at least and establish that it works. A bricks and mortar address is better.
- What are their motives? It will be very difficult to defend your actions or theirs if the motive is money. Do not pay for their information if you want to rely on it in court. They could also be motivated by revenge against say a company that has sacked them which would also call their credibility into question.
- Are they in a position to know what they claim to know?
- Has what they say happened, happened? Those infamous kiss and tell tales involve questioning which pulls no punches about whether two people have really had sex or not.
- Why do they need to be anonymous? Is their caution necessary?
- Would it be obvious the information had come from them?

Critique the information.

- What is the public interest in revealing the information they have? Apply your own "proportionality" test. Does it have public interest value in legal terms as well as being a story that will make you look good? Is that public interest sufficient to risk all.

- What other ways might there be of accessing it? Sometimes information that appears to be confidential is actually available openly if a journalist knows where to look which the source might not. Also, a confidential source can often be shielded from the risk of exposure by using their information as a "tip-off"; a steer on what questions to ask of attributable sources so that the eventual story need make no reference to the existence of any confidential information. It may well be possible to frame the questions so as to give the subject no inkling that they are inspired by inside information. This does not prevent further pursuit of the confidential source but it does make it less likely.
- Is there physical as well as oral evidence? Is any documentation authentic? How would you go about establishing that it is? Is the information in it reliable?
- Is the information in a form that would lead easily to identification of the source? This may not be obvious but the informant may know. Think what will be required to protect the identity.

Question yourself. If the story seems too good to be true, it probably is. Take enormous care not to read what you want to read into information.

- What are your motives? Do you want to believe your source because you like what they are telling you? Don't allow your enthusiasm for a good story to blur your judgment. Play devil's advocate with yourself.
- What other explanations could there be?
- What if you are being set up?
- What if the source, even if genuine, is just wrong?
- What makes the story credible?
- Could the story ever be run or are there simply too many legal obstacles?

Pause.

- Can you really protect the source's ID? Can your organisation? If the answer to either of those questions is no, you must not agree to try. Be clear that any confidentiality deal means you must not be prepared to say who isn't your source. Ruling people out may allow the source to be identified by process of elimination. If an organisation points the finger at the wrong person, you may be in an awkward position.
- Does the source realise what might happen next? Warn them of the possible outcomes of which they may not be aware. It is tempting not to in case it deters them from co-operating but it is the only fair way. The source may be taking a considerable risk themselves and might face civil or criminal action if you let them down. Sources

should be wary because of the threat of action on breach of confidence and under statutes such as the Data Protection Act, Official Secrets Act or Financial Services Act. The cases examined earlier in the chapter demonstrate that the source is more likely to be prosecuted than the journalist. A whistleblower would often also be risking dismissal from the organisation under investigation.

Consult your editor. This may be advisable before any agreement is entered into, depending on the level of authority permitted. An editor's instinct would be to be in the loop so as to be able to assess the source and the information personally and because it could be the editor's head on the block too. But the editor would be better off not knowing, especially if her news organisation would obey the law and comply with any disclosure order. It might be prepared to appeal it, but ultimately it would yield. Companies would be even more loath than an editor to defy a court order so, whether on principle or to protect the company from financial penalty, the editor also has to ask: If I join this agreement to protect a source, can I honour it? If the answer is no, the editor will have to trust the journalist and assess the risk based on the extent of that trust.

Decide what to do with any physical evidence. This is tricky. The physical evidence of documentation is important to the process of verification but hanging on to it can increase the risk of being forced to hand it over. The original would be more helpful in putting together, say, a justification defence against defamation but it is also likely to be more helpful in identifying the source. Destroying material could also be held to be in contempt if it were done to thwart the court.

One compromise is to scan a document, retain it stripped back to text only and return the original to the source. That provides the journalist with a working copy of the information and gives some evidence of the document's existence but makes it harder to trace the source from any identifying marks on the original.

The handling of confidential sources can be challenging for even the best-intentioned and well-briefed reporter. When the relationship breaks down it can have terrible consequences, as it did in the case of Dr David Kelly, the weapons expert who was found dead, having apparently taken his own life after being revealed as the confidential source of a BBC story challenging the basis of the Government's justification for attacking Iraq.

6. Access to Material

Editors are reluctant to come up with definitive answers on whether to hand over material demanded by a public agency. It depends. Like judges, they prefer to deal with the real circumstances of each case before reaching a conclusion. They too need to weigh the pros and cons of releasing material. Releasing footage, say of a riot, may well help to identify and prosecute rioters which the public might be very happy to see the news organisation play a part in. However, what would happen next time that news organisation sent a camera to a civil disturbance? Releasing material does definitely make a target of journalists, especially those with any sort of camera. More broadly, it is vital that a news organisation is not seen as, and certainly does not behave as, another arm of the State. The lesson must be not to hand over material lightly and certainly not to informal requests. The news media need to establish that disclosure is a "big deal" and that may mean insisting that a request is not only official but subject to judicial scrutiny to decide the proper balance of interests. Vital issues are at stake which rebound on journalists' ability to do an effective job. This is about safeguarding the free flow of information generally, not just in the case involved in a disclosure request. Again there is a danger that the importance of upholding freedom of expression rights will be discounted, and sometimes by journalists themselves.

7. Freedom of Information

It speaks volumes about the establishment's attitude to the Freedom of Information Act 2000 that, within two years of its 2005 introduction, the Government is trying to retreat from it by complaining about the cost of providing information and condemning journalists for being "serial" requesters of information.

Yet any self-respecting journalist should consider this a badge of honour. If journalists are to be condemned it should be for not making enough use of the Act given the massive backlog of information which is routinely released in other countries but rigidly kept under wraps in the UK. Journalists not making regular requests for information are surely failing in their pursuit of the public right to know.

But no, the Lord Chancellor is shocked by the demands journalists are making and, of course, dismisses requests as trivial. One, it is not for the Lord Chancellor to determine what is important and what is not. Two, the long list of revelations made possible by the Act by both national and regional media, make it obvious that revelations are far from inconsequential and that some significant strides towards openness have been made at many levels. Also, the law is "purpose blind" and the organisation holding the information requested has no right to ask why a requester wants it.

Then we have had the determined efforts by MPs to exempt themselves from the scope of the Act. It appears reasonable to a worryingly-large body of MPs that scrutiny should apply to run-of-the-mill public bodies and lower tiers of public officials but not to them, our most senior elected representatives. Worse, they have cloaked their arguments for secrecy in fallacious claims about the need to protect private correspondence from their constituents despite the fact that this already falls within the Data Protection Act. Do they not read the legislation they enact? It is for the House of Lords to challenge the approval of a Private Member's Bill which passed through the Commons after twice being talked out by a fine, but all-too-small group of MPs who believed the exemption was a "squalid" attempt to reduce the proper accountability of elected representatives.[38]

The combination of events helps to explain why figures such as Sir Christopher Meyer, the lay chairman of the Press Complaints Commission, feel the climate is becoming chillier.

There are various curbs on freedom of expression and we have focussed so far on those restricting what can be published or aired. One of the most fundamental curbs on freedom of expression is the secrecy that surrounds information so that we can't even access it, let alone air it. In terms of the public right to know, the Freedom of Information Act should be absolutely key to establishing a balance in a previously overly-secret system.

The Act, resisted by governments for 20 years, could really not be avoided any longer once the UK signed up to the European Convention on Human Rights which made many of the arcane blocks on the release of information from public bodies legally indefensible.

The system is not giving up its secrets without a fight. Despite being given a five-year run up from the creation of the Act in 2000 to its application from January 2005, many organisations have so far given little ground. It evidently takes more than the law of the land to change the habits of a lifetime within the government and other public bodies. The culture of secrecy is alive and well.

Maurice Frankel, whose lobbying with the Campaign for Freedom of Information over decades finally paid off with the passing of the Act, has discovered his work is far from over. In his response to the threatened clawback he wrote:

"What the government really wants is a bit more privacy from our prying eyes. FOI is beginning to put ministers under pressure. We are learning more about the costs of contentious policies like identity cards. We now know that the government considered weakening money laundering controls to encourage US style super casinos in the UK. Unwelcome information about ministers' meetings with commercial lobbyists has been disclosed. FOI has revealed that the apparent success of some academy schools, favoured by the government, is due not to better teaching but to the selection of pupils from better off backgrounds.

"At local level, the Act has been even more effective. Spending on contracts, consultancies and expenses has come under new scrutiny. FOI

[38] David Winnick (Labour MP for Walsall North), reported by the Guardian, May 18, 2007.

requests have revealed the success rates of individual heart surgeons, the failures of some restaurants to meet hygiene standards, the millions spent by councils employing temporary agency staff instead of full-time employees, the number of taxi drivers with drink-driving or assault convictions, the amounts hospitals make from parking charges and the care centres whose policy was to leave patients in their rooms during a fire, in the mistaken belief that they were fire-resistant."[39]

The important exhortation to journalists is to use the Freedom of Information Act and be prepared to persist in attempts to extend its limits. Frankel's Campaign for Freedom of Information website is a marvellous source of advice and inspiration at *www.cfoi.org.uk*. There is also a very useful book by Heather Brooke, *Your Right to Know*, which uses her experience in the more open American system to prise up a few establishment stones and see what crawls out from beneath them. It is packed with practical tips, information on sources and sample request letters, and provides a vocal challenge to the UK's obsession with secrecy.[40]

An amalgam of the advice from both includes the following:

- Find out who holds what information. Knowing your way around the system can save a lot of wasted time and energy. Talk to the organisation's information officer in the target organisation to establish what information is held and in what form before framing a request. Many information officers do believe in their role and may be allies in the process of persuading the organisation to be more open. Under s.16 of the Act organisations are obliged to "advise and assist."

  The organisation that generated the information is not necessarily the only, or easiest, target of a request. Consider which other organisations it shares information with which may have a different approach or a different way of storing the information to make it more accessible and more useful. It may be particularly helpful if material is shared with an organisation in the US, for instance, which has more liberal release laws.
- Work out what you need to know. If the information you want is not collated in that format, the information holder can argue that the necessary collation of data from more than one source would tip the request of over the cost cap.
- Be specific. Frame your request with just the right amount of detail so that it cannot easily be evaded and so that the necessary answer can again be provided within the cost cap. The common mistake is asking for too much information over too long a time frame.
- Be prepared to accept raw data rather than nothing and do the analysis yourself. Computer assisted reporting is a growth area and

[39] Maurice Frankel, director, Campaign for Freedom of Information, *www.cfoi.org.uk*.
[40] Brooke, Heather, *Your Right to Know, How to use the Freedom of Information Act and other access laws*.

investigative journalists are becoming more astute about finding stories from data which on the face of it is impenetrable and reveals nothing. And, where material is being withheld from within a document, ask for the original so it is at least clear where material has been deleted.

- Use successes in one area to press for equivalent information elsewhere. Many organisations now at least provide easy access to a disclosure log showing what has been released under the Act. Especially if the Information Commissioner has set a precedent, the pressure on organisations to give in becomes that much greater. The jobsworths can conclude that the cost in financial and reputation terms of releasing the information might at last be less than that of withholding it.
- Be persistent. Appeal to the Information Commissioner if blocked unreasonably.

The Freedom of Information Act in practice has not been particularly useful to overcome the reticence of response in the day-to-day whirl of breaking news. The long response times allowed may even have slowed down some replies. However, when reporters examine longer-term, underlying issues and pursue new angles, the Act has proved valuable.

One of the deterrent factors in making use of it is, however, that it does not allow for the protection of a scoop. A journalist can spend months working on an investigative piece, waiting for a key response under the terms of the Act. However, as soon as the agency involved decides to release that information, it is not released exclusively to the person who has inquired. It will often be posted straight onto a disclosure log so journalists, whose organisations have not invested in investigative reporting, gain the same advantage. Journalists have to be ready to move fast when a response arrives to keep a competitive edge.

There are various tiers of appeals procedure but given the long response times allowed at each stage, few cases have gone the distance so far. Here again it will be important to scrutinise adjudications to see where precedent is established which can be used to bring other organisations into line; or whether we have to concede defeat and try a different tack.

The danger is that disenchantment will set in. Journalists must not lose the war of attrition with public bodies that have yet to face up to their obligations. Heather Brookes, an American journalist who finds UK complacency over secrecy baffling, concludes:

"The public's right to know is not just a noble ideal for an enlightened society; it is thoroughly practical. Freedom of information is the most effective and inexpensive way to stop corruption and waste, and enhance efficiency and good governance."[41]

---

[41] ibid., p.243.

Therefore, whether in pursuit of principle or efficiency, journalists and indeed the general public should be exercising their rights under the Act to the full.

Governments need not resort to the mechanics of the marketplace to make our public bodies efficient. They could simply just try being open, honest and transparent with the public who pay for the services. This would be far more effective and a great deal cheaper. Scrutiny ensures that comparisons are made; that organisations and the individuals within them learn from their mistakes and that best practice is spread more easily.

It is up to journalists to keep pressing for public information to be made public. As Alan Rusbridger puts it in the Foreword to Heather Brooke's book:

"Inhabitants of the United States are much more aware than their British counterparts that the citizens own the government – and not the other way round."[42]

That's probably because the principle is easy to lose sight of in the fog of bureaucracy and secrecy engulfing our seats of power. Any "responsible" journalist needs to be doing their bit to encourage our public authorities to emerge blinking into the light of transparency and openness.

[42] ibid., Foreword.

CHAPTER 6
REGULATION

When it comes to upholding and challenging standards of journalism, the public has recourse to a range of regulatory bodies which broadly sit somewhere between the individual news source and the courts. So a person aggrieved by press coverage, for instance, might turn first to the "offending" newspaper; if not satisfied, the complaint can go to the next tier in the form of a regulatory body; and if not resolved there, can go to the courts for remedy. Although the hierarchy exists, a complainant need not follow it and can, for instance, proceed straight to law.

The main regulatory bodies we focus on here are the Press Complaints Commission (PCC), which covers newspapers and magazines and seems to crop up most frequently in media law judgments, and the Office of Communications (Ofcom) for broadcast. In terms of standard-setting it is also important to consider the BBC's own Editorial Guidelines and complaint-handling procedure.

One key distinction between the PCC and Ofcom; is that the latter is statutory while the former is not. In practice, the main difference is in the realm of sanction. The PCC relies on public reprimand, the ignominy of having to print hostile adjudications and the threat that being found against constitutes breach of contract for most working journalists and can lead to dismissal. Ofcom can impose fines on a broadcaster and, in worst cases, withdraw a licence to broadcast.

Not surprisingly, much of the establishment would like to see newspapers falling under the remit of Ofcom, or an organisation very much like it. The rich and powerful tend to dislike the media more than most and are often prepared to use their position to restrict its power. Somehow, this is portrayed by Parliament and the courts as motivated by pure public interest, whereas news organisations, and the journalists within them, are generally assumed to be driven entirely by self-interest. No-one—whether politician, celebrity or journalist—can claim to monopolise the moral high ground. At least let us accept that all sides are driven by a mix of pure and baser motives.

Generally, those calling for the PCC to be able to impose fines on news organisations are working on the basis that the only penalty that counts with newspapers is a financial one. Hit the watchdog where it hurts and it will come to heel. A journalist's view is that it would be a massively retrograde step in terms of pursuing pluralism and an appalling curb on freedom of expression if all media fell under such strict regulation whereby a statutory agent of Government could hold a newspaper hostage and remove its right to print. It would also make the PCC more like a court and restrict the flexibility it has as an interlocutor between the parties.

Also if we accept that money can be a motivator for the media, we must also accept that money can be a motivator for complainants. Famous people have agents and clipping services scouring the media for possible actionable material. How disappointing for them to have a press complaints commission that focuses on putting the record straight and upholding standards of conduct. They don't just want fines; they want damages.

1. Press Complaints Commission

The emergence of the legal concept of responsible journalism has put journalists' behaviour even more firmly in the spotlight. It is not enough that our stories are in the public interest; we must have pursued them and run them responsibly.

Cases such as *Moldova*, discussed in Chapter 1, stress that a journalist seeking to shield behind Art.10 rights must be able to demonstrate not just the reasonable accuracy of what was run but that it was the product of thorough processes of verification with an ethical underpinning. In the UK, the judges have looked to the codes of various regulatory bodies to provide the "ethics" test.

Lord Hoffmann, in *Jameel* at para.55, raises the issue specifically in terms of how to move to a definition of "responsible journalism" within a *Reynolds* public interest defence against defamation. He said:

"The standard of responsible journalism is as objective and no more vague than standards such as 'reasonable care' which are regularly used in other branches of the law. Greater certainty in its application is achieved in two ways. First, as Lord Nicholls said, a body of illustrative case law builds up. Secondly, just as the standard of reasonable care in particular areas, such as driving a vehicle, is made more concrete by extra-statutory codes of behaviour like the Highway Code, so the standard of responsible journalism is made more specific by the Code of Practice which has been adopted by the newspapers and ratified by the Press Complaints Commission. This too, while not binding upon the courts, can provide valuable guidance."

The prime ethical base for print journalism is the Press Complaints Commission Code of Practice with which any journalist in the dock is expected to have an intimate working relationship—another good reason for a journalist routinely to carry one of the creditcard-sized copies of it in purse or wallet.

The Press Complaints Commission (PCC), created in 1991 to replace the Press Council, is the name given to the regime of press self-regulation as a whole but it is in fact one of four bodies involved.

The PCC secretariat processes complaints and pursues resolution, by mutual agreement wherever possible. The Code of Practice itself was created and is maintained by the Editor's Code of Practice Committee comprising 14 editors from national and regional newspapers and magazines. Funding is channelled through the Press Standards Board of Finance, representing the publishers.

The Press Complaints Commission itself has 17 members, with seven editors and 10 lay members from outside the industry, including the chairman. The Commission oversees the system and adjudicates on complaints.

The target is to resolve complaints within 35 days so the secretariat works swiftly to broker resolution, often putting significant pressure on editors to respond. If the PCC regards the complaint as raising a possible issue under the Code, the editor has seven days to provide an initial response. The editor always represents the publication in the process. The PCC secretariat will assess the possibilities for conciliation, act as a go-between and attempt to secure a remedy acceptable to both parties. If conciliation fails, or is inappropriate, of if the case involves a major policy issue, the Commission will publish an adjudication. Where a complaint is upheld the publication must publish the adverse finding. No editor has ever failed to comply.

The code explicitly embraces the same sort of balancing act faced in the courts in weighing competing articles of the ECHR, attempting to protect both the rights of the individual and the public's right to know.

The PCC now carries extensive general guidance on its website and has produced an editor's codebook[1] to provide further guidance on its operation. This includes a useful checklist of its various means of resolving complaints without adjudication, which is predominantly the aim. These are:

- Clarification. A clarification might be appropriate where something has been omitted from the original article or if it is ambiguous or arguably misleading. It stops short of an admission by the editor that the article was wrong.

- Corrections and apologies. Straightforward factual errors are usually dealt with most cleanly and simply by the publication of a correction. In the case of serious errors, this might include an apology. The Code states that an apology should be published where appropriate.

- Letter for publication. This is particularly appropriate where the complainant is taking issue on a matter of opinion rather than fact.

- Follow-up article. An editor might offer to publish an interview with, or article by, a complainant, grudgingly although sometimes enthusiastically. A complainant may assume the newspaper is not amenable to challenging new material and complain direct to the PCC rather than approaching the editor. Just occasionally the complaint actually alerts the newspaper to interesting story developments which it is more than happy to cover.

[1] Beales, Ian, *The Editors' Codebook, the handbook to the Editors' Code of Practice*, p.10.

- Tagging newspaper records. This is an increasingly popular way of resolving complaints, either alone or as part of a package of remedies. The publication's electronic database and cuttings library is tagged with the complainant's objection to ensure the mistake is not repeated.

- Private letter of apology. Further publicity is often not an attractive option for the complainant, particularly in privacy cases or intrusion into grief.

- Private undertaking. Similarly, undertakings by the editor about the future conduct of the newspaper and its staff might also give a complainant some peace of mind.

Guardian readers, in particular, will be familiar with many of these remedies which the paper pursues for itself through its Readers' Editor as a first tier of recourse. Many regional newspapers take a similar approach but the Guardian has the most high-profile internal complaints-resolution procedure. This was a conscious policy to bolster the principle of self-regulation and provide evidence of accountability to readers.

2. Self-Regulation Myths

Journalists supposedly rule on other journalists

The myth is that self-regulation means complaints are handled by an "old boy" network where journalists shrug off problems and defend the indefensible. Press Complaints Commission panels reflect the balance of the commission so journalists are not in the majority.

The PCC is not noticeably kind to editors. The majority of adjudicators are lay members and the journalist members are not tolerant of other editors letting the side down. It has even been observed that the non-journalists are more sympathetic to the newspaper "excuses" and the other editors more sceptical and less forgiving. Also, given the highly-competitive nature of the media, especially at a national level, rival editors are not renowned for "cosying up" rather they arguably relish the discomfort of a competitor being shown up by being in breach of the code.

Those complaints resolved without adjudication have not just disappeared; they have involved the newspaper in various of the actions outlined above; most often by publishing a correction or apology.

The PCC supposedly has no teeth and imposes no penalty

For an editor, it is humiliating to have to print an adjudication which spells out exactly how her newspaper has fallen foul of the code. And in reaching settlement without adjudication, editors are often pressed into more fulsome apologies certainly than they would have chosen to run. Having a complaint upheld against the publication can be a dismissable offence. Compliance with the Code of Practice is now written in to many editors' and journalists' contracts. It is taken seriously. Working editors you don't want a complaint even to get as far as adjudication let alone be upheld.

Dealing with a complaint pursued by the PCC:

- Takes time and the editor, or a senior colleague, is expected to handle it;
- May require legal advice on remedies which is more time and expense;
- Often reveals that the publication's checking system and/or remedy procedures haven't worked and will need to be overhauled, with a commitment to complainant and PCC to do the overhauling;
- Means an editor may have to agree a remedy which isn't comfortable;
- Means an editor may be found against;
- Means the publication has to print the hostile adjudication;
- Means the editor and/or reporter may be sacked.

In agreeing to publish any hostile PCC adjudication, an editor is ceding power over content in a way which she would not for a proprietor, managing director or advertiser. This is a major concession. The PCC is not a minor irritant. Newspapers cannot just pay lip service to it even if they used to be inclined to.

Some opponents of self-regulation believe that with newspapers only money talks—that they will flout any regulations unless the penalty exceeds the potential benefit. Yet one of the reasons complainants dismiss the PCC route is not because it is all about money for the newspaper but because it is all about money for them.

The corrections demanded are supposedly buried so no-one sees them

The PCC's 2006 annual report[2] reveals that 74 per cent of corrections, clarifications or apologies appeared on the same page as the offending original, further forward in the publication or in a dedicated column.

The PCC supposedly does not handle third-party complaints

The PCC does now accept some what would be considered third-party complaints. Where a story concerns an individual, it is still up to that individual to complain. It is possible for the PCC to invite a complaint if

2 PCC Annual Report, 2006, *www.pcc.org.uk*.

its attention is drawn to a grievance but it remains for the individual to decide whether to pursue it or not.

However where the coverage complained of is more general the PCC may accept a complaint from someone not directly referred to in the piece, say on a claim of inaccuracy. This stance allows for more errors to be corrected without opening the PCC up wholesale to lobbyists.

Complainants may feel reticent about taking on a newspaper but genuinely anyone can approach the PCC. The service is free to the complainant. The secretariat does its utmost to ensure that ordinary people, who are not necessarily particularly articulate, are heard. Complainants do not need the weight of an organisation, nor of lawyers, behind them. Anyone really can complain. Complaints written honestly may well carry more weight than those crafted in legal jargon. Officers of the PCC will tease out the nature of the complaint and demand adequate responses from the editor. They pursue the complaint on behalf of the complainant and press for a resolution. A complaint to the Press Complaints Commission is the most common recourse for ordinary members of the public who feel they have had a raw deal in some way from the media. For many of those people, legal avenues are effectively closed to them, even with the spread of conditional fee arrangements.

The PCC supposedly allows newspapers to avoid ethical and legal responsibilities

The Code is not a watered-down version of legal obligations. It may require more than the law, but never less. It provides the cornerstone of ethical responsibilities.

The PCC supposedly stands idly by in the face of excess in the absence of a complaint

The PCC does generally have a reactive, rather than pro-active, remit but it can take initiatives by making public or private statements regarding required standards. The PCC can also be consulted—and often is—before publication to discuss the pros and cons of a story and how any particular treatment, of the inclusion of a particular photograph, might be treated within the code. It can also help to protect individuals from potential harassment and not just for royals (and their now-ex girlfriends). It offered advice to Suffolk police in the case of the Ipswich prostitute killings and to the Ministry of Defence from "stories for sale" over the military personnel detained by Iran. (The MoD didn't take it.) It also provides a hotline for anyone caught up in a "big" story which can be rung for advice on how to handle the situation.

The PCC investigated the circumstances and issues surrounding the jailing of the News of the World royal editor Clive Goodman for intercepting mobile phone messages and in May 2007 published new guidance for news organisations (see Chapter 4: Privacy).

The system of self-regulation supposedly does not prevent the excesses of popular tabloids

The fewer legal fetters on a free press the better. We have too many already. There is still arguably a gap between regional and national newspapers although numerically there are more complaints against regional and local newspapers because there are simply so many of them and they are read by so many people. As usual, most of the media debate focuses on a handful of popular tabloids or at best national newspapers as a whole. For the general public, local papers have at least as much, if not more, bearing on their lives. Regional papers work hard to honour the code in the way they gather and present news, and by responding to complaints—and from ordinary readers rather than celebrities. Local readers tend to be very ready to apply a "reality check" through the PCC if the newspaper is at all reticent in dealing with complaints about coverage within their community. For some of the nationals, the highly competitive tabloid market tempts them into excess but they are coming round to compliance with the Code. It was a chasm but it has narrowed.

The PCC is supposedly weak on safeguarding privacy

Genuine cases of infringement of privacy where a real personal hurt has been caused can be dealt with appropriately by the PCC and it has issued general guidance in this area as well as upholding various complaints, although they remain a small proportion of the total, which are predominantly about challenging accuracy.[3]

The PCC is driven by the same kinds of considerations as the courts in these issues. Its majority of lay members may weigh the "proportionality" issues slightly differently but the difference is not that great; the PCC could not afford for it to be otherwise the pressures to sacrifice self-regulation would become even greater.

Among its guiding principles on privacy, as quoted in The Editors' Codebook, are:

- Privacy is not an absolute right—it can be compromised by conduct or consent.

- Privacy is not a commodity which can be sold on one person's terms—the Code is not designed to protect commercial deals.

- Privacy does not mean invisibility—pictures taken in genuinely public places and information already in the public domain can be legitimate.

---

[3] ibid.

- Privacy may be against the public interest—such as when used to keep secret conduct that might reflect on a public figure or role model.[4]

The language and emphasis is different but there is clear recognition of issues surround Art.8 and Art.10 rights. The PCC even uses much of the same jargon as the court by referring to its "case law" as effectively setting boundaries in areas such as privacy. In this sense the Editors' Codebook as a whole provides a most useful summary of these precedents and indicates what implications they have for future coverage. Adjudications make it obvious that if another publication investigates or runs a story in a similar fashion its editor can expect to fall foul of the Code.

There are, however, several notorious cases in this area and certainly there are plenty of public figures who have dismissed the PCC, either by being dissatisfied by its handling of a complaint or by bypassing it completely and going straight to law. But these cases are not always as straightforward as they seem. The naked honeymoon photographs of DJ Sara Cox and her husband, which were an infringement of privacy, cost the People newspaper around £50,000 plus costs of more than twice that. Cox was portrayed as having been forced to court by the inadequacy of the PCC. But as the PCC's then director, Guy Black, pointed out, she accepted an apology brokered by the PCC. The issue never went to adjudication. If it had, the PCC may well have upheld the complaint. And when she sought a legal remedy, the case was settled out of court. No legal precedent was established.

Far more people (more than 200 in 2006) take privacy complaints to the PCC than to the courts. Privacy played a part in 19 adjudications and five privacy complaints were upheld during 2006. Chairman Sir Christopher Meyer said:

> "It is absolutely wrong to see the law and PCC as competitors. While every year you get three or four privacy cases rumbling through the courts, we have the speed and flexibility to deal with several hundred."[5]

Government Minister Ruth Kelly complained to the PCC when the Daily Mirror ran the news that she was sending one of her children to a private school for pupils with learning difficulties. Her complaint was not upheld but the adjudication was illuminating. It referred to the balance between the child's privacy and the public interest in the actions of her mother and there is clear proportionality at play. It said:

> "While there was unquestionably an intrusion felt by the complainant and her child, it was clear that the newspaper had taken steps to limit

---

[4] Beales, Ian, *The Editors' Codebook, the handbook to the Editors' Code of Practice*, p.34.
[5] Commenting on the Annual Report, reported in Press Gazette, April 25, 2007.

the nature of that intrusion in omitting the name of the child, his school and precise details of his condition.

"Had further details been included, the Commission may well have considered the intrusion to be unnecessary.

"It judged that the naming of the complainant herself – even though it carried with it an implicit identification of her child – was necessary in the context of the story and enabled a fuller, legitimate discussion of the issues at stake, including whether the State in general and Tower Hamlets Council in particular was able to offer appropriate schooling for children with special needs."[6]

The PCC is not a court, but it sounds very much like one. Primacy was given to the public interest in a Minister, particularly a former Education Minister, finding the state provision wanting when it came to her own child. How readers responded to her resolution of the dilemma was up to them. The story made an important contribution to the controversies around public/private education provision and it was run responsibly so as to keep the focus as much as possible on the issue and the Minister rather than the child.

The editor may even have discussed it with the PCC beforehand.

In May 2007, the PCC upheld a complaint against the Sun for intruding into singer Charlotte Church's privacy in its reporting of her pregnancy. To say merely that the pregnancy was "rumoured" was not enough to evade its Code obligations. The adjudication was printed on p.2 of the newspaper, hardly hidden away.

The PCC is also mirroring court judgments by upholding complaints where the degree of sexual detail provided is not justified in the weighing of Art.8 and Art.10 rights. A complaint over a story about a "Lady Chatterley" affair, published in two national newspapers, was not upheld against one but upheld against the other because it included lurid sexual detail.

The adjudication in one said: "The amount of information in the article was sufficient to enable the man's girlfriend to tell her story—as she was entitled to do—without including humiliating and gratuitously intrusive detail." The other said:

"When reporting one party's account of a relationship, newspapers must also have regard to the other person's private life. The complainant had not courted publicity and any limited public interest inherent in exposing adultery committed by someone who was married into an aristocratic family was insufficient to justify the level of detail in the piece."[7]

---

[6] Adjudications at *www.pcc.org.uk*.
[7] Adjudications on *www.pcc.org.uk*.

In an adjudication involving the daughter of motor racing magnate, Bernie Ecclestone, the PCC rejected complaints regarding some elements of the story based on an interview with the daughter's former boyfriend but upheld one saying:

"While it is noted that Miss Ecclestone has received publicity in the past on account of her lifestyle as the daughter of a very wealthy man, the commission made clear – as it always has done – that the previous publication of matters into the public domain dealing with a person's private life does not necessarily disentitle that person to any right of privacy."[8]

The extent of intimate detail, of a sexual nature, was not warranted. Sounds familiar.

There is supposedly no appeal from the PCC

The basic right of appeal from the PCC is to the courts. Under its predecessor body the Press Council, complainants had to grant a legal waiver—if their complaint was not upheld they could not go on to sue. That protection was removed when the PCC was created so dissatisfied complainants can, and do, proceed to the courts.

Within the PCC, there is now a Press Complaints Commissioner who handles complaints about the workings of the PCC but he safeguards procedural probity rather than challenging the substance of the adjudications.

Guardian editor Alan Rusbridger, a lead commentator on such issues, has called for the creation of an Ombudsman to act as a Court of Appeal from the PCC, so as to reduce further the need to have recourse to the courts.[9]

The PCC is supposedly weak, full stop

The PCC is not a draconian body. It is also not a professional body, such as the British Medical Council, because journalism is not a profession. That is one of the key features of journalism which makes the lighter touch of self-regulation appropriate and indeed vital. Freedom of expression and the need for plurality in a democracy means a journalist, unlike a dentist or lawyer, cannot be "struck off" and prevented from practising. This setting apart of journalists from many of the normal strictures of working life rankles in many quarters and the argument is often dismissed as being born out of the arrogance of journalists. But journalists are different; their role in society is different and in ways which the checks and balances of democratic society must recognise and learn to live with.

[8] ibid.
[9] *Evidence to Parliamentary inquiry into privacy and media intrusion*, reported Guardian, March 11, 2003.

3. Ofcom and the BBC

Broadcasters have historically needed access to limited airwaves, so the licensing of that access by the State has allowed for much stricter regulation of behaviour. Airwaves are relatively easy to regulate so the advantage is seized by the regulators.

Much of Ofcom's work is tied up in the practicalities of keeping the stations on air and with commercial aspects, such as the advertising of fatty foods to children. Recent focus has been on responding to the abuse of premium rate telephone quiz lines which extended even to Blue Peter. Is nothing sacred?

Ofcom has considerable powers and, as mentioned in the discussion of the PCC, represents the sort of model some politicians, lawyers and judges would like to see applied to the printed media. Ofcom cannot exercise prior restraint, but it can fine the operator, suspend or even revoke its licence to broadcast.

This makes it a very different animal from the PCC. Upholding standards of journalistic content and behaviour is only one element of its brief. Its remit also varies between commercial output and public service output, and more specifically the BBC.

Arguably the more obvious broadcast parallel with the PCC Code is the *BBC Editorial Guidelines* document.[10] This provides 230 pages of advice on how standards set out in the BCC Charter can be upheld in practice. The standards are similar in many respects to the PCC Code. The demands of impartiality are among the extra challenges facing the broadcast journalist but there is much common ground in the areas covered by this book, such as defamation, privacy and contempt. The level of detail offered is perhaps what inspired the PCC to produce its Editors' Codebook. So as not to be found wanting in comparison, it now provides a slimmer offering (at 104 pages) but it is a move towards providing more advice to editors on what the Code requires in practice.

Ofcom has a board with a chairman and both executive and non-executive members. Together they provide its strategic direction. It describes itself as the main statutory instrument of regulation with a fundamental role in the effective implementation of the Communications Act 2003.[11]

Of Ofcom's six specific duties it is the fifth and sixth that are most likely to come into play in terms of journalistic content.

"5. Applying adequate protection for audiences against offensive or harmful material—the taste and decency area.

6. Applying adequate protection for audiences against unfairness or the infringement of privacy—covering issues of accuracy, the opportunity to respond and intrusive coverage."

---

[10] *BBC Editorial Guidelines*, available to journalists and the public, *www.bbc.co.uk*.
[11] Available at *www.ofcom.org.uk*.

The Communications Act 2003 requires Ofcom to consider and where appropriate adjudicate on fairness and privacy complaints. The procedure for handling complaints is more formal than the PCC's but works along very similar lines. Ofcom expects the complaint to come from the "person affected"; it assesses the complaint to decide if it is going to "entertain"it; seeks a copy of the material and sets about trying to broker an appropriate resolution. This can include the editing of a programme where it is to be repeated; an undertaking not to repeat the programme; an apology or correction in writing and/or broadcast.

If the complainant accepts the resolution, that is the end of the matter. If the suggested redress is not accepted, Ofcom will proceed with consideration of the complaint. After appropriate submissions, there will be a hearing and the adjudication will normally be posted on the Ofcom website.

Where a complaint is upheld or partly upheld, the offending broadcaster may be required to broadcast a summary of the adjudication. We have probably all heard at least one but they are sporadic.

If the adjudication justifies consideration of statutory sanction, the complaint is referred back to the case leader to apply the published criteria for considering sanctions.

There is frequent reference to the Human Rights Act 1998 throughout the guidelines for complainants to make clear that the process is convention-compliant.

4. Multi-Platform News

It is difficult to see how the division between print and broadcast in terms of regulatory frameworks can be sustained in an era of growing convergence. So far, websites have been viewed as an adjunct to the host brand. The PCC has claimed authority over Guardian online and all other newspaper websites, even where they include broadcast format audio and video clips.

The EU is muscling in too creating the not unreasonable presumption that any rules it seeks to apply will be tighter, certainly for newspapers used to self-regulation. Given the UK civil service's tendency to "goldplate"EU directives, there would be a strong chance of British politicians using them as a pretext for even tougher interpretation.

This makes it even more likely that journalists will all end up under the most restrictive of the regimes. The PCC and the publications signed up to it can expect to come under increasing regulatory pressure over the coming years.

However, if the emergence of millions upon millions of bloggers makes us all part of the media now in the eyes of the law, the regulatory framework may simply become unsustainable and arguably already has.

The law may be platform-blind, but in reality there are websites galore breaching every kind of law and ethical code all the time. Unless they belong to a mainstream news organisation they have generally been action-proof. This is because any individual blogger is unlikely to have the assets to make it worth suing as there is little prospect of enforcing any damages award.

It operates rather like the Child Support Agency; the responsible news operations come under the cosh, while the irresponsible ones escape because they are too transient or have too few assets to worry about. That is rather how online is being treated so far.

Just as there are levels of accountability for public figures, it appears there are for individual news providers. The BBC and major newspaper groups live up to the highest standards of ethical and legal probity. For much of the rest, just about anything goes.

Perhaps soon, newsgathering operations will be regulated either as a condition of funding support or, in the case of newspapers, as a seal of quality and accountability to bolster credibility with the audience. The PCC could be used like a Fairtrade mark seal of approval, guaranteeing certain standards have been upheld in the production and content of the news provided.

Surely the system needs to find a way of rewarding those organisations which have a commitment to credible, reliable news output and are prepared to answer to their responsibilities rather than penalising them for being so obviously in the firing line. Compliance is costing the mainstream a fortune, whether in cash or restraint terms, while guerrilla publishers escape any effective control of standards or legality.

Is the only way to exercise freedom of expression to exercise it outside the system? That may make the journalist "purer" but where does it leave the general public and their right to know?

CHAPTER 7
REPORTING RESTRICTIONS

1. Children and Family Proceedings

Reporting restrictions in respect of the criminal courts are reasonably well known and relatively uncontroversial. The same cannot be said for those relating to children and the family justice system. The family justice system has been the subject of sustained criticism from pressure groups such as Fathers 4 Justice and Families Need Fathers for, among other things, its lack of transparency. This may be a simplistic comment, but that lack of transparency may well have its roots in the inability of the system to encompass even a modicum of publicity and standard press reporting. The principle of "open justice" has never really been a feature of the family system. The press may well be the eyes and ears of the public in relation to criminal cases where liberty may be at stake but the "seeing and hearing" process on behalf of the public has been conspicuously absent as far as family courts are concerned.

This is not meant as a criticism of the judges. They have to work within the legislation that imposes such restrictions. However, since the Human Rights Act came into force in October 2000, it is evident that many members of the judiciary would like to see significant changes in the law. Lord Justice Wall, a passionate advocate for change, put it this way in June 2006:

> "I am in favour of giving the media-and in practice this means the press-access to family proceedings, provided there are clear ground rules about what they can and cannot report. In practice this is mainly going to mean the extent to which, if at all, they are at liberty when reporting the proceedings, to identify the parties, and, in particular, the children concerned."[1]

He went on to say that ". . . the judiciary and practitioners should have nothing to fear from public scrutiny: indeed we should welcome it." Another judge who has campaigned for change is Mr Justice Munby. In giving evidence to Parliament's Constitutional Affairs Select Committee in 2006 he said:

---

[1] Sir Nicholas Wall, *Opening Up the Family Courts: An open or closed case*, 30/10/2006. Available at *www.judiciary.gov.uk*.

"I have come over the years . . . firmly to the view that the balance which is currently held between the confidentiality and privacy interests of the parties and the public interest in open justice is badly skewed, in the sense that the arguments in favour of confidentiality and privacy have left what I believe to be a very serious diminution of public confidence in the system. Any advantages which currently can be gained in terms of confidentiality and privacy proceedings are outweighed, and I believe fairly heavily outweighed, by the constantly eroding damage to public confidence in the system."[2]

To understand why there appears to be a large measure of consensus between the politicians and the judges it is necessary to look at the restrictions that have prevented the system from receiving greater exposure in the media. These are based upon two underlying assumptions. The first is that it is not in the best interests of children to receive press publicity. As the European Court of Human Rights said in *B and P* [2001][3]:

"The Court considers that such proceedings are prime examples of cases where the exclusion of the press and public may be justified in order to protect the privacy of the child and parties and to avoid prejudicing the interests of justice. To enable the deciding judge to gain as full and accurate a picture as possible of the advantages and disadvantages of the various residence and contact options open to the child, it is essential that the parents and other witnesses feel able to express themselves candidly on highly personal issues without fear of public curiosity or comment."[4]

The second is that proceedings dealing with family matters such as the breakdown of marriage or suspected child abuse should not be carried out in the full glare of publicity unless criminal charges result from the latter.

The first of these assumptions is also reflected in the criminal law. There are automatic reporting restrictions imposed by the Children & Young Persons Act 1933 on defendants appearing in the Youth Court.[5] The theory is that young people should not garner, because of press publicity, a reputation as a criminal when in fact there may be time for redemption. There may be restrictions imposed if a child is appearing in an adult court because of s.39 of the same Act. It all boils down to one question. Is the public interest in protecting the child from unwanted publicity greater than the public interest in revealing the information?

The developing law on privacy is a 'new' factor that is impinging upon this debate but equally it is true that in some circumstances publicity can be advantageous to the children involved. In child abduction cases for

---

[2] 6th Report-June 2006. Family Justice: The operation of the family courts revisited.
[3] [2001] ECHR 298.
[4] ibid., at para.38.
[5] Section 49.

example the press will usually offer maximum support in an endeavour to locate a missing child. Equally, there will be almost total agreement that publicity cannot possibly be in the best interests of a child. Adoption is the most obvious example. Publicity of a transfer of legal parentage at a very early age will not be likely to affect the child at that time but could quite easily do so as over time he or she becomes established in the local community.

2. Legislation

Let us look at the legislation that purports to impose restrictions upon the reporting of family cases. The term family proceedings for our purposes will embrace divorce, care proceedings, wardship proceedings, and to use the old terminology "custody" disputes when parents separate or divorce. There are three pieces of major legislation covering the reporting of family courts. The first is the Administration of Justice Act 1960 and in particular s.12. (As amended) It states:

"1. The publication of information relating to proceedings before any court sitting in private shall not of itself be contempt of court except in the following cases, that is to say—(a) where the proceedings—(i) relate to the exercise of the inherent jurisdiction of the High Court with respect to minors; (ii) are brought under the Children Act 1989; or (iii) otherwise relate wholly or mainly to the maintenance or upbringing of the child . . ."

The effect of s.12 said Munby J. in *Webster v Norfolk County Council* [2006][6] is:

". . . to prohibit the publication of accounts of what has gone on in front of the judge sitting in private, and also the publication of documents (or extracts or quotations from documents) such as affidavits, witness statements, reports, position statements, skeleton arguments or other documents filed in the proceedings, transcripts or notes of the evidence or submissions, and transcripts or notes of the judgment."[7]

That is what the press cannot do. This, according to Munby J., is what they can report:

- That a child is subject to proceedings under the Children Act 1989;
- The dates, times and places of past and future hearings;

[6] [2006] EWHC 2733 (Fam).
[7] ibid., para.59.

- The nature of the dispute in the proceedings;
- Anything seen or heard in the public precincts of the court in which the private hearing is taking place;
- The text or summary of any order made in such proceedings;
- Reveal the identity of a child;
- Publish photographs of the child, other parties or the witnesses;
- The party upon whose behalf the witness is giving or has given evidence.

Two things should at be emphasised at this point. The first is that the court may impose reporting restrictions and the media will be in contempt if the provisions of any such order are ignored. Secondly there is a distinction between proceedings held in *private* and those held *in camera*. Hearings in chambers are regarded as private but not secret and elements of the proceedings may be reported subject to the current interpretation of s.12.

Hearings in camera are regarded as secret and therefore normally reporting will not be allowed. Reference should be made to the statement of Lord Woolf M.R. in *Hodgson v Imperial Tobacco Ltd*[8] quoted with approval in *Allan v Clibbery* [2002][9]:

"However, it remains a principle of the greatest importance that, unless there are compelling reasons for doing otherwise . . . there should be public access to hearings in chambers and information available as to what happened at such hearings."

He went on:

"To disclose what occurs in chambers does not constitute a breach of confidence or amount to a contempt as long as any comment which is made does not substantially prejudice the administration of justice. (This) . . . does not apply to the exceptional situations identified in s.12 (1) of the Act of 1960 or where the court, with the power to do so, orders otherwise."

In summary therefore, chambers hearings are not secret hearings. Cases are held in chambers for administrative convenience. The press and pubic can be allowed in except in cases covered by s.12 of the 1960 Act. Yet as Munby J. has said, that does not prevent certain information about a case involving children reaching the public domain. The current view is that s.12 prevents the press from reporting on matters that are *integral* to the case being heard in chambers of the type referred to above. That is the case if the matter relating to children has been brought before the High Court under the inherent jurisdiction or the Children Act 1989. As

[8] [1998] EWCA 224.
[9] [2002] EWCA Civ 45.

Munby J. stated in the recent decision of *Ward v British Broadcasting Corporation* [2007][10] in respect of s.12:

"Section 12, although it prevents the publication of Judge Plumstead's judgment and imposes restrictions upon discussion of the facts and evidence in the case, does not prevent publication of the names of the parties, the child or witnesses: Re B (A child) (Disclosure) [2004] EWHC 411 (Fam)."

So the transcript of the judgment is private to the parties unless the court decides that it is in the interests of justice to make it public. Accordingly the press should not quote from a transcript without the authority of the court. Lord Justice Wall admitted that it had been his practice throughout his time in the family courts to give judgments in open court.

"Every judgment that I published was routinely made available to the press, which did not, I have to say, appear to be even remotely interested, despite some of the cases, on their facts, being quite extraordinary ... I have an element of cynicism abut the current press campaign for "transparency" in family justice. That cynicism derives from many years of trying, without any success at all, to encourage responsible press interest in the issues which regularly come before family courts."

3. Children Act 1989

The second piece of major legislation is s.97(2) of the Children Act 1989. This section makes it a criminal offence to put into the public domain the identity of a child who is involved in the proceedings:

"2. No person shall publish to the public at large or any section of the public any material which is intended, or likely, to identify—

a. any child as being involved in any proceedings before the High Court, a county court or a magistrates' court in which any power under this Act or the Adoption and Children Act 2002 may be exercised by the court with respect to that or any other child; or

b. an address or school as being that of a child being involved in any such proceedings."

This section was the subject of judicial scrutiny by the Court of Appeal in *Clayton v Clayton* [2006].[11] It decided that the prohibition imposed by

[10] [2007] EWHC 616 (Fam).
[11] [2006] EWCA Civ 878.

s.97(2) ends when the particular proceedings are concluded. Interestingly in the *Webster* case Munby J. admits that he, in common with his judicial colleagues, believed exactly the opposite to what was decided:

"The common belief (which I confess I shared) that the statutory pro-hibition outlasted the existence of the proceedings has now been exploded for what it always was-yet another of the many fallacies and misunderstandings which have tended to bedevil this particular area of law."[12]

In light of this "confession" it is perhaps understandable that:

1. The media shows little inclination to attempt to report family cases by focusing on the issues and not the personalities.

2. The media, perhaps almost subconsciously, believes that the legal restrictions prevent a story being told in a way that would be of inter-est to the public.

A court should consider, as a matter of good practice, whether the restrictions under 97(2) should be continued beyond the conclusion of the proceedings. If the court does not make a restraining order then the parties and the media will be free of the restrictions imposed. In *Clayton* the mother and father had a shared care arrangement after their divorce. The father who was actively involved in the fathers' rights campaign wished to discuss the way the case had proceeded through the family justice system. He wished to do so in a responsible and objective way and to involve the media.

However, at the conclusion of the proceedings the judge ruled that s.97(2) prevented identification of the child until her 18th birthday and made an order preventing him from discussing the case openly because it would identify the child. The Court of Appeal discharged the injunc-tion and held that s.97(2) applied only while the proceedings were "live." They had concluded in July 2005.

However, the court was concerned that the father wished to make a film about he case. One salient feature was that the father had abducted his daughter and this was a fact that meant in light of the new methodology in respect of privacy laws her Art.8 rights were engaged. In addition because her upbringing was at issue her welfare was paramount within the terms of s.1 of the Children Act 1989. As a result the court substituted a prohibited steps order under s.1 relating to the making of the film.

The impact of the decision in *Clayton v Clayton* is that once care pro-ceedings have been concluded the restrictions imposed by s.97(2) cease.

These two statutory provisions are referred to by Munby J. in the *Webster* case as "automatic restraints."[13]

---

[12] [2006] EWHC 2733, at para.52.
[13] ibid., para.53.

There are other statutes that deserve to be mentioned. Section 71 of the Magistrates' Courts Act 1980 sets out the reporting restrictions that automatically apply when reporting family proceedings in the Magistrates' Court. Newspapers, periodicals and broadcasters can only lawfully print, publish or include in programme service the following particulars:

- Names, addresses and occupations of the parties and witnesses
- Grounds of the application and concise statement of charges, defences and countercharges in support of which evidence is given,
- Submissions on any point of law arising in the course of the proceedings and decisions of the court on them
- The decision of the court and any observations made by the court in giving the decision.[14]

It will be apparent from the above that this legislation is aimed at permitting the media to publish a limited amount of information, theoretically enough to convey the gist of the case, but without identifying any children involved in the proceedings. This covers all family proceedings in the Magistrates' Court and not just those under the Children Act.

The Judicial Proceedings (Regulation of Reports) Act 1926 (as amended) restricts among other things reports of judicial proceedings for divorce or dissolution of civil partnerships. Originally introduced to prevent"medical"details of divorcing parties appearing the"1920's equivalent of the Sunday tabloids, the Act is showing its age. The Guardian reported in late 2006 "Trial by headline—McCartney divorce turns toxic as Mills documents published." The sub-heading was "Coverage may contravene reporting law." (i.e. the 1926 Act.). Duncan Lamont, media partner at Charles Russell LLP, was quoted as saying:

"But the floodgates are opening because the family courts have indicated they wish to be seen to be more transparent . . . and injunctions are no longer given to those who have already invaded their own privacy and regarded their relationship(s) as being in the public domain. Financial information remains confidential and there is an implied undertaking to the court by the parties that money matters must only be passed to professional advisers, not journalists . . . To lawyers it is not the allegations made by Heather Mills that are sensational: it is that they are being published at all. The break up of their marriage has seen the unexpected return of Edwardian-style reporting of divorce cases."[15]

It has to be said that since that statement was made the newspapers have not exactly been packed with salacious divorce court reporting, confirming perhaps that personality rather than principle will lead the editorial decision-making.

[14] Judicial Studies Board Guidelines: *www.jsboard.co.uk*.
[15] Guardian October 19, 2006.

4. Strasbourg Compliant?

The picture is one of little media interest in family proceedings, pressure group activity for more transparency in the system and increasing judicial and until recently governmental support for the idea. What has yet to be worked out is the substance. Before evaluating the challenges ahead consideration must be given to the impact of the current law upon the media. The media will never willingly turn down a good story that will sell newspapers. Assuming that the story involves a child or young person then it is likely that the media will attempt to plead that its Art.10 rights. That may indeed coincide with the young person who wishes to tell their own story, relinquishing their Art.8 rights and adopting Art.10.

Take the following example:

> Girl becomes pregnant at the age of 12. The putative father (X) is approximately the same age. The date is 1999. She was taken into the care of her English local authority and an injunction granted to protect the identities of the parents. Stories appeared in the Scottish press to the effect that the Catholic Church had paid her not to abort the child. The child (Y) was subsequently made subject to a care order and then placed for adoption. The existence of an injunction did not prevent both a local newspaper and then the Mail on Sunday from running the story that a 13-year-old mother was being "forced" to hand over her child for adoption.

The media clearly believed that there were points of public importance that could not be aired because of the "gagging order." In 2002, the mother had returned to her family and the care order was discharged in September 2003. The mother (A) approached the Mail on Sunday and agreed to talk about her experiences in the care system and the "consequences of having unprotected sex." The newspaper was willing to publish the story and confirmed that there was no intention to name the father (X) or the child (Y) in the article. It was in effect A's story. The local authority sought an order to protect Y's identity. The mother (A) was described as a "mature and articulate young person."

The case was heard by Munby J. and was one of the first to take the post-Human Rights Act approach to resolving such situations. The judge referred to his own statement, in the case of *Kelly v BBC* [2001][16] saying that when exercising the courts inherent jurisdiction or wardship jurisdiction in relation to the media there were three situations to consider:

1 The jurisdiction is not exercisable at all.
2 The jurisdiction is exercisable but the court is exercising only its *protective* jurisdiction and therefore the child's welfare is not the paramount consideration.

---

[16] [2001] Fam 59, at p. 74.

3 The court is exercising a "custodial" jurisdiction when the child's interests are paramount.

Having made this statement the judge then went on to say that the analysis had to be revisited in light of the Human Rights Act. He had the benefit of the Court of Appeal's decision in *Re S (A child)*[17] to the effect that the". . . child's rights under Article 8 must be taken into account by the court if it is to comply with its obligations under section 6 of the Act."[18] The other judges took the same view:

Hale LJ: "Now that the Human Rights Act is in force, the relevance of the jurisdiction may simply be to provide the vehicle which enables the court to conduct the necessary balancing exercise between the competing rights of the child under Article 8 and the media under Article 10."[19]

Lord Phillips M.R.: "It is necessary in the individual case to balance Article 8 rights which are engaged against Article 10 rights [. . . of the media]"[20]

Summarising the position Munby J. concluded:

"The exercise of the jurisdiction now requires the court first to decide whether the child's rights under Article 8 are engaged and, if so then to conduct the necessary balancing exercise between the competing rights under Articles 8 and 10, considering the proportionality of the potential interference with each right considered independently."[21]

After carrying out the balancing exercise, Munby J. ordered that the story could be published always providing that the father and the daughter were not identified. The story could be told without the Art.8 rights of either being breached. The court also focused on A because her Art.10 rights were engaged not just the media's. She wished to tell her story and was mature enough to understand the implications of so doing.

The House of Lords then delivered judgment in the *re S (A Child)* [2004][22] appeal confirming the approach taken by the Court of Appeal. Munby J. in the *Webster* case[23] asks how this exercise is to be performed when a number of conflicting rights and interests have to be balanced. The answer is provided by the well-known speech of Lord Steyn in the *Re S* case[24] which identifies the four propositions mentioned in Chapter (4, p. 127):

1 Neither article has precedence.
2 If there is conflict between the two articles there must be the intense focus on the comparative importance of the specific rights being claimed.

[17] [2003] EWCA Civ 963.
[18] ibid., per Latham L.J. at para.75.
[19] ibid., at para.40.
[20] ibid., at para.108.
[21] *Torbay BC v News Group Newspapers* [2003] EWHC 2927.
[22] [2004] UKHL 47.
[23] Op cit at para.54.
[24] See n.22 for reference: at para.17.

Justifications for interfering with or restricting each right.
Proportionality test must be applied to each. Referred to as the "ultimate balancing test."

Finally, let us return to s.97 of the Children Act 1989. We have examined the impact of s.97(2) but have so far ignored the wording of s.97(4). It states:

"The court may, if satisfied that the welfare of the child requires it, by order dispense with the requirements of subsection (2) to such an extent as may be specified in the order."

That section too must be interpreted by reference to Convention rights. Section 97 as a whole must be read in such a way as to comply with the Convention simply because the section constitutes a restriction upon the media's right to report under Art.10. So in practice it is not only in circumstances where the welfare of the child requires it that subs.2 should be dispensed with. As Munby J. put it in the *Webster* case:

". . . the statutory phrase 'if . . . the welfare of the child requires it' should be read as a non-exhaustive expression of the terms on which the discretion can be exercised, so that the power is exercisable not merely if the welfare of the child requires it but wherever it is required to give effect, as required by the Convention, to the rights of others."[25]

The point is also made in *Ward v BBC* [2007][26]:

". . . both the disclosure jurisdiction and the restraint jurisdiction have to be exercised in accordance with the principles explained by Lord Steyn in *Re S (A Child)* . . . and by Sir Mark Potter P in *A Local Authority v. W* . . .[27] that is, by a 'parallel analysis' of those of the various rights protected by the European Convention fort the Protection of Human Rights and Fundamental Freedoms which are engaged, leading to the ultimate balancing test reflecting the Convention principle of proportionality."[28]

5. Conclusion

Judges do have discretion to allow the media to have greater access to proceedings in family courts. It appears that the discretion is not used as much as some judges would like. Perhaps if the media showed a greater

[25] [2006] EWHC 2733 at para.58.
[26] [2007] EWHC 616 (Fam).
[27] [2005] EWHC 1564 (Fam).
[28] [2007] EWHC 616 (Fam) at para.13.

interest in family cases and challenged the failure to permit access more often then things would change. This is not to say that the media is invariably denied access. The celebrated "Baby Charlotte" case received a tremendous amount of media coverage when a hospital trust asked the court whether it was obliged to resuscitate a seriously ill baby.[29] In 2006, the High Court was asked to rule on whether a child suffering from severe spinal muscular atrophy should be ventilated. Holman J. permitted the media to attend and report the court proceedings but ruled that the media could not identify the parties.[30] The judge acknowledged this was a case that should be heard in public. He went on to thank the media for the "sensitivity they have shown, at any rate within the courtroom."

The Department of Constitutional Affairs has published a response to a consultation exercise entitled Improving Transparency and Privacy in Family Courts.[31] It will come as no surprise to discover that many professionals working within the family justice system would be concerned if their anonymity were to be lost. There was a guarded welcome for responsible media reporting but little enthusiasm from the media for a system of accredited family court reporters if that meant judges could decide what should or should not be published. The government has promised to bring forward recommendations later in 2007.

With respect to the statutory provisions, Munby J. has suggested that two things need to happen. First, that s.12 of the Administration of Justice Act 1960 should be revoked in respect of children cases. The press then would only have s.97(2) to contend with resulting in the ability to attend and report the courts but not having the power to identify the children involved in the case. Judges would still have discretion to impose other restrictions if appropriate. Secondly, the press but not the public should have the right to attend family courts. Yet care should be taken not to confuse two things. The ability of the press to be free from the yoke of anonymity provisions is one thing but naming children does nothing to convince the public that the family justice system is working as well as can be expected.

There needs to be a new beginning with the stakeholders and that includes the media each being clear about their respective roles in the family justice system. The debate should begin in earnest once the government's recommendations are published.

6. Reporting the Criminal Courts

There are a number of restrictions imposed upon the media in its reporting of the criminal courts of this country. The open justice principle and

---

[29] *Wyatt v Portsmouth Hospitals NHS Trust* [2005] EWCA Civ 1181.
[30] *An NHS Trust v MB (A child)* [2006] EWHC 507 Fam.
[31] March 22, 2007. Available via *www.dca.g.v.uk* website.

the media's Art.10 rights go hand in hand in this process. Any restrictions though will clash with Art.10(1) rights and, therefore, must be justified within the context of Art.10(2).[32]

Article 6 of the Convention states that everyone has the right to a fair trial and that means that everything should be done to avoid "trial by media." This aspect was touched upon in the chapter on contempt of court:

> "The general rule is that the administration of justice must be done in public. The media is in court to report the proceedings to the public, the majority of whom will be unable to be there in person but who have a right to be informed as to what has occurred. Accordingly, unless there is a good and lawful reason, nothing should be done to prevent the publication to the wider public of fair and accurate reports of proceedings by the media."[33]

7. Youth Court

Section 49 of the Children & Young Persons Act 1933 prevents the press from reporting anything that will lead to the identity of a young person appearing before the court being disclosed. There it is an offence to publish or broadcast:

a   the name, address or school or any particular leading to the identification of any child or young person involved in the proceedings as a defendant or a witness;

b   any photograph of or including, any such person.

Anonymity though can be lifted if there is a good public interest reason for so doing. The reasons are listed at s.49 (4A):

- To avoid injustice to the juvenile.
- The public interest requires that anonymity be lifted.
- If the authorities need to trace a juvenile in connection with a serious offence.

Section 44 of the 1933 Act reminds us that every court in dealing with a child or young person . . . shall have regard to the welfare of the child.

There are two important cases to consider in respect of s.49. The first is *McKerry v Teesdale and Wear Valley Justices* [2000].[34] The Divisional Court thought that it would be a relatively rare event for the anonymity ban to

---

[32] See Chapter 1, Freedom of Expression.
[33] Extract from Judicial Studies Board guidelines available at *www.jsboard.co.uk*.
[34] [2001] EMLR 127.

be lifted. Great care should be exercised before doing so. The court was adamant that lifting the ban in order to name and shame the youth was not part of the exercise. Nor should it be seen as imposing an additional punishment upon the individual.[35] From the media's point of view the court should invite any reporters who are present to make representations. (There are unlikely to be many because a story without a name hardly constitutes a basis for catching the public's attention in order to persuade them to buy a newspaper.) The balancing of Art.8 and 10 rights will come into the equation. One public interest reason for lifting a ban is protection of the public. The court may deem it important that a community is aware that this particular young person is in their midst especially if the appearance in the youth court is not his first and presumably not expected to be his last.

The second case is *T v Director of Public Prosecutions & North East Press* [2003].[36] In this case the defendant reached the age of 18 during the course of the proceedings. As the anonymity rules applied only to those under 18 the press sought clarification as to whether they could report his identity. Sullivan J. held that his identity could be revealed. The case also confirmed that the purpose of the s.49 restriction was to prevent the defendant from the "adverse consequences of publicity" without being explicit as to what those might be.

8. Anti-Social Behaviour Orders (Asbo)

The Anti-Social Behaviour Act 2003 made it clear that there is no automatic ban on identifying a person who is made the subject of an Asbo. The media needs to exercise caution because it is still possible for the court to impose an order under s.39 of the Children & Young Persons Act 1933. The general consensus is that publicity is necessary to assist with the enforcement of the order. If the local community is unaware that an order has been made it will be impossible to help with the enforcement. As with the Youth Court, identifying a person subject to an Asbo is not meant to be an exercise in naming and shaming. As Lord Justice Kennedy said in *Stanley v London Borough of Brent* [2004][37]:

> "it is clear to me that, whether publicity is intended to inform, to reassure, to assist in enforcing the existing orders by policing, to inhibit the behaviour of those against whom the orders have been made, or to

---

[35] Op cit Lord Bingham C.J. at para.17.
[36] [2003] EWHC 2408.
[37] [2004] EWHC 2229.

deter others, it is unlikely to be effective unless it includes photographs, names and at least partial addresses. Not only do the readers need to know against whom orders have been made, but those responsible for publicity must leave no room for mis-identification."

The current position is neatly summarised in the Home Office Guide to Anti-Social Behaviour Orders.[38] The following are the major points for the media to note:

- An order made against a child or young person is usually made in open court and not subject to reporting restrictions.
- The information is in the public domain and newspapers are entitled to publish it.
- If the young person made subject to an Asbo has previous convictions for example from the Youth Court and reporting restrictions were not lifted in that court, no mention of those convictions should be made in the report of the Asbo proceedings.
- On imposing an Asbo it is possible to refer to the behaviour for which he has previous convictions—but not the convictions themselves.
- The court making the Asbo may impose a s.39 order.
- A court must have a good reason for making a s.39 order as the restriction on publicity may render the order less effective than it would have been if the community was aware of its existence.
- Age alone is insufficient to justify reporting restrictions.
- Section 141 of the Serious Organised Crime and Police Act 2005 permits reporting of a hearing for the breach of an Asbo. Prior to 1 July, 2005, as the hearing was conducted in the Youth Court, the proceedings were covered by s.49 of the 1933 Act. That is no longer the case.
- However if reporting restrictions applied at the original Asbo hearing they will still be effective at the breach hearing unless lifted by the court.
- The working assumption is that unless the circumstances have changed dramatically in the intervening period then the restrictions will remain in place.
- Recent photographs of the subject of the Asbo may be published in order to assist with the enforcement of the order. A dated photograph will be of little use to the community. [39]

9. Section 39 Orders

Adult defendants in both the Magistrates' and Crown Court do not enjoy any form of anonymity from reporting. If children appear in the adult

[38] Youth Justice Board August 2006.
[39] Home Office Guide to Asbos August 2006. Section 15 p.55.

courts for example on a serious charge such as murder or manslaughter lawyers acting for the defendant may ask the court to issue a s.39 order. It must be stressed that the making of such an order is at the discretion of the judge taking account of all the relevant circumstances. Section 39 reads:

> "In relation to any proceedings in any court the court may direct that -
> a. no newspaper report of the proceedings shall reveal the name, address or school, or include any particulars calculated to lead to the identification, of any child or young person concerned in the proceedings (as either defendant or witness)
> b. no picture shall be published in any newspaper as being or including a picture of any child or young person so concerned in the proceedings except insofar as permitted by the court . . ."

Section 39 may also be used in Asbo proceedings. It should be noted that this provision applies only to those who are "concerned in the proceedings." So, a s.39 order would not be appropriate to prevent an adult defendant from being named in order to protect a child of the family from the consequences of potentially adverse publicity about his father. Courts are occasionally sympathetic to the plight of family members and may seek to impose a s.39 order even though there is no jurisdiction to do so. Journalists should be vigilant and determine exactly why and for whose benefit the reporting restriction has been imposed.

Judges prevented from this course of action under the terms of s.39 may resort to other legislation for a remedy most notably s.11 of the Contempt of Court Act. It would appear however; that once a defendant has been identified in court then s.11 is inappropriate, as the key information will be in the public domain. At the time of writing, a number of newspaper groups including the Times and Mirror are seeking to appeal a decision to impose a s.11 order on a convicted paedophile on the basis that his children would be adversely affected by the publicity. The order was made by Judge Warwick McKinnon sitting at Croydon Crown Court.

It transpired that previously an order had been made under s.4 (2) of the Contempt of Court Act 1981 which of course can only limit publication not prohibit it altogether. The s.11 order was an attempt to achieve what s.4(2) was never designed to do.

The key issue for the media is when, and in what circumstances, should a s.39 order be imposed? Guidance may be obtained from the decisions of the Court of Appeal Criminal Division. Watkins L.J. said in *R v Crown Court at Leicester Ex p.S* [1992][40] that the "mere fact" that a child or young person was before the court would:

> ". . . normally be a good reason for restricting reports of the proceedings . . . it will only be in rare and exceptional circumstances that

[40] [1992] 2 All E.R. 659 at p. 662 (j).

directions under s.39 will not be given or having been given will be discharged."

That statement was immediately doubted by the Court of Appeal in *R. v Lee* [1993] on the basis that it blurred the distinction between proceedings in the Youth Court and those in the Crown Court"... a distinction that Parliament clearly intended to preserve."[41] Perhaps the most important decision is that of Simon Brown LJ sitting in the Queen's Bench Divisional Court *in R. v Winchester Crown Court ex p.B* [2000].[42] He set out a number of principles that are relevant to the question of whether a section 39 order should be imposed. They are:

1 Are there good reasons for naming the defendant?
2 Considerable weight must be given to the age of the offender and the potential damage to any young person of public identification as a criminal before the offender has the benefit or burden of adulthood.
3 Regard must be had to the welfare of the child (s.44).
4 The court should consider the deterrent effect on others of any publicity as a legitimate objective to be achieved.
5 There is strong public interest in knowing what has occurred in court and that includes the identity of the defendant.
6 The weight attributed to these factors may vary at different stages in the proceedings. After a guilty plea or a finding of guilt the public interest in knowing the identity of the criminal may be the determining factor particularly if the crime is "serious or detestable."
7 There may be notice of an appeal. That may be a material factor in deciding to impose a s.39 order.

After considering all the factors relevant to the case, the court must *indicate the reasons* why an order is imposed or lifted. The above factors were included in the report and approved by the court in the case of *The Queen on the Application of T v St Albans Crown Court* [2002][43].

The first thing for the judge to decide is whether to make a s.39 order. Once the decision has been taken to impose it, the focus of attention switches to its content. The leading authority is *R.v Southwark Crown Court Ex p. Godwin* [1992].[44] Glidewell L.J. said:

"In our view s.39 as a matter of law does not empower a court to order in terms that the names of the defendants be not published . . . the order itself must be restricted to the terms of section 39 (12 either specifically using those terms or using words to the like effect and no more.'"[45]

41 [1993] 2 All E.R. 170 at p. 176 (b).
42 [2000] 1 Cr App Rep 11.
43 [2002] EWHC 1129 (Admin) at para.20 *per* Elias J.
44 [1992] 1 Q.B. 190.
45 ibid., pp. 196H–197B.

The court is sending out a clear message that it is not up to the judge to determine whether the defendant should not be named. It is an editorial decision to decide how to identify the defendant without causing any members of his or her family to be identified, assuming that the order has been made on the assumption of protecting a child of the family from adverse publicity resulting from the case.

In that respect the decision of the Court of Appeal (Criminal Division) in *R. v Teesside Crown Court Ex p. Gazette Media Company Ltd* [2005][46] is instructive. In this case the father (S) of an 11-year-old girl had sent indecent photographs of his daughter to another man (L). The two men shared an interest in indecent photographs of children. At a later stage, the father offered to facilitate sexual relations between L and his daughter. The men were charged with conspiracy to rape and offences contrary to the Protection of Children Act 1978. The trial judge made an order under s.39 even though the girl was not a party to the proceedings. It purported to prevent:

"... reporting of any proceedings in respect of Regina v. S and L. No identification of the defendant S by name or otherwise the nature of the case against him, the identification of the alleged victim (S's daughter) her age, place of abode or any circumstances that may lead to her identification in connection with these proceedings."[47]

The press were unhappy at the wording of the order and when the judge refused to amend it, appealed to the Court of Appeal pursuant to s.159 of the Criminal Justice Act 1988. The Court of Appeal accepted that the wording went beyond that which is permissible under s.39 and in so doing relied upon the *Godwin* case for authority. It was argued in the court that the effect of *Godwin* should be limited as a result of the Human Rights Act coming into force and in particular account should be taken of the daughter's Art.8 rights. The court would have been more sympathetic to the argument if Art.8 was the only provision from the Convention to be relevant. Article 10 had also to be taken into account. Lord Steyn in *Re S (A Child)* [2005] had been careful to point out that the "new methodology" should not be used to create "further exceptions to the general principle of open justice."[48]

Were there other options available rather than to quash the original order and institute a new s.39 order that was *Godwin*-compliant? The daughter's identity could be protected by resorting to s.1(2) of the Sexual Offences Amendment Act 1992. The offence of conspiracy to rape is covered by this provision and therefore the daughter, as the intended victim, is guaranteed anonymity for life. Unfortunately, there are two offences to be reported in this case. While the daughter's identity must not be revealed by the media in respect of the conspiracy charge,

---

[46] [2005] EWCA Crim 1983.
[47] ibid., para.3.
[48] [2005] UKHL 47 at para.20.

the 1992 Act does not apply to offences under the Protection of Children Act 1978.

Therefore, the only option was to "cover" the latter case with the new s.39 order and the conspiracy case with s.1(2) of the 1992 Act. The judges went on to issue a warning that to name the father and simply refer to the intended victim as an "11-year-old schoolgirl" would breach both orders. The reason being that if it is known that the defendant has an 11-year-old daughter it will be reasonable for the public to conclude she was indeed the intended victim. (See comment later in chapter.)

It should also be noted that the Court expressed dissatisfaction with the *Godwin* case but did not seek to distinguish it. Lord Justice Maurice Kay delivering the judgment of the court said:

"We make no secret of the fact that, if it were not for *Godwin*, we would have construed section 39 as enabling an express restriction of the naming of S and we would have included such an express restriction in the order . . . all this disposes us to the view that we regret the limitation which *Godwin* places on the drafting of orders . . ."[49]

Readers should note that s.39 may at some stage be replaced by s.45 of the Youth Justice and Criminal Evidence Act 1999. Section 45(3) states:

"The court may direct that no matter relating to any person concerned in the proceedings shall, while he is under the age of 18, be included in any publication if it is likely to lead members of the public to identify him as a person concerned in the proceedings."

Attention should also be focused on s.44 of the 1999 Act. This provides that once a criminal investigation has begun nothing is to be published about a person under 18 if it is likely to identify him as being a person involved in the offence.

Taken together, ss.44 and 45 offer a major challenge to the "open justice" remit of the media. It remains to be seen whether they will be brought into force or whether the government will use them as Swords of Damocles to urge more responsible media reporting in sensitive cases.

10. Sexual Offences

The Sexual Offences Act 2003 lists numerous offences of a sexual nature, some involving sexual contact others not, for example the crime of

[49] [2005] EWCA (Crim) 1983, para.19.

voyeurism.[50] The Sexual Offences (Amendment) Act 1992 as amended[51] provides anonymity for the complainant/victim of any of these offences. Once an *allegation* has been made but before an arrest:

> "No matter relating to that person shall during that person's lifetime be included in any publication if it is likely to lead members of the public to identify that person as the person against whom the offence is alleged to have been committed."

Once a person has been *accused* of an offence (in practice this means charged):

> "No matter likely to lead members of the public to identify a person as the person against whom the offence is alleged to have been committed shall during the complainant's lifetime be included in any publication."

A new subs.(3A) was inserted into the 1992 Act as a result of Sch.2 of the 1999 Act. It identifies matter that must be specifically excluded:

- Person's name
- Person's address
- Identity of any school or other educational establishment attended by the person
- Identity of any place of work
- Any still or moving picture of the person.

These changes became effective in October 2004.

The media by and large adhere to the rules but there are occasional lapses. In February 2006 the Daily Express and the Daily Telegraph were ordered to pay a total of £15,000 compensation and fined £4,700 after publishing photographs of the victim of an alleged sexual assault. The photographs had been taken from behind. The woman was a member of the military and in uniform when attending court and it was held that she could easily be recognised. Care needs to be taken with such photographs and it may be advisable for photographs to be modified to prevent identification taking place. For example, the colour of hair could be changed or height could be manipulated.

In December 2006, the Sunderland Echo was fined and had to pay compensation after a rape victim was identified from a description published by the newspaper. Newspapers need to be on their guard. With the availability of the vast resources of the internet it would not require too much effort on behalf of third parties to research information appearing in newspapers and make an informed judgment as to the identity of a victim.

[50] Section 67.
[51] By Section 48 and Sch.2 of the Youth Justice and Criminal Evidence Act 1999.

11. Preliminary Hearings

The Magistrates' Court Act 1980 (s.8) lists the 10 matters that *can* be published when reporting on preliminary proceedings as long as there is prospect of a jury trial. They are:

- Identity of the court
- Names of magistrates
- Names, address, occupation of the parties and witnesses and the ages of the accused and witnesses
- Offence or a summary of the offences
- Names of legal representatives
- Decision of the court
- Charges on which the accused is sent for trial
- If committal proceedings are adjourned, the date and place to which they are adjourned
- Arrangement for bail if granted
- Legal aid arrangements

These have a fundamental impact on reporting of Magistrates' Courts and their practical application will be discussed later in the chapter.

12. Pre-Trial Hearings

A pre-trial hearing can take place after the accused has been sent for trial or after proceedings for the trial have been transferred to the Crown Court and before the start of the trial.[52] There are automatic restrictions upon reporting these hearings and in particular rulings made as part of these hearings.[53] These restrictions will apply until the trial has concluded.

13. Preparatory Hearings

In respect of such hearings that may take place where cases are expected to be complex or relatively lengthy reporting is restricted to the following matters[54]:

---

[52] Criminal Proceedings and Investigations Act 1996, s.39.
[53] ibid., s.41.
[54] Criminal Proceedings and Investigations Act 1996, s.37(9).

- Identity of the court
- Name of the judge
- Names, ages, home addresses and occupations of the accused and witnesses
- Offences charged
- Names of counsel and solicitors
- If proceedings are adjourned, the date and place to which they are adjourned
- Bail arrangements if any
- Legal aid arrangements.

14. Reporting Restrictions in Practice

Journalists face a whole raft of restrictions embodied in various statutes, some specifically geared to reporting, others where the impact on media is incidental to the main thrust of the legislation.

The Acts generate relatively few challenges which reach the higher courts but the restrictions embodied in them do apply day in, day out to journalists particularly when covering court.

Every working journalist should have at least a basic knowledge of what the restrictions are so as not to fall foul of them inadvertently. An even more detailed knowledge is needed to understand their limits and how to avoid allowing them to hinder reporting more than need be.

That requires an appreciation of the purpose the legislation is designed to serve but also how it is actually framed and how it may now require realignment to satisfy the broad requirements of the Human Rights Act.

Journalists need to keep pushing and testing those limits. Orders made under the various statutes are challenged more frequently, and often successfully, by journalists. It is hard to say whether this is because more poor orders are being made or whether journalists are becoming more adept and confident in challenging them.

An invaluable record and interpretation of the restrictions is provided in two Judicial Studies Board booklets produced by Sir Igor Judge, as senior presiding judge for England and Wales, with the Society of Editors and the Newspaper Society, which represent newspaper editors and publishers respectively. One covers reporting restrictions in the magistrates' court; the other in crown court. They are most helpful in outlining and explaining the restrictions, but also in establishing a best practice expectation and so can be used persuasively with court officials although they may be due an update.

The guide also provides advice to magistrates when considering an order, including the following:

"If the court is asked to exclude the media or prevent it from reporting anything, however informally, do not agree to do so without first

checking whether the law would permit the court to do so. Then consider whether the court ought to do so. Invite submissions from the
media or its legal representatives. The prime concern is the interests
of justice."

Magistrates are told to consider if the action is necessary in the interests
of justice and, where restrictions are necessary, how far they should go.

The advice can be turned into a useful checklist for reporters. If con-
fronted with any unusual restriction, always aim to establish the statute
being employed to impose the ban; the grounds for making the ban; the
precise extent of the ban and how it serves the interests of justice. Ask
the court to make a submission to query or challenge the ban. A well-run
court will invite submissions, so every reporter in court should have a
sense of whether a ban is both lawful and appropriate in the particular
circumstances and be ready to challenge it, at least in outline. There is no
harm in respectful haggling to limit the encroachment on meaningful
reporting of the case.

15. Children and Family Proceedings in Practice

Moves to submit family proceedings to greater public scrutiny have to
be welcomed as an extension of the principle of open justice but journalists are likely to be underwhelmed by the changes envisaged.

The freedom to sit in the court is of limited use to a journalist, "accredited" or otherwise, if the restrictions on subsequent reporting are so tight
as to prevent the publication of a meaningful account of the hearing.

The welcome development is the rejection, spurred by Strasbourg, of
blanket regulations demanding, or even just allowing as the norm, hearings be held in private. A case by case approach is required.

On paper, the overlapping current regulations don't really make it
obvious that, in practice, it is rarely worth a journalist attempting to cover
family proceedings. Many courts routinely exercise their discretion to sit
in private and, even where a journalist is allowed in, the restrictions
make it generally an unrewarding experience.

Even where access is not denied, where restrictions allow for outcome
but no evidence, it is virtually impossible to make sense of the case for
readers. But the most common off-putting element for journalists is the
degree of anonymity required. Under the planned changes this could be
extended to all participants.

With rare exceptions, the powers-that-be in the UK consistently struggle to grasp why identity is important to journalists. At best, they understand it purely in commercial or self-interest terms as part of a desire to
sell more papers—which is clearly not considered a valid justification.

Or they see the thirst for names as part of an obsession with "human interest" (how awful) and a clear failure to engage with the issues.

What they fail to realise is that the only way most ordinary people are ever going to engage with the issues is through the experience of real people with whom they can identify. Abstract concepts even where played out in an individual case, if presented in "disembodied" form will not capture the audience's attention. Coverage written in the language of an argument over finer points of law will largely go unread and unnoticed, which rather defeats the purpose of opening up the hearings in the first place.

Also, part of the benefit of scrutiny is greater accountability and added pressure on all parties to provide reliable evidence. Without identities being revealed, the level of submission to any kind of "reality check" is limited.

There are genuine challenges over meeting Art.8 requirements of parties involved in family proceedings but the lack of journalistic enthusiasm for covering "anonymised" cases and rulings should hardly come as a great surprise to anyone.

Weight is reasonably being given to the concerns and interests of children caught up in proceedings and the extra load on them of having to give evidence in front of media representatives but concerns about whether coverage would be fair and accurate are bogus. These are basic requirements of any media reports of court proceedings which could otherwise be held in contempt. No extra restrictions are required.

This raises an entirely reasonable question asked by media organisations during the consultation. Why can't family courts be covered on the same basis as any other? The presumption across the board would be of open access. Any necessary restrictions could be imposed case-by-case as required to be Convention-compliant. That should surely be the starting point for any new approach.

The identity of children could be protected, as it is in Youth Courts if need be, or by use of s.39 orders.

As for "accrediting" journalists, this smacks of vetting and licensing which has to be unhealthy in a democracy. Credentials could be sought as in the Youth Court permission for "bona fide" journalists but there is no sense of having to seek approval, just that a journalist seeking entry should be able to demonstrate who they are and who they represent. The implication is evident that such accreditation could be withdrawn.

The decision in *Clayton* is an interesting one as it allows the identity restrictions to end when the proceedings end which seems remarkably generous in light of the concerns raised during the recent consultation. However in practice courts can elect to impose restrictions beyond the end of proceedings and can fairly easily go through the motions of considering each case individually, despite the expectation of an "intense focus" on competing Article rights. At least this is a move away from a wholesale ban to a situation where an order would have to be imposed—and justified—in each case and then be open to media challenge.

The culture of the family courts, which are even more secretive in practice than they are required to be by statute or case law, would have to relax considerably before any significant level of meaningful media coverage could be achieved.

The remarks by the newly-created Constitutional Affairs Secretary, Lord Falconer, in the Lord Williams of Mostyn Memorial Lecture at Gray's Inn in March 2007, hardly raised media expectations. He said:

"Over the course of the consultation well over 200 children gave their views. Overwhelmingly they rejected the idea—with clear support of key third-party organisations speaking up for the interests of children.

"They are clear, crystal clear, that they do not want the family court filled with people who have no involvement in the proceedings. They do not want people in the court hearing private details of their lives. They are worried about themselves or their families being identified by people whom they do not trust to report responsibly."[55]

He continued:

"There are concerns about a lack of openness yet we know we have a requirement to maintain confidentiality. We need to ensure that people know more about what goes on in the court room; for example the reasons conclusions are reached.

"We also need to be clear that families and children know what they rightly regard as private information, rightly remains private. That may well involve allowing the press or the public in only where the judge expressly agreed as an exception."[56]

It was a long way from Munby J.'s rousing evidence to the Commons Constitutional Affairs Committee in May 2006 where he said of care proceedings:

"They are proceedings where the state is seeking to take away somebody's child. In many care proceedings the outcome is an adoption order, so the stakes in many care cases are higher, I would like to think, than even in many very serious crown court cases.

"I have to say it seems quite indefensible that there should be no access by the media and no access by the public to what is going on in the courts where judges are day-by-day taking people's children away."[57]

---

[55] Lord Williams of Mostyn Memorial Lecture at Gray's Inn, March 2007, reported in Media Lawyer.
[56] ibid.
[57] Commons Constitutional Affairs Committee, May 2006, reported in Media Lawyer.

Yet, under the proposals as they stand, where the government gives a little away with one hand and takes more away with the other, there could be even less media coverage of family proceedings than there is now. Given the intensely private nature of the matters at stake and the central involvement of children, how often will judges really stand up for Art.10 rights over Art.8?

16. Reporting the Criminal Courts in Practice

Children in criminal cases

Children have for decades enjoyed special protection in the courts although general assumptions of anonymity have been through a state of flux since the introduction of Anti-Social Behaviour Orders. These were designed to be less serious than full-blown criminal convictions and it was hoped they would nip bad behaviour in the bud among those subject to them. In those circumstances youngsters made subject to Asbos could arguably deserve anonymity more than Youth Court defendants accused of more serious crimes. However, as the media logically argued, given that an Asbo is designed as a warning to the public as well as to its subject, it cannot be properly effective unless the general public are aware of exactly who is subject to it.

For some tearaways the macho culture in which they operate means an Asbo marks a kind of coming of age and in their circles may be viewed as a badge of honour. The cockiness often belies a much deeper vulnerability which is worth considering in so far as journalists get caught up in the contradictions of trying to be seen to be punishing young louts while also protecting their chances of turning over a new leaf.

In Magistrates' Court, one of the biggest challenges for a journalist is to keep track of the status of proceedings and the position of a juvenile within them. Watch out for the exceptional circumstances of Asbo hearings. This is an area where challenges have resulted in a great deal of freeing up over the issue of identity.

Is the court sitting as an adult court or youth court? Is an Asbo or a breach of Asbo involved where anonymity is not automatic? Has a s.39 (or s.45 order for the Asbo breach) been made to "restore" anonymity? Are there grounds to challenge it? (See p. 232 for a reminder of the permutations.)

If a juvenile is found guilty in youth court of criminal damage for spraying graffiti, there is an automatic ban on identifying him. The police then make an application for an Asbo. The magistrates then become civil rather than criminal and the press can name and give details of why the Asbo is being granted, but can't identify him as someone who has just been fined for criminal damage. Also, the magistrates may impose a s.39 order on the Asbo hearing.

So one minute a journalist will be taking special care not to print anything which could lead to identification of a juvenile. The next minute the same journalist will be considering grounds for challenging the s.39 order so the juvenile can be named.

Challenging the presumption of anonymity in Youth Court is harder but it can be done. If the defendant is guilty, anonymity can be withdrawn if the offending was persistent, or serious, or had an impact on a number of people or where alerting the public would prevent further offences.

Remember the sections of the Youth Justice and Criminal Evidence Act 1999 that give anonymity to children as soon as a crime is reported are not enforcible yet. A child only gets automatic anonymity when appearing in youth court as a defendant or witness. However the PCC Code urges a protective approach to the reporting of children to help the case for continuing to keep the provision in abeyance.

17. Section 39 Children and Young Persons Act 1933

Journalists will not spend long in court before being placed under the obligations of a s.39 order requiring anonymity for a child involved in the proceedings.

Journalists should remember that s.39 orders cannot be made just because the defendant, victim or witness is a child. The court has to justify the protection. Section 39 orders are much used and abused, and are subject to frequent challenge by journalists, sometimes successfully.

The Judicial Studies Board guidelines on reporting the courts state:

"Courts have accepted that very young children cannot be harmed by publicity of which they will be unaware and therefore section 39 orders are unnecessary. Orders cannot be made in respect of dead children. Naming a young offender who has been convicted might act as a deterrent to others or the public might wish to know the outcome of the trial in serious cases.

"The order must be restricted to the terms of section 39. The court cannot ban the naming of any adult, nor make any order relating to any child or young person who is not involved in the proceedings. The court can give guidance on the practical effect of the order and what, in its view, might and might not be caught by the order. However, this can only be guidance, which is not binding on the media.

"If a reporting restriction is imposed, the justices must make it clear in court that a formal order has been made. The order should use the words of section 39 and identify the child or children involved with clarity. A written copy should be drawn up as soon as possible after the order has been made orally. Copies must be made available for media inspection and communicated to those not present when the order was made (eg by inclusion in the daily list). The order only applies to the proceedings in the court by which it was made, but is not limited as to time."

Courts have the discretion to hear reporters in person, or their legal representatives. Indeed many courts have formally reconsidered orders or other reporting restrictions after media representations by letter or discussion with the magistrates' legal adviser.

If the courts do not follow these guidelines, an order can be challenged.

18. Sexual Offences in Practice

The main controversy in this area of media law is over the right of anonymity for alleged victims in sexual offences, most particularly rape. This has arisen from a handful of high-profile cases where allegations have received a great deal of publicity and not resulted in a guilty verdict. The vast majority of rape cases fail to end in conviction because the case is not proved beyond reasonable doubt. However, in the case that brought the issue back to prominence, the complainant was shown to have made false allegations and to have a history of it. The controversy was all the greater because it arose from the woman being named in the House of Lords which provoked debate not just about anonymity for women who claim to have been raped but over the extent of protection of parliamentary privilege whether for a Lord or the media, to breach the anonymity requirement imposed by the Sexual Offences (Amendment) Act 1992.

There has always been disquiet in some quarters over the imbalance created by the anonymity for the complainant in a rape case whereby the woman (or man) claiming to have been raped is anonymous throughout, indeed for life, whereas the accused is identified in the normal way as a defendant in court proceedings and is thus identified whether found guilty or acquitted.

Many men accused of rape are acquitted. It has one of the lowest conviction rates of any category of prosecution. But an acquittal does not mean the complainant was lying; just that the case was not proven beyond reasonable doubt. There are extreme cases such as those raised by Lord Campbell-Savours where the trial exposes blatant manufacturing of an accusation. But the alleged victim could be prosecuted for perjury at which point anonymity could be lifted. The trial judge has the powers already to lift anonymity either to induce evidence to come forward or where it is in the public interest, but not just because there is an acquittal.

The protection of anonymity is crucial for many rape victims who would not otherwise come forward at all. The case raised does not justify any attempt to remove that protection as a remedy already exists to cover such extremes. To remove all anonymity would be taking a sledgehammer to crack a nut. Not for the first time, an outraged Lord is lobbying for changes to legislation to cure a problem which already has a solution. The answer is to call for effective use of the powers that exist rather than demand new ones.

The second question raised by the naming concerned the extent of privilege if the media repeated the name outside Parliament. Any privilege in parliamentary reporting for journalists would provide protection against actions for defamation. It does not provide immunity from prosecution under other statutes. The legal advice, which most news organisations followed, was that it did not protect the media from the sanctions of the Sexual Offences (Amendment) Act so the woman's name should not have been reported.

The Attorney General also advised at the time that full blown privilege from any prosecution only attaches to the official record in Hansard or on the Parliament channel; not to a journalist's note.

19. Protecting Anonymity in Practice

A requirement to protect anonymity is imposed under various of the acts which restrict reporting, most commonly for children and complainants in sexual offences cases.

Protecting anonymity requires a great deal more than removing a name or even the other specific elements listed in s.49 of the Children and Young Persons Act 1933.

Any combination of detail used needs to be considered in the context of each particular case. The audience must not be able to use the coverage to put two and two together and work out the identity of the anonymous party. How the person is described is the first hurdle. A 13-year-old can be said to be from a large city but not from a tiny village. Then there is the evidence to consider, including where the offence took place. Is it safe to describe an occupation, a hobby, a pub visited regularly? If the person protected has a close link to the defendant, it can become nigh on impossible to outline the evidence as the relationship would become obvious. This is particularly problematic when protecting the alleged victims of sexual crimes which may have taken place over a number of years while the victim was in the care of the abuser.

Great attention must be paid to how anonymity is protected given the particulars of each case and rigorous processes must be in place for careful checking of such copy by staff sufficiently experienced to be alert to the pitfalls.

In the *Teesside* case [2005], discussed earlier in this chapter, the judges regretted not being able to order restriction on reporting the name of the defendant.

Yet identifying the defendant is central to operating within the spirit of open justice. We cannot have anonymous people being jailed and we cannot have them evading news of their crime being placed in the public domain. Anonymity for a defendant must surely be an absolute last resort. There are genuine dilemmas, although the court's stance and conclusion was unduly harsh.

At para.19 they say:

"Offences of the kind established in this case of S and L are frequently committed by fathers and stepfathers. The history of photography and the planning of further offences are indicative of a close relationship between the offender and the victim. If the offender is named and the victim is described as 'an 11-year-old schoolgirl' in circumstances in which the offender has an 11-year-old daughter, it is at least arguable that the composite picture presented embraces 'particulars calculated to lead to the identification' of the victim."

They considered, but for *Godwin*, that the solution would have been to withhold the identity of the defendant. The alternative, and for journalists preferable, conclusion is that greater care was needed in the degree of detail given from the proceedings. Because the public is now more aware that abuse takes place most often in the home, description of the offences and recording of the evidence has to be quite seriously curtailed.

Certainly it is established practice to avoid being precise about ages or, where offences come to light many years later, as to the exact timing of the offences, so that, as the judges say, the audience cannot follow the trail to the children. The victim cannot be shown to be in the care of the defendant and a string of offences over time makes this difficult to achieve.

The approach settled upon by the PCC is not to be derided. A commitment to naming the defendant and withholding details of relationship and more tends to deprive the media of the newsiest angle and is actually indicative of restraint in the interests of justice being seen to be done. It would be nice if the media were just occasionally given some credit in the courts for trying to operate in something other than naked self-interest.

20. Jigsaw Identification

Where more than one media organisation is going to run a case requiring anonymity, it is vital they take a consistent line on broadly what to include and what to omit so as to satisfy that requirement. The most crucial is for everyone to name the defendant but omit the relationship. Until very recently there was a great risk of a member of the public piecing identity together from multiple sources. Local newspapers have tended to identify the defendant on the ground of public accountability, but nationals were more likely to go for the storyline even if that meant sacrificing all identities. Eventually the Press Complaints Commission brought everyone in line.

The PCC code provides the guidance to ensure a consistent approach although, locally, it is always worth confirming that other media representatives are taking the same line.

1 The press must not, even if legally free to do so, identify children under 16 who are victims or witnesses in cases involving sex offences.

2 In any press report of a case involving a sexual offence against a child:
   i. The child must not be identified
   ii. The adult may be identified
   iii. The word "incest" must not be used where a child victim might be identified
   iv. Care must be taken that nothing in the report implies the relationship between the accused and the child.

Any reporter covering such a case needs to appreciate that this is one instance where collaboration with the competition is required. The court may well remind the press bench of the demands of anonymity. Reporters need to bear in mind the Code but also discuss, given the particular circumstances of the case, what can safely be included and what cannot so nobody subsequently goes beyond the agreed limits. Newsdesks should be aware of this and further discussion may be required between news organisations before publication.

21. Covering Court

A raft of reporting restrictions applies to coverage of adult courts. The ten-points of s.8 Magistrates' Court Act 1980 are the most frequently invoked and are worth remembering by rote together with the detail of the occasions when they do and do not apply.

The important guide to their application is to keep in mind their purpose. The restrictions on the various hearings in court in the run up to the trial are motivated by the same desires as the Contempt of Court Act. They are there to protect a defendant's Art.6 rights by safeguarding the integrity of the trial, most notably the role of the jury.

So the aim of the limits is to allow the public to know the basic details of who is in court, what they are accused of doing, where and when, and what is happening to them within the legal process. They specifically prevent use of any evidence at that stage which would suggest whether the defendant is guilty or innocent.

As long as there is a chance of a case ending up at jury trial, the restrictions will apply. So if a defendant enters a formal guilty plea or is acquitted, they do not apply. If a case is definitely going to be tried before magistrates they do not apply (with the exception of preliminary hearings to determine admissibility of evidence at trial by magistrates).

In practice, the restrictions are breached daily by court reporters embellishing their reports with extra detail beyond the ten points despite it being a criminal offence. The classic additions are uncontentious points such as what the defendant is wearing. There is also room to include a fair amount of information within the scope of "details of the charge" but anything that is presented as evidence or has a bearing on guilt is dangerous. Technically even a protestation of innocence is beyond the ten points but prosecution would be impossible to sustain given that the system assumes any defendant is innocent unless proven guilty.

However, a journalist reading these extended reports might be lulled into a false sense of security. Journalists need to be aware that, although prosecutions under the section are rare, any breach of the ten points is technically an offence. There is no requirement on the prosecution to prove that a trial was affected or that the journalist had any intent to prejudice proceedings. As ever, know your law and only ever take a calculated risk.

CONCLUSION—THE JOURNALIST

When the ECHR was incorporated into the Human Rights Act, the media fought to enshrine freedom of expression into what is the nearest construct Britain has to a written constitutional Bill of Rights.

There was a hope—expressed in S.12 (4) of the HRA—that freedom of expression being so crucial to democracy would edge it where the scales were otherwise evenly balanced, but this has been expressly ruled out by the courts. The Section states that the court must have regard to the importance which the Convention attaches to freedom of expression. In practice, the courts need only say they do but now work on the basis that the Section lends Art.10 no special consideration over any other.

It was perhaps also an attempt to capture the sense of collective rights. The whole basis of the ECHR and the UN Declaration of Human Rights is to protect the individual. In the wake of the Holocaust, this was entirely proper and understandable and its protection is needed as much across the world today as it ever was. However it inevitably downplays concepts of public good. In law, when a journalist goes up against the subject of an investigation, it is the individual right to freedom of expression up against the individual right to privacy or fair trial or whatever. Despite various nods to the vital role of a free press in a democracy—its vital contribution to the collective good—this is not enough to weigh the scales in our favour. No right is allowed to trump another.

Also the convention was designed to protect individuals against agents of the state. It was not originally envisaged as coming into play to resolve disputes between private parties but this is very much what it has become.

Indeed, as *Wainwright* and *Peck* demonstrate, claimants are actually finding it harder to achieve redress against public authorities. Other bodies, such as the media, which have somehow been embraced by the Act, are being called to account and paying for their infringements, but the very organisations the convention was designed to curb are still not feeling its force. It is remarkable how the State somehow manages to exempt itself from remedy even in an Act expressly targeted at its actions. One would have thought it applied perfectly to occasions such as the over-the-top stripsearches of the Wainwrights but no, somehow the related statutes cannot be "stretched" to fit; the requirements of the Human Rights Act cannot be "shoehorned" into existing legislation where agents of the state are involved.

No wonder journalists place so little confidence in the chances of Parliament coming up with an effective defence of Art.10 rights. Talk about being between a rock and a hardplace. Piecemeal, adhoc, judge-made restrictions on one hand; or, on the other, an explicit Privacy Act drawn up by a Parliament which attempts to wriggle out of its own responsibilities under the Act and resists attempts at greater accountability. Even if Parliament were persuaded to draw up a Privacy Act which was all-embracing rather than targeted only against the media, the Act would still be subject to the vagaries of judicial interpretation, as all statute is.

Privacy law would be drafted by MPs with a clear self-interest in gagging the press. The danger is that it would become more about set-tling old scores against the media and using their power to protect them-selves. These are the same MPs many of whom have battled to exempt themselves from the requirements of the Freedom of Information Act. If we cannot trust an independent judiciary to give sufficient weight to Freedom of Expression for the individual and society, what chance have we with Parliament?

Few journalists would attempt to defend their right to report on whether or not a celebrity is "good in bed" but there is no simple way to rule out whole categories of story. Who is to say what is important in society? What matters enough to become part of public discourse even if it causes an individual some embarrassment or inconvenience?

On a bad day it seems Art.10 hardly counts for anything. Far from Art.10 trumping other Articles it seems to be given less consideration. It is noted but rarely with any sympathy for those who want to exercise it and certainly no acknowledgment that a "hurt" is being caused by denying them those rights. It seems the media has to justify its very exist-ence; that the UK still works on a presumption that everything is secret unless there is a reason to make it public rather than vice versa.

Free and responsible media is not going to make life comfortable for those in positions of responsibility. Yet it is those people who set the boundaries. How do we protect justified ruffling of feathers, including those of the powerful?

Individuals deserve protection under Art.8 as a means of helping to develop every human being's personality. But individual rights to freedom of expression are being trampled underfoot. How can we pos-sibly comment upon and analyse our own existence without reference to other people, especially those with whom we have crossed paths and particularly where we have shared an intimate relationship? Where is the wringing of hands over the damage to "self" from being gagged?

Maybe defence of Art.8 rights will force the news media to rule out the celebrity-driven froth and, in doing so, bring more significant issues to the fore. The Mirror tried it under editor Piers Morgan as news of the Iraq war boosted sale. He pledged a celeb-free agenda and a focus on less trivial concerns, but it didn't last (and neither did he).

It would be lovely to imagine that if all newspapers confined them-selves to high-minded coverage of the workings of the formal public realm, that those millions of readers would make the switch and that the media would be allowed more room for manoeuvre to place significant stories in the public domain.

More likely, as privacy law elsewhere indicates, the media would be weakened across the board; hurdles would become even higher and the definitions of public interest even narrower.

Knock out "real" celebrity stories from the popular tabloids and they are more likely to be replaced with air-brushed, celebrity-endorsed image-enhancing coverage. How is that going to help raise the level of public debate? It will just reinforce the retreat from the public domain.

Yes, popular tabloids tread on toes, include large dollops of "tittle tattle" and on any given day do not obviously uphold the most noble traditions of "responsible journalism." That does not mean they should be prevented from doing what they do.

Tighter curbs on freedom of expression could drive even more of our audience into the fantasy world so many millions of us seem to prefer to the real one. We already live increasingly in virtual online environments where people express themselves to the hilt. It seems some people only feel they can be their true self when pretending to be someone else.

There was disappointment that *McKennitt v Ash* did not go to appeal. Privacy is being passed to and fro between judiciary, Parliament and Government and no-one wants to be left holding the baby. Maybe the Law Lords are looking for a case involving a mainstream news organisation from which it is easier to establish those general principles Browne has gone some way to spelling it out but we can expect more judgments in the privacy arena.

Meanwhile reporters are being murdered in countries all around the world for trying to tell it like it is; to provide the public with real information and fuller insight into what is going on in their world, especially but not exclusively through the actions of the powerful.

Over the past 12 months, the courts have significantly developed the laws relating to privacy; suggested that the family justice system should be opened up; re-stated the defence of public interest privilege and taken a more pragmatic approach on protection of sources. The message therefore is loud and clear. Journalists must keep a weather eye on the courts because the courts will continue to pass judgments on issues of fundamental importance to the media and its ability to maximise its rights to freedom of expression.

We hope this book will prove to be informative and help to stimulate debate about the relationship between the law and the media as they handle the challenges ahead.

Perhaps the last word should be left to Sedley LJ in the recent case of *Roberts & Another v. Gable & Others*[1]:

> "Where rights to reputation and privacy have wilted somewhat in the bright light of First Amendment jurisprudence, the English common law, now reinforced by the European Convention on Human Rights, seeks to hold the two in a sometimes difficult balance, calibrated by the concept of responsible journalism."

[1] [2007] EWCA Civ 721

APPENDIX 1

HUMAN RIGHTS ACT 1998

1998 CHAPTER 42

Sweet & Maxwell Ltd.

An Act to give further effect to rights and freedoms guaranteed under the European Convention on Human Rights; to make provision with respect to holders of certain judicial offices who become judges of the European Court of Human Rights; and for connected purposes.

[9th November 1998]

BE IT ENACTED by the Queen's most Excellent Majesty, by and with the advice and consent of the Lords Spiritual and Temporal, and Commons, in this present Parliament assembled, and by the authority of the same, as follows:—

Introduction

1.— The Convention Rights.

1 In this Act "the Convention rights" means the rights and fundamental freedoms set out in—
   a Articles 2 to 12 and 14 of the Convention,
   b Articles 1 to 3 of the First Protocol, and
   c [Article 1 of the Thirteenth Protocol][1],
   as read with Articles 16 to 18 of the Convention.

2 Those Articles are to have effect for the purposes of this Act subject to any designated derogation or reservation (as to which see sections 14 and 15).

3 The Articles are set out in Schedule 1.

4 The Secretary of State may by order make such amendments to this Act as he considers appropriate to reflect the effect, in relation to the United Kingdom, of a protocol.

5 In subsection (4) "protocol" means a protocol to the Convention—
   a which the United Kingdom has ratified; or
   b which the United Kingdom has signed with a view to ratification.

6 No amendment may be made by an order under subsection (4) so as to come into force before the protocol concerned is in force in relation to the United Kingdom.

2.— Interpretation of Convention rights.

1 A court or tribunal determining a question which has arisen in connection with a Convention right must take into account any—
   a judgment, decision, declaration or advisory opinion of the European Court of Human Rights,

---

[1] words substituted by Human Rights Act 1998 (Amendment) Order 2004/1574 art. 2(1)

b opinion of the Commission given in a report adopted under Article 31 of the Convention,

c decision of the Commission in connection with Article 26 or 27(2) of the Convention, or

d decision of the Committee of Ministers taken under Article 46 of the Convention, whenever made or given, so far as, in the opinion of the court or tribunal, it is relevant to the proceedings in which that question has arisen.

2 Evidence of any judgment, decision, declaration or opinion of which account may have to be taken under this section is to be given in proceedings before any court or tribunal in such manner as may be provided by rules.

3 In this section "rules" means rules of court or, in the case of proceedings before a tribunal, rules made for the purposes of this section—

a by [the Lord Chancellor or]² the Secretary of State, in relation to any proceedings outside Scotland;

b by the Secretary of State, in relation to proceedings in Scotland; or

c by a Northern Ireland department, in relation to proceedings before a tribunal in Northern Ireland—

i. which deals with transferred matters; and

ii. for which no rules made under paragraph (a) are in force.

Legislation

3.— Interpretation of legislation.

1 So far as it is possible to do so, primary legislation and subordinate legislation must be read and given effect in a way which is compatible with the Convention rights.

2 This section—

a applies to primary legislation and subordinate legislation whenever enacted;

b does not affect the validity, continuing operation or enforcement of any incompatible primary legislation; and

c does not affect the validity, continuing operation or enforcement of any incompatible subordinate legislation if (disregarding any possibility of revocation) primary legislation prevents removal of the incompatibility.

4.— Declaration of incompatibility.

1 Subsection (2) applies in any proceedings in which a court determines whether a provision of primary legislation is compatible with a Convention right.

2 If the court is satisfied that the provision is incompatible with a Convention right, it may make a declaration of that incompatibility.

3 Subsection (4) applies in any proceedings in which a court determines whether a provision of subordinate legislation, made in the exercise of a power conferred by primary legislation, is compatible with a Convention right.

4 If the court is satisfied—

a that the provision is incompatible with a Convention right, and

b that (disregarding any possibility of revocation) the primary legislation concerned prevents removal of the incompatibility,

it may make a declaration of that incompatibility.

5 In this section "court" means—

a the House of Lords;

b the Judicial Committee of the Privy Council;

c the Courts-Martial Appeal Court;

d in Scotland, the High Court of Justiciary sitting otherwise than as a trial court or the Court of Session;

e in England and Wales or Northern Ireland, the High Court or the Court of Appeal.

---

² words inserted by Transfer of Functions (Lord Chancellor and Secretary of State) Order 2005/3429 Sch. 1 para. 3

6   A declaration under this section ("a declaration of incompatibility")—
    a does not affect the validity, continuing operation or enforcement of the provision
    in respect of which it is given; and
    b is not binding on the parties to the proceedings in which it is made.

5.— Right of Crown to intervene.

1   Where a court is considering whether to make a declaration of incompatibility, the
    Crown is entitled to notice in accordance with rules of court.

2   In any case to which subsection (1) applies—
    a a Minister of the Crown (or a person nominated by him),
    b a member of the Scottish Executive,
    c a Northern Ireland Minister,
    d a Northern Ireland department,
    is entitled, on giving notice in accordance with rules of court, to be joined as a party
    to the proceedings.

3   Notice under subsection (2) may be given at any time during the proceedings.

4   A person who has been made a party to criminal proceedings (other than in
    Scotland) as the result of a notice under subsection (2) may, with leave, appeal to the
    House of Lords against any declaration of incompatibility made in the proceedings.

5   In subsection (4)—
    "criminal proceedings" includes all proceedings before the Courts-Martial Appeal
    Court; and
    "leave" means leave granted by the court making the declaration of incompatibility
    or by the House of Lords.

Public authorities

6.— Acts of public authorities.

1   It is unlawful for a public authority to act in a way which is incompatible with a
    Convention right.

2   Subsection (1) does not apply to an act if—
    a as the result of one or more provisions of primary legislation, the authority could
    not have acted differently; or
    b in the case of one or more provisions of, or made under, primary legislation which
    cannot be read or given effect in a way which is compatible with the Convention
    rights, the authority was acting so as to give effect to or enforce those provisions.

3   In this section "public authority" includes—
    a a court or tribunal, and
    b any person certain of whose functions are functions of a public nature,
    but does not include either House of Parliament or a person exercising functions in
    connection with proceedings in Parliament.

4   In subsection (3) "Parliament" does not include the House of Lords in its judicial
    capacity.

5   In relation to a particular act, a person is not a public authority by virtue only of sub-
    section (3)(b) if the nature of the act is private.

6   "An act" includes a failure to act but does not include a failure to—
    a introduce in, or lay before, Parliament a proposal for legislation; or
    b make any primary legislation or remedial order.

7.— Proceedings.

1   A person who claims that a public authority has acted (or proposes to act) in a way
    which is made unlawful by section 6(1) may—
    a bring proceedings against the authority under this Act in the appropriate court or
    tribunal, or
    b rely on the Convention right or rights concerned in any legal proceedings,
    but only if he is (or would be) a victim of the unlawful act.

2 In subsection (1)(a)"appropriate court or tribunal"means such court or tribunal as may be determined in accordance with rules; and proceedings against an authority include a counterclaim or similar proceedings.

3 If the proceedings are brought on an application for judicial review, the applicant is to be taken to have a sufficient interest in relation to the unlawful act only if he is, or would be, a victim of that act.

4 If the proceedings are made by way of a petition for judicial review in Scotland, the applicant shall be taken to have title and interest to sue in relation to the unlawful act only if he is, or would be, a victim of that act.

5 Proceedings under subsection (1)(a) must be brought before the end of—
a the period of one year beginning with the date on which the act complained of took place; or
b such longer period as the court or tribunal considers equitable having regard to all the circumstances,
but that is subject to any rule imposing a stricter time limit in relation to the procedure in question.

6 In subsection (1)(b)"legal proceedings"includes—
a proceedings brought by or at the instigation of a public authority; and
b an appeal against the decision of a court or tribunal.

7 For the purposes of this section, a person is a victim of an unlawful act only if he would be a victim for the purposes of Article 34 of the Convention if proceedings were brought in the European Court of Human Rights in respect of that act.

8 Nothing in this Act creates a criminal offence.

9 In this section"rules"means—
a in relation to proceedings before a court or tribunal outside Scotland, rules made by the [the Lord Chancellor or][3] Secretary of State for the purposes of this section or rules of court,
b in relation to proceedings before a court or tribunal in Scotland, rules made by the Secretary of State for those purposes,
c in relation to proceedings before a tribunal in Northern Ireland—
i. which deals with transferred matters; and
ii. for which no rules made under paragraph (a) are in force,
rules made by a Northern Ireland department for those purposes,
and includes provision made by order under section 1 of the Courts and Legal Services Act 1990.

10 In making rules, regard must be had to section 9.

11 The Minister who has power to make rules in relation to a particular tribunal may, to the extent he considers it necessary to ensure that the tribunal can provide an appropriate remedy in relation to an act (or proposed act) of a public authority which is (or would be) unlawful as a result of section 6(1), by order add to—
a the relief or remedies which the tribunal may grant; or
b the grounds on which it may grant any of them.

12 An order made under subsection (11) may contain such incidental, supplemental, consequential or transitional provision as the Minister making it considers appropriate.

13 "The Minister"includes the Northern Ireland department concerned.

8.— Judicial remedies.

1 In relation to any act (or proposed act) of a public authority which the court finds is (or would be) unlawful, it may grant such relief or remedy, or make such order, within its powers as it considers just and appropriate.

2 But damages may be awarded only by a court which has power to award damages, or to order the payment of compensation, in civil proceedings.

---

[3] words inserted by Transfer of Functions (Lord Chancellor and Secretary of State) Order 2005/3429 Sch. 1 para.3

3 No award of damages is to be made unless, taking account of all the circumstances of the case, including—
a any other relief or remedy granted, or order made, in relation to the act in question (by that or any other court), and
b the consequences of any decision (of that or any other court) in respect of that act, the court is satisfied that the award is necessary to afford just satisfaction to the person in whose favour it is made.

4 In determining—
a whether to award damages, or
b the amount of an award,
the court must take into account the principles applied by the European Court of Human Rights in relation to the award of compensation under Article 41 of the Convention.

5 A public authority against which damages are awarded is to be treated—
a in Scotland, for the purposes of section 3 of the Law Reform (Miscellaneous Provisions) (Scotland) Act 1940 as if the award were made in an action of damages in which the authority has been found liable in respect of loss or damage to the person to whom the award is made;
b for the purposes of the Civil Liability (Contribution) Act 1978 as liable in respect of damage suffered by the person to whom the award is made.

6 In this section—
"court" includes a tribunal;
"damages" means damages for an unlawful act of a public authority; and
"unlawful" means unlawful under section 6(1).

9.— Judicial acts.

1 Proceedings under section 7(1)(a) in respect of a judicial act may be brought only—
a by exercising a right of appeal;
b on an application (in Scotland a petition) for judicial review; or
c in such other forum as may be prescribed by rules.

2 That does not affect any rule of law which prevents a court from being the subject of judicial review.

3 In proceedings under this Act in respect of a judicial act done in good faith, damages may not be awarded otherwise than to compensate a person to the extent required by Article 5(5) of the Convention.

4 An award of damages permitted by subsection (3) is to be made against the Crown; but no award may be made unless the appropriate person, if not a party to the proceedings, is joined.

5 In this section—
"appropriate person" means the Minister responsible for the court concerned, or a person or government department nominated by him;
"court" includes a tribunal;
"judge" includes a member of a tribunal, a justice of the peace and a clerk or other officer entitled to exercise the jurisdiction of a court;
"judicial act" means a judicial act of a court and includes an act done on the instructions, or on behalf, of a judge; and
"rules" has the same meaning as in section 7(9).

Remedial action

10.— Power to take remedial action.

1 This section applies if—
a a provision of legislation has been declared under section 4 to be incompatible with a Convention right and, if an appeal lies—
i. all persons who may appeal have stated in writing that they do not intend to do so;
ii. the time for bringing an appeal has expired and no appeal has been brought within that time; or

iii. an appeal brought within that time has been determined or abandoned; or

b it appears to a Minister of the Crown or Her Majesty in Council that, having regard to a finding of the European Court of Human Rights made after the coming into force of this section in proceedings against the United Kingdom, a provision of legislation is incompatible with an obligation of the United Kingdom arising from the Convention.

2 If a Minister of the Crown considers that there are compelling reasons for proceeding under this section, he may by order make such amendments to the legislation as he considers necessary to remove the incompatibility.

3 If, in the case of subordinate legislation, a Minister of the Crown considers—

a that it is necessary to amend the primary legislation under which the subordinate legislation in question was made, in order to enable the incompatibility to be removed, and

b that there are compelling reasons for proceeding under this section,

he may by order make such amendments to the primary legislation as he considers necessary.

4 This section also applies where the provision in question is in subordinate legislation and has been quashed, or declared invalid, by reason of incompatibility with a Convention right and the Minister proposes to proceed under paragraph 2(b) of Schedule 2.

5 If the legislation is an Order in Council, the power conferred by subsection (2) or (3) is exercisable by Her Majesty in Council.

6 In this section "legislation" does not include a Measure of the Church Assembly or of the General Synod of the Church of England.

7 Schedule 2 makes further provision about remedial orders.

Other rights and proceedings

11. Safeguard for existing human rights.

A person's reliance on a Convention right does not restrict—

a any other right or freedom conferred on him by or under any law having effect in any part of the United Kingdom; or

b his right to make any claim or bring any proceedings which he could make or bring apart from sections 7 to 9.

12.— Freedom of expression.

1 This section applies if a court is considering whether to grant any relief which, if granted, might affect the exercise of the Convention right to freedom of expression.

2 If the person against whom the application for relief is made ("the respondent") is neither present nor represented, no such relief is to be granted unless the court is satisfied—

a that the applicant has taken all practicable steps to notify the respondent; or

b that there are compelling reasons why the respondent should not be notified.

3 No such relief is to be granted so as to restrain publication before trial unless the court is satisfied that the applicant is likely to establish that publication should not be allowed.

4 The court must have particular regard to the importance of the Convention right to freedom of expression and, where the proceedings relate to material which the respondent claims, or which appears to the court, to be journalistic, literary or artistic material (or to conduct connected with such material), to—

a the extent to which—

i. the material has, or is about to, become available to the public; or

ii. it is, or would be, in the public interest for the material to be published;

b any relevant privacy code.

5 In this section—

"court" includes a tribunal; and

"relief" includes any remedy or order (other than in criminal proceedings).

13.— Freedom of thought, conscience and religion.

1 If a court's determination of any question arising under this Act might affect the exercise by a religious organisation (itself or its members collectively) of the Convention right to freedom of thought, conscience and religion, it must have particular regard to the importance of that right.

2 In this section "court" includes a tribunal.

Derogations and reservations

14.— Derogations.

1 In this Act "designated derogation" means any derogation by the United Kingdom from an Article of the Convention, or of any protocol to the Convention, which is designated for the purposes of this Act in an order made by the [Secretary of State][4].

3 If a designated derogation is amended or replaced it ceases to be a designated derogation.

4 But subsection (3) does not prevent the [Secretary of State][5] from exercising his power under subsection (1) to make a fresh designation order in respect of the Article concerned.

5 The [Secretary of State][6] must by order make such amendments to Schedule 3 as he considers appropriate to reflect—
   a any designation order; or
   b the effect of subsection (3).

6 A designation order may be made in anticipation of the making by the United Kingdom of a proposed derogation.

15.— Reservations.

1 In this Act "designated reservation" means—
   a the United Kingdom's reservation to Article 2 of the First Protocol to the Convention; and
   b any other reservation by the United Kingdom to an Article of the Convention, or of any protocol to the Convention, which is designated for the purposes of this Act in an order made by the [Secretary of State][7].

2 The text of the reservation referred to in subsection (1)(a) is set out in Part II of Schedule 3.

3 If a designated reservation is withdrawn wholly or in part it ceases to be a designated reservation.

4 But subsection (3) does not prevent the [Secretary of State][8] from exercising his power under subsection (1)(b) to make a fresh designation order in respect of the Article concerned.

5 The [Secretary of State][9] must by order make such amendments to this Act as he considers appropriate to reflect—
   a any designation order; or
   b the effect of subsection (3).

[4] words substituted by Secretary of State for Constitutional Affairs Order 2003/1887 Sch. 2 para. 10(1)
[5] words substituted by Secretary of State for Constitutional Affairs Order 2003/1887 Sch. 2 para. 10(1)
[6] words substituted by Secretary of State for Constitutional Affairs Order 2003/1887 Sch. 2 para. 10(1)
[7] words substituted by Secretary of State for Constitutional Affairs Order 2003/1887 Sch. 2 para. 10(1)
[8] words substituted by Secretary of State for Constitutional Affairs Order 2003/1887 Sch. 2 para. 10(1)
[9] words substituted by Secretary of State for Constitutional Affairs Order 2003/1887 Sch. 2 para. 10(1)

16.— Period for which designated derogations have effect.

1   If it has not already been withdrawn by the United Kingdom, a designated derogation ceases to have effect for the purposes of this Act, at the end of the period of five
years beginning with the date on which the order designating it was made.

2   At any time before the period—
  a   fixed by subsection (1), or
  b   extended by an order under this subsection,
comes to an end, the [Secretary of State][10] may by order extend it by a further period
of five years.

3   An order under section 14(1) ceases to have effect at the end of the period for consideration, unless a resolution has been passed by each House approving the order.

4   Subsection (3) does not affect—
  a   anything done in reliance on the order; or
  b   the power to make a fresh order under section 14(1).

5   In subsection (3) "period for consideration" means the period of forty days beginning with the day on which the order was made.

6   In calculating the period for consideration, no account is to be taken of any time
during which—
  a   Parliament is dissolved or prorogued; or
  b   both Houses are adjourned for more than four days.

7   If a designated derogation is withdrawn by the United Kingdom, the [Secretary of
State][11] must by order make such amendments to this Act as he considers are
required to reflect that withdrawal.

17.— Periodic review of designated reservations.

1   The appropriate Minister must review the designated reservation referred to in
section 15(1)(a)—
  a   before the end of the period of five years beginning with the date on which section
1(2) came into force; and
  b   if that designation is still in force, before the end of the period of five years beginning with the date on which the last report relating to it was laid under subsection
(3).

2   The appropriate Minister must review each of the other designated reservations (if
any)—
  a   before the end of the period of five years beginning with the date on which the
order designating the reservation first came into force; and
  b   if the designation is still in force, before the end of the period of five years beginning with the date on which the last report relating to it was laid under subsection
(3).

3   The Minister conducting a review under this section must prepare a report on the
result of the review and lay a copy of it before each House of Parliament.

Judges of the European Court of Human Rights

18.— Appointment to European Court of Human Rights.

1   In this section "judicial office" means the office of—
  a   Lord Justice of Appeal, Justice of the High Court or Circuit judge, in England and
Wales;

---

[10] words substituted by Secretary of State for Constitutional Affairs Order 2003/1887 Sch. 2
para. 10(1)
[11] words substituted by Secretary of State for Constitutional Affairs Order 2003/1887 Sch. 2
para. 10(1)

   b judge of the Court of Session or sheriff, in Scotland;

   c Lord Justice of Appeal, judge of the High Court or county court judge, in Northern Ireland.

2 The holder of a judicial office may become a judge of the European Court of Human Rights ("the Court") without being required to relinquish his office.

3 But he is not required to perform the duties of his judicial office while he is a judge of the Court.

4 In respect of any period during which he is a judge of the Court—

   a a Lord Justice of Appeal or Justice of the High Court is not to count as a judge of the relevant court for the purposes of section 2(1) or 4(1) of the Supreme Court Act 1981 (maximum number of judges) nor as a judge of the Supreme Court for the purposes of section 12(1) to (6) of that Act (salaries etc.);

   b a judge of the Court of Session is not to count as a judge of that court for the purposes of section 1(1) of the Court of Session Act 1988 (maximum number of judges) or of section 9(1)(c) of the Administration of Justice Act 1973 ("the 1973 Act") (salaries etc.);

   c a Lord Justice of Appeal or judge of the High Court in Northern Ireland is not to count as a judge of the relevant court for the purposes of section 2(1) or 3(1) of the Judicature (Northern Ireland) Act 1978 (maximum number of judges) nor as a judge of the Supreme Court of Northern Ireland for the purposes of section 9(1)(d) of the 1973 Act (salaries etc.);

   d a Circuit judge is not to count as such for the purposes of section 18 of the Courts Act 1971 (salaries etc.);

   e a sheriff is not to count as such for the purposes of section 14 of the Sheriff Courts (Scotland) Act 1907 (salaries etc.);

   f a county court judge of Northern Ireland is not to count as such for the purposes of section 106 of the County Courts Act (Northern Ireland) 1959 (salaries etc.).

5 If a sheriff principal is appointed a judge of the Court, section 11(1) of the Sheriff Courts (Scotland) Act 1971 (temporary appointment of sheriff principal) applies, while he holds that appointment, as if his office is vacant.

6 Schedule 4 makes provision about judicial pensions in relation to the holder of a judicial office who serves as a judge of the Court.

7 The Lord Chancellor or the Secretary of State may by order make such transitional provision (including, in particular, provision for a temporary increase in the maximum number of judges) as he considers appropriate in relation to any holder of a judicial office who has completed his service as a judge of the Court.

7A The following paragraphs apply to the making of an order under subsection (7) in relation to any holder of a judicial office listed in subsection (1)(a)–

   a before deciding what transitional provision it is appropriate to make, the person making the order must consult the Lord Chief Justice of England and Wales;

   b before making the order, that person must consult the Lord Chief Justice of England and Wales..

7B The following paragraphs apply to the making of an order under subsection (7) in relation to any holder of a judicial office listed in subsection (1)(c)—

   a before deciding what transitional provision it is appropriate to make, the person making the order must consult the Lord Chief Justice of Northern Ireland;

   a before making the order, that person must consult the Lord Chief Justice of Northern Ireland.

7C The Lord Chief Justice of England and Wales may nominate a judicial office holder (within the meaning of section 109(4) of the Constitutional Reform Act 2005) to exercise his functions under this section.

7D The Lord Chief Justice of Northern Ireland may nominate any of the following to exercise his functions under this section—

   a the holder of one of the offices listed in Schedule 1 to the Justice (Northern Ireland) Act 2002;

   b a Lord Justice of Appeal (as defined in section 88 of that Act).

J[12]

Parliamentary procedure

19.— Statements of compatibility.

1 A Minister of the Crown in charge of a Bill in either House of Parliament must, before Second Reading of the Bill—
a make a statement to the effect that in his view the provisions of the Bill are compatible with the Convention rights ("a statement of compatibility"); or
b make a statement to the effect that although he is unable to make a statement of compatibility the government nevertheless wishes the House to proceed with the Bill.
2 The statement must be in writing and be published in such manner as the Minister making it considers appropriate.

Supplemental

20.— Orders etc. under this Act.

1 Any power of a Minister of the Crown to make an order under this Act is exercisable by statutory instrument.
2 The power of the Lord Chancellor or the Secretary of State to make rules (other than rules of court) under section 2(3) or 7(9) is exercisable by statutory instrument.
3 Any statutory instrument made under section 14, 15 or 16(7) must be laid before Parliament.
4 No order may be made by [the Lord Chancellor or][13] the Secretary of State under section 1(4), 7(11) or 16(2) unless a draft of the order has been laid before, and approved by, each House of Parliament.
5 Any statutory instrument made under section 18(7) or Schedule 4, or to which subsection (2) applies, shall be subject to annulment in pursuance of a resolution of either House of Parliament.
6 The power of a Northern Ireland department to make—
a rules under section 2(3)(c) or 7(9)(c), or
b an order under section 7(11),
is exercisable by statutory rule for the purposes of the Statutory Rules (Northern Ireland) Order 1979.
7 Any rules made under section 2(3)(c) or 7(9)(c) shall be subject to negative resolution; and section 41(6) of the Interpretation Act (Northern Ireland) 1954 (meaning of "subject to negative resolution") shall apply as if the power to make the rules were conferred by an Act of the Northern Ireland Assembly.
8 No order may be made by a Northern Ireland department under section 7(11) unless a draft of the order has been laid before, and approved by, the Northern Ireland Assembly.

21.— Interpretation, etc.

1 In this Act—
"amend" includes repeal and apply (with or without modifications);
"the appropriate Minister" means the Minister of the Crown having charge of the appropriate authorised government department (within the meaning of the Crown Proceedings Act 1947);
"the Commission" means the European Commission of Human Rights;
"the Convention" means the Convention for the Protection of Human Rights and Fundamental Freedoms, agreed by the Council of Europe at Rome on 4th November 1950 as it has effect for the time being in relation to the United Kingdom;

---

[12] added by Constitutional Reform Act 2005 c. 4 Sch. 4(1) para. 278
[13] words inserted by Transfer of Functions (Lord Chancellor and Secretary of State) Order 2005/3429 Sch. 1 para. 3

"declaration of incompatibility" means a declaration under section 4;
"Minister of the Crown" has the same meaning as in the Ministers of the Crown Act 1975;
"Northern Ireland Minister" includes the First Minister and the deputy First Minister in Northern Ireland;
"primary legislation" means any—
a public general Act;
b local and personal Act;
c private Act;
d Measure of the Church Assembly;
e Measure of the General Synod of the Church of England;
f Order in Council—
    i. made in exercise of Her Majesty's Royal Prerogative;
    ii. made under section 38(1)(a) of the Northern Ireland Constitution Act 1973 or the corresponding provision of the Northern Ireland Act 1998; or
    iii. amending an Act of a kind mentioned in paragraph (a), (b) or (c);
and includes an order or other instrument made under primary legislation (otherwise than by the Welsh Ministers, the First Minister for Wales, the Counsel General to the Welsh Assembly Government, a member of the Scottish Executive, a Northern Ireland Minister or a Northern Ireland department) to the extent to which it operates to bring one or more provisions of that legislation into force or amends any primary legislation;
"the First Protocol" means the protocol to the Convention agreed at Paris on 20th March 1952;
"the Eleventh Protocol" means the protocol to the Convention (restructuring the control machinery established by the Convention) agreed at Strasbourg on 11th May 1994;
"the Thirteenth Protocol" means the protocol to the Convention (concerning the abolition of the death penalty in all circumstances) agreed at Vilnius on 3rd May 2002;
"remedial order" means an order under section 10;
"subordinate legislation" means any—
a Order in Council other than one—
    i. made in exercise of Her Majesty's Royal Prerogative;
    ii. made under section 38(1)(a) of the Northern Ireland Constitution Act 1973 or the corresponding provision of the Northern Ireland Act 1998; or
    iii. amending an Act of a kind mentioned in the definition of primary legislation;
b Act of the Scottish Parliament;
(ba) Measure of the National Assembly for Wales; (bb) Act of the National Assembly for Wales;
c Act of the Parliament of Northern Ireland;
d Measure of the Assembly established under section 1 of the Northern Ireland Assembly Act 1973;
e Act of the Northern Ireland Assembly;
f order, rules, regulations, scheme, warrant, byelaw or other instrument made under primary legislation (except to the extent to which it operates to bring one or more provisions of that legislation into force or amends any primary legislation);
g order, rules, regulations, scheme, warrant, byelaw or other instrument made under legislation mentioned in paragraph (b), (c), (d) or (e) or made under an Order in Council applying only to Northern Ireland;
h order, rules, regulations, scheme, warrant, byelaw or other instrument made by a member of the Scottish Executive, [Welsh Ministers, the First Minister for Wales, the Counsel General to the Welsh Assembly Government,][14] a Northern Ireland Minister or a Northern Ireland department in exercise of prerogative or other executive functions of Her Majesty which are exercisable by such a person on behalf of Her Majesty;

---

[14] words inserted by Government of Wales Act 2006 c. 32 Sch. 10 para. 56(4)

"transferred matters" has the same meaning as in the Northern Ireland Act 1998; and

"tribunal" means any tribunal in which legal proceedings may be brought.

2 The references in paragraphs (b) and (c) of section 2(1) to Articles are to Articles of the Convention as they had effect immediately before the coming into force of the Eleventh Protocol.

3 The reference in paragraph (d) of section 2(1) to Article 46 includes a reference to Articles 32 and 54 of the Convention as they had effect immediately before the coming into force of the Eleventh Protocol.

4 The references in section 2(1) to a report or decision of the Commission or a decision of the Committee of Ministers include references to a report or decision made as provided by paragraphs 3, 4 and 6 of Article 5 of the Eleventh Protocol (transitional provisions).

5 Any liability under the Army Act 1955, the Air Force Act 1955 or the Naval Discipline Act 1957 to suffer death for an offence is replaced by a liability to imprisonment for life or any less punishment authorised by those Acts; and those Acts shall accordingly have effect with the necessary modifications.

22.— Short title, commencement, application and extent.

1 This Act may be cited as the Human Rights Act 1998.

2 Sections 18, 20 and 21(5) and this section come into force on the passing of this Act.

3 The other provisions of this Act come into force on such days as the Secretary of State may by order appoint; and different days may be appointed for different purposes.

4 Paragraph (b) of subsection (1) of section 7 applies to proceedings brought by or at the instigation of a public authority whenever the act in question took place; but otherwise that subsection does not apply to an act taking place before the coming into force of that section.

5 This Act binds the Crown.

6 This Act extends to Northern Ireland.

7 Section 21(5), so far as it relates to any provision contained in the Army Act 1955, the Air Force Act 1955 or the Naval Discipline Act 1957, extends to any place to which that provision extends.

SCHEDULE 1

THE ARTICLES

Section 1(3)

PART I

THE CONVENTION

RIGHTS AND FREEDOMS

Right to life

Article 2

1. Everyone's right to life shall be protected by law. No one shall be deprived of his life intentionally save in the execution of a sentence of a court following his conviction of a crime for which this penalty is provided by law.

2. Deprivation of life shall not be regarded as inflicted in contravention of this Article when it results from the use of force which is no more than absolutely necessary:
a in defence of any person from unlawful violence;
b in order to effect a lawful arrest or to prevent the escape of a person lawfully detained;
c in action lawfully taken for the purpose of quelling a riot or insurrection.

Prohibition of torture

Article 3

No one shall be subjected to torture or to inhuman or degrading treatment or punishment.

Prohibition of slavery and forced labour

Article 4

1. No one shall be held in slavery or servitude.
2. No one shall be required to perform forced or compulsory labour.
3. For the purpose of this Article the term "forced or compulsory labour" shall not include:
a any work required to be done in the ordinary course of detention imposed according to the provisions of Article 5 of this Convention or during conditional release from such detention;
b any service of a military character or, in case of conscientious objectors in countries where they are recognised, service exacted instead of compulsory military service;
c any service exacted in case of an emergency or calamity threatening the life or well-being of the community;
d any work or service which forms part of normal civic obligations.

Right to liberty and security

Article 5

1. Everyone has the right to liberty and security of a person. No one shall be deprived of his liberty save in the following cases and in accordance with a procedure prescribed by law:

a the lawful detention of a person after conviction by a competent court;

b the lawful arrest or detention of a person for non-compliance with the lawful order of a court or in order to secure the fulfilment of any obligation prescribed by law;

c the lawful arrest or detention of a person effected for the purpose of bringing him before the competent legal authority on reasonable suspicion of having committed an offence or when it is reasonably considered necessary to prevent his committing an offence or fleeing after having done so;

d the detention of a minor by lawful order for the purpose of educational supervision or his lawful detention for the purpose of bringing him before the competent legal authority;

e the lawful detention of persons for the prevention of the spreading of infectious diseases, of persons of unsound mind, alcoholics or drug addicts or vagrants;

f the lawful arrest or detention of a person to prevent his effecting an unauthorised entry into the country or of a person against whom action is being taken with a view to deportation or extradition.

2 Everyone who is arrested shall be informed promptly, in a language which he understands, of the reasons for his arrest and of any charge against him.

3 Everyone arrested or detained in accordance with the provisions of paragraph 1(c) of this Article shall be brought promptly before a judge or other officer authorised by law to exercise judicial power and shall be entitled to trial within a reasonable time or to release pending trial. Release may be conditioned by guarantees to appear for trial.

4 Everyone who is deprived of his liberty by arrest or detention shall be entitled to take proceedings by which the lawfulness of his detention shall be decided speedily by a court and his release ordered if the detention is not lawful.

5 Everyone who has been the victim of arrest or detention in contravention of the provisions of this Article shall have an enforceable right to compensation.

Right to a fair trial

Article 6

1 In the determination of his civil rights and obligations or of any criminal charge against him, everyone is entitled to a fair and public hearing within a reasonable time by an independent and impartial tribunal established by law. Judgment shall be pronounced publicly but the press and public may be excluded from all or part of the trial in the interest of morals, public order or national security in a democratic society, where the interests of juveniles or the protection of the private life of the parties so require, or to the extent strictly necessary in the opinion of the court in special circumstances where publicity would prejudice the interests of justice.

2 Everyone charged with a criminal offence shall be presumed innocent until proved guilty according to law.

3 Everyone charged with a criminal offence has the following minimum rights:

a to be informed promptly, in a language which he understands and in detail, of the nature and cause of the accusation against him;

b to have adequate time and facilities for the preparation of his defence;

c to defend himself in person or through legal assistance of his own choosing or, if he has not sufficient means to pay for legal assistance, to be given it free when the interests of justice so require;

d to examine or have examined witnesses against him and to obtain the attendance and examination of witnesses on his behalf under the same conditions as witnesses against him;

e to have the free assistance of an interpreter if he cannot understand or speak the language used in court.

No punishment without law

Article 7

1 No one shall be held guilty of any criminal offence on account of any act or omission which did not constitute a criminal offence under national or international law at the time when it was committed. Nor shall a heavier penalty be imposed than the one that was applicable at the time the criminal offence was committed.

2 This Article shall not prejudice the trial and punishment of any person for any act or omission which, at the time when it was committed, was criminal according to the general principles of law recognised by civilised nations.

Right to respect for private and family life

Article 8

1 Everyone has the right to respect for his private and family life, his home and his correspondence.

2 There shall be no interference by a public authority with the exercise of this right except such as is in accordance with the law and is necessary in a democratic society in the interests of national security, public safety or the economic well-being of the country, for the prevention of disorder or crime, for the protection of health or morals, or for the protection of the rights and freedoms of others.

Freedom of thought, conscience and religion

Article 9

1 Everyone has the right to freedom of thought, conscience and religion, this right includes freedom to change his religion or belief and freedom, either alone or in community with others and in public or private, to manifest his religion or belief, in worship, teaching, practice and observance.

2 Freedom to manifest one's religion or beliefs shall be subject only to such limitation as are prescribed by law and are necessary in a democratic society in the interests of public safety, for the protection of public order, health or morals, or for the protection of the rights and freedoms of others.

Freedom of expression

Article 10

1 Everyone has the right to freedom of expression. This right shall include freedom to hold opinions and to receive and impart information and ideas without interference by public authority and regardless of frontiers. This Article shall not prevent States from requiring the licensing of broadcasting, television or cinema enterprises.

2 The exercise of these freedoms, since it carries with it duties and responsibilities, may be subject to such formalities, conditions, restrictions or penalties as are prescribed by law and are necessary in a democratic society, in the interests of national security, territorial integrity or public safety, for the prevention of disorder or crime, for the protection of health or morals, for the protection of the reputation or rights of others, for preventing the disclosure of information received in confidence, or for maintaining the authority and impartiality of the judiciary.

Freedom of assembly and association

Article 11

1 Everyone has the right to freedom of peaceful assembly and to freedom of association with others, including the right to form and to join trade unions for the protection of his interests.

2 No restrictions shall be placed on the exercise of these rights other than such as are prescribed by law and are necessary in a democratic society in the interests of national security or public safety, for the prevention of disorder or crime, for the protection of health or morals or for the protection of the rights and freedoms of others. This Article shall not prevent the imposition of lawful restrictions on the exercise of these rights by members of the armed forces, of the police or of the administration of the State.

Right to marry

Article 12
Men and women of marriageable age have the right to marry and to found a family, according to the national laws governing the exercise of this right.

Prohibition of discrimination

Article 14
The enjoyment of the rights and freedoms set forth in this Convention shall be secured without discrimination on any ground such as sex, race, colour, language, religion, political or other opinion, national or social origin, association with a national minority, property, birth or other status.

Restrictions on political activity of aliens

Article 16
Nothing in Articles 10, 11 and 14 shall be regarded as preventing the High Contracting Parties from imposing restrictions on the political activity of aliens.

Prohibition of abuse of rights

Article 17
Nothing in this Convention may be interpreted as implying for any State, group or person any right to engage in any activity or perform any act aimed at the destruction of any of the rights and freedoms set forth herein or at their limitation to a greater extent than is provided for in the Convention.

Limitation on use of restrictions on rights

Article 18
The restrictions permitted under this Convention to the said rights and freedoms shall not be applied for any purpose other than those for which they have been prescribed.

PART II

THE FIRST PROTOCOL

Protection of property

Article 1
Every natural or legal person is entitled to the peaceful enjoyment of his possessions. No one shall be deprived of his possessions except in the public interest and subject to the conditions provided for by law and by the general principles of international law.

The preceding provisions shall not, however, in any way impair the right of a State to enforce such laws as it deems necessary to control the use of property in accordance with the general interest or to secure the payment of taxes or other contributions or penalties.

Right to education

Article 2
No person shall be denied the right to education. In the exercise of any functions which it assumes in relation to education and to teaching, the State shall respect the right of parents to ensure such education and teaching in conformity with their own religious and philosophical convictions.

Right to free elections

Article 3
The High Contracting Parties undertake to hold free elections at reasonable intervals by secret ballot, under conditions which will ensure the free expression of the opinion of the people in the choice of the legislature.

PART III

[Abolition of the death penalty
The death penalty shall be abolished. No one shall be condemned to such penalty or executed.][16]

---

[15] substituted by Human Rights Act 1998 (Amendment) Order 2004/1574 art. 2(3)
[16] substituted by Human Rights Act 1998 (Amendment) Order 2004/1574 art. 2(3)

APPENDIX 2

DEFAMATION ACT 1996

[. . .]¹

Responsibility for publication

1.— Responsibility for publication.

   1 In defamation proceedings a person has a defence if he shows that—
   a he was not the author, editor or publisher of the statement complained of,
   b he took reasonable care in relation to its publication, and
   c he did not know, and had no reason to believe, that what he did caused or contributed to the publication of a defamatory statement.

   2 For this purpose "author", "editor" and "publisher" have the following meanings, which are further explained in subsection (3)—
   "author" means the originator of the statement, but does not include a person who did not intend that his statement be published at all;
   "editor" means a person having editorial or equivalent responsibility for the content of the statement or the decision to publish it; and
   "publisher" means a commercial publisher, that is, a person whose business is issuing material to the public, or a section of the public, who issues material containing the statement in the course of that business.

   3 A person shall not be considered the author, editor or publisher of a statement if he is only involved—
   a in printing, producing, distributing or selling printed material containing the statement;
   b in processing, making copies of, distributing, exhibiting or selling a film or sound recording (as defined in Part I of the Copyright, Designs and Patents Act 1988) containing the statement;
   c in processing, making copies of, distributing or selling any electronic medium in or on which the statement is recorded, or in operating or providing any equipment, system or service by means of which the statement is retrieved, copied, distributed or made available in electronic form;
   d as the broadcaster of a live programme containing the statement in circumstances in which he has no effective control over the maker of the statement;
   e as the operator of or provider of access to a communications system by means of which the statement is transmitted, or made available, by a person over whom he has no effective control.

In a case not within paragraphs (a) to (e) the court may have regard to those provisions by way of analogy in deciding whether a person is to be considered the author, editor or publisher of a statement.

   4 Employees or agents of an author, editor or publisher are in the same position as their employer or principal to the extent that they are responsible for the content of the statement or the decision to publish it.

¹ Note not available

5 In determining for the purposes of this section whether a person took reasonable care, or had reason to believe that what he did caused or contributed to the publication of a defamatory statement, regard shall be had to—
a the extent of his responsibility for the content of the statement or the decision to publish it,
b the nature or circumstances of the publication, and
c the previous conduct or character of the author, editor or publisher.
6 This section does not apply to any cause of action which arose before the section came into force.

Offer to make amends

2.— **Offer to make amends.**

1 A person who has published a statement alleged to be defamatory of another may offer to make amends under this section.
2 The offer may be in relation to the statement generally or in relation to a specific defamatory meaning which the person making the offer accepts that the statement conveys ("a qualified offer").
3 An offer to make amends—
a must be in writing,
b must be expressed to be an offer to make amends under section 2 of the Defamation Act 1996, and
c must state whether it is a qualified offer and, if so, set out the defamatory meaning in relation to which it is made.
4 An offer to make amends under this section is an offer—
a to make a suitable correction of the statement complained of and a sufficient apology to the aggrieved party,
b to publish the correction and apology in a manner that is reasonable and practicable in the circumstances, and
c to pay to the aggrieved party such compensation (if any), and such costs, as may be agreed or determined to be payable.
The fact that the offer is accompanied by an offer to take specific steps does not affect the fact that an offer to make amends under this section is an offer to do all the things mentioned in paragraphs (a) to (c).
5 An offer to make amends under this section may not be made by a person after serving a defence in defamation proceedings brought against him by the aggrieved party in respect of the publication in question.
6 An offer to make amends under this section may be withdrawn before it is accepted; and a renewal of an offer which has been withdrawn shall be treated as a new offer.

3.— **Accepting an offer to make amends.**

1 If an offer to make amends under section 2 is accepted by the aggrieved party, the following provisions apply.
2 The party accepting the offer may not bring or continue defamation proceedings in respect of the publication concerned against the person making the offer, but he is entitled to enforce the offer to make amends, as follows.
3 If the parties agree on the steps to be taken in fulfilment of the offer, the aggrieved party may apply to the court for an order that the other party fulfil his offer by taking the steps agreed.
4 If the parties do not agree on the steps to be taken by way of correction, apology and publication, the party who made the offer may take such steps as he thinks appropriate, and may in particular—

    a make the correction and apology by a statement in open court in terms approved by the court, and

    b give an undertaking to the court as to the manner of their publication.

5 If the parties do not agree on the amount to be paid by way of compensation, it shall be determined by the court on the same principles as damages in defamation proceedings. The court shall take account of any steps taken in fulfilment of the offer and (so far as not agreed between the parties) of the suitability of the correction, the sufficiency of the apology and whether the manner of their publication was reasonable in the circumstances, and may reduce or increase the amount of compensation accordingly.

6 If the parties do not agree on the amount to be paid by way of costs, it shall be determined by the court on the same principles as costs awarded in court proceedings.

7 The acceptance of an offer by one person to make amends does not affect any cause of action against another person in respect of the same publication, subject as follows.

8 In England and Wales or Northern Ireland, for the purposes of the Civil Liability (Contribution) Act 1978—

    a the amount of compensation paid under the offer shall be treated as paid in bona fide settlement or compromise of the claim; and

    b where another person is liable in respect of the same damage (whether jointly or otherwise), the person whose offer to make amends was accepted is not required to pay by virtue of any contribution under section 1 of that Act a greater amount than the amount of the compensation payable in pursuance of the offer.

9 In Scotland—

    a subsection (2) of section 3 of the Law Reform (Miscellaneous Provisions) (Scotland) Act 1940 (right of one joint wrongdoer as respects another to recover contribution towards damages) applies in relation to compensation paid under an offer to make amends as it applies in relation to damages in an action to which that section applies; and

    b where another person is liable in respect of the same damage (whether jointly or otherwise), the person whose offer to make amends was accepted is not required to pay by virtue of any contribution under section 3(2) of that Act a greater amount than the amount of compensation payable in pursuance of the offer.

10 Proceedings under this section shall be heard and determined without a jury.

4.— Failure to accept offer to make amends.

1 If an offer to make amends under section 2, duly made and not withdrawn, is not accepted by the aggrieved party, the following provisions apply.

2 The fact that the offer was made is a defence (subject to subsection (3)) to defamation proceedings in respect of the publication in question by that party against the person making the offer. A qualified offer is only a defence in respect of the meaning to which the offer related.

3 There is no such defence if the person by whom the offer was made knew or had reason to believe that the statement complained of—

    a referred to the aggrieved party or was likely to be understood as referring to him, and

    b was both false and defamatory of that party. but it shall be presumed until the contrary is shown that he did not know and had no reason to believe that was the case.

4 The person who made the offer need not rely on it by way of defence, but if he does he may not rely on any other defence. If the offer was a qualified offer, this applies only in respect of the meaning to which the offer related.

5 The offer may be relied on in mitigation of damages whether or not it was relied on as a defence.

Limitation

5.— Limitation of actions: England and Wales.

☐1 The Limitation Act 1980 is amended as follows.

☐2 For section 4A (time limit for action for libel or slander) substitute—

"**4A. Time limit for actions for defamation or malicious falsehood.**
The time limit under section 2 of this Act shall not apply to an action for—
a libel or slander, or
b slander of title, slander of goods or other malicious falsehood. but no such action shall be brought after the expiration of one year from the date on which the cause of action accrued. ".

☐3 In section 28 (extension of limitation period in case of disability), for subsection (4A) substitute—

"(4A) If the action is one to which section 4A of this Act applies, subsection (1) above shall have effect—
a in the case of an action for libel or slander, as if for the words from 'at any time' to 'occurred)' there were substituted the words 'by him at any time before the expiration of one year from the date on which he ceased to be under a disability'; and
b in the case of an action for slander of title, slander of goods or other malicious falsehood, as if for the words 'six years' there were substituted the words 'one year'.".

☐4 For section 32A substitute—
"Discretionary exclusion of time limit for actions for defamation or malicious falsehood

32A.— Discretionary exclusion of time limit for actions for defamation or malicious falsehood.

☐1 If it appears to the court that it would be equitable to allow an action to proceed having regard to the degree to which—
a the operation of section 4A of this Act prejudices the plaintiff or any person whom he represents, and
b any decision of the court under this subsection would prejudice the defendant or any person whom he represents,
the court may direct that that section shall not apply to the action or shall not apply to any specified cause of, action to which the action relates.

☐2 In acting under this section the court shall have regard to all the circumstances of the case and in particular to—
a the length of, and the reasons for, the delay on the part of the plaintiff;
b where the reason or one of the reasons for the delay was that all or any of the facts relevant to the cause of action did not become known to the plaintiff until after the end of the period mentioned in section 4A—
i. the date on which any such facts did become known to him, and
ii. the extent to which he acted promptly and reasonably once he knew whether or not the facts in question might be capable of giving rise to an action; and
c the extent to which, having regard to the delay, relevant evidence is likely—
i. to be unavailable, or
ii. to be less cogent than if the action had been brought within the period mentioned in section 4A.

☐3 In the case of an action for slander of title, slander of goods, or other malicious falsehood brought by a personal representative—
a the references in subsection (2) above to the plaintiff shall be construed as including the deceased person to whom the cause of action accrued and any previous personal representative of that person; and
b nothing in section 28(3) of this Act shall be construed as affecting the court's discretion under this section.

4 In this section"the court" means the court in which the action has been brought.".

5 In section 36(1) (expiry of time limit no bar to equitable relief), for paragraph (aa) substitute—

"(aa) the time limit under section 4A for actions for libel or slander, or for slander of title, slander of goods or other malicious falsehood;".

6 The amendments made by this section apply only to causes of action arising after the section comes into force.

6.— Limitation of actions: Northern Ireland.

1 The Limitation (Northern Ireland) Order 1989 is amended as follows.

2 In Article 6 (time limit: certain actions founded on tort) forparagraph (2) substitute—

"(2) Subject to Article 51, an action for damages for—
  a libel or slander, or
  b slander of title, slander of goods or other malicious falsehood,
  may not be brought after the expiration of one year from the date on which the cause of action accrued.".

3 In Article 48 (extension of time limit), for paragraph (7) substitute—

"7. Where the action is one to which Article 6(2) applies, paragraph (1) has effect—
  a in the case of an action for libel and slander, as if for the words from "at any time" to "occurred" there were substituted the words "by him at any time before the expiration of one year from the date on which he ceased to be under a disability"; and
  b in the case of an action for slander of title, slander of goods or other malicious falsehood, as if for the words "six years" there were substituted the words "one year".".

4 For Article 51 substitute—

51.—

1 If it appears to the court that it would be equitable to allow an action to proceed having regard to the degree to which—
  a the provisions of Article 6(2) prejudice the plaintiff or any person whom he represents; and
  b any decision of the court under this paragraph would prejudice the defendant or any person whom he represents,
  the court may direct that those provisions are not to apply to the action, or are not to apply to any specified cause of action to which the action relates.

2 In acting under this Article the court is to have regard to all the circumstances of the case and in particular to—
  a the length of, and the reasons for, the delay on the part of the plaintiff;
  b in a case where the reason, or one of the reasons, for the delay was that all or any of the facts relevant to the cause of action did not become known to the plaintiff until after the expiration of the period mentioned in Article 6(2)—
    i. the date on which any such facts did become known to him, and
    ii. the extent to which he acted promptly and reasonably once he knew whether or not the facts in question might be capable of giving rise to an action; and
  c the extent to which, having regard to the delay, relevant evidence is likely—
    i to be unavailable, or
    ii to be less cogent than if the action had been brought within the time allowed by Article 6(2).

3 In the case of an action for slander of title, slander of goods or other malicious falsehood brought by a personal representative—
  a the references in paragraph (2) to the plaintiff shall be construed as including the deceased person to whom the cause of action accrued and any previous personal representative of that person; and

b nothing in Article 48(3) shall be construed as affecting the court's discretion under this Article.

4 In this Article "the court" means the court in which the action has been brought."

5 The amendments made by this section apply only to causes of action arising after the section comes into force.

The meaning of a statement

7. Ruling on the meaning of a statement.
In defamation proceedings the court shall not be asked to rule whether a statement is arguably capable, as opposed to capable, of bearing a particular meaning or meanings attributed to it.

Summary disposal of claim

8.— Summary disposal of claim.

1 In defamation proceedings the court may dispose summarily of the plaintiff's claim in accordance with the following provisions.

2 The court may dismiss the plaintiff's claim if it appears to the court that it has no realistic prospect of success and there is no reason why it should be tried.

3 The court may give judgment for the plaintiff and grant him summary relief (see section 9) if it appears to the court that there is no defence to the claim which has a realistic prospect of success, and that there is no other reason why the claim should be tried.
Unless the plaintiff asks for summary relief, the court shall not act under this sub-section unless it is satisfied that summary relief will adequately compensate him for the wrong he has suffered.

4 In considering whether a claim should be tried the court shall have regard to—
a whether all the persons who are or might be defendants in respect of the publication complained of are before the court;
b whether summary disposal of the claim against another defendant would be inappropriate;
c the extent to which there is a conflict of evidence;
d the seriousness of the alleged wrong (as regards the content of the statement and the extent of publication); and
e whether it is justifiable in the circumstances to proceed to a full trial.

5 Proceedings under this section shall be heard and determined without a jury.

9.— Meaning of summary relief.

1 For the purposes of section 8 (summary disposal of claim) "summary relief" means such of the following as may be appropriate—
a a declaration that the statement was false and defamatory of the plaintiff;
b an order that the defendant publish or cause to be published a suitable correction and apology;
c damages not exceeding £10,000 or such other amount as may be prescribed by order of the Lord Chancellor;
d an order restraining the defendant from publishing or further publishing the matter complained of.

2 The content of any correction and apology, and the time, manner, form and place of publication, shall be for the parties to agree.
If they cannot agree on the content, the court may direct the defendant to publish or cause to be published a summary of the court's judgment agreed by the parties or settled by the court in accordance with rules of court.
If they cannot agree on the time, manner, form or place of publication, the court may direct the defendant to take such reasonable and practicable steps as the court considers appropriate.

[(2A) The Lord Chancellor must consult the Lord Chief Justice of England and Wales before making any order under subsection (1)(c) in relation to England and Wales.

(2B) The Lord Chancellor must consult the Lord Chief Justice of Northern Ireland before making any order under subsection (1)(c) in relation to Northern Ireland.

(2C) The Lord Chief Justice may nominate a judicial office holder (as defined in section 109(4) of the Constitutional Reform Act 2005) to exercise his functions under this section.

(2D) The Lord Chief Justice of Northern Ireland may nominate any of the following to exercise his functions under this section—

a the holder of one of the offices listed in Schedule 1 to the Justice (Northern Ireland) Act 2002;

b a Lord Justice of Appeal (as defined in section 88 of that Act).]²

3 Any order under subsection (1)(c) shall be made by statutory instrument which shall be subject to annulment in pursuance of a resolution of either House of Parliament.

10.— Summary disposal: rules of court.

1 Provision may be made by rules of court as to the summary disposal of the plaintiff's claim in defamation proceedings.

2 Without prejudice to the generality of that power, provision may be made—

a authorising a party to apply for summary disposal at any stage of the proceedings;

b authorising the court at any stage of the proceedings—

i. to treat any application, pleading or other step in the proceedings as an application for summary disposal, or

ii. to make an order for summary disposal without any such application;

c as to the time for serving pleadings or taking any other step in the proceedings in a case where there are proceedings for summary disposal;

d requiring the parties to identify any question of law or construction which the court is to be asked to determine in the proceedings;

e as to the nature of any hearing on the question of summary disposal, and in particular—

i. authorising the court to order affidavits or witness statements to be prepared for use as evidence at the hearing, and

ii. requiring the leave of the court for the calling of oral evidence, or the introduction of new evidence, at the hearing;

f authorising the court to require a defendant to elect, at or before the hearing, whether or not to make an offer to make amends under section 2.

11. Summary disposal: application to Northern Ireland.

In their application to Northern Ireland the provisions of sections 8 to 10 (summary disposal of claim) apply only to proceedings in the High Court.

Evidence of convictions

12.— Evidence of convictions.

1 In section 13 of the Civil Evidence Act 1968 (conclusiveness of convictions for purposes of defamation actions), in subsections (1) and (2) for "a person" substitute "the plaintiff" and for "that person" substitute "he"; and after subsection (2) insert—

"(2A) In the case of an action for libel or slander in which there is more than one plaintiff—

a the references in subsections (1) and (2) above to the plaintiff shall be construed as references to any of the plaintiffs, and

b proof that any of the plaintiffs stands convicted of an offence shall be conclusive evidence that he committed that offence so far as that fact is relevant to any issue arising in relation to his cause of action or that of any other plaintiff.".

² added by Constitutional Reform Act 2005 c. 4 Sch. 4(1) para. 255

The amendments made by this subsection apply only where the trial of the action begins after this section comes into force.

2 In section 12 of the Law Reform (Miscellaneous Provisions) (Scotland) Act 1968 (conclusiveness of convictions for purposes of defamation actions), in subsections (1) and (2) for "a person" substitute "the pursuer" and for "that person" substitute "he"; and after subsection (2) insert—

"(2A) In the case of an action for defamation in which there is more than one pursuer—

a the references in subsections (1) and (2) above to the pursuer shall be construed as references to any of the pursuers, and

b proof that any of the pursuers stands convicted of an offence shall be conclusive evidence that he committed that offence so far as that fact is relevant to any issue arising in relation to his cause of action or that of any other pursuer.".

The amendments made by this subsection apply only for the purposes of an action begun after this section comes into force, whenever the cause of action arose.

3 In section 9 of the Civil Evidence Act (Northern Ireland) 1971 (conclusiveness of convictions for purposes of defamation actions), in subsections (1) and (2) for "a person" substitute "the plaintiff" and for "that person" substitute "he"; and after subsection (2) insert—

"(2A) In the case of an action for libel or slander in which there is more than one plaintiff—

a the references in subsections (1) and (2) to the plaintiff shall be construed as references to any of the plaintiffs, and

b proof that any of the plaintiffs stands convicted of an offence shall be conclusive evidence that he committed that offence so far as that fact is relevant to any issue arising in relation to his cause of action or that of any other plaintiff.".

The amendments made by this subsection apply only where the trial of the action begins after this section comes into force.

Evidence concerning proceedings in Parliament

13.— Evidence concerning proceedings in Parliament.

1 Where the conduct of a person in or in relation to proceedings in Parliament is in issue in defamation proceedings, he may waive for the purposes of those proceedings, so far as concerns him, the protection of any enactment or rule of law which prevents proceedings in Parliament being impeached or questioned in any court or place out of Parliament.

2 Where a person waives that protection—

a any such enactment or rule of law shall not apply to prevent evidence being given, questions being asked or statements, submissions, comments or findings being made about his conduct, and

b none of those things shall be regarded as infringing the privilege of either House of Parliament.

3 The waiver by one person of that protection does not affect its operation in relation to another person who has not waived it.

4 Nothing in this section affects any enactment or rule of law so far as it protects a person (including a person who has waived the protection referred to above) from legal liability for words spoken or things done in the course of, or for the purposes of or incidental to, any proceedings in Parliament.

5 Without prejudice to the generality of subsection (4), that subsection applies to—

a the giving of evidence before either House or a committee;

b the presentation or submission of a document to either House or a committee;

c the preparation of a document for the purposes of or incidental to the transacting of any such business;

d the formulation, making or publication of a document, including a report, by or pursuant to an order to either House or a committee; and

e any communication with the Parliamentary Commissioner for Standards or any person having functions in connection with the registration of members' interests.
In this subsection "a committee" means a committee of either House or a joint committee of both House of Parliament.

Statutory privilege

14.— Reports of court proceedings absolutely privileged.

1 A fair and accurate report of proceedings in public before a court to which this section applies, if published contemporaneously with the proceedings, is absolutely privileged.

2 A report of proceedings which by an order of the court, or as a consequence of any statutory provision, is required to be postponed shall be treated as published contemporaneously if it is published as soon as practicable after publication is permitted.

3 This section applies to—
a any court in the United Kingdom,
b the European Court of Justice or any court attached to that court,
c the European Court of Human Rights, and
d any international criminal tribunal established by the Security Council of the United
Nations or by an international agreement to which the United Kingdom is a party.
In paragraph (a) "court" includes any tribunal or body exercising the judicial power of the State.

4 In section 8(6) of the Rehabilitation of Offenders Act 1974 and in Article 9(6) of the Rehabilitation of Offenders (Northern Ireland) Order 1978 (defamation actions: reports of court proceedings), for "section 3 of the Law of Libel Amendment Act 1888" substitute "section 14 of the Defamation Act 1996".

15.— Reports, &c. protected by qualified privilege.

1 The publication of any report or other statement mentioned in Schedule 1 to this Act is privileged unless the publication is shown to be made with malice, subject as follows.

2 In defamation proceedings in respect of the publication of a report or other statement mentioned in Part II of that Schedule, there is no defence under this section if the plaintiff shows that the defendant—
a was requested by him to publish in a suitable manner a reasonable letter or statement by way of explanation or contradiction, and
b refused or neglected to do so.
For this purpose "in a suitable manner" means in the same manner as the publication complained of or in a manner that is adequate and reasonable in the circumstances.

3 This section does not apply to the publication to the public, or a section of the public, of matter which is not of public concern and the publication of which is not for the public benefit.

4 Nothing in this section shall be construed—
a as protecting the publication of matter the publication of which is prohibited by law, or
b as limiting or abridging any privilege subsisting apart from this section.

Supplementary provisions

16. Repeals.
The enactments specified in Schedule 2 are repealed to the extent specified.

17.— Interpretation.

1 In this Act—
"publication" and "publish", in relation to a statement, have the meaning they have for the purposes of the law of defamation generally, but "publisher" is specially defined for the purposes of section 1;
"statement" means words, pictures, visual images, gestures or any other method of signifying meaning; and "statutory provision" means —
   a a provision contained in an Act or in subordinate legislation within the meaning of the Interpretation Act 1978, [. . .]³
   [(aa) a provision contained in an Act of the Scottish Parliament or in an instrument made under such an Act, or]⁴
   b a statutory provision within the meaning given by section 1(f) of the Interpretation Act (Northern Ireland) 1954.
2 In this Act as it applies to proceedings in Scotland—
"costs" means expenses; and
"plaintiff" and "defendant" mean pursuer and defender

General provisions

18.—

1 The following provisions of this Act extend to England and Extent. Wales—
   section 1 (responsibility for publication),
   sections 2 to 4 (offer to make amends), except section 3(9),
   section 5 (time limit for actions for defamation or malicious falsehood).
   section 7 (ruling on the meaning of a statement),
   sections 8 to 10 (summary disposal of claim),
   section 12(1) (evidence of convictions),
   section 13 (evidence concerning proceedings in Parliament),
   sections 14 and 15 and Schedule 1 (statutory privilege).
   section 16 and Schedule 2 (repeals) so far as relating to enactments extending to England and Wales,
   section 17(1) (interpretation),
   this subsection,
   section 19 (commencement) so far as relating to provisions which extend to England and Wales, and
   section 20 (short title and saving).
2 The following provisions of this Act extend to Scotland—
   section 1 (responsibility for publication),
   sections 2 to 4 (offer to make amends), except section 3(8),
   section 12(2) (evidence of convictions),
   section 13 (evidence concerning proceedings in Parliament),
   section 14 and 15 and Schedule 1 (statutory privilege).
   section 16 and Schedule 2 (repeals) so far as relating to enactments extending to Scotland, section 17 (interpretation),
   this subsection,
   section 19 (commencement) so far as relating to provisions which extend to Scotland, and
   section 20 (short title and saving).
3 The following provisions of this Act extend to Northern Ireland—
   section 1 (responsibility for publication).
   sections 2 to 4 (offer to make amends), except section 3(9),
   section 6 (time limit for actions for defamation or malicious falsehood),
   section 7 (ruling on the meaning of a statement),

³ added by Scotland Act 1998 c. 46 Sch. 8 para. 33(2)
⁴ added by Scotland Act 1998 c. 46 Sch. 8 para. 33(2)

sections 8 to 11 (summary disposal of claim),
section 12(3) (evidence of convictions),
section 13 (evidence concerning proceedings in Parliament),
sections 14 and 15 and Schedule 1 (statutory privilege),
section 16 and Schedule 2 (repeals) so far as relating to enactments extending to Northern Ireland,
section 17(1) (interpretation), this subsection,
section 19 (commencement) so far as relating to provisions which extend to Northern Ireland, and
section 20 (short title and saving).

19.— Commencement.

1 Sections 18 to 20 (extent, commencement and other general provisions) come into force on Royal Assent.
2 The following provisions of this Act come into force at the end of the period of two months beginning with the day on which this Act is passed—
section 1 (responsibility for publication),
sections 5 and 6 (time limit for actions for defamation or malicious falsehood),
section 12 (evidence of convictions),
section 13 (evidence concerning proceedings in Parliament),
section 16 and the repeals in Schedule 2, so far as consequential on the above provisions, and
section 17 (interpretation), so far as relating to the above provisions.
3 The provisions of this Act otherwise come into force on such day as may be appointed—
a for England and Wales or Northern Ireland, by order of the Lord Chancellor, or
b for Scotland, by order of the Secretary of State, and different days may be appointed for different purposes.
4 Any such order shall be made by statutory instrument and may contain such transitional provisions as appear to the Lord Chancellor or Secretary of State to be appropriate.

20.— Short title and saving.

1 This Act may be cited as the Defamation Act 1996.
2 Nothing in this Act affects the law relating to criminal libel.

SCHEDULE 1

QUALIFIED PRIVILEGE

Section 15.

PART I

STATEMENTS HAVING QUALIFIED PRIVILEGE WITHOUT EXPLANATION OR CONTRADICTION

1.
A fair and accurate report of proceedings in public of a legislature anywhere in the world.

2.
A fair and accurate report of proceedings in public before a court anywhere in the world.

3.
A fair and accurate report of proceedings in public of a person appointed to hold a public inquiry by a government or legislature anywhere in the world.

4.
A fair and accurate report of proceedings in public anywhere in the world of an international organisation or an international conference.

5.
A fair and accurate copy of or extract from any register or other document required by law to be open to public inspection.

6.
A notice or advertisement published by or on the authority of a court, or of a judge or officer of a court, anywhere in the world.

7.
A fair and accurate copy of or extract from matter published by or on the authority of a government or legislature anywhere in the world.

8.
A fair and accurate copy of or extract from matter published anywhere in the world by an international organisation or an international conference.

PART II

STATEMENTS PRIVILEGED SUBJECT TO EXPLANATION OR CONTRADICTION

9.—

1 A fair and accurate copy of or extract from a notice or other matter issued for the information of the public by or on behalf of—
a a legislature in any member State or the European Parliament;
b the government of any member State, or any authority performing governmental functions in any member State or part of a member State, or the European Commission;
c an international organisation or international conference.
2 In this paragraph "governmental functions" includes police functions,

10.
A fair and accurate copy of or extract from a document made available by a court in any member State or the European Court of Justice (or any court attached to that court), or by a judge or officer of any such court.

11.—

1 A fair and accurate report of proceedings at any public meeting or sitting in the United Kingdom of—
a a local authority, local authority committee or in the case of a local authority which are operating executive arrangements the executive of that authority or a committee of that executive;
b a justice or justices of the peace acting otherwise than as a court exercising judicial authority;
c a commission, tribunal, committee or person appointed for the purposes of any inquiry by any statutory provision, by Her Majesty or by a Minister of the Crown, a member of the Scottish Executive [, the Welsh Ministers or the Counsel General to the Welsh Assembly Government]⁵ or a Northern Ireland Department;
d a person appointed by a local authority to hold a local inquiry in pursuance of any statutory provision;

⁵ words inserted by Government of Wales Act 2006 c. 32 Sch. 10 para. 40

e any other tribunal, board, committee or body constituted by or under, and exercising functions under, any statutory provision.

(1A) In the case of a local authority which are operating executive arrangements, a fair and accurate record of any decision made by any member of the executive where that record is required to be made and available for public inspection by virtue of section 22 of the Local Government Act 2000 or of any provision in regulations made under that section.

2 In sub-paragraphs (1)(a) and (1A)—

"executive" and "executive arrangements" have the same meaning as in Part II of the Local Government Act 2000;

"local authority" means —

a in relation to England and Wales, a principal council within the meaning of the Local Government Act 1972, any body falling within any paragraph of section 100J(1) of that Act or an authority or body to which the Public Bodies (Admission to Meetings) Act 1960 applies,

b in relation to Scotland, a council constituted under section 2 of the Local Government etc. (Scotland) Act 1994 or an authority or body to which the Public Bodies (Admission to Meetings) Act 1960 applies,

c in relation to Northern Ireland, any authority or body to which sections 23 to 27 of the Local Government Act (Northern Ireland) 1972 apply; and

"local authority committee" means any committee of a local authority or of local authorities, and includes—

a any committee or sub-committee in relation to which sections 100A to 100D of the Local Government Act 1972 apply by virtue of section 100E of that Act (whether or not also by virtue of section 100J of that Act), and

b any committee or sub-committee in relation to which sections 50A to 50D of the Local Government (Scotland) Act 1973 apply by virtue of section 50E of that Act.

3 A fair and accurate report of any corresponding proceedings in any of the Channel Islands or the Isle of Man or in another member State.[6]

12.—

1 A fair and accurate report of proceedings at any public meeting held in a member State.

2 In this paragraph a "public meeting" means a meeting bona fide and lawfully held for a lawful purpose and for the furtherance or discussion of a matter of public concern, whether admission to the meeting is general or restricted.

13.—

1 A fair and accurate report of proceedings at a general meeting of a UK public company.

2 A fair and accurate copy of or extract from any document circulated to members of a UK public company—

a by or with the authority of the board of directors of the company,

b by the auditors of the company, or

c by any member of the company in pursuance of a right conferred by any statutory provision.

3 A fair and accurate copy of or extract from any document circulated to members of a UK public company which relates to the appointment, resignation, retirement or dismissal of directors of the company.

4 In this paragraph "UK public company" means—

a a public company within the meaning of section 1(3) of the Companies Act 1985 or Article 12(3) of the Companies (Northern Ireland) Order 1986 or

b a body corporate incorporated by or registered under any other statutory provision, or by Royal Charter, or formed in pursuance of letters patent.

---

[6] In relation to England: para. 11 is modified: [See Westlaw UK].

5 A fair and accurate report of proceedings at any corresponding meeting of, or copy of or extract from any corresponding document circulated to members of, a public company formed under the law of any of the Channel Islands or the Isle of Man or of another member State.

14.
A fair and accurate report of any finding or decision of any of the following descriptions of association, formed in the United Kingdom or another member State, or of any committee or governing body of such an association—

a an association formed for the purpose of promoting or encouraging the exercise of or interest in any art, science, religion or learning, and empowered by its constitution to exercise control over or adjudicate on matters of interest or concern to the association, or the actions or conduct of any person subject to such control or adjudication;

b an association formed for the purpose of promoting or safeguarding the interests of any trade, business, industry or profession, or of the persons carrying on or engaged in any trade, business, industry or profession, and empowered by its constitution to exercise control over or adjudicate upon matters connected with that trade, business, industry or profession, or the actions or conduct of those persons;

c an association formed for the purpose of promoting or safeguarding the interests of a game, sport or pastime to the playing or exercise of which members of the public are invited or admitted, and empowered by its constitution to exercise control over or adjudicate upon persons connected with or taking part in the game, sport or pastime;

d an association formed for the purpose of promoting charitable objects or other objects beneficial to the community and empowered by its constitution to exercise control over or to adjudicate on matters of interest or concern to the association, or the actions or conduct of any person subject to such control or adjudication.

15.—

1 A fair and accurate report of, or copy of or extract from, any adjudication, report, statement or notice issued by a body, officer or other person designated for the purposes of this paragraph—
a for England and Wales or Northern Ireland, by order of the Lord Chancellor, and
b for Scotland, by order of the Secretary of State.

2 An order under this paragraph shall be made by statutory instrument which shall be subject to annulment in pursuance of a resolution of either House of Parliament.

PART III

SUPPLEMENTARY PROVISIONS

16.—

1 In this Schedule—
"court"includes any tribunal or body exercising the judicial power of the State;
"international conference" means a conference attended by representatives of two or more governments;
"international organisation" means an organisation of which two or more governments are members, and includes any committee or other subordinate body of such an organisation; and
"legislature"includes a local legislature.

2 References in this Schedule to a member State include any European dependent territory of a member State.

3 In paragraphs 2 and 6"court"includes—
a the European Court of Justice (or any court attached to that court) and the Court of Auditors of the European Communities,

b the European Court of Human Rights,

c any international criminal tribunal established by the Security Council of the United Nations or by an international agreement to which the United Kingdom is a party, and

d the International Court of Justice and any other judicial or arbitral tribunal deciding matters in dispute between States.

4 In paragraphs 1, 3 and 7"legislature"includes the European Parliament.

17.—

1 Provision may be made by order identifying—

a for the purposes of paragraph 11, the corresponding proceedings referred to in sub-paragraph (3);

b for the purposes of paragraph 13, the corresponding meetings and documents referred to in sub-paragraph (5).

2 An order under this paragraph may be made—

a for England and Wales or Northern Ireland, by the Lord Chancellor, and

b for Scotland, by the Secretary of State.

3 An order under this paragraph shall be made by statutory instrument which shall be subject to annulment in pursuance of a resolution of either House of Parliament.

SCHEDULE 2

REPEALS

Section 16

Chapter	Short title	Extent of repeal
1888 c. 64.	Law of Libel Amendment Act 1888.	Section 3.
1952 c. 66.	Defamation Act 1952.	Section 4. Sections 7, 8 and 9(2) and (3). Section 16(2) and (3). The Schedule.
1955 c. 20.	Revision of the Army and Air Force Acts (Transitional Provisions) Act 1955.	In Schedule 2, the entry relating to the Defamation Act 1952.
1955 c. 11 (N.I.).	Defamation Act (Northern Ireland) 1955.	Section 4. Sections 7, 8 and 9(2) and (3). Section 14(2). The Schedule.
1972 c. 9 (N.I.).	Local Government Act (Northern Ireland) 1972.	In Schedule 8, paragraph 12.
1981 c. 49.	Contempt of Court Act 1981.	In section 4(3), the words "and of section 3 of the Law of Libel Amendment Act 1888 (privilege)".
1981 c. 61.	British Nationality Act 1981.	In Schedule 7, the entries relating to the Defamation Act 1952 and the Defamation Act (Northern Ireland) 1955.
1985 c. 43.	Local Government (Access to Information) Act 1985.	In Schedule 2, paragraphs 2 and 3.
1985 c. 61.	Administration of Justice Act 1985.	Section 57.
S.I. 1986/594 (N.I. 3).	Education and Libraries (Northern Ireland) Order 1986.	Article 97(2).
1990 c. 42.	Broadcasting Act 1990.	Section 166(3). In Schedule 20, paragraphs 2 and 3.

APPENDIX 3

CONTEMPT OF COURT ACT 1981
1981 CHAPTER 49

An Act to amend the law relating to contempt of court and related matters.

[27th July 1981]

Strict liability

1. The strict liability rule.
In this Act "the strict liability rule" means the rule of law whereby conduct may be treated as a contempt of court as tending to interfere with the course of justice in particular legal proceedings regardless of intent to do so.

2.— Limitation of scope of strict liability.

1 The strict liability rule applies only in relation to publications, and for this purpose "publication" includes any speech, writing, [programme included in a cable programme service][1] or other communication in whatever form, which is addressed to the public at large or any section of the public.

2 The strict liability rule applies only to a publication which creates a substantial risk that the course of justice in the proceedings in question will be seriously impeded or prejudiced.

3 The strict liability rule applies to a publication only if the proceedings in question are active within the meaning of this section at the time of the publication.

4 Schedule 1 applies for determining the times at which proceedings are to be treated as active within the meaning of this section.

5 In this section "programme service" has the same meaning as in the Broadcasting Act 1990.][2]

3.— Defence of innocent publication or distribution.

1 A person is not guilty of contempt of court under the strict liability rule as the publisher of any matter to which that rule applies if at the time of publication (having taken all reasonable care) he does not know and has no reason to suspect that relevant proceedings are active.

2 A person is not guilty of contempt of court under the strict liability rule as the distributor of a publication containing any such matter if at the time of distribution (having taken all reasonable care) he does not know that it contains such matter and has no reason to suspect that it is likely to do so.

3 The burden of proof of any fact tending to establish a defence afforded by this section to any person lies upon that person.

4 [...][3]

---

[1] Words substituted by Broadcasting Act 1990 (c.42), s.203(1), Sch.20 para.31(1)(a).
[2] Section 2(5) inserted by Broadcasting Act 1990 (c.42), s.203(1), Sch.20, para.31(1)(b).
[3] Repeals Administration of Justice Act 1960 (c. 65), s.11.

4.— Contemporary reports of proceedings.

1 Subject to this section a person is not guilty of contempt of court under the strict liability rule in respect of a fair and accurate report of legal proceedings held in public,
published contemporaneously and in good faith.

2 In any such proceedings the court may, where it appears to be necessary for avoiding a substantial risk of prejudice to the administration of justice in those proceedings, or in any other proceedings pending or imminent, order that the publication
of any report of the proceedings, or any part of the proceedings, be postponed for
such period as the court thinks necessary for that purpose.

2A Where in proceedings for any offence which is an administration of justice offence
for the purposes of section 54 of the Criminal Procedure and Investigations Act 1996
(acquittal tainted by an administration of justice offence) it appears to the court that
there is a possibility that (by virtue of that section) proceedings may be taken against
a person for an offence of which he has been acquitted, subsection (2) of this section
shall apply as if those proceedings were pending or imminent.

3 For the purposes of subsection (1) of this section […]⁴ a report of proceedings shall
be treatedas published contemporaneously—
a in the case of a report of which publication is postponed pursuant to an order
under subsection (2) of this section, if published as soon as practicable after that
order expires;
b in the case of a report of committal proceedings of which publication is permitted by virtue only of subsection (3) of section 8 of the Magistrates' Courts Act 1980,
if published as soon as practicable after publication is so permitted.

5. Discussion of public affairs.

A publication made as or as part of a discussion in good faith of public affairs or other
matters of general public interest is not to be treated as a contempt of court under the strict
liability rule if the risk of impediment or prejudice to particular legal proceedings is merely
incidental to the discussion.

6. Savings.

Nothing in the foregoing provisions of this Act—
a prejudices any defence available at common law to a charge of contempt of court
under the strict liability rule;
b implies that any publication is punishable as contempt of court under that rule
which would not be so punishable apart from those provisions;
c restricts liability for contempt of court in respect of conduct intended to impede
or prejudice the administration of justice.

7. Consent required for institution of proceedings.

Proceedings for a contempt of court under the strict liability rule (other than Scottish proceedings) shall not be instituted except by or with the consent of the Attorney General or
on the motion of a court having jurisdiction to deal with it.

Other aspects of law and procedure

8.— Confidentiality of jury's deliberations.

1 Subject to subsection (2) below, it is a contempt of court to obtain, disclose or solicit
any particulars of statements made, opinions expressed, arguments advanced
or votes cast by members of a jury in the course of their deliberations in any legal
proceedings.

---

⁴ Words repealed by Defamation Act 1996 (c.31), Sch.2, para.1.

2 This section does not apply to any disclosure of any particulars—
 a in the proceedings in question for the purpose of enabling the jury to arrive at their verdict, or in connection with the delivery of that verdict, or
 b in evidence in any subsequent proceedings for an offence alleged to have been committed in relation to the jury in the first mentioned proceedings,
or to the publication of any particulars so disclosed.

3 Proceedings for a contempt of court under this section (other than Scottish proceedings) shall not be instituted except by or with the consent of the Attorney General or on the motion of a court having jurisdiction to deal with it.

9.— Use of tape recorders.

1 Subject to subsection (4) below, it is a contempt of court—
 a to use in court, or bring into court for use, any tape recorder or other instrument for recording sound, except with the leave of the court;
 b to publish a recording of legal proceedings made by means of any such instrument, or any recording derived directly or indirectly from it, by playing it in the hearing of the public or any section of the public, or to dispose of it or any recording so derived, with a view to such publication;
 c to use any such recording in contravention of any conditions of leave granted under paragraph (a).

2 Leave under paragraph (a) of subsection (1) may be granted or refused at the discretion of the court, and if granted may be granted subject to such conditions as the court thinks proper with respect to the use of any recording made pursuant to the leave; and where leave has been granted the court may at the like discretion withdraw or amend it either generally or in relation to any particular part of the proceedings.

3 Without prejudice to any other power to deal with an act of contempt under paragraph (a) of subsection (1), the court may order the instrument, or any recording made with it, or both, to be forfeited; and any object so forfeited shall (unless the court otherwise determines on application by a person appearing to be the owner) be sold or otherwise disposed of in such manner as the court may direct.

4 This section does not apply to the making or use of sound recordings for purposes of official transcripts of proceedings.

10. Sources of information.
No court may require a person to disclose, nor is any person guilty of contempt of court for refusing to disclose, the source of information contained in a publication for which he is responsible, unless it be established to the satisfaction of the court that disclosure is necessary in the interests of justice or national security or for the prevention of disorder or crime.

11. Publication of matters exempted from disclosure in court.
In any case where a court (having power to do so) allows a name or other matter to be withheld from the public in proceedings before the court, the court may give such directions prohibiting the publication of that name or matter in connection with the proceedings as appear to the court to be necessary for the purpose for which it was so withheld.

APPENDIX 4

NEWSPAPER AND MAGAZINE PUBLISHING IN THE UK

Editors' Code of Practice

This is the newspaper and periodical industry's Code of Practice. It is framed and revised by the Editors' Code Committee made up of independent editors of national, regional and local newspapers and magazines. The Press Complaints Commission, which has a majority of lay members, is charged with enforcing the Code, using it to adjudicate complaints. It was ratified by the PCC on the 7 August 2006. Clauses marked* are covered by exceptions relating to the public interest.

The Code

All members of the press have a duty to maintain the highest professional standards. This Code sets the benchmark for those ethical standards, protecting both the rights of the individual and the public's right to know. It is the cornerstone of the system of self-regulation to which the industry has made a binding commitment.

It is essential that an agreed code be honoured not only to the letter but in the full spirit. It should not be interpreted so narrowly as to compromise its commitment to respect the rights of the individual, nor so broadly that it constitutes an unnecessary interference with freedom of expression or prevents publication in the public interest.

It is the responsibility of editors and publishers to implement the Code and they should take care to ensure it is observed rigorously by all editorial staff and external contributors, including non-journalists, in printed and online versions of publications.

Editors should co-operate swiftly with the PCC in the resolution of complaints. Any publication judged to have breached the Code must print the adjudication in full and with due prominence, including headline reference to the PCC.

1 Accuracy

i. The press must take care not to publish inaccurate, misleading or distorted information, including pictures.
ii. A significant inaccuracy, misleading statement or distortion once recognized must be corrected, promptly and with due prominence, and – where appropriate – an apology published.
iii. The press, whilst free to be partisan, must distinguish clearly between comment, conjecture and fact.
iv. A publication must report fairly and accurately the outcome of an action for defamation to which it has been a party, unless an agreed settlement states otherwise, or an agreed statement is published.

2 Opportunity to reply

A fair opportunity for reply to inaccuracies must be given when reasonably called for.

3* Privacy

i.   Everyone is entitled to respect for his or her private and family life, home, health and correspondence, including digital communications. Editors will be expected to justify intrusions into any individual's private life without consent.
ii. It is unacceptable to photograph individuals in a private place without their consent. *Note – Private places are public or private property where there is a reasonable expectation of privacy.*

4* Harassment

i.   Journalists must not engage in intimidation, harassment or persistent pursuit.
ii.   They must not persist in questioning, telephoning, pursuing or photographing individuals once asked to desist; nor remain on their property when asked to leave and must not follow them.
iii. Editors must ensure these principles are observed by those working for them and take care not to use non-compliant material from other sources.

5 Intrusion into grief or shock

i.   In cases involving personal grief or shock, enquiries and approaches must be made with sympathy and discretion and publication handled sensitively. This should not restrict the right to report legal proceedings, such as inquests.
*ii. When reporting suicide, care should be taken to avoid excessive detail about the method used.

6* Children

i.   Young people should be free to complete their time at school without unnecessary intrusion.
ii.   A child under 16 must not be interviewed or photographed on issues involving their own or another child's welfare unless a custodial parent or similarly responsible adult consents.
iii. Pupils must not be approached or photographed at school without the permission of the school authorities.
iv.   Minors must not be paid for material involving children's welfare, nor parents or guardians for material about their children or wards, unless it is clearly in the child's interest.
v.   Editors must not use the fame, notoriety or position of a parent or guardian as sole justification for publishing details of a child's private life.

7* Children in sex cases

1   The press must not, even if legally free to do so, identify children under 16 who are victims or witnesses in cases involving sex offences.
2   In any press report of a case involving a sexual offence against a child—
    i.   The child must not be identified.
    ii. The adult may be identified.
    iii. The word "incest" must not be used where a child victim might be identified.
    iv. Care must be taken that nothing in the report implies the relationship between the accused and the child.

8* Hospitals

i   Journalists must identify themselves and obtain permission from a responsible executive before entering non-public areas of hospitals or similar institutions to pursue enquiries.
ii   The restrictions on intruding into privacy are particularly relevant to enquiries about individuals in hospitals or similar institutions.

9* Reporting of Crime

i   Relatives or friends of persons convicted or accused of crime should not generally be identified without their consent, unless they are genuinely relevant to the story.

ii Particular regard should be paid to the potentially vulnerable position of children who witness, or are victims of, crime. This should not restrict the right to report legal proceedings.

10* Clandestine devices and subterfuge

i   The press must not seek to obtain or publish material acquired by using hidden cameras or clandestine listening devices; or by intercepting private or mobile telephone calls, messages or emails; or by the unauthorized removal of documents or photographs.

ii Engaging in misrepresentation or subterfuge can generally be justified only in the public interest and then only when the material cannot be obtained by other means.

11 Victims of sexual assault

The press must not identify victims of sexual assault or publish material likely to contribute to such identification unless there is adequate justification and they are legally free to do so.

12 Discrimination

i   The press must avoid prejudicial or pejorative reference to an individual's race, colour, religion, gender, sexual orientation or to any physical or mental illness or disability.

ii Details of an individual's race, colour, religion, sexual orientation, physical or mental illness or disability must be avoided unless genuinely relevant to the story.

13 Financial journalism

i.   Even where the law does not prohibit it, journalists must not use for their own profit financial information they receive in advance of its general publication, nor should they pass such information to others.

ii. They must not write about shares or securities in whose performance they know that they or their close families have a significant financial interest without disclosing the interest to the editor or financial editor.

iii. They must not buy or sell, either directly or through nominees or agents, shares or securities about which they have written recently or about which they intend to write in the near future.

14 Confidential sources

Journalists have a moral obligation to protect confidential sources of information.

15 Witness payments in criminal trials

i.   No payment or offer of payment to a witness—or any person who may reasonably be expected to be called as a witness—should be made in any case once proceedings are active as defined by the Contempt of Court Act 1981. This prohibition lasts until the suspect has been freed unconditionally by police without charge or bail or the proceedings are otherwise discontinued; or has entered a guilty plea to the court; or, in the event of a not guilty plea, the court has announced its verdict.

*ii. Where proceedings are not yet active but are likely and foreseeable, offer payment to any person who may reasonably be expected to be called as a witness, unless the information concerned ought demonstrably to be published in the public interest and there is an over-riding need to make or promise payment for this to be done; and all reasonable steps have been taken to ensure no financial dealings influence the evidence those witnesses give. In no circumstances should such payment be conditional on the outcome of a trial.

*iii. Any payment or offer of payment made to a person later cited to give evidence in proceedings must be disclosed to the prosecution and defence. The witness must be advised of this requirement.

16* Payment to criminals

i. Payment or offers of payment for stories, pictures or information, which seek to exploit a particular crime or to glorify or glamorise crime in general, must not be made directly or via agents to convicted or confessed criminals or to their associates—who may include family, friends and colleagues.

ii. Editors invoking the public interest to justify payment or offers would need to demonstrate that there was good reason to believe the public interest would be served. If, despite payment, no public interest emerged, then the material should not be published.

The public interest

There may be exceptions to the clauses marked * where they can be demonstrated to be in the public interest.

1 The public interest includes, but is not confined to:
   i Detecting or exposing crime or serious impropriety.
   ii Protecting public health and safety.
   iii Preventing the public from being misled by an action or statement of an individual or organisation.

2 There is a public interest in freedom of expression itself.

3 Whenever the public interest is invoked, the PCC will require editors to demonstrate fully how the public interest was served.

4 The PCC will consider the extent to which material is already in the public domain, or will become so.

5 In cases involving children under 16, editors must demonstrate an exceptional public interest to over-ride the normally paramount interest of the child.

PCC Guidance Notes

Court Reporting (1994)
Reporting of international sporting events (1998)
Prince William and privacy (1999)
On the reporting cases involving paedophiles (2000)
The Judiciary and harassment (2003)
Refugees and Asylum Seekers (2003)
Lottery Guidance Note (2004)
On the reporting of people accused of crime (2004)
Data Protection Act, Journalism and the PCC Code (2005)
Editorial co-operation (2005)
Financial Journalism: Best Practice Note (2005)
On the reporting of mental health issues (2006)
Copies of the above can be obtained online at **www.pcc.org.uk**
Press Complaints Commission
Halton House, 20/23 Holborn, London EC1N 2JD
Telephone: 020 7831 0022 Fax: 020 7831 0025
Textphone: 020 7831 0123 (for deaf or hard of hearing people)
Helpline: 0845 600 2757

BIBLIOGRAPHY

Websites

5 Raymond Buildings: *www.5rb.co.uk*.

British and Irish Legal Information Institute: *www.bailii.org*.

British Broadcasting Corporation: *www.bbc.co.uk*.

Campaign for Press and Broadcasting Freedom: *www.cpbf.org.uk*.

Department for Constitutional Affairs: *www.dca.gov.uk*.

Media Lawyer: *www.medialawyer.press.net*.

Office of Public Sector Information: *www.opsi.gov.uk*.

Books

Barendt, Eric, *Freedom of Speech*, Oxford University Press (2007).

Barendt and Hitchens, *Media Law: Cases and Materials*, Longman (2000).

Beales, Ian, *The Editors' Codebook*, the handbook to the Editors' Code of Practice, Newspaper Publishers Association, The Newspaper Society, Periodical Publishers Association, The Scottish Daily Newspaper Society and Scottish Newspaper Publishers Association (2005).

Bloy, Duncan, *Media Law*, Sage Publications (2007).

Brooke, Heather, *Your Right to Know: How to use the Freedom of Information Act and other access laws*, Pluto Press (2005).

Caddell, Richard and Johnson, Howard, *Blackstone's Statutes on Media Law*, Oxford University Press (2006).

Carey, Peter and Sanders, Jo, *Media Law* (3rd edn.), Sweet & Maxwell (2004).

Greenwood, Walter, Welsh, Tom & Banks, David (2007) *Essential Law for Journalists* (19th edn.) Oxford University Press (2007).

Hadwin, Sara Real readers, real news: the work of a local newspaper editor, in Franklin, Bob ed., *Local Journalism and Local Media*, Routledge (2006).

Hargreaves, Ian, *Journalism: Truth or dare?* OUP, Oxford (2003).

Kovach, Bill and Rosenstiel, Tom, *The Elements of Journalism*, Atlantic Books (2003).

Lapping, Brian, *The bounds of freedom*, Constable in collaboration with Granada Television (1980).

Mill, John Stuart, *On Liberty & Others Essays*, Oxford World Classics (1991).

PCC (2006) Annual Report, Press Complaints Commission, London and Code and adjudications (1998).

Randall, David, *The Universal Journalist*, Pluto Press (2007).

Robertson, Geoffrey and Nicol, Andrew, *Media Law* (4th edn.) Penguin (2002).

Rosenberg, Joshua, *Privacy and the Press* Oxford University Press (2004).

Press Complaints Commission:Code of Practice: *www.pcc.org.uk.*

Office of Communication: Broadcasting Code: *www.ofcom.org.uk.*

BBC Editorial/ Producers' Guidelines: *http://www.bbc.co.uk.* (Then search"editorial guidelines").

INDEX

LEGAL TAXONOMY
FROM SWEET & MAXWELL

This index has been prepared using Sweet and Maxwell's Legal Taxonomy. Main index entries conform to keywords provided by the Legal Taxonomy except where references to specific documents or non-standard terms (denoted by quotation marks) have been included. These keywords provide a means of identifying similar concepts in other Sweet & Maxwell publications and online services to which keywords from the Legal Taxonomy have been applied. Readers may find some minor differences between terms used in the text and those which appear in the index. Suggestions to *sweetandmaxwell.taxonomy@thomson.com*.

(All references are to page number)

LAW AND THE MEDIA

AUSTRALIA
Law Book Co.
Sydney

CANADA AND USA
Carswell
Toronto

HONG KONG
Sweet & Maxwell Asia

NEW ZEALAND
Brookers
Wellington

SINGAPORE and MALAYSIA
Sweet & Maxwell Asia
Singapore and Kuala Lumpur